The UN Human Rights Council

Elgar Practical Guides

Rich in practical advice, *Elgar Practical Guides* are handy, concise guides to a range of legal practice areas.

Combining practical insight and step-by-step guidance with the relevant substantive law and procedural rules, the books in this series focus on understanding and navigating the issues that are likely to be encountered in practice. This is facilitated by a range of structural tools including checklists, glossaries, sample documentation and recommended actions.

Elgar Practical Guides are indispensable resources for the busy practitioner and for the non-specialist who requires a first introduction or a reliable turn-to reference book.

For a full list of Edward Elgar published titles, including the titles in this series, visit our website at www.e-elgar.com.

The UN Human Rights Council

A Practical Anatomy, Second Edition

ERIC TISTOUNET

Independent Human Rights Expert, Former Head of the Human Rights Council Branch, Office of the United Nations High Commissioner for Human Rights, Creator and Moderator of the Lake Room Initiative, and lecturer and invited professor of practice in various universities and institutes

Elgar Practical Guides

EE Edward Elgar
PUBLISHING

Cheltenham, UK • Northampton, MA, USA

Published by

Edward Elgar Publishing Limited
The Lypiatts
15 Lansdown Road
Cheltenham
Glos GL50 2JA
UK

Edward Elgar Publishing, Inc.
William Pratt House
9 Dewey Court
Northampton
Massachusetts 01060
USA

Authorised representative in the EU for GPSR queries only: Easy Access System Europe – Mustamäe tee 50, 10621 Tallinn, Estonia, gpsr.requests@easproject.com

A catalogue record for this book is available from the British Library

Library of Congress Control Number: 2025941103

This book is available electronically in the **Elgar**online
Law subject collection
https://doi.org/10.4337/9781035323616

MIX
Paper | Supporting responsible forestry
FSC® C014540

ISBN 978 1 0353 2360 9 (cased)
ISBN 978 1 0353 2361 6 (eBook)
ISBN 978 1 0353 7023 8 (ePub)

Printed and bound in the UK by Short Run Press Ltd, Exeter EX2 7LW

Contents

Biography

Eric Tistounet, born in 1961, lives in Geneva, Switzerland. He joined the United Nations human rights system in 1987 and since then he has occupied various functions in the Office of the High Commissioner for Human Rights. In particular, he provided support to several treaty bodies and special rapporteurs and joined the Executive Office of the High Commissioner as external relations officer and later senior adviser on issues relating to the human rights multilateral system. He served as the last Secretary of the Commission on Human Rights from 2003 to 2006 and as the first secretary of the Human Rights Council from 2006 to 2008. He was appointed Head of the Human Rights Council Branch in 2008 to the end of 2023. Since then, he has been lecturing, writing and teaching about the UN human rights system and human rights diplomacy as invited professor of practice in various universities. He is also advising various stakeholders on these matters and has launched a Lake Room Initiative (also known as the Space for Dialogue) to help bridges between delegations on human rights matters.

Foreword

Omar Zniber

It is well established that working in the field of human rights is not easy. On the contrary, it is a demanding job that requires rigour and, above all, an in-depth knowledge of legal literature, accumulated experience and an open-mindedness capable of grasping the various issues involved in this work. This is why Mr. Eric Tistounet's work is commendable.

Mr. Tistounet, well known in the field of human rights in Geneva and beyond, has exceptional experience of more than 35 years of work in the service of the Council and for the human rights community more generally.

Throughout his career, he has ensured that the Council is on the right track and that the Council's relationship with its infrastructure and ecosystem, including the Office of the High Commissioner for Human Rights, is as coordinated and organised as possible.

We must therefore pay tribute to this work, which is certainly not the first, but which confirms Mr. Tistounet's desire to work tirelessly and in perfect collaboration with all the actors in this field.

Mr. Tistounet has long demonstrated his invaluable knowledge in the service of the Member States of the Human Rights Council. He is known for having steered his Members clear of numerous pitfalls, but also for his open-mindedness and for the many wise recommendations and advice that he has constantly lavished on all the States and also on the Council's related mechanisms, in particular the special procedures.

We should therefore be pleased that all those committed to the promotion of and respect for human rights have been able to benefit from this precise cooperation and the added value to which Mr. Tistounet has always contributed.

The present work therefore restores, in part, but also in a very illustrative way, this exceptional career. He was a promoter, in his own way, of human rights and the universal values they represent. It is therefore important to bear in mind the need for very high-level skills in such a complex field, which requires nuance and a great deal of sacrifice, as human rights work is more demanding than ever before. If we bear in mind the need to maintain a better life for the world's population, it is necessary to have highly qualified and specialised profiles such as Mr. Tistounet.

Having recently left his post, Mr. Tistounet remains mobilised and makes an extremely valuable contribution, in a way accentuating the benevolence he has towards the Human Rights Council, building bridges with academic circles in Geneva and far beyond.

Today, it has created a framework for reflection that helps Member States, also at their request, to better orient their dialogues and overcome the significant difficulties we all face in a more troubled world, heavily burdened by geopolitical conflicts related to key human rights issues, whether thematic issues or those relating to situations in Member States.

The present work provides an overview of the current situation, but also a new stage in the work of Mr Tistounet who, I am convinced, will continue to strengthen his contribution, which is necessary to build peace and stability through human rights.

Omar Zniber
President of the 18th Human Rights Council cycle, Permanent Representative of the Kingdom of Morocco to the United Nations and to the other international organizations in Geneva

Foreword

Fabian Salvioli

This book could be written in two ways: by convening a group of a dozen people, divided into two parts: experts in international human rights law, and experts in the daily practice of the United Nations Human Rights Council.

The other possibility was to summon Eric Tistounet to write it.

Only with the solid theoretical knowledge and practical expertise of the author can this book be the work of a single person.

Eric Tistounet has walked through the anatomy of the most important bodies of the United Nations human rights system for more than three decades. He began his career in 1987, assisting and serving as the secretariat of several treaty bodies, particularly the Human Rights Committee, the body that interprets and applies the International Covenant on Civil and Political Rights. He was also Chief of Staff of the United Nations High Commissioner for Human Rights.

He served as the last Secretary of the Commission on Human Rights and was a privileged actor in the process by which it was decided to replace that body with the Human Rights Council in 2006, to assume as its first Secretary. From there, he continued to serve in strategic roles, including Chief of the Human Rights Council Branch at the Office of the United Nations High Commissioner for Human Rights.

Tistounet speaks to us based on a high theoretical knowledge but 'from the kitchen', where mere theory finds a limit that it cannot cross due to lack of access. He exposes each topic addressed with the right alchemy between legal idealism and political pragmatism, without omitting details and allowing himself very useful critical reflections.

All this makes this book an exquisite and essential text for anyone who wishes to know deeply the life of the Human Rights Council, its strengths, weaknesses, and the challenges in a world that, vertiginously, escalates into conflicts that put at risk the system of founding values of the United Nations Organization.

Tistounet is committed to multilateralism, dialogue, objective, expert and prudent examination of each situation that comes to the Council's attention; it proposes fluid interaction with other human rights spaces within the system, and the optimization of resources.

The chapters of the book take a didactic walk through a presentation of the Council, the process of its creation – its genesis – the complex satellite machinery that navigates around the body, the functions of the body, the government and the role of the presidency and the bureau, and the relations between 'the world of New York and the world of Geneva' – postulating the establishment of a solid bridge that allows a permanent connection.

Later on, the book highlights the interlocutors who day by day come to the Council with their interests; the individual positions of the Member States, collective action – groups of States – the possibilities for States that have the status of observers, and Non-Governmental Organizations.

Likewise, the book accurately describes the different sessions – ordinary and special – and the activities between sessions of the Council, as well as the side events.

Decision-making in the Council is one of the most important issues due to the public repercussion of the resolutions that are adopted, and the impact on the work of the Organization. Tistounet devotes a chapter that contemplates not only the formal procedure, but also the factors that influence States or Groups of States to present, support, abstain from, or oppose a project.

The author wonders whether the Council has learnt from the history of the former Commission and underlines the body's constant effort to reform itself, to adapt to the challenges presented by an evolving system of human rights, traversed by permanent political debates.

The book ends with a profound reflection, which the author hastens to point out as 'imperfect'; it details a list of success stories that can illustrate the functioning of the Human Rights Council over time and warns of the tension between flexibility, realism and transparency – on the one hand – and confusion and lack of visibility – on the other.

I am privileged to enjoy the author's friendship and to have followed his work closely over the past 15 years, when I was a member of the United Nations Human Rights Committee and later when I served as Special Rapporteur. I do not want to end this foreword without saying that Eric Tistounet, through his professionalism, his knowledge, his commitment to human rights, and his ethical behaviour, has earned respect and recognition inside and outside the United Nations human rights system.

Fabian Salvioli
Professor, National University of La Plata
Former UN Special Rapporteur on the Promotion of Truth, Justice, Reparations and Guarantees of Non-Recurrence

Preface to the second edition

By the end of February 2020, I was deeply involved in supporting the 43rd Session of the Human Rights Council, which had just started its work with its usual cohort of dignitaries attending the High-Level Segment as well as a succession of numerous interactive dialogues, panels and general debates. Obviously, many crises were to be dealt with, and there was a general lack of serenity among all stakeholders due to the tense atmosphere prevailing outside Room XX with the accumulation of worrying news linked to the rapidly developing COVID-19 pandemic.

Nevertheless, I was also proudly preparing for a side event that the Geneva Academy had planned to organize by mid-March to mark the launch of the first edition of the book, which Elgar Publishing had just released.

Little did I know that the cases of the Coronavirus, which had been detected in December 2019 and spread to other countries across the world, would lead the World Health Organization (WHO) to characterize the Public Health Emergency of International Concern that it had declared on 30 January as a full-fledged pandemic on 11 March 2020. Two days later, the Council, for the first time in its existence, had to suspend its session given the enactment of severe measures restraining the holding of public events by the Host Country. This was unprecedented. What would follow in the next few years had a considerable impact on the Council's work and functioning as well as its perceived status.

The mere idea of launching a book in these conditions vanished almost instantaneously, not to re-emerge before 20 October 2020 – but in a virtual manner. In the meantime, together with my extremely able colleagues and against the tide of the atrocious virus and its vicious impact on the world population, I worked as hard as I could, from a Secretariat standpoint, to ensure that the Council would not halt its work. I knew that a machine of its nature might be stopped by extraneous measures and that if and when it did, rebooting or restarting it would take a considerable amount of time. What was bothering me considerably were the considerations that when the Commission on Human Rights had been abolished and the Human Rights Council established in 2006, it took no less than two years for the intergovernmental human rights system to resume its due course. I did not want the Council to face another parenthesis of the same duration.

Fortunately for the Council and the human rights programme, the two Council Presidents who led the Council during the two years of the pandemic, assisted by their energetic Vice-Presidents and with the support of many representatives and States or NGO delegates, as well as a fully committed Secretariat, managed to keep the Council working and within an extremely short period of time to rise and blossom again.

What followed were three incredibly heavy and somewhat chaotic years, featuring a Council extremely adept at confronting the consequences of the stringent measures righty taken to preserve the population from succumbing to this harsh disease, thus avoiding the fate of so many other international bodies that almost halted their work. Alone among the international bodies established by the United Nations or other international organizations, the Council found itself complying with all its requirements, fulfilling all its duties and implementing its full its programme of work. The Council found innovative ways and means to meet in a hybrid and/or virtual manner, held all its regular sessions, organized Special Sessions and urgent debates, created new mandates, expanded its activities, and lengthened its sessions. For instance, during this period, the Council organized no fewer than five urgent debates – more than in the previous 14 years – and eight Special Sessions.

While the rest of the UN system was lost in byzantine and sterile discussions about creating an environment conducive to resuming its meetings, the Council simply proceeded and adopted a large number of resolutions, considered numerous amendments, dealt with procedural motions, and, when there was no other choice, used an electronic voting system that had been created initially for the New York bodies but which none of them managed to use, even once. It also proceeded with elections and the adoption of Presidential Statements or Decisions intersessionally.

The methodology used was based on the flexibility which I described at length in the first edition of this book, with an attempt at focusing on the 'what' rather than the 'how'. While others were trying to develop sophisticated – and costly - electronic systems which eventually collapsed or proved to be of no significant use, the Council Secretariat used whatever was at its disposal in the public domain. When this proved not to be fully supported by the UN technocracy, semantics came to its recourse. The platforms which were not initially blessed by the organization were nevertheless used informally and vaguely described as 'remote participation platforms' or similar obscure terminology with proper acronyms beloved by the UN machinery. Eventually, when the experience became successful, the Council's activities served as examples or precedents and those platforms which had not been approved before became the new standards, while those being developed at great cost were left aside.

As a result of these unique characteristics and the energy deployed to consider all human rights issues, whether country-specific or thematic ones, and against the background of an almost paralysed intergovernmental system, the Council emerged as one – if not the only – remaining credible voices able to deal with any type of emergency, thus attracting attention from all stakeholders and raising its visibility to a previously unknown level.

When the pandemic finally and most fortunately ran its course with a much-revived Council, other clouds appeared immediately on the horizon. On 24 February 2022, the Russian Federation launched what it described as a special military operation in Ukraine, as a result of which war reappeared on a continent that had proudly considered it had been eradicated forever from its own soil. Once again, the Council, which was preparing for its February/March 2022 Session, became fully engaged, and a new cycle of initiatives and actions took place with urgent debates, Special Sessions, creation of new mandates as well as the suspension of the Russian Federation's rights of membership. This increase of activities, read against the background of a revitalized human rights intergovernmental machinery, further boosted the visibility of the Council in public opinion and served as testimony that the international community remained relevant when gross and massive human rights violations were perpetrated and dealt with by the Council.

In the months that followed, the Council's relevance remained tested on multiple occasions, particularly when less visible human rights situations or conflicts unfolded, often without the same level of scrutiny by the international media, social network and consequently public opinion. Additionally, its propensity to deal with an increasing number of issues and set up new mechanisms, mandates and tools added to the complexity of its work and functioning, further burdeningr small delegations.

And then, 7 October happened, with its outrageous violence both on that day and the days, weeks and months that followed. Millions of civilians were affected by multiple and intersecting forms of gross and massive human rights violations, war crimes, violations of imperative human rights and humanitarian norms. Gaza today, as well as other occupied territories, echoes the torment and descent of Dante's Inferno, each layer revealing a deeper level of suffering. The ICJ as well as the ICC, the ultimate guardians of international humanitarian and human rights law, were fully seized of the matters and their pronouncements are awaited with the faint hope that all those concerned will eventually be held accountable for their crimes.

As a result of such utter violence and its atrocious toll on civilians in these two and many other conflicts, and the subsequent resentment that occurred against the placidity or lack of action by the international community epitomized by the blockage of the Security Council, the Human Rights Council was once again considered as a lieu and place where action could be triggered – or not.

Those participating in the work of the Council and all those following its work noted the cruel contradictions in the statements by many stakeholders, with terminology being used or action requested in one situation but not necessarily the other, with a different approach depending not on the situation of the human rights victims but the States' allegiances. They also noted that the whole world's attention seemed to be focusing on two situations, forgetting the other 57 conflicts often referred to by the High Commissioner for Human Rights, that were prevailing in less visible spots but with a comparable level of tragedy, suffering and inhumanity.

They also noticed a decrease in attention to the imperative nature of human rights by a number of its previously most ardent supporters, as well as a deterioration in the level of implementation of human rights at the domestic level in countries from the Global North or Global South that had so far considered themselves exempt from any criticism. As a result, terms like 'double standards' or 'hypocrisy' resurfaced from where they had been left 15 years ago.

What seemed to be an impossible postulate to challenge – that multilateralism was the only realistic path to managing complex situations in international law, especially in the fields of human rights and humanitarian law – has suddenly and brutally been called into question. The achievements of decades of human rights diplomacy have abruptly appeared to falter, revealing a fragility that had gone unnoticed. Given that this work is titled 'Anatomy', the analogy that comes to mind is that of a person who considers themselves to be in relatively good health, only to be informed that they are, in fact, suffering from a serious disease thought to have been eradicated for a long time.

When assessing the work of the Council and the outcome of its deliberations, and envisaging its future, it is important to bear in mind a number of contingencies and uncertainties tainting today's international reality. A systemic contradiction endures between, on the one hand, the quest for simple and almost binary answers to the numerous questions raised by both the general and specialized public and, on the other hand, a constant and inexorable complexification of the processes at play.

As was mentioned, since the eruption of the COVID-19 pandemic into our lives, a conjunction of circumstances led to the strengthening of the standing of the Council into a de facto main United Nations body. It accelerated the expansion of its activities, strengthened its credibility and increased its visibility.

The fact that the Council remained fully active throughout the pandemic, combined with its relevance in confronting some of the crises that plagued the world in recent years propelled the Council into another dimension.

The Council is rightly considered as an ever-expanding body approached by a multiplicity of stakeholders trying to elevate their causes among many other ones with which it is dealing. At the same time, the Council is also constantly engaged in an introspective process aiming at rationalizing its work, which is a euphemism to state that its ultimate desire is to contain the said expansion, reduce the number of weeks of meetings, and provide more space for a comprehensive analysis of the multiple thematic or country crises the world is facing.

The resulting deep contradictions and the utter complexification of the Council's work and functioning as well as the political, legal and administrative environment in which it tries to navigate, made a review of this book an absolute necessity.

Against the background of my decision to leave the Organization after 37 years of activity and open myself to new challenges, I rapidly came to realize that the Anatomy I had written only a few years ago required a systemic revamping with proper consideration given to the tectonic changes I was witnessing and an attempt to analyse and appraise the changes which had occurred in the working methods, the modus operandi, the action and operations of the Council in just four years. With the enthusiastic response by Elgar Publishing and the encouragement of many readers in the Council's circles and beyond, I resumed my work as a legal anatomist.

I sincerely hope that this second edition will allow all those interested in the work of the Council and consequently – and unfortunately – lost in deciphering its manifold manifestations given the opacity of its public documentation, to understanding better what is currently at stake, namely what the future of human rights protection at the international level may be against the background of a vacillating multilateralism, and more importantly, whether to characterize it in an optimistic or pessimistic manner. But this is a conclusion I will once again leave to the readers to reach.

For my part, I do consider that the underlying trends observed since the end of the horrific tragedy of the Second World War and the subsequent tragedies towards a progressive recognition and implementation of human rights norms worldwide remain relevant. Even if some would undoubtedly prefer to disregard multilateralism and bury it somewhere between the Congress of Vienna and Yalta, it seems to me that reason will ultimately prevail, that massive violations of human rights, wherever they occur, will continue to be condemned with increasing fervour and effectiveness, and that the centrality of victims of human rights violations, regardless of their race, gender, nationality, religion, or other characteristics, will continue to be recognized. The only boundaries that exist in the field of human rights are not those marked by force and weaponry, but those established by norms agreed upon for decades by the international community, inspired by all those whose wish was to elevate humanity above selfish and materialistic interests. Despite all the hostile manifestations and setbacks currently observed, there is, in my view, one certainty and one only: trust in humanity.

There is no other choice.

Geneva, 31 December 2024

Acknowledgements

The initial project which led to the publication of the first edition of this book was conducted by the author with the support of the United Nations Sabbatical Leave Programme and the Office of the High Commissioner for Human Rights during a period of 4 months in 2018/2019. The second edition was prepared during the year 2024 and is up-to-date as of the end of 2024.

The author expresses his gratitude to the successive High Commissioners for Human Rights with whom he had the opportunity to work with and who greatly supported him in his endeavour He is indebted to his former colleagues within the Secretariat of the Human Rights Council – which he led for many years – and whose competence always amazed him. Many of whom became his friends over the years.

The author is grateful to the Geneva Academy who hosted him during his Sabbatical Leave and to the Geneva Human Rights Platform which welcomed him as a member of its Advisory Board upon his reconversion. His deep thanks thus go to Gloria Gaggioli and Felix Kirchmeier for their gracious and efficient welcome.

The author expresses his deep gratitude to the current and previous Council's Presidents and Bureau members as well as co-facilitators and focal points with whom he had the privilege to work since the Council's establishment. This extends to all Council's stakeholders with whom he cooperated for many years and continues to do so albeit in a different capacity.

The author also expresses his gratitude to all Ambassadors who attended the Lake Room Meetings, also known as the Space for Dialogue Initiative, which he created in February 2024 with a view to build bridges between

States on sensitive human rights issues at a time when multilateralism is in crisis.

The author wishes to express appreciation for the constant support and excellent advice provided by his mentor and friend Bertrand Ramcharan, former Acting and Deputy High Commissioner for Human Rights.

Finally, the author wishes to express his deep gratitude to his immediate family for their unwavering support over the years, particularly when the pressure of stewarding the Council work or managing the complexity of a large international organization became especially heavy.

Introduction

During the Western European Middle Ages, there was no rational medicine. Surgery was the province of barbers, executioners and bath-keepers. Dissecting dead bodies was not authorized and those who tried to behave as scientists had no other choice but to carry on their anatomical research in secret. Ideas about biology were certainly odd and surely not even remotely connected to reality. It was considered that, for instance, women had more water in their bodies than men and thus, if there were frequent rains during pregnancy, the baby was more likely to be born female. In the same vein, the liver was supposed to secrete yellow bile, the spleen black bile and the heart blood. Contrary to Greek philosophers, it was taught that the brain was merely a phlegm-secreting gland. Persons with disabilities were regarded as possessed by evil spirits and medicine was carried out using exorcism, consecrated bells, relics, readings of holy texts and even torture.[1]

Fortunately for all concerned, reason emerged from the darkness of time and, over the forthcoming centuries, the doctrine of the Middle Ages was seriously challenged and progressively abandoned. The antique knowledge came back to light and breakthroughs were achieved with the study of anatomy, which started flourishing in the seventeenth and eighteenth centuries.

Several centuries later, in a totally different set of circumstances, the general discourse about the Human Rights Council and its mechanisms was opened to interpretation, theories, concepts and conclusions or recommendations, without a deep and thorough knowledge of what the

1 See, for instance the teaching of St. Thomas Aquinas. More generally, see 'A Short History of Medicine' by Erwin Ackerknecht.

Council is all about, how it operates and why certain procedures were established or practices developed and others not. The vast magnitude of the Council's activities and its complexification over the years are too often neglected and, at times, rudimentary statements are offered with no particular effort to shed light on its activities, as well as its role and responsibilities. As a result, whatever the outcome of such efforts, it may be marred by imprecision, inaccuracy and inappropriateness.

Should this be the result of well-understood and self-proclaimed – or not – political bias, there is surely not much that can be done about it, and the following 450 or so pages will not serve any purpose. However, more often than not, it is the consequence of the increased complexity and opacity of the Council's working methods, which are marked by a frequent resort to uncodified precedents.

There exists a vast array of practices, tools and mechanisms which have been progressively and patiently established by the Council. Facing successive human rights crises and organizational obstacles in a highly politically charged environment, the Council developed its practices with a high level of flexibility. It used every possible entry point or sleight of hand in order to reach a goal which otherwise would never have been achieved.

Given the practical impossibility of reaching a general consensus on a broad range of matters resulting from the high level of polarization between all concerned, it did so with persistence and determination, adjusting its working methods, creating numerous new processes, envisaging multiple areas of development and working tirelessly on all matters which it had to tackle with a step-by-step strategy. Despite its relatively young age, or because of it, it never displayed any form of reluctance to conceive new tools or instruments.

When improvements could not be agreed upon, new avenues were explored; when precedents could not be resorted to, it envisaged new ones; when no existing mechanism or tool was available, new ones were simply created. It did so with patience and realism, always keeping what existed and leaving a large space for interpretation and a margin of manoeuvre for future consideration.

Quite understandably, it reached these goals by resorting to a vast array of legal and policy means. Sometimes it altered its procedure in a clear and comprehensive manner, but in the vast majority of cases, it did so in an extremely pragmatic manner by adopting decisions, resorting to practices initiated or proposed by the successive Presidents and their Bureaux, and agreeing informally to set up new procedures proposed by concerned stakeholders.

Given this fragmentary approach, it is extremely hard to grasp fully what the Council is all about, what it did, when it did so, and obviously why and how it privileged one convoluted and complex method rather than a much simpler and obvious one.

In such a context, it should also be pointed out that any piece of information on the Council is scarce and hard to identify or isolate. Despite the very transparent approach favoured by the Council from its inception, elements of information are spread across multiple media, from the Council's reports, resolutions, decisions, or Presidential Statements to the minutes of the Bureaux meetings, the letters by or to the Presidents, the webcast archives, the Council website or Extranet, or even worse, a well-formed but unwritten practice.

The purpose of *The UN Human Rights Council: A Practical Anatomy* is thus to study meticulously the structure of the Council and its mechanisms with a view to enabling the readers to formulate opinions and recommendations and propose informed decisions. In a manner not entirely different from a biological anatomy, such an approach requires a simultaneously macroscopic and microscopic approach, describing the detailed procedures and overall context, the specific and the general, the trends and the underlying factors.[2]

2 Readers are advised to consult books and essays on the Human Rights Council such as: *The UN Human Rights Council* (Routledge, Abingdon), *The Law, Policy and Politics of the UN Human Rights Council* (Brill-Nijhoff, Leiden), *The UN and Preventive Diplomacy* and *Contemporary Human Rights Ideas: Rethinking Theory and Practice*, all by Bertrand Ramcharan (Routledge, Abingdon); *The United Nations Human Rights Council: A Critique and Early Assessment*, by Rosa Freedman (Routledge, Abingdon); *New Challenges for the UN Human Rights Machinery: What Future for the UN Treaty Body System and the Human Rights Council* Procedures, by Cherif Bassiouni and William Schabas (Intersentia, Cambridge); *In Defence of Politicization of Human Rights: The UN Special*

- The first chapter (by analogy, 'the body') describes in a nutshell what the Council is all about ('The Human Rights Council in a nutshell').
- The second chapter ('the skeleton') aims at dissecting the multiple functions of the Council by resorting to a fractional analysis of the Council's predecessor, the Commission on Human Rights, and developing what the author refers to as a 'Human Rights geology'. This describes the various mechanisms and procedures that were layered one on top of another over time. Since the Council continues to resort to every single one of them, understanding this process is of crucial importance ('The Human Rights Council functions').
- The third chapter ('The Nervous System') envisages the specificity of the Council's governance with largely known and unknown responsibilities assigned to its President and Bureau ('The Human Rights Council Governance: The Role and Functions of the President and His/Her Bureau').
- In the fourth chapter ('the organs'), an account is made of all of the Council's stakeholders, including those who are seldom met in the work of other universal or regional intergovernmental bodies. It studies how they may – or may not – interact with the Council and its mechanisms ('The Human Rights Council stakeholders').
- The fifth chapter ('The Circulatory System') details the complex structure of the Council's sessional or intersessional activities. Given the exponential increase in the Council's activities and its inventiveness, it is a rather complex endeavour to cluster them and underline their various modus operandi ('The Structure of Sessional and Intersessional Activities').
- The way the Council adopts its decisions or acts upon procedural motions is studied in the sixth chapter ('the digestive system'). Although this may seem the simplest of all efforts since, after all, the Council is following the General Assembly's rules of procedure, the irrepressible nature of its inventiveness makes it significantly more

Procedures, by Elvira Dominguez-Redondo (Oxford University Press); *The United Nations Commission on Human Rights: A Very Great Enterprise*, by John Pace (Oxford University Press) *The UN Human Rights Council Achievements and Challenges in its First Decade*, by Cantu Rivera (Springer), *An International Relations Perspective on the Reform Needs of the Human Rights Council*, by W.S Heinz (German Yearbook of International Law).

complicated ('The Human Rights Council voting procedure and procedural motions').

- The seventh chapter ('the respiratory system') envisages how the Council has attempted to and is still attempting to reform itself, constantly reviewing its work and functioning and stimulating more efficient and effective working methods ('The change management process as it applies to the Council and previously the Commission').
- In the guise of what can only be considered, by necessity, an imperfect conclusion, the author dwells upon the positive outcomes of the Council's work, the impact of an ever-expanding number of mechanisms and bodies, and the fluctuating nature of the frustrations which intergovernmental human rights trigger. Since science is a never-ending process, there is a moment when humility obliges questions to be left to others – particularly the readers – to address, now or in the future, and this will be how the Anatomy will end.

When the first edition of this book was published in early 2020, the author could not anticipate that the whole human rights ecosystem would be seriously shaken in the years that followed by the COVID-19 pandemic and thereafter by a series of conflicts of huge magnitude with considerable impact on its operation. Changes were so abrupt and far-reaching that it made it important to rapidly update the Anatomy and provide support to all the Council's stakeholders in their endless quests to grasp its modus operandi, effectiveness, status, work and functions.

It is thus the author's sincere hope that the second edition of *The UN Human Rights Council: A Practical Anatomy* will provide readers with the necessary information to develop an awareness and understanding of the Council and its mechanisms, and thus enable them to reach conclusions and pass judgements, whatever they may be.

1 The Human Rights Council in a nutshell

The study of the human anatomy, quite clearly, starts with an analysis of the body as a whole. It is not possible to conjecture what lies within a body if there is no understanding of the overall body being studied. Insofar as the Human Rights Council is concerned, this will be done succinctly, based on an overall description of the Council and its main mechanisms. The aim of this chapter is to offer some general considerations that are necessary to understand their main features.

The Human Rights Council (the Council) was established by the United Nations (UN) General Assembly (the Assembly) in its Resolution 60/251 of 15 March 2006 to replace the Commission on Human Rights (the Commission). Its status, which is supposed to be reviewed on a regular basis, is that of a subsidiary organ of the Assembly.

It is composed of 47 Members, who are elected directly and individually by secret ballot by the majority of the members of the Assembly. The Members of the Council serve for a period of three years and are not eligible for immediate re-election after two consecutive terms. Candidates are expected to make voluntary pledges and commitments reflecting their contribution to the promotion and protection of human rights, which are published on the website of The Assembly. Members are requested to uphold the highest standards in the promotion and protection of human rights. The Assembly, by a two-thirds majority present and voting, may suspend the rights of membership of a Member that commits gross and systematic violations of human rights.

The Council meets regularly throughout the year for a total duration of no less than ten weeks. Three regular sessions are thus scheduled every year, in February/March (known as the Main Session, attended by government high officials in its High-level Segment of three days), June/July and September. At the request of a member of the Council, with the support of one-third of its membership, namely a total of 16 States, the Council may also meet in the context of Special Sessions.

The Council upon its establishment inherited the mandates, mechanisms, functions, and responsibilities of the Commission, which it has assumed, reviewed, improved and rationalized by way of its Institutions-building Package comprising Human Rights Council Resolutions 5/1 and 5/2, adopted one year after the holding of its first session on 18 June 2007. Human Rights Council Resolution 16/21, adopted at the end of the review of its work and functioning five years after its establishment on 15 March 2011, should also be included in this list of basic documents.

The Council's functions and responsibilities are very broad and relate, inter alia, to the promotion of all human rights and fundamental freedoms for all people, without distinction of any kind and in a fair and equal manner; the consideration of violations of human rights, including gross and systematic violations; and the effective coordination and mainstreaming of human rights within the UN system.

Its work is based on the principles of universality, impartiality, objectivity and non-selectivity, constructive international dialogue and cooperation with a view to enhancing the promotion and protection of all human rights, as well as civil, political, economic, social and cultural rights, including the right to development.

Its working methods are expected to be transparent, fair, and impartial, enabling dialogue, being results-oriented, and allowing for subsequent follow-up discussions on recommendations and their implementation. They should also allow for substantive interaction with Special Procedures and mechanisms.

In order to achieve the goals assigned to it, the Council promotes human rights education and learning, as well as advisory services, technical assistance, and capacity-building, serves as a forum for dialogue on thematic issues on all human rights, makes recommendations to the Assembly for the further development of international law in the field of human rights, promotes the full implementation of human rights obligations undertaken by States and follow-up to the goals and commitments related to the promotion and protection of human rights emanating from UN Conferences and Summits, undertakes a Universal Periodic Review (UPR), contributes through dialogue and cooperation to the prevention of human rights violations, responds promptly to human rights emergencies and makes recommendations with regard to the promotion and protection of human rights.

The Council also assumed the role and responsibilities of the Commission regarding the work of the Office of the UN High Commissioner for Human Rights and inherited from it a system of Special Procedures, expert advice, and a Complaints Procedure, as delineated in its Resolution 5/1.

The Council works in close cooperation with governments, regional organizations, national human rights institutions, and civil society. It applies the rules of procedure established for committees of the Assembly, as complemented by the rules developed in its Resolution 5/1 and in practice. The participation of and consultation with observers, including States that are not members of the Council, specialized agencies, other intergovernmental organizations, and national human rights institutions (NHRIs), as well as non-governmental organisations (NGOs), are well established. This work is based on arrangements like the Economic and Social Council Resolution 1996/31 of 25 July 1996, as well as practices observed by the Commission, and ensures the most effective contribution of these entities.

The Council submits an annual report to the Assembly. In accordance with the Assembly Resolution 65/281 of 17 June 2011, the agenda item entitled 'Report of the Human Rights Council' is allocated to the plenary of the Assembly and to the Third Committee. The President of the Council (the President) presents the Council's Annual report in his/her capacity as President to the plenary of the Assembly and the Third Committee. An interactive dialogue is organized with him/her at the time of the presentation of the report to the Third Committee.

1.1 The UPR mechanism

Upon its creation, the UPR represented a new and unique feature of the human rights architecture. The UPR, which is based on objective and reliable information, enables the fulfilment by each Member State of the United Nations of its human rights obligations and commitments to be reviewed in a manner that ensures universality of coverage and equal treatment with respect to all States. It is a cooperative mechanism based on an interactive dialogue with the full involvement of the country concerned.

Since the inception of the UPR, without exception, all UN Member States have been reviewed by the Council (see the calendar of UPR Review for the third UPR Cycle at www.ohchr.org). The periodicity of the review for the first cycle was four years, while the second and subsequent reviews, it was four and a half years. During the first cycle, 48 States were reviewed per year. From the second cycle onwards, 42 States were reviewed per year.

The consideration of these States takes place during three sessions of two weeks each, held by the UPR Working Group. The Working Group is composed of the 47 Members of the Council and is chaired by the President. Although the working modalities and procedures of the Working Group resemble in every respect those of the Council, the two should not be confused, as the Working Group remains a subsidiary body of the Council. This being stated, the UPR is a universal mechanism, with the Council being involved in it heavily at every step of the procedure.

Each review is based on three documents called 'reports':

- The first one[1] is presented by the State itself (although it is usually in a written format, it can be also done in an oral manner, as has been done on an exceptional basis).
- The second and third ones[2] are presented by the Office of the High Commissioner for Human Rights (OHCHR).

The second report combines the information provided by treaty bodies, Special Procedures, and other official UN documents.

The last one is a summary of 'additional, credible and reliable' information provided by NHRIs and NGOs. If there is an NHRI of the State

1 Which does not exceed a number of words corresponding to 20 pages.

2 Which do not exceed a number of words corresponding to ten pages each.

under review that is accredited as being in full compliance with the Paris Principles,[3] it benefits from a separate section in this report.

The UPR is a peer-review mechanism. Accordingly, only States may participate in the interactive dialogue organized by the Working Group. Other stakeholders may attend the review without the possibility of taking the floor.

For each review, a troika of three rapporteurs is selected by drawing of lots among the Members of the Council and from different regional groups. They are formed to facilitate each review, in particular the preparation of the report of the Working Group. OHCHR provides the necessary assistance to the troikas.

A complex process was set into motion in order to guide the selection of each troika. It includes the following elements:

- The country concerned may request that one of the rapporteurs be from its own regional group.
- It may also request the substitution of a rapporteur but only on one occasion.
- A rapporteur may request to be excused from participation in a specified review process.

Member and Observer States may transmit issues or questions prior to the review to the concerned State to facilitate and focus the review.

Since the start of the second UPR cycle, the duration of the review has been three and a half hours - with variations stemming out of the liquidity crisis, of which one-third is made available to the State under Review. The modalities for the establishment of lists of speakers are quite complex, as they require all interested parties to register with the Secretariat during the week preceding the UPR Working Group session. Upon its closure at 6 p.m. on the Thursday, the Secretariat arranges the list by alphabetical order. The following day, the Council Bureau meets, and its members proceed with the drawing of lots for the first speaker for each item on the list.

---

3 Usually referred to as A-status NHRI.

All those inscribed on the lists of speakers are entitled to speak. Given that the time set aside for each review is exactly the same and cannot, under any circumstances, be extended, the speaking time per speaker may be significantly reduced. In practical terms, speaking time is often approximately one minute.

At the end of the review by the Working Group, a report is prepared. It includes all recommendations made by all of the speakers. Only those recommendations made orally in the context of the public meeting are included. If the speaker is interrupted before the end of their statement, the portion of the recommendations or statement that was not delivered formally is not included in the report.

The State under review must identify the recommendations that enjoy its support. All the others are considered to be noted. In other words, those recommendations are not really accepted and in certain instances are utterly rejected by the State under review, although UN terminology does not use such terms. Although an inventive terminology may be used, the Council proceeds on the assumption that there are only two categories of recommendations.[4] The States under review may decide to inform the Working Group about its decision at any point in time, either at the Working Group or at the Council plenary Level. The latest moment for this is when the final outcome of its review is adopted by the Council.

The final outcome of the review is adopted by the plenary of the Council. The Council dedicates a one-hour segment to each State under review, divided into three parts of 20 minutes each. The State under review is provided with 20 minutes, which it may organize as it wishes. The Council Members and Observers also have 20 minutes. The list of speakers for the second segment is organized by a drawing of lots at the Bureau level, with the understanding that those unable to speak may have their written statements posted on the Internet.

Contrary to the UPR Working Group peer-review modalities, the plenary of the Council proceeds based on its own working methods, thus enabling everyone to speak. Hence, the other stakeholders, namely NHRIs and NGOs, are provided with the possibility of commenting on the outcome of the review and are set aside a total time of the remaining

---

4 Para. 32 of HRC Resolution 5/1.

20 minutes. The list of speakers for other stakeholders is organized on a first-come, first-served basis, it being understood that the national NHRI, when it exists will always speak first.

From the second review onwards, the reviews were expected to focus on the implementation of the preceding cycle. Additionally, the Council considers the UPR under its agenda item 6, during which all stakeholders may participate and comment on the mechanism itself.

The efficiency and effectiveness of the UPR have been widely applauded. Despite its flaws linked to the number and nature of the recommendations made during a relatively short process, there is a general recognition that the universality of this mechanism combined with the cooperative and constructive nature of the dialogue make it a very powerful tool. A lot was said, and unsaid, about the UPR, but the assessment that it is one of the most, if not the most, successful Council's features is shared by all.

Almost all stakeholders have expressed their firm belief that it serves as a triggering mechanism, enabling significant progress at the domestic level. What often goes unnoticed is the 'psychology' of the UPR according to which States under Review often feel the pressure of supporting at least the same percentage of recommendations as their neighbours or members of the groups they belong to. This average is about two-thirds, which is remarkably high. States are in most cases led to support more recommendations that they would have anticipated initially. This immediately provides an entry point for all stakeholders to enter into a process of dialogue and implementation at the domestic level.

Another undeniable positive impact of the UPR is that States under Review are eager to cooperate with those concerned at the domestic level with a view to implementing specific UPR recommendations. It is rare that the same openness exists for other mechanisms. This leads to the striking remark that national authorities may be reluctant to engage in discussing the necessary follow-up to the recommendations of Special Procedures or treaty bodies, whereas they may have absolutely no difficulty in doing so for similar or comparable recommendations made under the UPR process.

The UPR may thus be considered as a process that prioritizes action over quasi-legal consideration. While it may be far more superficial, it is far more likely to secure concrete results at the domestic level.

Lastly, also largely unnoticed is the fact that the UPR represents the most comprehensive and objective mapping of the human rights situation in the world. Since all States participate in the reviews over a period of four and a half years, it is the broadest and most comprehensive assessment which can be anticipated at the international level without being suspected of its partiality. There are, however, two shortcomings. First this process spans four and a half years rather than being conducted on an annual basis.Second, the related documentation cannot easily be condensed into a user-friendly report.

The UPR is however increasingly weakened both by an apparently never-ending expansion of the number of recommendations made and an obvious inability of the Council to instil changes into its UPR modus operandi. Perceived and presented – together with the Special Procedures – as the Council's jewel in the crown, there is a sense of immutability in how the UPR should work and proceed. Very little can therefore be made to contain the expansion process, establish proper working links with the treaty bodies and Special Procedures and more importantly dwell on implementation and follow up. In a very changing and unstable world, when a process, whichever it may be, is perceived as the ultimate success by absolutely all concerned, wherever they come from and whatever political groups they are part of, who would actually dare to changing its working premises? The author is among those who dare to consider that it may be the moment to adjust the working modalities of the UPR, not its substance or its architecture, to avoiding it becoming hostage of its own rituals.

1.2 Special procedures

A number of individuals or groups have been appointed to serve as Special Procedures mandate holders. All of the special rapporteurs are individual experts or working groups composed of five experts. All are independent and serve in their personal capacity. They contribute to the development of the international understanding of thematic or country situations, they conduct thematic studies, they undertake country visits and send communications to concerned governments when allegations of violations or abuses have been brought to their attention. Additionally, they engage in promotional activities such as convening seminars, participating in conferences and providing advice for technical cooperation.

Mandate holders report to the Council on a yearly basis on the implementation of their mandates or at other times deemed appropriate by the Council. They deploy every possible activity to fulfil their mandates, yet they do not receive a salary, making this function particularly challenging. Mandate holders consult all relevant parties, participate in conferences, organize seminars and/or study thoroughly the matters at stake to provide the Council with the most accurate assessment of current or future trends. The modus operandi of the Special Procedures involves the initiation, with the assistance of the OHCHR, of country visits to analyse the human rights situation at the national level and report back to the Council. States are encouraged to extend standing invitations to all thematic Special Procedures. By doing so they announce their permanent willingness to accept requests for visits from all Special Procedures.[5]

Special Procedures may also intervene directly with governments regarding allegations of human rights violations within their mandates by means of letters, including urgent appeals and other communications.[6] Summaries of all communications received, as well as responses, are brought to the attention of the Human Rights Council on a yearly basis.

Special Procedures mandates are usually compartmentalized into two categories: at the time of writing of this Anatomy, there coexisted 46 thematic and 14 country mandates. All mandate holders, however, adhere to the same rules and practices, and their participation in the Council's work follows the same procedures.

The selection of mandate holders was refined and conceptualized in the Council Resolutions 5/1 and 16/21. When nominating, selecting and appointing mandate holders, emphasis is placed on the expertise, experience, independence, impartiality, personal integrity and objectivity of

5 As of 2023, 128 Member States and one non-Member Observer had extended standing invitations to Special Procedures. The updated list is available at https://spinternet.ohchr.org/_Layouts/SpecialProceduresInternet/StandingInvitations.aspx.

6 Before the COVID-19 pandemic, Special Procedures sent 655 communications to countries and other actors. They conducted 84 visits in all regions of the world. They submitted a total of 181 reports, attended more than 90 forums or consultations and issued 441 press releases or comparable products.

the candidates. A Consultative Group, composed of five State representatives selected by the five Regional Groups of the United Nations, although serving in their personal capacity, considers all applications, which are publicly listed online. Candidates may be nominated by governments, regional groups, international organizations, the OHCHR, NHRIs and NGOs, and by individuals.

A careful selection process is set into motion that includes interviews of the shortlisted candidates by the Consultative Group. The selection follows a three-tiered approach. Upon receipt of the recommendations of the Consultative Group, the Council President engages in consultations with all States and others, particularly regional coordinators. Upon completion of the consultations, the President issues a public list of candidates. The appointment of mandate holders is completed with the Council's subsequent approval of this list. If difficulties arise regarding the selection of a particular person as a mandate holder, all appointments are postponed to a later stage during the session or the intersessional period.

The tenure of mandate holders in a given function cannot exceed six years. There is a general rule of non-accumulation of human rights functions, which implies that a Special Procedure mandate holder cannot hold comparable functions within the UN system or other international organizations. Individuals holding decision-making positions in a government, any other international organization or entities such a NHRI or a NGO are excluded from the selection process due to potential conflicts of interest. Mandate holders are not paid and act in their personal capacity.

In accordance with the Code of Conduct included in Council Resolution 5/2, States are expected to: 'cooperate with and assist Special Procedures in the performance of their tasks'. Conversely, it is incumbent on mandate holders to exercise their functions in accordance with their mandates and in compliance with the Code of Conduct.

Given the ongoing expansion in the number of Special Procedures mandates, it was deemed necessary to initiate a formal coordination process through the establishment of a Coordination Committee of Special Procedures. The Committee's mandate includes enhancing the effectiveness and independence of mandate holders, raising their concerns in discussions of the Human Rights Council, proactively identifying issues of concern to groups of mandates, and facilitating joint action on cross-cutting issues or issues of shared concern, exchanging information. It also facilitates the sharing of experience concerning methods of work among mandate holders, identifying innovative ways to raise awareness about Special Procedures and their work, encouraging States to cooperate with Special Procedures, and proposing a draft agenda for the Annual Meeting of the Special Procedures, which is held annually.

The reports of the Special Procedures are reviewed in the context of interactive dialogues with the Council. These dialogues take the form of an introduction by the concerned mandate holders followed by a series of questions and comments to which he/she may respond on the spot or at the end of the list of speakers. While all stakeholders may participate in the process, contributions from NGOs are restricted to a specific amount of time.[7]

Special Procedures may also be invited on an ad hoc basis to participate in Council proceedings as panellists. When Special Sessions are being held, a representative of the Special Procedures[8] takes the floor immediately after the High Commissioner to frame the discussion.

The growing number of mandates is often mentioned as an impediment to their effectiveness and visibility. It is, however, fair to observe that the world is shaped by human beings and thus faces an increasing number of challenges, the nature of which makes it necessary to have specific and focussed lenses on any given situation. The landscape continuously changes and that which is not of specific urgency today may become a priority tomorrow, and vice-versa. Accordingly, the prospects for rationalizing the system of Special Procedures look quite dim, whereas a possible expansion of that system to include new activities requiring attention from the human rights system seems unfortunately high. How to respond to the challenges faced by the Council in dealing with an increasing number of country or thematic situations while shaping better the system of Special Procedures is thus an immense challenge, the responses to which remain to be identified.

---

7 Fifteen minutes for individualized dialogues, 30 minutes for clustered dialogues.

8 Normally a representative of the Coordinating Committee.

The system of Special Procedures is sophisticated and capable of responding to both thematic country-specific emergencies. It addresses a wide variety of rights and freedoms and fosters rich discussions that are not always free from tension. The richness of the recommendations, the flexibility of the system, the independence of the mandate holders, their ability to conduct field visits and organize consultations on a variety of subjects, and the high number of initiatives conducted each year, are all highly commendable and considered key to the Human Rights Council's activities. In short, they provide the Council with a sense of accomplishment and meaning.

This is not altered by the fact that the high number of procedures generates difficulties of an organizational nature and does prevent the Council from giving due credit and adequate timing to their work. Similarly, the larger the special procedures system is, the more complex it is to coordinate among its various dismemberments and ensure that priority is granted to the protection of human rights in the field and not to endless discussions at the UN headquarters. Regardless of the complexity of these issues, they must ultimately be addressed within the framework of the efficiency process outlined below.[9]

1.3 Commissions of inquiry, commissions on human rights, fact-finding missions and other ad hoc investigations

In addition to the activities of Special Procedures mandates, certain particularly grave violations of human rights and international humanitarian law require the urgent intervention of the Council. Such crises can be abrupt and may trigger a prompt response from the Council, which may vary from an analysis of the facts to some form of identification of those responsible for violations and crimes. The structure of each mandate differs, but there are some commonalities, which are emerging with time. In the early years of the Council, these mandates did not follow an easily defined pattern, with scope, composition and nature varying from case to case. More recently, despite the continued inventiveness in terminology, the Council has de facto initiated a process of harmonization of their terms of reference.

---

9 See Chapter 7, Section 7.2.

While the Commission on Human Rights established only two such bodies in its existence, the Council has created no less than 38 of them in its relatively short existence. The fact that these bodies were of an exceptional nature at the time of the abolishment of the Commission explains why their nature, composition and modus operandi were left out of the Institutions-Building Package (IBP).

These investigation mechanisms are usually composed of three independent, international experts. While they are usually appointed by the Council President, the High Commissioner may also be tasked with their appointment and act as an interface with the Council. The experts are usually tasked with establishing the facts and circumstances surrounding the alleged violations and abuses, with a view to ensuring accountability for perpetrators, justice for the victims and an end to impunity. They are also expected to formulate recommendations to the Council, particularly regarding whether the alleged facts constitute international crimes or war crimes, and what accountability measures can be taken. In addition, they are expected to engage with the concerned authorities or other international actors with a view to providing support and the expertise to secure the immediate improvement of the human rights situation.

They are typically required to report back orally at the next regular Council session after their appointment and in a written manner in the subsequent ones. The duration of their mandates is one year. However, if the grave human rights situation persists, it is not uncommon for these mechanisms to have their mandates extended on a yearly basis for an unspecified duration.

At the time of completion of the first edition of this *Anatomy* there were six such mechanisms in place.

As a comparison, 11 such mechanisms existed at the end of 2024, including a thematic one to advance racial justice and equality in law enforcement (EMLER).The full list of all investigations established since the creation of the council is available on the website of the Council.[10]

---

10 See International Commissions of Inquiry, Commissions on Human Rights, Fact-Finding missions and other Investigations | OHCHR

Figure 1.1 below shows the increase in the number of investigations mechanisms since the establishment of the Council.

The significant increase that marked the past ten years is therefore of considerable interest. Their reports are often regarded as the highlights of the Council sessions, and the subject of intense media reporting, with a specific focus on their conclusions. Their impact on the rest of the UN system is not to be neglected.

However, some questions would eventually have to be looked into, such as the possible duplications that may arise between these investigation mechanisms and the system of special rapporteurs, not to mention the work of the High Commissioner and his/her Office. Also, as will be referred to in other parts of this *Anatomy*, particularly its conclusion, polarization plays its role, and it is hard not to notice that certain situations are investigated while others, similar or comparable, are not. Omissions are sometimes more important than actions.

1.4 The Human Rights Council Advisory Committee and the Complaints Procedure

At the time of the abolishment of the Commission on Human Rights, there existed two other important mechanisms advising it, namely the

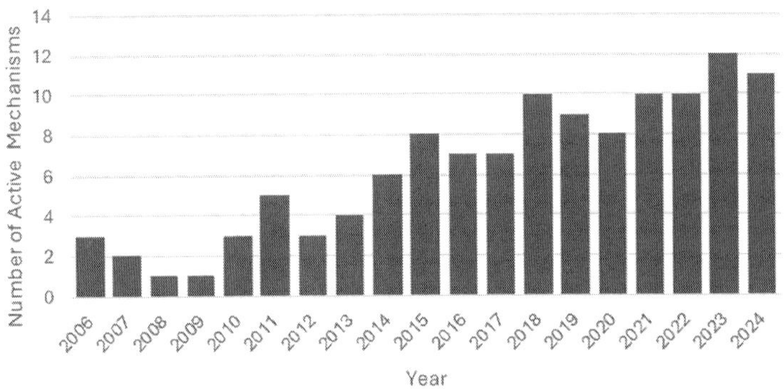

Figure 1.1 Number of active mechanisms per year

Sub-Commission on the Promotion and Protection of Human Rights and the so-called 1503 procedure.[11] The former provided advice to the Commission on a whole range of issues through the preparation of studies and reports, as well as the consideration of matters in a public format. It also addressed country-specific situations, particularly those not under the Commission's direct scrutiny. However, in its final years of activity, it was deprived of its ability to adopt country-specific resolutions.[12]

The 1503 procedure was established to enable the Commission to examine, in a confidential manner, a consistent pattern of reliably attested violations of human rights and fundamental freedoms occurring in any country of the world. It is the oldest human rights complaint mechanism under the UN system.

When the Assembly established the Human Rights Council to replace the Commission, even if it maintained the system of Special Procedures as it was, it did not proceed in the same way insofar as the Sub-Commission and the 1503 procedure were concerned. The Assembly simply referred to the need to maintain expert advice and a Complaints Procedure. This implied that the Council had to conceptualize new systems that would not necessarily replicate the terms or mandates of these two mechanisms. Likewise, the former Sub-Commission's advisory bodies[13] were detached from the Committee and replaced by Forums[14] responding directly to the Council.

By way of Sections III and IV of the Council Resolution 5/1, the Council established, after lengthy negotiations, the Human Rights Council Advisory Committee and the Complaints Procedure.

11 See ECOSOC Resolution 1503 (XLVII) of 27 May 1970.

12 See paragraph 52 of Commission's decision 2000/109 of 26 April 2000.

13 The Working Group on Indigenous Populations; Contemporary Forms of Slavery; Minorities and the Social Forum.

14 The Working Group on Contemporary Forms of Slavery's functions and responsibilities were taken up by a new mandate of the Special Rapporteur on Contemporary Forms of Slavery, including their causes and consequences.

1.4.1 The Human Rights Council Advisory Committee

The Advisory Committee (the Committee) was established to serve as a 'think-tank' for the Council.

The Committee is composed of 18 experts, serving in their personal capacities, who are elected by the Council through a secret ballot, each of them proposed or endorsed by a UN Member State. The system is thus fundamentally different from that of the selection of Special Procedures through a three-tier process. Elections take place at the Council level, and the vote is secret if the number of candidates exceeds the number of seats allocated to each region.[15]

Provisions similar to those governing the system of Special Procedures apply with regard to the principles of non-accumulation of functions and conflict of interest. Members serve a term of three years and are eligible for re-election once, allowing for a maximum of six consecutive years of service, as is the case for members of the Council or Special Procedures mandate holders. However, a former member may be eligible for candidacy again after a one-year gap.

The functions of the Committee are clearly described as aiming to provide expertise to the Council in the manner and form requested by the Council, focussing mainly on studies and research-based advice. More importantly, such expertise may only be rendered upon the request of the Council and in compliance with its resolutions and under its guidance. It is also explicitly mentioned that the Committee should not adopt resolutions or decisions. It may, however, propose, within the scope of the work set out by the Council for the latter's consideration and approval, suggestions for further enhancing its procedural efficiency as well as further research proposals within the scope of the work set out by the Council.

The former Sub-Commission advisory bodies were detached from the Committee and replaced by Forums responding directly to the Council. By depriving the Committee of the ability to adopt decisions or resolutions, the Council triggered a margin of uncertainty insofar as the

15 The geographic distribution is as follows: African States, 5; Asian States, 5; Eastern European States, 2; Latin American and Caribbean States, 3; and Western European and other States, 3.

Committee's *raison d'être* and working modalities were concerned. For example, even if the Committee must follow the Council's requests, the Council is not specifically requested to respond to any responses, suggestions, studies or reports emanating from the Committee. The 2011 review intended to clarify this aspect by requiring the Council to strengthen its interaction with the Committee and engage more systematically with it through work formats such as seminars, panel working groups and sending feedback on the inputs of the Committee. The Council is also requested to clarify the mandates given to the Committee. The dates of the two annual one-week sessions of the Committee were also rescheduled to bring them closer to those of the Council in the expectation that this will enable proper interaction. The Committee is also invited to interactively dialogue with the Council.

Over the years, the Advisory Committee and the Council have intensified their relationship through formal meetings between the plenary of the former and the Bureau of the latter. Letters were sent to the Council President, including proposals for new activities, studies and research. The responses to such letters are, however, left to the individual initiatives of Member States which, may or may not trigger a response to these suggestions or more often than not propose entirely new subjects for the Committee's consideration.

This management hiatus, which it is hoped will be overcome sooner or later, should however not hide the importance of the Committee, which has played a leading role in drafting instruments later revisited and adopted or considered by the Council. It has also submitted an impressive number of studies and amount of research for the Council's consideration. The mandates which the Council, has given it, are of importance[16] and its proposals for new action, have been considered of great value.

---

16 The following studies are currently being considered by the Committee: the human rights implications of new and emerging technologies in the military domain; the impact of disinformation on the enjoyment and realization of human rights; technology-facilitated gender-based violence; implications of plastic pollution for the full enjoyment of human rights; and the impact of artificial intelligence systems on good governance. For a list of past mandates see https://www.ohchr.org/en/hr-bodies/hrc/advisory-committee/mandates.

It is however self-evident that the Committee in its current structure and modus operandi is not able to respond to the various potential demands of the international community and consequently is often left aside when important research or studies are envisioned by sponsors of resolutions at the Council level. Given the fact the Committee's mandates do not entail any financial implications the working methods and the appointment process may deserve to be looked into in the context of any future review as alluded to below in Chapter 7.

1.4.2 The Complaints Procedure

While there was no agreement to designate the Advisory Committee as the successor to the Sub-Commission, the Complaints Procedure was established based on the former 1503 procedure. Improvements were introduced to ensure that the Procedure emphasizes the impartiality, objectivity, efficiency and victim-oriented character of its work, along with a timely response to requests.

The procedure is confidential in nature. It is not an individual complaint mechanism, as with certain human rights treaties. Under this procedure, a person or a group, including NGOs, claiming to be victims of violations of human rights and fundamental freedoms may submit complaints to the Council. The fundamental difference between this procedure and the individual communications' procedures under several treaty bodies lies in the political nature of the Council. It thus addresses consistent patterns of 'gross and reliably attested violations of human rights and all freedoms occurring in any part of the world and any circumstances. These terms were never – and probably will never be – the subject of consensual agreement on their definition. From the *travaux préparatoires* of the former so-called '1503 procedure' of the Commission which was replaced by the Complaints Procedure, it appears that a 'pattern of gross and reliably attested violations of human rights involve[s] several victims, a certain number of breaches spread over a minimum period of time, which are particularly inhuman or degrading in character'. Incidentally, this definition is one of the rarest available in the public domain concerning grave cases of human rights violations. It is however up to each concerned body to build up its own jurisprudence on a case-by-case manner.

The current Complaints Procedure follows a three-tier approach.

- The Working Group on Communications (WGC), composed of five members appointed by the Advisory Committee,[17] is the first step in initiating the Complaints Procedure. Each member is appointed for a three-year mandate.
- An initial pre-screening of communications received is carried out jointly by the Chair of the WGC and the Secretariat to filter out manifestly ill-founded or anonymous submissions. Their list is however shared with the WGC for consideration if deemed appropriate. The WGC decides on the admissibility of a communication and assesses the merits of the allegations, particularly as to whether the communication reveals a consistent pattern of gross and reliably attested violations of human rights and fundamental freedoms. It may decide to dismiss the communication, keep it under review, or channel it to the Working Group on Situations, which is the third step in the proceedings.
- The Working Group on Situations (WGS) is composed of five members, each appointed for one year by each regional group. They serve in their personal capacity, and their mandate may be renewed once. Based on the recommendations of the WGC, the WGS is tasked with presenting a report to the Council on consistent patterns of gross and reliably attested violations of human rights and fundamental freedoms and to make appropriate recommendations, normally in the form of a draft resolution or decision. It may also choose to keep the case pending or dismiss it.
- Each Working Group meets at least twice a year, with each session lasting five working days.
- The reports of the WGS are reviewed by the plenary of the Council, in closed sessions, as often as necessary, but at least once per year. At the conclusion of the process, the Council may decide to discontinue the consideration of the situation, keep it under review and appoint an independent and highly qualified expert to monitor the situation and report back to the Council, discontinue the review or recommend

17 This is an interesting anomaly. The Council's resolution 5/1 disconnected entirely the Advisory Committee from what might otherwise been considered as its predecessor, the Sub-Commission. However, the members of the Working Groups continue to be selected among members of the Committee in a similar manner to the selection process at the 1503 procedure level.

that OHCHR provide additional technical cooperation, capacity-building assistance, or advisory services to the State concerned.

It is important to note that the Complaints Procedure, at every stage, promotes dialogue between the body (WGC or Council) with the concerned Member States where the violations would have occurred. This is particularly the evident when the Working Groups decide to keep cases under review, aiming specifically to foster such dialogue. There is an extremely high rate of responses to the Complaints Procedure requests. Similarly, when a specific case is brought before the Council, delegations from the concerned countries are invited to participate. The delegations engage substantively in discussions while the matter is under consideration. When decisions are adopted, they may take the floor, but only after the decision is adopted.

Although the procedure is, by definition, confidential in nature, it remains victim-oriented. Hence both the author of the communication and the State concerned are informed at key stages of the proceeding: when the communication is deemed inadmissible, when it is taken up for consideration by the WGS, when it is kept under review by one of the two working groups or the Council, and upon the final outcome.

Of significant importance, whenever the Council has considered a report by the WGS, the Council President refers to it the following morning, detailing the conclusions reached and the countries considered. This means that despite the fact that the procedure is of a confidential nature, those participating in the procedures are made aware of the situations which are being discussed behind closed doors.

Since its establishment in 2007, the Council has discussed the following human rights situations at the plenary level: Cameroon (2014), the Democratic Republic of Congo (2009, 2011 and 2012), Eritrea (2012), Guinea (2009 and 2010), Iraq (2012), Kyrgyzstan (2006), Maldives (2008), Tajikistan (2011), Turkmenistan (2008, 2009 and 2012).

Of particular interest, the consideration of all these cases was eventually discontinued with the following caveats:

In the case of the Democratic Republic of Congo and of Iraq, recommendations were made to the OHCHR to increase technical cooperation, capacity-building assistance and advisory services. However, the confidentiality of the procedure creates a catch-22 situation regarding the follow-up of such recommendations. How can the Council revisit the matter if the case has been de jure dismissed? The Institutions-Building Package (IBP) offers no provision to clarify this. Any initiative under the public procedure rests with Member or Observer States. However, the confidential procedure operates solely through recommendations by the Working Group on Situations. Once a case is dismissed, the Working Group cannot reopen it. Nor can Member States or the Secretariat bring it back to the plenary, as the IBP does not grant them that authority. Accordingly, no-one is formally empowered to monitor the implementation of such technical cooperation recommendations, creating a vacuum that arguably deserves further consideration when and where appropriate.

As far as the human rights situation in Eritrea, the Council decided to discontinue the consideration of the case under the Complaints Procedure in order to take up public consideration of the same in the context of the implementation of the Council resolution 20/20 of 6 July 2012 which established the mandate of a special rapporteur. This remains the only case when the Council's consideration of a complaint under the Confidential Procedure led to the establishment of a public mandate.

Despite the above-mentioned results, the Complaints Procedure suffers from a lack of understanding about its working methods and the concurrence of other procedures. Complainants may prefer to submit their case to a Special Procedure, in the hope of triggering an urgent appeal. The presumed victim could alternatively address a treaty body in the expectation that the case will lead to a final quasi-judicial decision. The Complaints Procedure also faces challenges due to the confidential nature of its proceedings. Nevertheless, it is rarely mentioned that the percentage of comprehensive responses from concerned States, including concrete action at the domestic level, is exceptionally high compared with that for other procedures. Additionally, the level of participation at the plenary level is extremely high, and the procedure's outcomes gain significant weight when cases are submitted by the Working Group on Situations.

Notwithstanding these positive remarks, taking into consideration the constant increase of the Council's activities the question may soon arise as to the relevance of this procedure in the grand scheme of things. Given the fact that between 2014 and 2024 not a single case was referred to the plenary for its action and considering the imperious nature of dealing efficiently and effectively with all types of human rights violations, it would appear timely to consider new working methods or revisiting the current stratification. From the author's point of view, it would make perfect sense to, for instance, reduce the number of bodies involved in the procedure from three to two, namely a single Working Group of experts or, alternatively, a hybrid body including experts and States' representatives.

1.5 The intergovernmental working groups, groups of experts, forums and High Commissioner's designated experts

Since its establishment the Council has established quite a number of other subsidiary or ad hoc mechanisms to help it perform its functions under resolution 60/251.

The most traditional bodies which it has established are very traditional to the intergovernmental world, namely open-ended intergovernmental working groups whose main purpose is to negotiate new legal instruments or consider the best ways to implement existing international instruments.

According to Rule 18 as contained in resolution 5/1 the Council may indeed set up 'working groups and other arrangements'. Participants in these bodies shall be decided upon by the members based on rule 7. The rules of procedure of these bodies shall follow those of the Council, as applicable, unless decided otherwise by the Council. At the outset, it should be underlined that these bodies being composed of the UN Members without distinction between Council Members and observers, cannot in practical terms take decisions other than by consensus. This results partly from the absence at the Palais des Nations of an electronic voting system that would be extended in general to the UN membership. But, more importantly, this comes from the fact that the attendance at such working groups is usually such that it would enable the required quorum under rule 108 of the GA rules of procedure.[18]

---

[18] Rule 108 of the UNGA rules of procedure states that 'the presence of a majority of the members shall be required for any decision to be taken'. Hence, when a working group is meeting and a decision

Accordingly, when disagreements occur during a working group session, this is settled by having the Chairperson/rapporteur introduce a section in the report where he/she shared his/her own conclusions which are thus by definition considered not to be supported by the Working Group as a whole.

As per the duration of these working groups, it is of importance that there is no time-limit established by the Council for the completion of the purpose for which the relevant working group was established. Accordingly, as per common practice, the relevant rules in this regard are those of the Council's predecessor. In this regard, the only reference of interest lies in Operative Paragraph 60 of Decision 2000/109[19] of the Commission on Human Rights which states:

> In creating any standard-setting working group, the Commission should consider a specific timeframe within which the group would be called upon to complete its task. This could vary, depending on the complexity of the issue and the nature of the instrument. However, in most instances, the established timeframe should not in principle exceed five years. If, by the end of this timeframe, the working group has not been able to achieve the desired result, the Commission should consider the following options: (i) Extending the mandate; (ii) Providing for a period of reflection (such as one or two years); during this period, chairpersons should continue to consult widely and where possible provide the Commission with papers on an envisaged outcome; (iii) Examining the working methods of the particular working group (taking into account the format of the report, annexes to the report, chairperson's perception paper, etc.).

In practical terms, the five year timeframe is purely indicative and was never considered as a compelling practice.

The open-ended intergovernmental working groups currently in existence are the (i) Intergovernmental Open-Ended Working Group on the

---

contemplated, 97 delegations would need to be represented in the room which is never the case in practical terms. Additionally, there would be a need for the credentials of each participants to be checked which is never done for a working group of this nature, all those having a proper badge to enter the UN premises being entitled to get into the room.

19 See https://www.ohchr.org/sites/default/files/Documents/HRBodies/HRCouncil/CompilationDocuments1999-2005.pdf.

Right to Development, (ii) the Intergovernmental Working Group on the Effective Implementation of the Durban Declaration and Programme of Action, (iii) the Ad Hoc Committee on Complementary Standards to the International Convention on the Elimination of All Forms of Racial Discrimination, (iv) the Open-ended Intergovernmental Working Group on Regulatory framework of Activities of Private Military and Security Companies, and (v) the Intergovernmental Working Group on Transnational Corporations and Other Business Enterprises.

Aside the traditional open-ended intergovernmental working groups, the Council established a number of hybrid bodies. The first Forums to be established where the (i) Forum on Minority Issues and (ii) the Social Forum. Both provided a space for discussing issues stemming from the relevant Council resolutions and based on the experience gathered by the previous Sub-Commission on the Promotion and Protection of Human Rights which was abolished in 2006 and partly replaced by the Council's Advisory Committee.

The participation in these forums is guided by the enabling resolutions and their chairpersons are selected by the Council President. They usually attract quite a considerable number of participants from all horizons, expanding beyond the scope of those attending the regular sessions of the Council – thus creating at times issues in relation to statements made in the course of the discussion. As is the case with the above-mentioned open-ended intergovernmental working groups, rules applicable in these circumstances cannot easily be implemented in view of the lack of quorum. Additionally, given the lack of clarity as to who may be considered members of a Forum, there are no convenient procedures to settle difficulties that may arise during debates.

Aside from the Forum on Minority and the Social Forum, three additional Forums were established: (i) the Forum on Business and Human Rights, (ii) the Forum on Human Rights, Democracy and the Rule of Law and (iii) the Permanent Forum of People of African Descent.

There are important nuances between some of these forums. In particular, the Working Group on Business and Human Rights is guiding and chairing the relevant Forum. More importantly, the Permanent Forum on People of African Descent, which was established by UNGA resolution 75/134 is composed of ten members thus moving it slightly away from the legal status of the other forums.

As is clearly visible from the evolution of Forums over time, the Council in establishing new subsidiary bodies is increasingly relying on the input of experts. This is even more noticeable when it comes to two expert mechanisms: the meetings of which are open-ended and attended by many participants. The Expert Mechanism on the Rights of Indigenous Peoples (EMRIP) is composed of seen experts while the Expert Mechanism on the Right to Development (EMRTD) is composed of five.

This move away from the traditional Council's modus operandi is also underlined by a comparable trend towards the creation of hybrid mechanisms whereby the High Commissioner is requested to designate experts monitoring the human rights situation in three countries, namely Sudan, Haiti and Colombia.[20] The legal standing of these experts is hard to define. On the one hand they cannot be considered as Special Procedures since they are not established following the usual modalities contained in resolutions 5/1 and 16/21 and, as a result, they are not taking part of the annual meetings of mechanisms. On the other hand, their working methods and modus operandi resemble in every respect that of the special rapporteurs or independent experts.

1.6 Interaction between the various human rights bodies and mechanisms

As outlined, there coexists a large variety of extra-conventional mechanisms established by the Council or its predecessor. In parallel, further to the latter recommendations, the General Assembly adopted a number of human rights instruments, some of which have created treaty bodies. There exist at present ten such bodies composed of independent experts monitoring the implementation of core international human rights treaties.[21] Given the number of bodies and mechanisms dealing with human rights matters within the human rights system, one of the most frequently asked question relates to the interaction – or lack of – between these various conventional and extra-conventional bodies or mechanisms.

---

20 See Council's resolutions S-32/1, 52/39 and 53/22 respectively.

21 See https://www.ohchr.org/EN/HRBodies/Pages/TreatyBodies.aspx.

There is no obvious response to this question. Depending on the circumstances, some might argue that there is ample coordination while others may refute this conclusion. This is probably because there are no easily identified criteria enabling cooperation or coordination, which are mostly subjective elements, to be gauged.

In reality, the issues or themes addressed by these bodies or mechanisms often overlap or relate to similar matters. Immediate examples include the ill-treatment of persons and the deprivation of liberty, the rights of women, the struggle against any form of discrimination, the right to development and the right to life. Many other examples come to mind and it is actually possible to consider that any of the rights enshrined in the Universal Declaration could be addressed by three or more mechanisms. As far as States are concerned, they may be subjected to reviews or investigations initiated almost simultaneously by several bodies or mechanisms, which represents a serious problem, particularly for small delegations.

This rationale behind the juxtaposition and coexistence of so many different layers is explained below[22] and almost unavoidable in a multilateral context. Efforts to streamline these bodies or mechanisms have been largely unsuccessful. Considerable energy is often expended on the negotiation processes, which ultimately result in little or no substantial change to the existing landscape. For instance, it is difficult to realistically foresee any future scenario in which human rights bodies are merged or their working methods aligned and fully synchronized. There are simply too many obstacles to such an endeavour, from legal impediments to political or bureaucratic considerations.

What is striking, however, is that only a few practical steps have been taken to ensure an adequate level of cooperation and coordination. At the outset, it should be borne in mind that the co-existence of a variety of bodies or mechanisms has inherent value, as the repetition of similar or comparable recommendations can create a leitmotif and generating public focus on a particular theme or situation. However, this value becomes meaningless if there is no real or genuine coordination, cooperation, or even sharing of information between the various actors. Additionally,

---

22 See Chapter 2.

when this becomes the rule rather than the exception, it defeats the purpose – if there is any.

It is extremely difficult not to lament the inadequate level of interaction between all concerned parties, a shortcoming which is probably linked to the 'silo' mentality prevalent in so many large international or national public or private organizations. However, over the years, genuine but modest efforts have been undertaken to strengthen the complementarity of these bodies and mechanisms, reduce the possible level of duplication, and instil practical modalities for cooperation and coordination in their working methods. Some results were achieved, such as the establishment and strengthening over the years of a Coordinating Committee of Special Procedures, the stimulation of dialogues between the Human Rights Council Advisory Council and its parent body as well as the holding of annual meetings of Special Procedures mandate holders and chairpersons of treaty bodies. However, this is far from the setting up of a practical mechanism of interaction and cooperation.

The picture thus remains one of a system that, in the author's opinion, frequently misses opportunities to develop meaningful synergies and coordination. In addition to the 'silo' mentality, it is probably rooted in the conjunction of political and psychological considerations which are often difficult to describe.

It is for instance quite obvious that States may prefer the status quo rather than opening Pandora's box and renegotiating what was agreed years earlier in long and arduous negotiations with the risk of regressing or reaching an unsatisfactory outcome.

Similarly, concerned bodies or mechanisms, preoccupied with and overwhelmed by fulfilling their own mandates, may lose sight of the importance and complementarity nature of activities performed by others. Also, it may be extrapolated that independent experts within these various bodies or mechanisms at times display a specific reluctance to change, coupled with a fear of the unknown or their own powers.

In concrete terms, at least five distinct types of mechanisms coexist to assess the human rights situations at the country level, namely: (a) the UPR where UN Member States review the situation of all human rights in all countries of the world; (b) the treaty bodies which monitor the implementation of specific human rights in the territory of States parties, either via the reporting or communications procedures; (c) the Special Procedures which report and advise on human rights at the country level from a thematic or country-specific perspective; (d) the various commissions of inquiry, fact-finding missions and investigation mechanisms; and (e) the Complaints Procedure which deals with consistent patterns of gross and reliably attested violations of all human rights in any part of the world. To this list, the experts designated by the High Commissioner at the request of the High Commissioner, which were alluded to in the previous section, should be added. There are however and most regrettably almost no coordination or harmonization processes between them.

In a comparable manner, three mechanisms coexist which consider substantive matters, namely (a) the Human Rights Council Advisory Committee, which operates as a think-tank for the Council, (b) the thematic Special Procedures, and (c) the treaty bodies, which interpret the provisions of the relevant Covenant or Convention in their general comments or decisions on individual communications.

There is, however, no single opportunity for these mechanisms to meet and exchange information, let alone develop mutually agreed strategies. Special Procedures mandate holders meet once per year, and the Coordinating Committee ensures some form of continuity throughout the year. However, none of the other bodies or mechanisms are participating on a continuing basis. It would appear quite logical that representatives of treaty bodies, commissions of inquiry, the Advisory Committee and the Complaints Procedure (Working Group on Communications) attend the meetings, at least partially and join in the consideration of substantive and organizational matters. This may represent the first step towards generating a culture of communication and coordination among the various components of the human rights system.

It is quite regrettable to note that instead of trying to build bridges between them, the various expert mechanisms have displayed little interest to work together on specific projects. This may be understandable and quite common in the international human rights world given the subjective nature of each stakeholder and the lack of objective requirements for these different mechanisms to meet, cooperate or dialogue. It is however simply incomprehensible from an external point of view not to consider it in the interest of the human programme as a whole. Should the mechanisms not be in a position to organize such meetings by themselves, the author would not find it inappropriate for the Council itself to take the initiative of organizing such meetings on an intersessional basis in the context of roundtables or seminars.

Another step would be to systematize the exchange of information and dialogue when substantive human rights provisions undergo interpretation or commentary by a Committee or a special rapporteur. Practical measures could include the establishment of a virtual platform accessible by all members of treaty bodies, Special Procedures mandate holders and experts of the Advisory Committee. This could be complemented by systematizing the invitation of other mechanisms' experts to any such discussion led by a mechanism, whatever it is.

The UPR is at times perceived as weakening the status of conclusions of treaty bodies and Special Procedures. This comes from what appears to the author as a pure misconception of the modus operandi of the UPR. Indeed, it is considered that their conclusions and recommendations are often included into recommendations by peers in the context of the UPR review. Since the reviewed States are given the opportunity to support or simply note the said recommendations, it is advanced that, by not supporting the treaty bodies' recommendations, this represents a de facto rejection of mandatory documents.[23]

What is not taken into account is that the recommendations made by States in the context of the UPR, although they are often taken from the outcome of the work of treaty bodies or special rapporteurs, almost never quote a specific recommendation. Hence, when noted and not supported by the State under Review, the legal effect, if any, is limited to the bilateral relationship between the latter and the State having made the concerned recommendations. If it were to be organized differently, the UPR mechanism may easily transform itself into an appeal's court against treaty bodies or special procedures' conclusions and recommendations.

However, considering that an average of two-thirds of all recommendations made in a review are supported by the concerned State and that a significant number of them are directly linked to a treaty body or Special Procedure recommendation, this implies that their content was blessed by the State under Review in a formal manner. This strengthens their implementability. Having been supported by the State under Review,

23 See above, Chapter 1, Section 1.1.

they may easily be referred to at the domestic level and subjected to discussion and follow-up action. They provide extremely helpful entry points enabling all concerned, from civil society to UN entities, to engage substantively in the implementation and follow-up process. A proactive approach would thus be for Special Procedures and treaty bodies to build up their follow-up work partly on those recommendations, which incorporate their own conclusions. Providing a conceptual basis for such an activity would require appropriate funding and impact on organizational matters. It would, however, maximize the implementation of such important recommendations and uphold the complementary nature of the mechanisms.

Lastly, it is at times regretted that the various mechanisms produce many documents which are not easily accessible, and are sometimes partly duplicative and/or of a contradictory nature. Their overwhelming nature is considered as shedding doubt on the possibility of implementing the numerous recommendations they include. However, this corpus of documents also represents the deepest and broadest charting of human rights, which currently exists at the universal level. Some efforts have been made to categorize and index these documents, but this remains a complex and somewhat cumbersome exercise. It could be envisioned that this could be further refined using AI tools – provided that an appropriate level of funding is made available.

2 The Human Rights Council functions

The skeleton is the body part that forms the supporting structure of an organism and the framework that provides support, shape and protection to the organs. By furthering the analogy to a biological anatomy, this chapter aims to analyse the fundamental structure of the Council and its mechanisms. This will consist of a quasi-dissection of the multiple functions of the Council. It will also include a rapid and fragmentary discussion of what the author considers one of the main weaknesses or deficiencies of the Commission, as this is the body that preceded the Council and built the foundations upon which it was built. The text will also show how some of these weaknesses have been corrected. This will be done against the background of decrypting the multilayered structure of the intergovernmental human rights machinery.

The General Assembly Resolution 60/251 spells out the Council's functions and terms of reference. However, being the result of intense and arduous negotiations, the text is rather brief and includes a number of provisions that had to be clarified by the Council in the Institutions Building Package[1] and its own practice.

Before its eventual abolition, the Commission faced serious challenges in adjusting its modus operandi to the pressing nature of circumstances. In contrast, since its inception, the Council has developed an array of mechanisms, tools and procedures and it has done so in a pragmatic and extremely subtle manner. Often, these efforts were not encapsulated in a resolution, decision or Presidential Statement owing to the difficulties

1 HRC Resolutions 5/1 and 5/2 of 18 June 2017 are to be read in conjunction with HRC Resolution 16/21 of 25 March 2011.

faced in reaching consensus on a written document, a fact that makes it difficult to analyse the outcome of the Council's work in a comprehensive manner.

Very often, the Council's areas of responsibility are analysed and distributed into two baskets. The first one includes activities aimed at promoting and protecting human rights as well as preventing human rights violations. The second is more generic and includes dialogue on thematic issues as well as the development of international human rights law. This is the general background of this study.

To this static model – which does not necessarily give credit to the multiple activities of the Council and, in particular its flexibility in dealing with the challenges it may face – an evolving approach deriving from the complex evolution of the intergovernmental human rights system will be privileged. This approach may be referred to as 'human rights geology'.[2] Beyond the apparent awkwardness of referring to geology in an anatomical description of a human rights body, the intent is to apprehend the multiplicity of layers constituting the intergovernmental human rights system, each layer requiring a specific lens of understanding and reading.

Over the 76 years that have elapsed since the adoption of the Universal Declaration of Human Rights, various procedures, mechanisms and bodies have been established by the intergovernmental machinery. Each generation added at least one, and often more, new tools to the existing toolbox, and as is customarily the case with universal international organizations, none of them were or could be abolished.[3] This is due to the fact that the process of adopting amendments or revisions to a given

2 According to Wikipedia, geology is an Earth science concerned with the solid Earth, the rocks of which it is composed, and the processes by which they change over time. By analogy, the human rights geology is tantamount to analysing the various human rights intergovernmental mechanisms and tools established over the past decades and, in particular, the processes by which they have changed over time.

3 With the noticeable exception of the Commission, which was abolished in 2006, this was, however, the result of a convergence of criticisms going much beyond the usual political or policy acrimony and falling outside the scope of the present study.

text, not to mention its abolition, is so complex, cumbersome and heavy that it is considered much easier, politically and legally speaking, to work on an altogether new text.[4] Whether the former tools or mechanisms may become obsolete over the years is usually not taken into account.

This human rights geology is of crucial importance in decrypting the functions and activities of the Council to date. Indeed, when the Council sets up an intergovernmental working group with a view to preparing a new Declaration or Convention, it is actually replicating the approach of the former Commission in its early years. When it is looking into human rights situations at the country level, the Council is actually following the lead of the Commission when it initiated the very first country public mandates or dealt with such matters under the 1503 procedure in the 1970s. When it is considering new thematic areas of work or expanding on existing ones, it is replicating the work initiated with the establishment of the first thematic mandate on enforced or involuntary disappearances in that same decade. When it deliberates on the importance of the promotion of human rights or of technical cooperation and advisory services, the Council is in reality following priorities which were identified by the intergovernmental machinery in the 1980s. When it is contemplating the establishment of an investigation mechanism, it is building on activities that were privileged in the 1990s and further developed later. When it is expanding and deepening its relations with the Office of the High Commissioner and interacts with the High Commissioner on country, thematic or other matters, it follows what was contemplated and set into motion in the 1990s.[5]

---

4 This observation extends to the setting up of international human rights norms. Whereas regional organizations have often privileged the adoption of Optional Protocols, this proved to be extremely hard to achieve at the universal level. Consequently, with few exceptions, new norms were usually dealt with in the context of new instruments, and accordingly, new monitoring bodies.

5 This may easily be testified by considering a document entitled 'Compilation of recent documents in relation to the enhancement of the working methods of the Commission on Human Rights from 1999 to 2005' available on the Council website. At least 12 documents and five other relevant documents have been meticulously compiled. The Commission's ambitions to revisit and enhance the effectiveness of its own mechanisms, as they were initially referred to in the Chairperson's statement of 29 April 1999, proved to be largely

This is partly explained by the fact that among the factors that led to the abolition of the Commission was a certain inability to reform, review or revisit its tools and mechanisms in a meaningful manner. Unlike the Commission, the Council, at the direction of its Presidents and Bureaux, opted for a flexible and pragmatic approach, putting on hold what could not be improved at a given moment but seizing opportunities whenever possible.

The segments included in the programme of work of any Council session are intermingled in a complex array of tools and mechanisms. Accordingly, understanding the complexity of the overall human rights system as well as the specificity of each single mechanism requires a very thorough understanding of the Council's and Commission's actions and intentions at the time any of the considered tools or mechanisms were contemplated and/or established.

The multiple tools and mechanisms allow the international community to react to situations or issues in an appropriate manner. This dense and complex patchwork allows those aiming to bring a given situation or theme to the attention of the Council to avail themselves of the luxury of resorting to many different precedents to reach an agreement on a specific course of action. Without this accumulation of tools and mechanisms, there would be much less flexibility and consequently more difficulty in contemplating a way out of intense and delicate political negotiations.

---

unsuccessful. Against this background, the Commission proceeded with the adoption of documents of an increasingly technical nature, touching on such matters as speaking time limits, the organization of the High-Level Segment, and the structure of interactive dialogues. Nevertheless, it is fair to note that most of the innovations or changes introduced by the Council in its short existence were considered but implemented without success by the Commission. The Council is, however, still struggling with following up on some of the ambitious steps analysed by the Commission, such as the support to, 'rationalizing' of and cooperation with the network of Special Procedures, the follow-up to the mechanisms' findings, the consideration of emergencies or urgent matters, the structure of the complaints' procedure and the advisory body, or the purpose, methodology and timeframe of the adoption of resolutions.

Consequently, when one particular tool cannot be implemented in a specific case, the Council may turn to another one previously used in different sets of circumstances, the existence of which is resorted to as a precedent. The Council may also envisage a totally new tool, given the Council's longstanding appetite for new tools and mechanisms. Similarly, although a procedure or tool may be deemed to be on the verge of obsolescence by commentators, it may suddenly arise from the ashes and prove its usefulness in dealing with cases that would otherwise be left unattended because of the inadequacy of other mechanisms otherwise considered more effective or efficient.[6]

Beforehand, however, it is important to give attention to the weaknesses or deficiencies of the Commission in dealing with gross and massive human rights violations. Whether this is specifically acknowledged or not, it is quite obvious that the ability, or lack of ability, of the Commission to deal appropriately with gross and massive human rights violations underpins efforts made to reform the Commission and later define the Council.

2.1 The inadequacy of the responses of the Commission on Human Rights to gross and massive violations of human rights

The fact that the international community has had to expand the scope, nature and number of human rights tools and mechanisms on a continuing basis since the 1960s may be considered a testimony to the lack of adequacy of the then-existing system in dealing with serious human rights country or thematic situations. The most striking and regrettable example of this inadequacy relates to the difficulties faced by the Commission on Human Rights in addressing gross and massive human rights situations in certain specific cases.

When envisaging the effectiveness of today's Human Rights Council functions, it is important to acknowledge the heritage of the Commission on Human Rights, its predecessor. In this regard, comments are often restricted to the very last decade of the Commission's existence and

6 The most obvious example is that of the Complaints Procedure.

the analysis made against the political prism prevailing at the time.[7] However, this is limited in scope since it does not focus on the previous five decades. A much broader assessment is thus topical, particularly one that takes into account the Commission's lack of responses to some of the worst human tragedies post-Second World War.

Indeed, it should be expected that the most important intergovernmental body dealing with human rights would have considered these matters as promptly and efficiently as possible. This is particularly the case in view of the fact that the United Nations was established after the Second World War and the genocides perpetrated by the Nazi regime on the clear understanding and commitment that such an atrocious situation would never be tolerated again.

Unfortunately, this was not the case.

Pinpointing the failures of the intergovernmental machinery in two of the worst situations[8] that have arisen in recent decades is therefore topical since it sheds light on how the Council is interpreting its mandate today.

2.1.1 The Cambodian Genocide

The Cambodian genocide took place in the 1970s, from 1975 to 1979. It was carried out by the Khmer Rouge Regime and caused the deaths of approximately 1.5–3 million Cambodians – about a quarter of the population. Millions fell victim to the regime by being sent to labour camps or subjected to forced labour, torture, inhuman treatment, arbitrary detention, starvation, harsh living conditions and being denied all the rights and freedoms set forth in the Universal Declaration.

It would have been expected that the Commission on Human Rights, the then main UN human rights body, would have devoted time and

7 The issues most often referred to relate to the impact of the events of 11 September 2001, the Durban Conference, the composition and agenda of the Commission, the non-re-election of a prominent Security Council Member, and the undue weight of certain States that were constantly re-elected compared to others.

8 On the understanding that more or less the same comments could unfortunately be offered regarding other cases of genocide.

attention to considering the matter, analysed the situation from the very beginning and alerted all other relevant UN bodies about the unfolding tragedy. It would have further been expected that, when the situation reached the qualification of a gross and massive human rights situation degenerating into a genocide, the Commission would have deployed every possible means to consider the situation, planned immediate remedial action and summoned other relevant UN bodies to take meaningful action.

Unfortunately, this did not happen far from it.

The main reason behind this inaction was the impossibility for the international community to overcome the politics of the Cold War and post-Cold War eras and coming to terms with such atrocities. The following developments shed light in a chronological manner on the actions by the Commission and its subsidiary body, the Sub-Commission on Prevention of Discrimination and Protection of Minorities.

The first (unsuccessful) attempt at establishing a mandate on this matter was made at the March 1978 Session of the Commission, three years after the start of the genocide.[9] At the initiative of the Secretariat, the matter was brought to light and several members of the Commission supported the suggestion that an impartial investigation into the reports of 'extensive violations of human rights in Democratic Kampuchea' be undertaken forthwith. However, other members felt that the information available was not sufficient to warrant such an investigation, particularly since the government of Democratic Kampuchea had not been informed that such allegations had been brought before the Commission and had not had an opportunity to provide information to the Commission concerning them. In view of this disagreement, the Chairperson proposed a draft decision 9 (XXXIV) which was adopted and provided for the documents and summary records of the 34th session to be shared with the said government for it to be able to respond to them through the Sub-Commission.

In response to this call, the Sub-Commission considered the matter in September 1978, at which time 1,000 pages of materials were received and

9 See the Commission's draft resolution E/CN.4/L.1402.

analysed.[10] During the discussion that ensued, several members of the Sub-Commission 'expressed their deep concern over reports of alleged systematic and flagrant violations of human rights and fundamental freedoms in Democratic Kampuchea, which allegedly had brought about the death of hundreds of thousands, if not millions, of people from all walks of life, men, women and children, since 1975 and voiced fear that on the basis of the information before the Sub-Commission the alleged atrocities were still being perpetrated'.[11] They went on to propose that a working group or at least a rapporteur of the Sub-Commission should analyse the evidence and report to the Commission as a matter of the highest priority. One member, however, objected to the distribution of relevant documents, observing that 'they consisted of slanderous propaganda disseminated by political refugees hostile to the present regime of Democratic Kampuchea... and that neither the Sub-Commission nor any other UN body had the right to intervene in the domestic affairs of that country, such interference being a violation of Article 2, paragraph 7, of the Charter of the United Nations'. Eventually, the Sub-Commission decided to request its Chairperson to analyse these materials and present a report to the following session of the Commission. The Chairperson's analysis was circulated on 30 January 1979 and contained an account of terrible testimonies channelled to the Sub-Commission by refugees and NGOs, as well as some governments.[12]

---

10 See document E/CN.4/1335.

11 Ibid., para 4.

12 Section IV of the Chairperson's analysis included interesting developments on the reliability of the allegations received. Of interest, however, the report contains also a summary of one of the experts who analysed the information's views according to which 'while not claiming that refugee accounts are always false or grossly inaccurate... many considerations might have a bearing on the accuracy of these accounts, including in particular the fact that many refugees coming from the middle or upper class in the old society and those who were connected with the previous regime are strongly motivated to portray the situation in Cambodia in the worst possible light have not been sufficiently taken into account' (para 22). The Chairperson's analysis also indicates that

> no reliable information concerning the number of persons who have lost their lives in Democratic Kampuchea since 17 April 1975 through executions or through other acts or omissions of the Government is

Despite the dire accounts in the materials received by the Sub-Commission and shared with the Commission, the latter did not take any action on the matter at its 35th session in 1979. After the collapse of the Khmer Rouge regime, it adopted its Resolution 29 (XXXVI) of 11 March 1980 in which it condemned 'all the gross and flagrant violations of human rights which have occurred in Kampuchea' as well as the 'invasion and occupation of parts of Kampuchea by foreign forces and the violations of human rights that have ensued'. It further decided to keep the matter under review as a matter of priority and requested a member of the Sub-Commission to review any further material on the subject at the 33rd session of the Sub-Commission and submit it back to the Commission together with appropriate recommendations to.[13]

Eventually, the Sub-Commission adopted its last resolution on the matter, which recommended to the Commission 'that it should keep the situation of human rights in Kampuchea under continuing review and to this end to consider inviting the Secretary-General to designate a Special Representative to assist in restoring full respect for human rights and fundamental freedoms as speedily as possible in Kampuchea'.[14] The Commission did not take any action on the Sub-Commission's request.

The mandate of the Special Rapporteur on the situation of human rights in Cambodia was established by the Commission Resolution 1993/6, adopted more or less 15 years after the end of the genocide.

---

available in the materials. Several estimates refer to the execution of at least 100,000 persons and the death from this and other causes especially disease, starvation and exhaustion are said to total 1 million or more persons in all. The materials reflect a general belief that the loss of life from epidemics and endemic diseases such as malaria and from physical hardships and privations has been several times greater than that from executions. At the same time, there are several references in the materials to the fact that executions may have been more frequent and the conditions of life more difficult in the areas of the country from which most of the refugees providing accounts have come than in certain other areas.

13 See paras 2, 3 and 10 of Resolution 29 (XXXVI).

14 See para 3 of the Sub-Commission Resolution 24 (XXXIII) of 12 September 1980.

2.1.2 The Rwandese Genocide

On 6 April 1994, the plane carrying the Rwandese and Burundi Heads of State was shot down on its descent into Kigali. The genocide started the following day and ended in July 1994 with the defeat of government forces. Close to one million Rwandans were killed during this 100-day period. The extent of the killings and accompanying terror is unchallenged in human history. As mentioned by Jean Hatzfeld in his book *Machete Season*,[15] the number of deaths occurring every day far exceeded that of Nazi Germany, with close to 10,000 deaths every day.

Retrospectively, it would have been expected that, given the lessons of the past, the inadequacy of the response of the international community, and in particular the Commission, to previous genocides and massive human rights violations, it would have taken the lead in trying to prevent these violations from occurring, or at least ring alarm bells forcefully with the UN political bodies and alert them to the extent of the killings, the terrible cost in human lives, and the gross and massive human rights violations.

However, this did not happen.

Of particular importance in this case is the fact that, contrary to the genocide in Cambodia, information was shared with the Commission on the extent of human rights violations in Rwanda several years before the start of the genocide, and the special mechanisms that had been established since the middle of the 1970s were by then fully operational and played an extremely important early-warning role.

As early as 1992, Amos Wako, the Special Rapporteur on Extrajudicial, Summary or Arbitrary Executions, reported[16] to the Commission on cases he had brought to the attention of the Rwandese authorities the previous year. In 1992, the situation worsened and the Working Group on Enforced or Involuntary Disappearances shared with the Commission in 1993 five reported cases of disappearances which it had transmitted to the government for its clarification.[17] Similarly, the Special Rapporteur

---

15 2003, Editions du Seuil.
16 See E/CN.4/1992/30, paras 461–467.
17 See E/CN.4/1993/25, paras 441–446.

on the Question of Torture referred to reports of prisoners who had been subjected to torture following the mass arrests of 1990. He also mentioned further cases of maltreatment by the military, as well as arrests and the mistreatment of members of the Tutsi ethnic minority.

In view of the foregoing, as well as allegations brought to his attention, the new Special Rapporteur on Extrajudicial, Summary or Arbitrary Executions, Bacre Ndiaye, requested an invitation to visit Rwanda. He undertook his visit from 8 to 17 April 1993, one year before the start of the genocide, and reported on his mission to the Commission. The report was made available on 11 August 1993.[18]

In his report, the Special Rapporteur indicated that he had used as his main working document the report of an international commission of inquiry which gave 'an idea of the scale of Rwanda's problems as regards human rights in general and extrajudicial, summary or arbitrary executions in particular. It (went) in detail into the mechanisms behind the massacres and describe(d) the methods used by the perpetrators of violations; it also clearly identifie(d) those responsible for violating the right to life'.[19]

Describing the situation as he had witnessed it, he stated that:

> a climate of mistrust and terror currently prevails in Rwanda. Although rumour is largely responsible for this situation, violence is none the less a feature of everyday life. There is an alarming increase in crime, fuelled by the profusion of weapons in circulation... and the destitute condition of a whole sector of the population exacerbated by displacements of the population as a result of the war. But the prevalence of crime is also sometimes used to cover up acts of political violence... The situation has become particularly explosive with the distribution of weapons to civilians by the authorities officially to combat the forces of the FPR... Massacres of civilian populations have been perpetrated either by the Rwandese security forces or by certain sectors of the population.[20]

Analysing the factors that had facilitated the violations of human rights, the Special Rapporteur pinpointed the absence of the rule of law, the

18 See E/CN.4/1994/7/Add.1.
19 Ibid., para 7.
20 Ibid., paras 22 and 28.

tradition of impunity, the failings of the judicial system, the absence of any system for the protection of ethnic minorities and injurious propaganda.[21]

In offering its conclusions and recommendations, the Special Rapporteur underlined that 'Rwandese citizens, whatever their ethnic group, political affiliations or social origin, had the same fundamental rights as all other citizens throughout the world' and that 'the international community (could) not remain indifferent to their situation and must provide its assistance wherever that of the Rwandese State (was) inadequate or non-existent'.

The Special Rapporteur then went on to make 12 recommendations on various aspects of the struggle against extrajudicial, summary and arbitrary executions. His eleventh recommendation related to the 'genocide question'. As to the question of whether the massacres which he had previously described could be termed genocide, he proposed an initial reply according to which the violations of the right to life described in his report could fall within the purview of article III of the Convention on the Prevention and Punishment of the Crime of Genocide.[22]

It is fair to state that never before had a UN expert mechanism been so clear in alerting the international community about a situation which it indicated fell within the purview of the Genocide Convention and offered such rich and comprehensive conclusions and recommendations. Contrary to what had happened two decades earlier, the early warning signs were there, and clearly depicted in the experts' public reports. The Commission was alerted in depth on the situation (which already qualified as a genocide a year before it degenerated even further into atrocities of the worst possible nature and prevalence).

---

21 Ibid., paras 44–58.

22 Article III of the Genocide Convention states that 'the following acts shall be punishable: (a) genocide; (b) conspiracy to commit genocide; (c) direct and public incitement to commit genocide; (d) attempt to commit genocide; and (e) complicity in genocide'. The Special Rapporteur also referred to article IV which states that 'Persons committing genocide or any of the other acts... shall be punished, whether they are constitutionally responsible rulers, public officials or private individuals'.

The special mechanisms thus played their early warning role in an adequate and effective manner. The international community, as it gathered in the Commission on Human Rights, unfortunately did not respond in time or in a meaningful and adequate manner to the early warning. Soon afterwards, the situation deteriorated further into the abomination of genocide. In particular, there was no call for a Special Session on the situation of human rights in Rwanda in the period of time that followed the issuing of the report and prior to the 50th session that took place from 31 January to 11 March 1994.

Of significant relevance is thus the fact that the Commission on Human Rights, at its 50th Session, failed to consider the situation of Rwanda as reported to it by the Special Rapporteur, whereas it did consider the situation of human rights in many countries of the world, including Burundi[23] and the Democratic Republic of Congo.[24] No proposal was tabled by any country on the situation and thus no action was contemplated on this matter.

The very first High Commissioner for Human Rights, José Ayala-Lasso, assumed his functions on 5 April 1994. Almost immediately, he addressed a memorandum on the situation of human rights in Rwanda to the Secretary-General,[25] which he followed up with requests for urgent information from a wide range of UN agencies on 26 April 1994. Based on the information gathered, he called on members of the Commission, on 4 May 1994, to consider the advisability of convening a Special Session. He then visited the country on 11 and 12 May, accompanied by Louis Joinet, Special Rapporteur of the Sub-Commission on the question of impunity and Chairperson of the Working Group on Arbitrary Detention. In his report to the Commission, he detailed the tragic situation he had witnessed firsthand, condemning the wanton killings of more than 200,000 persons, and called for effective international action to prevent a further escalation of human rights violations. He invited the Commission on Human Rights to consider the appointment of a special rapporteur who would examine all human rights aspects of the situation, including the root causes and responsibilities for the recent atrocities, and report thereon as early as possible, and periodically thereafter.

---

23 Resolution 1994/86.

24 Resolution 1994/87.

25 On 14 April 1994, see E/CN.4/S-3/3.

In his conclusions, the High Commissioner further stated that:

28. The situation in Rwanda can be characterized as a human rights tragedy. The wanton killing of more than 200,000 innocent civilians, including women, children and elderly persons, calls for the strongest condemnation by the international community.
29. The struggle for power in Rwanda has obvious political connotations which transcend the framework of human rights. However, long-standing and persistent human rights violations have been committed in a climate of disrespect for basic human rights principles and impunity for the perpetrators of major crimes.
30. Effective international action to prevent a further escalation of human rights violations is urgently required. Killings of civilians must stop immediately.
31. At the same time, every effort must be made to achieve a cease-fire or at least temporary cessation of hostilities in order to create the conditions necessary for humanitarian assistance to reach the 2 million displaced, as well as other persons in need. Furthermore, all those who are trapped between lines or detained in places which they do not consider safe must be given the possibility of moving to areas of their own choice with the assistance and protection of UNAMIR.
32. The authors of the atrocities must be made aware that they cannot escape personal responsibility for criminal acts they have carried out, ordered or condoned.
33. All relevant international human rights instruments to which Rwanda is a party, including the Convention on the Prevention and Punishment of the Crime of Genocide, as well as international humanitarian law, must be fully respected.
34. Both parties to the conflict should immediately implement the abovementioned steps and measures.
35. The Commission on Human Rights, for its part, may wish to consider the appointment of a special rapporteur who would examine all human rights aspects of the situation, including root causes and responsibilities for the recent atrocities, and report thereon as early as possible, and periodically thereafter.
36. The Commission on Human Rights may also wish to decide that the special rapporteur should be assisted in the collection and analysis of information by a team of human rights field officers acting in close cooperation with UNAMIR and other UN agencies and programmes from within Rwanda, as well as from neighbouring countries where Rwandan refugees are located.
37. It should be noted in this regard that both the Special Representative of the Secretary-General for Rwanda and the Force Commander of UNAMIR have pledged their full cooperation with UN human rights monitors, following a decision by the Commission on Human Rights in this regard.
38. The Commission on Human Rights may further wish to endorse the suggestion that future UN efforts aimed at conflict resolution and

> peacebuilding in Rwanda should be accompanied by a strong human rights component and that this process should be effectively supported by a comprehensive programme of human rights assistance.

Eventually, but extremely late, when the genocide was well underway and close to its ending, the Commission met in the context of its third Special Session on 24 and 25 May 1994, as a result of which a Special Rapporteur was appointed to investigate the human rights situation in Rwanda.[26]

It should be borne in mind that the Commission on Human Rights could not deal with the above matters in the absence of broad agreement among its members and that a variety of factors prevented it from stepping in. However, it remains that the absence of a proper modus operandi to circumvent these blockages was a tragedy in itself.

These two situations highlight the impossible practical situation in which the Commission found itself in dealing with the worst types of human rights violations that may be registered. The political standstill, the absence of means to overcome political blockages, the considerable delays in responding to urgent human rights and humanitarian crises, the inadequacy of the tools used in this regard and the lack of coordination between the various concerned bodies were ingredients of a deafening silence in dealing with human rights disasters. Analysed together with other comparable tragedies, the inadequacy of the responses and the powerlessness of the Commission had a lasting influence on the perception of the intergovernmental human rights machinery by the public at large. Indeed, questions were often raised about what the rationale of an intergovernmental human rights body might be if it is not in a position to raise its voice loud and clear and call all concerned to action in situations of this nature. The following section attempts to respond to this question insofar as the Council is concerned.

---

26 See CHR Resolution S-3/1 included in the report of the 3rd Session (E/CN.4/S-3/3).

2.2 Elements of a human rights geology: how the Council addresses human rights issues

The very complex human rights geology linked to the responses – or lack of responses – proposed by the international community to deal with human rights violations and address human rights thematic issues since the creation of the United Nations shapes to a large extent the functions of the Council.

The multilayered institutional structure that exists today is the result of decades of efforts made to identify which responses may be proposed to country or thematic human rights issues. A plethora of mechanisms and tools have been set in motion and continue to operate even if the usefulness and contribution of each one taken separately may be questioned. Taken as a whole, this system has become very sophisticated and complex, yet has an appropriate network of tools, bodies and mechanisms, which may be used or resorted to when needed. Their nature may be different, but their ultimate goals remain the same: providing responses to human rights issues, whatever they may be.

This geology, complicated as it may be, is composed of multiple layers of contributions by generations of stakeholders who tried to identify possible steps forward and answers to emerging problems. It must be read as a whole in order to decipher the modus operandi of today's Council. It would indeed be extremely difficult, if not impossible, to analyse the Council's working methods and functioning without understanding the articulation of this multiplicity of layers.

While attempting to describe this system, it is important to recall that each one of its components remains in place and may be used at any point in time. Precedents in the human rights world are commonly referred to in order to articulate a response to a situation or issue.

It is also of significant importance to bear in mind that, from the end of the Cold War and following the devastation that occurred in several countries and regions during the 1990s, the desire of the international community, or the vast majority of its members, was to identify new solutions or reshape old ones with a view to overcoming possible standstills and addressing directly or indirectly the issues at stake. It is undeniable that the wish not to replicate the mistakes and deficiencies of the past featured high in the collective mind and was behind the Council's activities from its inception.

Indeed, changes in the manner in which the international community addressed human rights violations or issues could not have been more striking since the establishment of the Council. It recaptured and re-conceptualized the existing tools and mechanisms or it created new ones. It did so by resorting to an extremely flexible approach.

Accordingly, it is particularly difficult to disassociate the functions of the Council – as they were described in a very careful but succinct manner by the General Assembly Resolution 60/251 – from the toolbox of mechanisms and practices which were developed over time. Understanding the multilayered human rights system requires a detailed reading of each layer. It represents, in the author's opinion, a sine qua non in order to assess today's Council and its mechanisms.

The complex human rights geology is described in the following section, each section briefly describing one of the layers and linking it to the current Council functions and activities.

2.2.1 Standard Setting[27]

The first decades of activities of the Commission on Human Rights were almost entirely devoted to the development of norms and standards. This was based upon the conviction that without them it would be futile to consider human rights. Indeed, with no recognized and universally agreed standards, there would be no framework against which to gauge in an objective manner a specific human rights situation and ensure that human rights benefit fully and fairly all humans with no distinction whatsoever.

Standard setting remains of particular importance in clarifying the boundaries beyond which States may not venture and delineating and clarifying the meaning of some societal issues at the universal level. It also serves as a framework allowing States to set goals and purposes for

---

27 See OP 5(c) of the General Assembly Resolution 60/251 of 15 March 2006.

themselves which otherwise would remain mostly subjective or of a vanishing nature.

Of interest but outside the scope of the present study, the drafters of the Universal Declaration on Human Rights and of consecutive international instruments were somewhat convinced that by agreeing on norms and standards in the same manner that domestic legislators enacted laws and governments deduced regulations, this would by itself trigger concrete action in terms of respect and consequently protection and promotion of human rights. Experience shows that this particular viewpoint left much to be desired and that some of the worst abuses committed in recent decades were initiated and carried out directly or indirectly by governments otherwise bound by a vast network of international human rights instruments. This does not diminish the fundamental importance of standard setting but acts as a reminder that this activity must be linked to an array of mechanisms and tools in order to ensure their effectiveness in the jurisdiction of States parties and beyond.

From the creation of the United Nations to the establishment of the Council, a large variety of international human rights instruments were adopted by the Commission on Human Rights. They established the foundations upon which the international community built the current international human rights system. These yardsticks derive from the Universal Declaration in an inverted pyramidal manner, from the Universal Declaration to the International Bill of Human Rights, the other Conventions, their Protocols and the ensuing Declarations or Guidelines. The main human rights treaties established monitoring bodies[28] entrusted with the task of monitoring their implementation via the

28 The Human Rights Committee (CCPR) monitors the implementation of the International Covenant on Civil and Political Rights (1966) and its optional protocols; the Committee on Economic, Social and Cultural Rights (CESCR) monitors the implementation of the International Covenant on Economic, Social and Cultural Rights (1966); the Committee on the Elimination of Racial Discrimination (CERD) monitors the implementation of the International Convention on the Elimination of All Forms of Racial Discrimination (1965); the Committee on the Elimination of Discrimination against Women (CEDAW) monitors the implementation of the Convention on the Elimination of All Forms of Discrimination against Women (1979) and its optional protocol

consideration of States' reports, individual or inter-State communications, and in certain cases, field visits. The general comments or observations adopted by these monitoring bodies constitute a fundamental body of interpretation; although they cannot be considered as mandatory in accordance with the letter and spirit of the relevant conventions, they represent the most astute, objective and comprehensive comments on selected provisions of the relevant international human rights texts. In this regard, they may not be of a mandatory nature, but rejecting them or refusing to abide by them is surely a matter of serious concern and a hint that the concerned country may not be in full compliance with the concerned treaty.[29]

In paragraph 5(d) of Resolution 60/251 establishing the Council, the General Assembly decided that the Council 'shall (...) make

(1999); the Committee against Torture (CAT) monitors the implementation of the Convention against Torture and Other Cruel, Inhuman or Degrading Treatment (1984); the Committee on the Rights of the Child (CRC) monitors the implementation of the Convention on the Rights of the Child (1989) and its optional protocols (2000); the Committee on Migrant Workers (CMW) monitors the implementation of the International Convention on the Protection of the Rights of All Migrant Workers and Members of Their Families (1990); the Committee on the Rights of Persons with Disabilities (CRPD) monitors the implementation of the International Convention on the Rights of Persons with Disabilities (2006); the Committee on Enforced Disappearances (CED) monitors the implementation of the International Convention for the Protection of All Persons from Enforced Disappearance (2006); and the Subcommittee on Prevention of Torture and other Cruel, Inhuman or Degrading Treatment or Punishment (SPT) established pursuant to the Optional Protocol of the Convention against Torture (OPCAT) (2002) visits places of detention in order to prevent torture and other cruel, inhuman or degrading treatment or punishment.

29 Referring to its findings in response to the individual communications and the General Comments of the Human Rights Committee, the ICJ acknowledged the 'considerable body of interpretative case law', stating that it should 'ascribe great weight to the interpretation adopted by this independent body that was established specifically to supervise the application of that treaty.' (AHMADOU SADIO DIALLO (JUDGMENT OF 30 NOVEMBER 2010), para 66.

recommendations to the General Assembly for the further development of international law in the field of human rights'. Of interest, the two very first resolutions adopted by the Council related to the adoption of human rights instruments. This was a clear recognition that standard setting would remain of importance despite the fact that numerous instruments had already been adopted. This was to a certain extent in contradiction to voices that considered that the age of standard setting was over and thus advocated a move from standard setting to implementation. Such a call was made on the perception that all energy had to be devoted to the implementation of standards and not their elaboration and that the existing network of international human rights instruments and treaty bodies was sufficient to cover all possible grounds.

The age of standard setting was and is, however, not over. The international community through the Council found it of importance to adopt the following conventions or declarations:

- Further to the adoption of the HRC Resolution 1/1 of 29 June 2006, the International Convention for the Protection of All Persons from Enforced Disappearances was submitted to the General Assembly which adopted it by virtue of its Resolution 61/177 of 20 December 2006.
- Further to the adoption of the HRC Resolution 1/2 of 29 June 2006, the United Nations Declaration on the Rights of Indigenous Peoples was submitted to the General Assembly which adopted it by virtue of its Resolution 61/295 of 13 September 2007.
- Further to the adoption of the HRC Resolution 8/2 of 18 June 2008, the Optional Protocol to the International Covenant on Economic, Social and Cultural Rights was submitted to the General Assembly which adopted it by virtue of its Resolution 63/117 of 10 December 2008.
- Further to the adoption of the HRC Resolution 17/18 of 14 July 2011, the Optional Protocol to the Convention on the Rights of the Child on a communications procedure was submitted to the General Assembly which adopted it by virtue of its Resolution 66/138 of 19 December 2011.
- Further to the adoption of the HRC Resolution 16/1 of 23 March 2011, the United Nations Declaration on Human Rights Education and Training was submitted to the General Assembly which adopted it by virtue of its Resolution 66/137 of 19 December 2011.

- Further to the adoption of the HRC Resolution 32/28 of 1 July 2016, the Declaration on the Right to Peace was submitted to the General Assembly which adopted it by virtue of its Resolution 71/189 of 2 February 2017.
- Further to the adoption of the HRC Resolution 39/12 of 28 September 2018, the United Nations Declaration on the Rights of Peasants and Other People Working in Rural Areas was submitted to the General Assembly which adopted it on 28 November 2018.

Additionally, it should be borne in mind that a number of intergovernmental working groups are currently in place and working on drafts relating to:

- Transnational corporations and other business enterprises with respect to human rights;
- Complementary Standards to the International Convention on the Elimination of All Forms of Racial Discrimination; and
- An international regulatory framework on the regulation, monitoring and oversight of the activities of private military and security companies (new/revised intergovernmental working group mandate as per HRC res 36/11).

Also, it is important to recall that existing working groups such as the Working Group on the Right to Development or the Intergovernmental Working Group on the Effective Implementation of the Durban Declaration and Programme of Action are engaged in activities that may or will ultimately culminate in the adoption of new standards. The Human Rights Council Advisory Committee is also dealing with matters of a similar nature.

Looking forward, it may be assumed that quite a number of additional matters, touching mostly on societal issues, will require intense discussion as well as possible standard setting in the near future. Special Rapporteurs and the Council's Advisory Committee have, at times, suggested in reports submitted to the Council the necessity of deepening the conversation on important thematic issues[30] in a prelude to the elaboration of appropriate norms and standards.

---

30 See A/HRC/37/37, 34/34, 31/39 and 28/41.

Considering the state of our contemporary society at the end of the first quarter of the twenty-first century, it may well be assumed that, inter alia, the development of artificial intelligence, the many challenges raised by the Internet, bioethics, climate change, the impact of the exponential growth of modern technology on many aspects of human lives, the struggle against terrorism and its impact on human rights, and the omnipotence of transnational corporations and other non-State actors in many aspects of our lives may sooner or later require systematic and comprehensive consideration. This will require an appropriate framework to be drawn for the development of such matters while fully respecting the human rights of all individuals. The more humanity will get out of its twentieth-century boundaries, the more questions will be raised as to the adequacy of the existing norms and their interpretation with the new environment in which it is evolving and the increasing challenges it may face. It is the author's opinion that increasingly new norms and mechanisms will be needed to balance the existing set of rights with the emerging obstacles faced in trying to stretch the interpretation of the Universal Declaration and the ten existing international human rights instruments and accompanying protocols and declarations to the new paradigms. It is quite reasonable to consider that the Universal Declaration's drafters did not and could not have in mind the systemic – or even tectonic – changes that the artificial intelligence and beyond, the datafication of human existence, and the undue weight of artificial intelligence would bring about. The same applies, inter alia, to pervasive and enduring changes that Earth's climate has faced in the past decade due to human activity.

Standard setting is thus a key aspect of the work of the Council and will remain so for a long time. As mentioned above, the Council has established intergovernmental working groups which are in place and work on the elaboration of related instruments. Their annual consideration takes place during one of the three sessions of the Council and their work is presented to the Council plenary. This gives publicity to the work of the working groups.

2.2.2 Procedures for Dealing with Violations of Human Rights[31]

The Commission on Human Rights faced difficulties in diversifying its activity after the initial years of exclusive standard setting. Heavily impacted by the Cold War, the international community struggled for decades to consider how and when to deal with violations of human rights and fundamental freedoms. If not placed against such a context and the historical events surrounding it, it would be difficult nowadays to understand the adoption of documents such as the Economic and Social Council (ECOSOC) Resolution 728F (XXVIII) of 30 July 1959, which bluntly approved the statement that 'the Commission on Human Rights recognizes that it has no power to take any action in regard to any complaints concerning human rights'.

The ensuing decade was marked by prodigious developments in the consideration of human rights violations, which were mostly the consequences of the irruption of new actors in the wake of the decolonization process. Resolutions of considerable importance were adopted at the initiative of the newly independent countries and mechanisms were established in the 1960s to deal with human rights violations. These were the prelude to the development of what is now a dense and efficient network of mechanisms. They also led to the establishment of mechanisms to consider communications revealing gross and reliably attested violations of human rights and fundamental freedoms.

In the context of the current study, it is sufficient to refer to the yardstick resolutions adopted by the Commission on Human Rights and the ECOSOC, which enabled the said Commission to inscribe in its agenda items relating to the public consideration of the question of human rights and fundamental freedoms (ECOSOC Resolution 1235 (XLII)) as well as the confidential consideration of complaints (ECOSOC Resolution 1503 (XLVIII)).[32]

A very fine political balance was reached between the consideration of human rights violations in all countries and the need to focus attention

31 See OP 5 (d), (f), and (i) of the General Assembly Resolution 60/251 of 15 March 2006.

32 See also Commission Resolutions 6, 8 and 9 (XXIII).

on the situation in specific territories. This is testified by the letter of Resolution 1235, which referred to cases revealing a consistent pattern of violations of human rights, 'as exemplified by the policy of apartheid as practised in the Republic of South Africa and in the Territory of South West Africa under the direct responsibility of the United Nations and now illegally occupied by the Government of the Republic of South Africa, and racial discrimination as practised notably in Southern Rhodesia'.

Country Mandates

As a result of this focus, the first-ever Special Procedures were established to deal with specific territories. The first one was on the apartheid regime in South Africa, and the second on the situation of human rights in the occupied Palestinian territories. Thus, the Commission established the Ad Hoc Working Group of Experts on South Africa and the Special Rapporteur on the question of Apartheid in 1967. This was followed two years later by the creation of the Working Group on the Situation of Human Rights in the Occupied Palestinian Territories. Both mechanisms were the subject of specific agenda items. When the apartheid regime came to an end, the attached mechanisms were abolished, thus leaving the situation of human rights in the Occupied Palestinian Territories as the only territory subjected to a specific agenda item both at the time of the Commission and at that of the Council.

From these very specific situations, the Commission moved to others in the following decade with the creation in 1975 of an Ad Hoc Working Group on the Situation of Human Rights in Chile, which was transformed in 2000 into a Special Rapporteur on the situation of human rights in Chile.[33] From then on, the Commission and later the Council created a number of other country Special Procedures.

As of 31 December 2024, there were 14 such mechanisms,[34] established under agenda item 4 of the Council (human rights situations that require the Council's attention) or agenda item 10 (technical assistance and capacity building). The latter are often referred to as independent

33 Commission Resolution 2000/33 of 20 April 2000.

34 https://spinternet.ohchr.org/_Layouts/SpecialProceduresInternet/ViewAllCountryMandates.aspx.

experts to mark the difference between the two items and consequently the approach followed.

One of the major subjects of confrontation between various stakeholders relates to the relevance of country mandates to the current circumstances.

Some argue that the Council should avoid confrontation of a political nature and gear towards consensus in any possible manner. Country mandates – and for this purpose, Commissions of Inquiry, Fact-Finding Missions, and comparable mechanisms – are often imposed upon certain States, but their impact is extremely limited. Double standards and finger-pointing are often mentioned in this context as the result of the overly 'aggressive' behaviour of certain States within the Council (notably the Global North) against other more vulnerable ones (mostly from the Global South).

Others emphasize the key role played by country mandate-holders and the inherent contradiction in seeking the consent of concerned countries when modelling a possible mandate to address human rights violations of a broad and significant nature. Should the Council not create such mandates, it would soon become irrelevant and miss its most important goals, tackling gross and massive human rights violations.

In the context of the present Anatomy, it is sufficient to state that the contenders of both arguments are partly right – and consequently partly wrong – in developing their cases. It is undoubtable that only a segment of the existing gross and massive human rights violations throughout the world are addressed by the Council. In this context, 14 country mandates, to which a comparable number of commissions of inquiry or similar tools should be added, do not account for the numerous cases of gross and massive human rights violations in the world. Covering the whole number of situations would be impossible in practical terms since it would multiply by a significant factor the existing number of mandates. Hence, facing this practical (and political) impossibility, the Council is selective. How this is operationalized is obviously doubtful and depends on whether a State or group of States takes the initiative of tabling a draft resolution creating a new mandate. The goodwill of the international community is therefore key to this undertaking. In certain cases, there is absolutely no doubt that such an operation is essential and responds to an unchallengeable set of gross and massive human rights violations. In other cases, this may be questionable compared to situations left untouched – either because a resolution on these matters would fail or because no State is interested or in a position to draft a text on the situation at stake because of the international 'weight' of the concerned State or States. This level of subjectivity is quite clearly embarrassing for the Council and by extension to the international community and the United Nations.

Fortunately, there is nothing set in stone in the Council's realm. Flexibility, the greatest asset and leitmotif of the Council, as will be exemplified in the sections and chapters to come, allows the Council to privilege a pragmatic approach over dogmatic ones. Accordingly, it is the author's opinion that a way to mitigate the above-mentioned contradictory approach towards country mandates would be to add a new layer in between special procedures or commission of inquiry and the universal periodic review.

In an ideal world, which is presumably not the one in which we are living, there would be room for the Council to establish, as a complement to the existing procedures and mechanisms, five regional working groups composed of five experts each, which would have the role of reporting every year on the situation of human rights in the geographic region of which they are in charge. Obviously, this would not encompass the countries covered by individual mandates. They would also be tasked with bridging with States and the UN system on how to tackle the implementation of numerous UPR and thematic special procedures mechanisms. The ultimate result would be for all countries to be subjected to some forms of combined scrutiny and assistance, thus enabling the Council to deal, for instance, with the situation of human rights in the Global North – something which it has always failed to do. This would also mitigate one of the constant criticisms against the Council that it is driven by political forces that lead to the utter polarization of its work.

Thematic Mandates

The creation of country mandates has always been a very delicate and politicized process. After the setting up of a mechanism on Chile, the intention was to reproduce this step concerning the situation of human rights in Argentina. However, due to intense lobbying by Argentina, this could not be achieved, and instead, the Commission developed a new type of mechanism, the Working Group on Enforced or Involuntary Disappearances, in 1980. Needless to say, the majority of the cases dealt with by the said Working Group referred to Argentina at the moment of its creation, but officially the mandate was said to be 'thematic' and not country-oriented.

This thematic approach was of great significance since it allowed for the consideration of thematic issues with a focus on specific countries. The nature of the thematic procedure was therefore understood from the beginning as a principled approach focusing on the comprehensive study of a given theme. A specific focus was on the situation in selected countries subjected to field visits[35] by the concerned rapporteurs. Further to this very first thematic mandate, others followed, starting with the Special Rapporteur on Extrajudicial, Summary and Arbitrary Executions in 1982 and the Special Rapporteur on Torture and Other Cruel, Inhuman or Degrading Treatment in 1985. The mandates were given, in accordance with the political will of the moment, to individuals or to groups of individuals constituted in a Working Group.[36] As of 31 December 2024, there were 46 thematic working groups or special rapporteurs, all of them known under the common name 'Special Procedures'.

The Network of Special Procedures

At present, there are 60 Special Procedures and 90 mandate-holders.[37] It is quite striking to note that in the last three decades, the number of country mandates slightly increased (from eight to 14, or 75 per cent) whereas the number of thematic mandates expanded in a quasi-exponential manner (from five to 46, or 780 per cent). This testifies to the difficulties faced by the intergovernmental community in dealing with human rights violations at the country level. This question is often linked to the principle of non-interference in domestic affairs. There is not, and cannot be, any clear and universally agreed set of criteria for the establishment of country-specific mechanisms. This very fact leads to accusations of bias, finger-pointing or double-standards, since two comparable situations may lead to the establishment of a mandate, or not, depending on political circumstances, which by definition are of a variable and

35 Through the preparation of mission reports and the sending of urgent appeals or communications.

36 Not to be confused with the intergovernmental standard setting working groups.

37 Working Groups are composed of five independent experts.

volatile nature. Those States that strongly oppose the creation of a given country mandate may support them in another set of circumstances. The background to this lies with short- or long-term geopolitical trends.

Whereas most of the first thematic mandates related to civil and political rights, those established at a later stage were mostly of an economic, social and cultural rights nature.

The Council plenary considers all the reports produced by the Special Rapporteurs. A very advanced form of cooperation which can be adopted by a given State is to issue 'standing invitations' to all the Special Procedures. This corresponds to a political declaration that this State accepts automatically a field visit by any Special Rapporteur at his or her request. This shows openness and willingness to cooperate with human rights mechanisms.

The consideration of thematic mandates' reports follows the format of interactive dialogues on a combination (commonly known as 'cluster') of two thematic Special Rapporteurs while the consideration of country-specific mandates remains individualized. The modus operandi for both dialogues is the same, with mandate-holders being given the opportunity to present their reports and consequently address questions or comments raised by Member and Observer States. A few NGOs also contribute to the dialogue.[38]

On average, the interactive dialogues with Special Procedures represent more than a third of any given session. Special Procedures are the eyes and ears of the Council and their contribution to the Council's work is crucial. They are often referred to as the Council's jewels in the crown. Their independence and expertise enable them to depict a thematic or country situation in a very knowledgeable and objective manner. They assist the Council in reaching specific conclusions and adopting relevant recommendations that require appropriate follow-up.

It is, however, important not to hide the fact that questions may arise in practical terms regarding the full adequacy of the procedure for the selection of mandate-holders concerning the requirements of independence,

---

38 The duration of the NGO segment is 15 minutes for individual interactive dialogues and 30 minutes for clustered interactive dialogues.

integrity and high competence. Similarly, questions may also be raised about the impact of a multiplicity of mandates on their effectiveness in the field as well as their visibility and coherence. In an ideal world, this might require a review of a substantive review. In the current circumstances and against a backdrop of a complex and unstable geopolitical environment, it is probably better for such questions to be borne in mind but left to future consideration.

2.2.3 The Confidential Consideration of Patterns of Gross and Reliably Attested Violations of Human Rights and Fundamental Freedoms

The public consideration of human rights violations, as envisioned in 1967 under Resolution 1235, was complemented by a confidential procedure set up by Resolution 1503 of the ECOSOC on 27 May 1970. This should be read against the background of significant difficulties faced by potential sponsors of such initiatives in proposing the consideration of a specific situation in a public setting under the equivalent of the current Council's agenda items 2, 4, 7 or 10. Hence, the possibility of considering a situation in a confidential setting was considered, by default, fully appropriate for those advocating a focus on human rights violations at the country level. Those facing difficulties with the public consideration of human rights situations based on their perception of double standards and finger-pointing were reassured by the confidential nature of the procedure.

Initially, this was anticipated by some as the main medium for considering human rights violations. Currently, it has evolved into a complementary or alternative approach that is governed by strict rules and procedures, the foundations of which rest on Resolution 1503, now the Complaints Procedure.

When situations are referred to the plenary under the Complaints Procedure, they are considered in two steps – firstly, a confidential dialogue with representatives of the country to which the procedure is dedicated, and secondly, the adoption of one or more decisions in a confidential meeting. Should there be no specific situation submitted to its review, the plenary considers the report of the working group on situations at least once per year, at the Council's September Session.[39]

---

39 See Chapter 1.

As proposed in the first chapter, there would be merit in considering the possibility of the two Working Groups to be replaced by a single body the composition of which, in the author's opinion, should rely on independent expertise or be of a hybrid nature with independent experts working alongside State representatives.

2.2.4 Broadening the Landscape: Promotion of Human Rights, Human Rights Education, Advisory Services and Technical Cooperation[40]

Having met serious challenges in the consideration of human rights situations, the international community moved in the 1980s and later decades towards activities that were of a lesser level of political connotation than the establishment of country or thematic mandates. They were nevertheless considered to have a significant and positive impact on the state of human rights in the world. This helped in gathering some forms of broad agreement in the field of human rights, a process that continues to this date.

The promotion of human rights through such media as human rights education, the development of promotional and educational materials in the field of human rights, and the provision of advisory services, technical cooperation and capacity-building thus became priorities and mirrored the development of the network of special rapporteurs. Whereas this may be presented as a carrot-and-stick policy, it goes much deeper into the very conceptualization of human rights. Human rights do not proceed in a vacuum and cannot be restricted to a dichotomy between human violators and others. There is no human rights paradise on Earth and each country and society faces its own challenges in the field. Some may be rectified through education, promotion, and capacity-building while others may require a higher level of engagement with the international community. In all cases, there is no simple solution to a very complex equation.

40 See OP 5 (a), (b) and (i) of the General Assembly Resolution 60/251 of 15 March 2006.

Efforts in these specific areas were deepened at the Council level as epitomized by the adoption of the United Nations Declaration on Human Rights Education and Training in 2011.[41]

Technical cooperation and advisory services represent the core activities of the Council. The reports of the Voluntary Fund for Technical Cooperation are considered at the Council's March Sessions while annual thematic discussions on technical cooperation are organized at the June Sessions, further to Council Resolutions 18/18 and 36/28.

An important issue which the Council has faced since its creation relates to how it may address issues raised at the country level either in the context of what is often perceived as 'aggressive' mandates or under the banner of technical cooperation and advisory services. On the one hand it may be advanced that certain issues warrant being looked into given their serious nature by way of a dedicated mandate under the Council's agenda items 2, 4 or 7. On the other hand, it may be considered that given the lack of cooperation by many concerned countries with the mandate-holders established against their will, a less stringent approach may be privileged which includes a certain level of cooperation with them under agenda item 10.

This duality has led to serious but so far fruitless conversations about which approach should be privileged. Some, basing themselves on the imperious need to address gross and massive human rights violations, consider that dedicated Special Procedures need to be established whether the concerned countries are involved in and in agreement with their setting up or not. Others, considering the importance of not infringing on the sovereignty of States, arguing about the effectiveness factor that is increased with a technical cooperation mandate, or rejecting the finger-pointing flaw disclosed by the Western hemisphere, privilege the cooperative approach.

The author has always considered that what matters is the interest of the subjects of international human rights law, namely the individuals. Should they be better served by a specific country mandate under agenda

41 See also the high-level panel discussion on the implementation of the United Nations Declaration on Human Rights Education and Training held on 14 September 2016 at the Council's 33rd Session.

items 2, 4 or 7, then that course of action should be followed. Should a technical cooperation mandate be better suited to them, then item 10 is a perfectly reasonable solution, especially since there is not much difference in the modus operandi of the mandate-holders whatever the agenda items under which they were established. Should, in the future, other innovative options be found, then so be it.

2.2.5 Dealing with Emergencies and Setting up Investigatory Mechanisms

Having significantly expanded its role and functions in the context of its regular sessions, the Commission faced various dilemmas in relation to its own programme of work. Meeting only once per year, in March/April, the Commission was not in a situation to respond to human rights emergencies from May to February. This anomaly could not be easily rectified since it represented one of the strongest areas of disagreement that prevailed during the Cold War about the possibility of the Commission taking action on country situations. The fall of the Berlin Wall and the end of the Cold War by the end of the 1980s allowed the Commission to progressively strengthen its toolbox of procedures and mechanisms by agreeing to meet intersessionally in the context of Special Sessions when the circumstances so requested. This possibility was, however, strictly limited in practice by the requirements that half of the members of the Commission had to express their formal agreement with a request for a Special Session to be convened. Hence, a State or group of States that wanted to convene such a Special Session had to obtain at least 27 signatures, which was a very high threshold. Consequently, only five Special Sessions could be organized[42] from 1992 to the abolishment of the Commission.

42 First Special Session on the situation of human rights in the territories of the former Yugoslavia (13–14 August 1992); Second Special Session on the situation of human rights in the territories of the former Yugoslavia (30 November to 1 December 1992); Third Special Session on the situation of human rights in Rwanda (24–25 May 1993); Fourth Special Session on the situation in East Timor (23–27 September 1999); and Fifth Special Session on the grave and massive violations of the human rights of the Palestinian people by Israel (17–19 October 2000).

The negotiations that led to the adoption of General Assembly Resolution 60/152 and the creation of the Council were marked by lengthy and tense discussions on a number of issues, in particular the modalities for convening Special Sessions read in conjunction with the provisions relating to the size of the Council and the possible suspension of a member from the Council.

The upgrading of the status of the Council from a subsidiary organ of ECOSOC to that of the General Assembly meant, in practical terms, that the distribution of seats between the five regional groups had to be aligned with that of the Assembly. Consequently, those States that were predominantly initiators of requests for a Special Session faced the prospect of no longer being in a position to do so. Hence, there was a fear that there would be even fewer Special Sessions with the establishment of the Council. The same group of States also recommended that the membership of the future Council be significantly reduced and that, by a simple majority, the General Assembly may suspend the right to membership in the Council of a member that committed gross and systematic violations of human rights.

Another group of States held a completely opposing view, according to which the size of the Council should remain close to that of the former Commission, that the Commission's practice in relation to the holding of Special Sessions should be upheld and that the right of membership could not be suspended.

An agreement was reached between these positions. Thus, the provisions in operative paragraphs 7, 8 and 10 of Resolution 60/251 should be read conjunctly. Accordingly, the size of the Council was reduced marginally from that of the Commission (47 members vs. 53 members) and a two-thirds majority of the General Assembly members was required to suspend the rights of membership of a Council member (a possibility that did not exist before). In return, the support of only a third of the membership to the convening of a Special Session was agreed upon as the threshold.

The subsequent Council resolution developed these provisions and Resolution 5/1 devoted an entire sub-section[43] to the modalities for the

43 See paras 119–128 of the Council Resolution 5/1 of 18 June 2007.

holding of Special Sessions. From its establishment to 31 December 2024, the Council had held 36 Special Sessions. An overwhelming majority of them concerned country situations (34), while two only touched upon thematic issues.[44] The country Special Sessions related to the human rights situations in 16 countries or territories[45] and two non-State actors.[46]

Special Sessions are by definition held intersessionally. Hence, it became necessary to decide how to deal with an emergency that may arise during a regular session. Given the rather rigid structure and heavy nature of the regular sessions, it was initially felt that when an issue of importance arose during these sessions, it was to be dealt with in the context of the general debates under a relevant agenda item. This, however, did not provide for a high level of visibility to the matter at stake and did not lead to the immediate adoption of any specific resolution.

Therefore, the Council decided to revisit the practice of the Commission in comparable situations. Indeed, shortly before being abolished, the Commission approved a set of practices enabling it to organize 'Special Sittings' during a regular session whenever circumstances so required. As a result, the Council decided to follow a comparable practice which it entitled 'Urgent Debates'. The requirements for holding an urgent debate are quite simple: the request to hold an urgent debate must be made by a Member State; that request is considered by the Bureau which proposes a date for the holding of the debate; and the final decision (with or without a vote) is taken by the Council and the debate takes place soon after. At the end of the debate, a resolution is adopted, thus departing from the

44 See below developments on the seventh and 10th Special Sessions on the negative impact of the worsening of the right to food and on the impact of the global economic and financial crises on the universal realization enjoyment of human rights, respectively. The 13th Special Session held immediately after the earthquake in Haiti referred to the support for the recovery process in Haiti; this is a human rights approach and is therefore of a mixed character.

45 In descending order: Israel/Palestine (8), Syrian Arab Republic (5), Myanmar (3), Sudan (3), Israel/Lebanon (1), South Sudan (1), Burundi (1), Central African Republic (1), Libya (1), Côte d'Ivoire (1), the Democratic Republic of Congo (1), Haiti (1), Sri Lanka (1), Afghanistan (1), Ethiopia (1) and Ukraine (1).

46 Boko Haram (1) and ISIS (1).

practice of having all resolutions adopted during the last two days of the regular sessions. So far, the Council has organized nine urgent debates.[47]

As far as the outcome of a consideration of a country's situation beyond the establishment of country Special Procedures is concerned, the Council also expanded on the hesitant practice of the Commission in this regard and developed an array of bodies entrusted with in-depth analysis of the facts and addressing recommendations to the Council. In the early stage of the Council's work, the appointment of a Commission of Inquiry (COI) or a Fact-finding Mission (FFM) or a request to the High Commissioner to dispatch an investigation mission was normally agreed upon at the conclusion of a Special Session. More recently, the establishment of such ad hoc mechanisms was the result of resolutions adopted during regular Council sessions, thus providing more time for sponsors to discuss the format and terms of reference of such mechanisms.

No less than 38 such mechanisms have been set into motion by the Council since its establishment,[48] which can be considered a significant number given their cost and complexity. The terminology may differ significantly from one to the other, but their terms of reference usually include the investigation of alleged violations of international human rights law, the establishment of the facts and circumstances of such violations and of the crimes committed, as well as the ensuing accountability. The inventiveness of the Council in identifying terms describing the bodies in charge of the investigations often leaves readers with a sense of perplexity. It should, however, be recalled that the Council, although a human rights body, remains an intergovernmental machine operating within the United Nations parameters. Resolutions establishing such procedures need to be adopted, generally by vote, and whatever may be done to broaden the support for these mandates is used by the main sponsors and the penholder(s). If semantics is a proper way to deal with this matter and a slight adjustment to the name or title of the considered entity is necessary, so be it. What matters is the ultimate gain of the international community regarding the consideration of certain matters.

Beyond the terminology used, the author also considered that certain thematic matters, given their importance, deserve to be covered by

---

47 See Chapter 5, Section 5.1.4.

48 See https://www.ohchr.org/en/hr-bodies/hrc/list-hrc-mandat.

investigations similar to or at least comparable with the country COIs or FFMs. The establishment of the Expert Mechanism to Advance Justice and Equality in Law Enforcement[49] is an excellent model of what may be done by the Council in this regard. Ultimately, given the increasing complexity of the world we are living in, there is no longer a clear dichotomy between country and thematic mandates, and nothing should prevent the Council from launching investigations into so-called thematic issues when the situation warrants it.

The COI/FFM are normally requested to report back to the Council at each of its following sessions, with a final report normally requested one year down the road. They are usually provided with a short timespan to present an oral report at the following session, an interim report at the next one and a final one a year later.

While the first of such mechanisms were mostly of an unspecified and even ad hoc nature,[50] the practice progressively emerged for these mechanisms to be composed of three independent experts appointed by the President of the Council, from a list of names suggested by the Office of the High Commissioner for Human Rights.[51] It is important to note that the Council has not yet conceptualized the modus operandi of such bodies. The nomination process is an ad hoc one that differs from that of Special Procedures mandate-holders. Accordingly, there remains a level of uncertainty in the manner in which the COI/FFM are established and

49 See HRC Resolution 47/21 adopted on 13 July 2021

50 See for instance RES/S-2/1 (high-level commission of inquiry comprising eminent experts on human rights and international humanitarian law); RES/S-3/1 (high-level fact-finding mission to be appointed by the President); RES/S-4/1 (high-level mission to assess the human rights situation in Darfur composed of five highly qualified persons and the Special Rapporteur on the situation of human rights in the Sudan); and RES/S-9/1 (Special Procedures mandates holders to urgently seek and gather information and submit their reports to the Council).

51 It is of interest to note that the IBP provisions applied to the appointment of special rapporteurs do not apply in these circumstances. This was deemed necessary to ensure that a new mechanism of this nature is set up as soon as possible given the emergency of the situation.

how they operate. To date, there has been no real attempt to address this matter.

COI and FFM also exacerbate tensions with the concerned countries, which often describe them as political in nature and the result of the Council's polarization marked by finger-pointing and double standards. Their reactions may thus be quite firm and at times unacceptable. For instance, in 2018, the High Commissioner was prompted to issue a public comment in response to attacks against the report of the independent international Commission of Inquiry on Burundi and personal attacks against the Chair of the Commission, Mr. Doudou Diene.[52] The President of the Council also reacted to personal attacks against Mr. Diene after the

---

52 See the comments by the High Commissioner dated 25 October 2018:

> Yesterday's statement by Burundi's Ambassador (...) attacking the report of the independent international Commission of Inquiry established by the UN HRC is deeply regrettable in both tone and substance. The threat to prosecute the members of the Commission for the work they have done at the express request of the Council – a subsidiary body of the General Assembly – is unacceptable and should be immediately withdrawn. And the personal attack on the Chair of the Commission of Inquiry, Mr. Doudou Diène, comparing him to a participant in the slave trade, was a disgrace. As a Member State of the United Nations, Burundi should show respect to its institutions and the various bodies, laws and mechanisms it has established. Burundi's belligerent and defamatory response to the findings of the Commission of Inquiry, and its repeated and wholly unsupported assertions that the Commission was the puppet of mysterious external forces, as well as the Government's complete failure to address the very serious findings of the Commission of Inquiry, are reprehensible. I urge the Government of Burundi to issue an immediate retraction of this inflammatory statement and to offer a full apology to Mr. Diène and the other Commissioners, as well as to the Council, which created the Commission, and its President who selected and appointed the three Commissioners. Burundi is currently one of the 47 member States sitting on the Human Rights Council.

https://www.ohchr.org/SP/NewsEvents/Pages/DisplayNews.aspx?NewsID=23777&LangID=E.

concerned country's statement at the 40th session.[53] Similar extremely strong personal attacks were often directed at members of the investigations dealing with the human rights situation in Israel and the OPT.

Additionally, facing political challenges and difficulties inherent to the establishment of a fact-finding mission or a commission of inquiry, mostly of a political nature, the Council, true to its tradition and practice, conceived other mechanisms with different titles and settings. While their terms of reference and working methods remained largely similar to those of classic COI and FFM, the title used to refer to them, their level of independence and the way they were appointed may vary considerably.

In view of the difficulties faced in getting support to set up a COI or FFM, the very first such mechanism was established shortly after the Council's fourth Special Session on the situation of human rights in Darfur[54] and was entitled 'High-Level Mission'.[55] Given the inherent difficulties faced by this Mission, it did not serve as a precedent.

More recently, the Council created an investigation of a hybrid nature with the Office of the High Commissioner for Human Rights being tasked to report back to the Council on a given situation[56] or with the High Commissioner or her/his Office requested to dispatch a mission of independent and/or international experts whose precise title differs from

---

53 At the Bureau meeting held on 22 February 2019, the President recalled past instances of delegations using their interventions during interactive dialogues to make personal attacks against Special Procedures mandate-holders and members of the Council's fact-finding and other investigative bodies. The Bureau agreed on the need to be vigilant about this and to remind speakers that personal remarks against Council mandate holders would not be tolerated.

54 See A/HRC/RES/S-3/1.

55 It was composed of six Members serving in their personal capacities, including two Ambassadors. For the difficulties faced by the Mission, see Section 7 of 'The UN HRC' Bertrand Ramcharan, Routledge. For the report of the Mission, see A/HRC/4/80.

56 See HRC resolutions S-16/1 (Mission to the Syrian Arab Republic), S-22/1 (Mission to Iraq), 28/30 (Investigation on Libya), 29/13 (Mission to improve human rights, accountability, and reconciliation in South Sudan), and 37/41 (human rights situation in Libya).

one case to another based on the delineation of the mandate or, broadly speaking, on political considerations.[57]

It is interesting to point out a voluntary omission: indeed, in what may prima facie appear as an anomaly, the Council rarely requested country and/or thematic Special Procedures to examine a specific human rights situation as part of or in cooperation with a COI/FFM.[58] This may, however, be explained by the heavy workload of the Special Procedures, the difficulties in coordinating the participation of several mandate-holders and, more importantly, the desire not to impose additional time-consuming responsibilities on the work of Special Rapporteurs.

More recently, the Council expanded the scope of intervention of the COI/FFM beyond that of gathering facts, analysing the situations in depth and proposing recommendations. Echoing the General Assembly's establishment of an International Impartial and Independent Mechanism (IIIM) on Syria,[59] the Council decided to establish, based on the recommendation of the existence of a COI, 'an ongoing independent mechanism to collect, consolidate, preserve and analyse evidence of the most serious international crimes and violations of international law committed in Myanmar since 2011 and to prepare files in order to facilitate and expedite fair and independent criminal proceedings, in accordance with international law standards, in national, regional or international courts or tribunals that may in the future have jurisdiction over these crimes in accordance with international law'.[60] This Accountability Mechanism, once established by the Secretary-General, was requested to report annually to the Council and the General Assembly.

57 A mission by independent experts on Burundi (UNIIB – S-24/1), a team of international experts on the Kasai Region of the DRC (A/HRC/RES/35/33 and 39/16), a group of eminent international and regional experts on Yemen (A/RES/HRC/36/31 and 39/16), and a team of three experts on Burundi (A/HRC/RES/36/2).

58 See A/HRC/RES/S-8/1.

59 Which, in a nutshell, could be identified as a pre-trial evidence collecting and evidence conservation mechanism.

60 See Council Resolution 39/2 of 27 September 2018.

2.2.6 Dialoguing with the High Commissioner for Human Rights and her/his Office[61]

The creation of the post of High Commissioner for Human Rights[62] further to the Vienna Conference on Human Rights, was the culmination of efforts initiated more than a decade before.

The UN human rights architecture was significantly transformed with the General Assembly's decision to appoint a UN senior official with principal responsibility for UN human rights activities. Previously, this responsibility lay with the Chief of the Centre for Human Rights, who was at the assistant-secretary-general level, while the High Commissioner post was upgraded to that of under-secretary-general. The Centre for Human Rights was a relatively small department located in Geneva with limited external visibility. Even though the Chiefs of the Centre had a serious influence on the human rights programme and had been instrumental in several important policy as well as legal and political decisions by the intergovernmental machinery, their authority was far too easily and successfully challenged by various stakeholders.[63]

Raising the level of the High Commissioner and, more importantly altering the appointment process by deciding that the High Commissioner would be appointed by the Secretary-General and approved by the General Assembly ensured that, aside from the charter-based and treaty-based bodies, there would henceforth be a strong secretarial authority responding directly to the Secretary-General.

The General Assembly decided by the same resolution that the High Commissioner would operate within the framework of the overall competence, authority and decisions of the General Assembly, the ECOSOC and the Commission on Human Rights. This provision was introduced to ensure complementarity between the various actors, particularly the High Commissioner and the Commission, later the Council.

---

61 See OP 5 (g) of General Assembly Resolution 60/251.

62 See General Assembly Resolution 48/141 of 20 December 1993.

63 See for instance, *The Advent of Universal Protection of Human Rights* Theo Van Boven and *The Transformation of the UN Role* by Bertrand Ramcharan.

The influence and independence of the successive High Commissioners were profound and significant. As a result, the shape and structure of the human rights programme were changed and the High Commissioner's Office expanded to a level probably unexpected at the time of the adoption of Resolution 48/141.

The relationship between the High Commissioner and the Commission, later the Council, has been, at times, somewhat complex. This is due to the conjunction of responsibilities over comparable, if not identical issues or situations. In most cases, however, the coexistence of both entities has been harmonious and mutually beneficial. In particular, the High Commissioner's actions on the ground and/or in the areas of technical cooperation and capacity-building have often interplayed with those of the Commission, later the Council.

The High Commissioner also plays a leading role in implementing the resolutions or decisions adopted by the Council. This is particularly the case concerning the submission of an average of 100 reports per year, often on complex or delicate thematic issues. The High Commissioner also plays a leading role in establishing and supporting the COIs/FFMs and all other investigation mechanisms.

Also, the High Commissioner inherited the previous responsibilities of the Centre for Human Rights in terms of secretarial and substantive support to the charter-based and treaty-based bodies. However, such a high level of synergy did not necessarily expand to the consideration of country or thematic situations or issues, and the independent voice and role of the High Commissioner in these areas was at times challenged.

Upon its creation, the Council inherited the roles and responsibilities of the Commission on Human Rights relating to the work of the Office of the United Nations High Commissioner by virtue of operative paragraph 5 (g) of the General Assembly Resolution 60/251. Since these roles and responsibilities had been left somewhat vaguely defined, it should not appear as a surprise that the Council had to struggle with how it should interact with the High Commissioner.

As far as institutional matters were concerned, the synergy between the two entities was clarified by the adoption of several Presidential Statements, which followed dense and lengthy negotiation processes:

- The PRST/15/2 of 1 October 2010 described the level of interaction which should exist between the Council and the Office insofar as the strategic programme 19, human rights, was concerned.[64]
- The PRST 18/2 of 30 September 2011 clarified the information which the Council invited – not requested – the High Commissioner to include in her annual report.
- The PRST 19/1 of 22 March 2012 described the modalities according to which the information referred to in PRST 18/2 would be conveyed.[65]

Further to these Presidential Statements, the modalities of the formal interaction of the High Commissioner with the Council were also agreed upon and systematized in the years that followed. This was sometimes done without a formal decision by the Council. One example is the Annual Report of the High Commissioner, which is always presented during the first or second week of the March Session of the Council and is followed one day later by a comprehensive interactive dialogue. Furthermore, the High Commissioner presents updates at the start of the June and September Sessions which are considered in the format of a general debate (namely without a questions-and-answers modus operandi).[66]

The presentation of the HC Annual Report or Updates constitutes one of the milestones of any given session. It is in the context of such a statement that the High Commissioner takes a position on thematic or country-based human rights issues as well as on matters relevant to the UN human rights architecture and his/her activities as well as those of her/his office.

Other reports submitted by the High Commissioner at the request of the Council are presented immediately before the start of the general debate on the relevant agenda item. Although their nature varies considerably

64 This PRST refers to the strategic framework format which was replaced in 2016 by a one-year programme plan.

65 Such interaction takes place in informal meetings with states and other stakeholders outside the regular sessions of the Council.

66 These arrangements are based on the draft programme of work for the Human Rights Council for the first year as foreseen by Council decision 1/105 of 30 June 2006.

from one to the other depending on the Council's requests, these reports often touch on important thematic matters.

The possibility for the High Commissioner to report to the Council on his/her own volition was at times challenged based on the presumption that this would systematically require a formal Council request. However, the reading of the General Assembly Resolution 48/141 tells a different story and provides a very clear basis for the High Commissioner to proceed independently and refer to the Council with any issues s/he may find appropriate. As early as 2005, the Acting High Commissioner for Human Rights referred to the then Commission a report on the situation of human rights in Iraq[67] and another one on the situation of human rights in the Darfur region of the Sudan.[68] These unchallenged precedents provided the basis for any future report of the High Commissioner to the Council based solely on her/his mandate. In his previous capacity, the author often recalled these precedents and argued that these two cases might serve as precedents and that absolutely nothing would argue against the presentation of ad hoc reports by the High Commissioner to the Council. This would enable the High Commissioner to raise his/her voice on issues which otherwise remain within the constraints of oral updates at the beginning of the Council's sessions. Although unfruitful, these efforts contributed to leading the way to other courses of action less formal in nature. It is, however, important to bear such precedents in mind for future consideration when the time comes.

Furthermore, the need emerged to provide opportunities for the High Commissioner to address the Council either during or between sessions. In accordance with General Assembly Resolution 48/141, the High Commissioner may address the Council at any point in time during the regular Council sessions on any issue she considers appropriate.

However, with time, it was considered appropriate to expand this level of interaction beyond the boundaries of regular sessions. A practice emerged of holding so-called 'informal conversations' with the members and Observers of the Council, allowing the High Commissioner to brief them informally on any issues deemed necessary. Despite the very informal nature of such briefings, their impact is not negligible: the enhanced

67 E/CN.4/2005/4.
68 E/CN.4/2005/3.

interactive dialogue on the human rights of migrants organized on 15 June 2015 and the 24th Special Session on preventing the deterioration of the human rights situation in Burundi held on 17 December 2015 are linked with the conversations held beforehand.[69]

Other, more informal briefings may be organized by the High Commissioner on his/her own volition. The difference between an informal conversation and a briefing lies in the channelling of the request. In the former case, the High Commissioner addresses the invitation to the conversation through the President, thus giving the perception that the Council is somewhat involved in the process, whereas in the latter case, s/he addresses such an invitation directly to the Member State, with the President and his/her Bureau not involved in this matter at all.

Lastly, as mentioned above, the High Commissioner and her/his Office implement the Council's resolutions or decisions. In particular, the High Commissioner has increasingly been asked to investigate, directly or through the medium of a group of experts which she/he was to set into motion, delicate country-based human rights issues.

As with many other aspects of the Council's work, the typology of actions requested from the High Commissioner and the ensuing responses by the Council have constantly expanded.

At the border between formal reporting on and/or investigation of human rights situations and mere briefing on the activities of the Office at headquarters or in the field, the High Commissioner has been requested to present the Office's reports on specific human rights situations, on the work of relevant field presences or on developments relating to technical cooperation projects, in the context of agenda items 2.[70]

---

69 See Chapter 3. Since the informal conversations are not taking place in formal settings, there is no need to adopt any formal decision in this regard. Informal conversations were held on 26 May and 15 December 2015, 30 November 2016, 28 August 2018, 4 February, 6 September 2019, 9 April 2020 in the context of the COVID-19 pandemic, and on 22 February 2023 (on the preparations for the 75th Anniversary of the UDHR).

70 In 2018, such interaction under item 2 concerned inter alia the following projects or situations: Guatemala, Honduras, and Colombia

Recently, the Council also invited the High Commissioner to present the findings on the situation of human rights in Ukraine in an atypical manner. In accordance with the terms of Resolution 29/23[71] as subsequently reiterated by the Council, the High Commissioner was invited to present orally to the States Members of the Council and observers the findings of each of the periodic reports of the Office of the High Commissioner on the situation of human rights in Ukraine, as part of the interactive dialogues, and through the modalities of the Council, in accordance with its Resolution 5/1 of 18 June 2007. Of interest, since the said periodic reports of the Office on the human rights situation in Ukraine are produced on a quarterly basis and given the fact that the Council is only meeting three times per year, the last report of the year is presented in the context of an ad hoc and informal Council format. They are presented in the Council Chamber in December,[72] are presided over by the Council President, but since these are not formal meetings of the Council, there are no specific room arrangements and the rules and practices of the Council work are not applicable.[73]

Recently, at its September 2019 Session, the Council made a quite comparable request to the High Commissioner on the human rights situation in the Bolivarian Republic of Venezuela, further to Resolutions A/HRC/RES/42/4 and 42/25 of 26 and 27 September 2019, respectively. The main difference with the resolution on the human rights situation in Ukraine was that the said report was requested to be made to the Council in a formal manner. This precedent was also used when adopting Resolution 46/2 of 23 March 2021 on the situation of human rights in Nicaragua,.

(A/HRC/37/3 and Add.1 to 3), Cyprus (A/HRC/37/22), the Islamic Republic of Iran (GA Resolution 72/189), Sri Lanka (A/HRC/37/23), the Occupied Palestinian Territory, including East Jerusalem (A/HRC/37/42), the occupied Syrian Golan (A/HRC/37/43), Libya (oral update and A/HRC/37/46), Cambodia (A/HRC/37/64), Afghanistan (A/HRC/37/45), Haiti (oral update and A/HRC/38/30), Yemen (oral update), Georgia (oral update and A/HRC/39/44), and the DRC (A/HRC/39/42).

71 See A/HRC/RES/29/23 of 3 July 2015.

72 They were presented on 9 December 2015, 12 December 2016, 15 December 2017 and 19 December 2018.

73 Particularly those in relation to points of order or rights of reply. However, States may always request the floor to clarify the matter at stake in the format of a point of clarification.

Since comparable reports were subjected to significantly different formats, the Council decided to upgrade its consideration of the last report of the Office on the situation of human rights in Ukraine by Resolution 53/30 of 14 July 2023. Henceforth, the Office report was submitted to a formal meeting of the Council and not only an informal one.

2.2.7 The Universality of Human Rights[74]

The Universal Periodic Review

Considering country situations through the exclusive prism of country mandates (either Special Procedures or investigation mechanisms) did not give enough credit to the universality of human rights as set forth in the Vienna Declaration and Programme of Action. Indeed, the current number of country-specific mandate-holders is 11 and that of mandated investigations is 11, whereas gross and massive violations of human rights unfortunately prevail in all continents in a much larger number of countries. Hence, when the Council was established, the General Assembly decided that a universal peer review mechanism would be established, thus ensuring that the situation of human rights in all UN Member States would be scrutinized on a regular and equitable basis. This new mechanism was added to the other forms of monitoring in order to overcome, at least partly, the criticisms raised against double standards at the Council level.

At the outset, the Universal Periodic Review (UPR) appears as a rather puzzling process divided into three consecutive periods of time (preparation, conduct and follow-up of each review), articulated in two different steps (UPR Working Group and plenary), involving different stakeholders (State under Review, UN Member and Observer States, the so-called 'troikas', other 'relevant' stakeholders and civil society), based on an array of documents (information provided by the State concerned, a compilation of UN information and a summary of stakeholders' information) and following an intricate set of procedures. This convoluted mechanism is, in reality the result of a negotiation process which was arduous and delicate, and marked by serious misunderstandings or disagreements on the scope, nature and depth of the review. Hence, some of the existing features or oddities may only be explained by the challenges faced during

74 See OP 5 (e) of the General Assembly Resolution 60/251.

the negotiations, particularly insofar as the UPR process at the plenary is concerned.

In order to grasp fully the manifold aspects of the plenary's consideration of the outcome of the UPR mechanism, it may be of relevance to consider one of the numerous documents circulated during the negotiation phase, namely the contribution by the then High Commissioner for Human Rights, Louise Arbour.[75] In her contribution to the discussion, the High Commissioner proposed several key features based on the operations of treaty bodies and special rapporteurs and the experience gained by other peer-review processes. The key elements of her input related to the need for independent expertise to be instilled into the UPR process uphill from the plenary consideration of the States under the Review's reports, as well as the need to secure an appropriate role for civil society. This led her to suggest a two-pronged approach with, on the one hand, a working group composed of independent experts who would be entrusted with the task of pre-screening the reports, articulating questions and entering into dialogue with the States under Review with the active participation of civil society and, on the other hand, the plenary entrusted with the task of reviewing the report of the Working Group of Experts and adopting the outcome of the review.

Although largely debated by the various groups and States involved in the negotiations, this non-paper was not endorsed by the Council. On the eve of the adoption of the 5/1 Resolution, the President and his Bureau requested a formal meeting with the High Commissioner – a rather exceptional situation – to inform her that her position paper did not rally enough support to be adopted.

However, the various elements proposed by the High Commissioner were echoed in Resolution 5/1, particularly regarding the awkward division of responsibilities between a working group – composed of 'the 47 Members States of the Council'[76] – and the plenary. Similarly, the 'troikas', the role of which is described in the IBP as facilitating each review, 'including

75 See also Louise Arbour's foreword to the first edition of the present Anatomy.

76 See para 18 of HRC Resolution 5/1.

the preparation of the report of the Working Group',[77] is a reminder of the expertise envisioned by the High Commissioner, although in this instance, this does not emanate from independent experts but from three members of the Council. Furthermore, whereas the review by the Working Group is conceptualized as a peer-review process with inputs by States and other relevant stakeholders – namely all concerned but civil society – the latter may contribute to the UPR by providing written information[78] and commenting orally on the outcome of the review.[79]

Accordingly, the insistence of several key players during the negotiations phase that the UPR should be considered strictly as a peer-review process, and conversely their reluctance to have the contribution of civil society intruding into the process, led to the division of the plenary process into two clearly defined phases: the first part is constituted by the outcome of the review, which includes the Working Group report 'together with the views of the State under review concerning the recommendations and/or conclusions, as well as voluntary commitments made by the State under review and replies presented by the State under review before the adoption of the outcome by the Council at its plenary session to questions or issues that were not sufficiently addressed during the interactive dialogue in the Working Group'.[80] The second phase includes the statements made by the States under Review, Member and Observer States on the outcome of the Review as well as the general comments by other relevant stakeholders (i.e., NGOs).

Ms. Louise Arbour continued to play a leading role in proposing, developing and conceptualizing what would become the UPR Mechanism. This mechanism's modalities were clarified in the Institution-Building Package (Resolution 5/1) and further refined during the Review of the work and functioning of the Council.[81]

---

77 See paras 18–21 of Resolution 5/1. For the process of selection of troika members, see the Presidential Statement included in document A/HRC/OM/L.1 of 28 February 2008 as well as the PRST 8/1 of 9 April 2008.

78 See para 15 c of HRC Resolution 5/1.

79 See paras 28–31 of HRC Resolution 5/1.

80 See ibid., paras 13 and 14.

81 With one caveat, namely that the format of the UPR working group review reports was not agreed upon at the start of the first UPR

A great deal of effort was deployed to ensure that the system would treat all countries equally, thus translating into deeds the principle of universality of consideration of all UN Member States. The agreed rules and regulations[82] described in a meticulous manner the various stages of the process, from the selection of 'troikas'[83] or the documents prepared by the Secretariat to the format of the outcome document or the input by NGOs. No exception to these rules is permitted.

With the advent of the UPR, despite the criticism of its mild nature as it is a peer review, the situation in all countries has thus been considered at least twice[84] with no selectivity or double standard. The same modalities are applied to Small Island Developing States, Least Developed Countries, Permanent Members of the Security Council and wealthy industrialized countries. This has enabled the Council to develop a formidable mapping of the human rights situation in the world and allowed all States to develop their capacities in the field of human rights. Given the high proportion of recommendations[85] supported by the States under the UPR, this has also enabled all stakeholders, including UN components and the Specialized Agencies as well as civil society, to dialogue with the concerned States on issues which otherwise would have remained in many respects taboo or too delicate to raise at the domestic level.

The universality of human rights as enshrined in the Universal Declaration and reiterated in various instruments, in particular the Vienna Declaration and Programme of Action, was also considered through other prisms.

Working Group. The manifold problems faced in how to report the comments and recommendations made by States in the context of that report kept negotiators extremely busy until an agreement was reached only a few hours only before the first such report was presented to the Working Group for its adoption.

82 See Section I of the Council Resolutions 5/1 and 16/21.

83 Troika: group of representatives from three Member States who are in charge of preparing the reports adopted by the UPR Working Group after each review.

84 At the time of drafting this study, a bit more than half of the membership had gone through the third cycle of the UPR.

85 Two-thirds of the recommendations are, on average supported by SURs.

Civil and Political Rights vs. Economic, Social and Cultural Rights

The first thematic special mechanisms were predominantly focused on civil and political rights. Upon the appointment of High Commissioner Mary Robinson, the discourse changed: it became clear that in order for both the Commission and the High Commissioner to perform their functions adequately and in conformity with the letter and spirit of the Universal Declaration, as well as underlying principles, it was crucial to broaden the horizon and consider groups in focus as well as economic, social and cultural rights.

Despite political assumptions, it is hard to differentiate between the various mandates given the interplay between all sets of rights in theory and practice. It is, however, noticeable that from 1995 to 2002, the Commission established successively new mandates on toxic waste, structural adjustment policies, foreign debt, extreme poverty, education, food, adequate housing and health. This approach was furthered by the Council, which established additional mandates on, for instance, albinism, cultural rights, the right to development, international order, human rights and transnational corporations, leprosy, unilateral coercive measure and water and sanitation.

Small States

Beyond the nature of the Special Procedures mandates, from the establishment of the Council, issues arose regarding the representation of all countries in the Council on an equal footing. Indeed, the principles of universality of human rights may not be fully implemented if some States are excluded, in practical terms, from participating in the work of the Council because of their size, particularly their non-representation or inadequate representation in Geneva.

The last sentence in paragraph 7 of the General Assembly Resolution 60/251 provided that members of the Council would serve for a period of three years and should not be eligible for immediate re-election after two consecutive terms. The intention was extremely clear, namely ensuring that some members would not be de facto permanent members of the Council as they had been members of the Commission in the previous decades. However, this prescription was not complemented by practical means that would have ensured that small States, particularly Small Island Developing States (SIDS) and Least Developed Countries (LDCs), were provided with the means to participate actively in Council sessions and on a par with other countries – not to mention becoming members of the Council. This was especially the case for those States that did not have a Permanent Mission in Geneva, so their physical participation was thus even more complicated.

At the initiative of Mauritius and the Maldives, the Council rectified this anomaly and created, by way of Resolution 19/26 of 23 March 2012, the Voluntary Technical Assistance Trust Fund to Support the Participation of LDCs and SIDS in the work of the Council. The Trust Fund became operational in 2014. It was expected to: (a) to develop training and capacity-building, including e-learning; (b) fund the travel and accommodation for SIDS/LDCs delegates; (c) support three-month work placements of fellows in their respective delegations; and (d) organize induction training sessions to benefit SIDS/LDCs. At the time of completion of the present study, the operations of the Trust Fund have been extremely successful, ensuring the participation of a total of 143 delegates[86] and fellows from 69 SIDS/LDC countries.[87,88]

86 Eighty-nine women and 54 men.

87 Thirty-five from Africa, 22 from Asia and the Pacific and 14 from the Caribbean and Latin American regions.

88 Council Resolution 34/40 of 24 March 2017 broadened the scope of the Trust Fund's terms of reference by encouraging it to support the conduct of at least one briefing on the outcomes of the regular and Special Sessions each year in New York prior to the commencement of each session of the General Assembly with a view to supporting the engagement of these delegations in the work of the Third Committee. It further encouraged the Trust Fund to support the conduct of a workshop in Africa, Asia and the Pacific, and in the Caribbean before its tenth anniversary, reflecting on its achievements, identifying where further improvements might be made, and assessing the value of its activities in fulfilling its training and capacity-building mandate. The first regional workshop took place in Georgetown, Guyana, in cooperation with CARICOM, on 19 and 20 November 2018 with the participation of the Council's President. At the conclusion of the workshop, the SIDS/LDCs participating delegates adopted the Georgetown declaration, spelling out a plan of action for the forthcoming years. The second such workshop will take place from 19 to 21 November 2019 in Nadi, Fiji, also with the participation of the Council's President.

Beyond this interaction of SIDS/LDCs with the Council, there was a specific need for these countries to be in a position to participate in the UPR. Indeed, the underlying principle of the UPR mechanism is the presence of *all* UN Member States during their UPR. It would have been impossible to ensure the participation of SIDS/LDCs in the mechanism and consequently the universality of the UPR without the establishment of another Trust Fund, namely that to Facilitate the Participation of Developing Countries, Particularly the Least Developed Countries, in the UPR by virtue of the Council's Resolution 6/17 of 28 September 2007.

2.2.8 Broadening Further the Landscape: Thematic Discussions, Panels, Forums and Intersessional Activities

Should there be dates to remember in the context of the present study, three would be of particular relevance, namely the establishment of the Commission on 16 February 1946, the dissolution of the Soviet Union on 26 December 1991 – the unofficial date of the end of the Cold War – and the establishment of the Council on 15 March 2006. From this, it is easy to deduce that the Commission operated for exactly three-quarters of its existence against the background of an East/West divide – or rift. Considering further that the years following the dissolution of the Soviet Union were marred with difficulties in fully apprehending the consequences of the end of the Cold War, and that the Commission on Human Rights entered into serious political difficulties at the turn of the twenty-first century, one may be tempted to conclude that the modus operandi of the then-main UN human rights body was built against the background of the East/West divide.

One may further be tempted to note that, when the Council was established, it tried to build itself against a totally different background. By then, the Cold War had been over for 15 years, the world had entered into another era, several conflicts of a different nature were proceeding in various parts of the world, the international economy had changed its paradigms and the social architecture of the past was already seriously challenged. Hence, that which had characterized the half-century existence of the Commission was no longer prevalent and new challenges had to be faced by the nascent Council. At the risk of oversimplifying the situation, the underlying rifts were no longer East/West and Communism/Capitalism, but North/South and Conservatives/Liberals.

Accordingly, adjusting itself to this new situation, the Council had to broaden its scope of action. New ways had to be found to discuss issues which were/are divisive among the members of the international community. The existing mechanisms or tools, as they had been inherited – and slightly adjusted – from the Commission, were no longer sufficient to deal with these societal and related issues. In short, the Council had to identify ways and means to dialogue on non-consensual issues and it did so with flexibility and pragmatism.

It would be extremely hard to be comprehensive in mapping the areas of tension between different sets of rights and/or freedoms since the Council's creation. However, some of them may be easily be identified as follows:

Thematic matters:

- The tension between the concept of 'defamation' of religion, seen as the protection of a religion or belief against attacks deemed insulting or offensive, and the freedom of religion and belief as well as expression and opinion, which are human rights enjoyed by individuals,[89] was palpable from the establishment of the Council. The adoption of Resolution 16/18 of 24 March 2011 on Combatting Intolerance, Negative Stereotyping and Stigmatization of, and Discrimination, Incitement to Violence and Violence Against, Persons Based on Religion or Belief settled the dispute at least for a while.[90] The factors that enabled a consensus to emerge at the time on these sensitive matters were US President Obama's 2009 Cairo Speech and the start of the 'Arab Spring'.[91] The events that emerged in Europe in July 2023 in relation to the burning of the Holy Quran revived these difficulties and more generally underlined the continuing difficulties posed by

89 See Council Resolutions 4/9 of 30 March 2007, 7/9 of 27 March 2008, 10/22 of 26 March 2009 and 13/16 of 25 March 2010 on condemning defamation of religions.

90 Reaffirmed by the Council in subsequent years, the resolution marked a shift from the protection of religions and beliefs to that of the persons professing a religion or belief.

91 See also Council's Resolution 12/16 of 2 October 2009 tabled by Egypt and the USA as an aftermath of President Obama's Remarks to the Muslim World delivered on 4 June 2009 in Cairo.

the interpretation of the role of religions in societies as well as their impacts on human rights. They led to the convening of the ninth Urgent Debate on 'the alarming rise in premeditated and public acts of religious hatred as manifested by recurrent desecration of the Holy Quran in some European and other countries'.[92] It goes without stating that, at the time of writing this second edition, the events in the Middle East are triggering a revisiting of these issues.

Serious misunderstandings on issues relating to the protection against violence and discrimination based on sexual orientation and gender identity remain. The appointment of an Independent Expert on these issues did not settle the controversy.[93] Thus, all resolutions on the matter[94] were/are the subject of an extremely delicate adoption process. The last resolution on the matter was adopted with 23 votes in favour and 17 against, with seven abstentions. However, it was subjected to no fewer than 13 amendments some of them being defeated with a very narrow margin.[95]

The question of the death penalty remains a divided issue although the resolutions on the matter are generally adopted with a large majority:[96]

- The follow-up to the 2001 Durban Declaration and Programme of Action adopted at the World Conference against Racism, Racial Discrimination, Xenophobia and Related Intolerance and the outcome document of the Durban Review Conference also remain

92 See section 5.1.4 below.

93 See Council's Resolution 32/2 of 30 June 2016.

94 Ibid. See also Council's Resolution 17/19 of 17 June 2011 and 27/32 of 26 September 2014.

95 See https://hrcmeetings.ohchr.org/HRCSessions/RegularSessions/50/Pages/resolutions.aspx

96 The most recent resolution on the question of the death penalty was adopted on 5 October 2023 with a majority of 28 in favour and 11 against, with seven abstentions. However, an amendment referring to the importance of holding domestic debates at the national level was rejected with a thin majority of 19 in favour and 21 against, with seven abstentions. Another amendment on the reaffirmation of the sovereign rights of all States to develop their own legal systems, including determining appropriate legal penalties, was defeated with 19 votes in favour, 19 against, and nine abstentions.

a highly divisive matter. More broadly, there is little agreement on many issues linked to the struggle against racism. Controversial State positions hamper the work of such bodies as the Ad-Hoc Committee on the Elaboration of Complementary Standards, the Working Group of Experts on People of African Descent, and the Intergovernmental Working Group on the Effective Implementation of the Durban Declaration and Programme of Action in charge of setting the standards in this area.

- Issues relating to terrorism and human rights have often led to controversies between those focusing attention on the protection of human rights and fundamental freedoms while countering terrorism[97] and those prioritizing the consideration of the effects of terrorism on the enjoyment of all human rights.[98] After years of efforts by proponents of both alternatives, a consensus recently emerged, as encapsulated in Resolution 37/27 of 23 March 2018 on Terrorism and Human Rights.[99]
- There does not seem to be any palpable progress on a divide relating to the impact of the activities of transnational corporations on the enjoyment of human rights. Some countries focus their attention on the effective implementation of the Guiding Principles on Business and Human Rights and appropriate support for the Working Group on Business and Human Rights and the Forum on Business and Human Rights.[100] Other countries wish to move ahead by elaborating an internationally legally binding instrument to regulate the activities of transnational corporations and other business enterprises and accordingly focus their attention on the work of the Open-ended Intergovernmental Working Group on Transnational Corporations.[101]
- More generally, there are multiple other political divides on issues that would otherwise look perfectly compatible to an external observer, such as the right to the development and full enjoyment of all human rights, particularly economic, social and cultural rights, including the effects of foreign debt and other international

97 See Council's Resolutions 35/34 of 23 June 2017 and 41/18 of 12 July 2019.

98 See Council's Resolution 34/8 of 23 March 2017.

99 See also Council's Resolution 42/18 of 26 September 2019.

100 See, inter alia, Council's Resolution 17/4 of 6 July 2011, 26/22 of 27 June 2014 and 35/7 of 22 June 2017.

101 See Council's Resolution 26/9 of 26 June 2014.

obligations, the negative impact of corruption, human rights and unilateral coercive measures, the promotion of mutually beneficial cooperation in the field of human rights, human rights and international solidarity, and international cooperation in the field of human rights.[102] Even issues relating to the digital age or climate change are facing challenges of a substantive nature when they are discussed at the Council. Furthermore, the adoption of the Declarations on the Right to Peace[103] and the Declaration on the Rights of Peasants and Other People Working in Rural Areas[104] were extremely sensitive and marked by comparable rifts.
- The space allocated to civil society, the protection of human rights defenders, the safety of journalists and the cooperation with the United Nations, its representatives and mechanisms in the field of human rights are also matters triggering friction between and within groups of States.[105]

Country situations:

- As mentioned in previous sections, there are significant divergences of views on the course of action to be followed in dealing with country situations. Although this is not linked with societal issues, they form a background against which some of the above controversial areas are being considered or interpreted.

Some are thus arguing for strong responses from the Council, including the setting up of Commissions of Inquiry or Special Rapporteurs under agenda item 4. If this is not possible for political reasons linked to the interpretation of item 4 as having an accusatory nature, they suggest doing so under agenda items 2 or 10, which are considered as more 'technical' in nature. In general terms, they perceive the consideration of such matters as central to the work and the *raison d'être* of the Council

102 See, inter alia, Council's Resolutions 37/11 of 22 March 2018, 37/19, 37/21 and 37/23 of 23 March 2018, 38/2 and 38/3 of 5 July 2018, and 39/9 of 27 September 2018.

103 See General Assembly Resolution 71/189.

104 See Council's Resolution 39/12 of 28 September 2018.

105 See, inter alia, Council's Resolutions 31/32 of 24 March 2016, 38/12 of 6 July 2018, 39/6 of 27 September 2018, and 40/11 of 21 March 2019.

and regret the politicization and what they perceive as the resulting filibustering. They also consider item 7 as an anomaly since it focuses on one country situation alone in the Council's agenda, all other country situations are theoretically considered under the other items, which were crafted in a generic manner.

Others consider that the principle of State sovereignty should apply whatever the circumstances, thus privileging a consensual and non-confrontational approach. They vilify a practice that they consider as revealing a pattern of finger-pointing and double standards which they believe is neither efficient nor effective. They are, as a matter of principle, opposed to any given country mandate, unless the concerned country is in agreement with it, and are supporters of the UPR Mechanism or of technical cooperation and advisory services under agenda item 10. As per item 7, they consider it as the continuation of the Commission's own agenda item on the same topic established after the Six-Day War in 1967 and a reflection of the specificity of the situation.[106] They also consider it as a 'thematic' matter since it concerns a foreign occupation condemned by a large number of United Nations resolutions.

There are thus unambiguous divergences of views within the international community on how it should address societal issues and country-related matters. These controversies often echo similar divides at the national and regional levels.

It is, however, of fundamental importance to underline that a number of matters which were very controversial at the time of the Commission are no longer of such a nature. For instance, matters or issues relating to torture, the death penalty, summary executions, arbitrary detention or enforced and involuntary disappearances, which were a source of serious tension between States and groups of States at the time of the

106 The Commission on Human Rights included items 8 and 9, which read as follows: item 8: Question of the violation of human rights in the occupied Arab territories, including Palestine; and item 9: Question of the violation of human rights and fundamental freedoms in any part of the world, including: (a) Question of human rights in Cyprus; and (b) Procedure established in accordance with Economic and Social Council resolutions 1503 (XLVIII) and 2000/3.

Commission, are now discussed with much less acrimony and the ensuing outcomes are generally adopted[107] without significant difficulties. This is no small achievement.

It is also important to note the intense efforts deployed in a constructive and cooperative manner with a view to dealing with emerging or pressing thematic matters. Members of the Council are rallying on an increasing scale in order to conceptualize and face new or persistent challenges and consider appropriate solutions to increasingly complex problems which arise.

In order to deal with issues of this complexity and the many serious divergences which our world has been struggling with since the turn of the century, the Commission deployed some introspective and soul-searching efforts. The documents[108] which it adopted in the last years of its existence represented an attempt at defining a comprehensive framework within which societally and politically charged issues could be handled with a minimum of understanding and acceptance. In other words, the Commission tried to agree on a set of rules or practices which would enable delegations to agree to disagree and thus move forward, albeit slowly and often reluctantly.[109] The Commission did not succeed in its endeavour.

As far as the Council is concerned, it has, since its establishment, set numerous tools in motion and refined its modus operandi to cope with these matters. Flexibility has become a leitmotif in its approach to complex problems and cooperation and dialogue are often emphasized. As

107 With or without a vote.

108 See the compilation of recent documents in relation to the enhancement of the working methods of the Commission on Human Rights (1999–2005) available on the website of the HRC at https://www.ohchr.org/Documents/HRBodies/HRCouncil/CompilationDocuments1999-2005.pdf.

109 The above-mentioned Commission's documents included proposed rules and regulations encouraging joint statements, framing interactive dialogues with mandate-holders, limiting the exercise of the rights of reply, biennializing resolutions, informing about drafts to be tabled and publicizing the informals held in this regard, rationalizing the participation of dignitaries, clarifying the voting procedure or strengthening the role of the Bureau.

examples of such efforts, it is of interest to note that the President of the 18th Human Rights Council cycle established eight clusters of issues affecting the Council's work, including (i) the contribution of the Council to the review of its status by the General Assembly, (ii) new technologies, artificial intelligence and the digital divide, (iii) rationalization of initiatives, (iv) use of modern technology by the Council, (v) efficiency of the UPR process, (vi) challenges faced by small and developing States and least developed countries, (vii) participation of women in the Council's activities and sexual harassment, and (viii) accessibility.

2.2.9 Reaching out to the Outside World and Becoming More Transparent[110]

At the risk of oversimplification, it is hard not to observe that far too often intergovernmental gatherings tend to operate in their own bubble and dramas with little, if any, impact on the ground. This is probably linked to the growing complexity and sophistication of their programmes, discussions and agenda, the difficulty of translating abstract norms into implementable action points, and/or the closed nature of their working environment. The Council is not impermeable to such a situation and the numerous and often uninformed media reports on the activities of the Commission before its abolition made it even more topical. It had thus to make its activities understandable, implementable and known by all of its stakeholders, as well as the public at large.

To be fair, the Commission on Human Rights tried to reach out to the outside world but with limited success. Its main and possibly sole achievement in this regard was providing civil society with a significant role during its work, thereby using it as a medium for the dissemination of information. Indeed, contrary to most other UN intergovernmental bodies, particularly the General Assembly and its main Committees, the Commission boosted the participation of NGOs with ECOSOC by extending to them prerogatives similar to those of Observer States – with the noticeable exception of points of order or rights of reply. The participation of hundreds of NGO representatives during the Commission's sessions was a real success, although it was not deprived of polemics. This opening up to civil society had a profound and durable impact on the

110 See General Assembly Resolution 60/251, para 5 (i) and (j).

operations of the Commission and was extended to the Council by virtue of paragraph 11 of Resolution 60/251.

The Commission was, however, much less successful in developing relations with the outside world, particularly the media and consequently the public at large. Its activities were at times rudely mischaracterized. At the turn of the century, it was bluntly referred to in media reports as the 'discredited' or 'outrageous' Commission. The Commission was, however, unresponsive to such criticisms due to a lack of appropriate means and expertise.

The Commission's debates were public in the UN sense of the term, meaning that anyone duly accredited could attend its plenary. However, there was little information available, if any, about its work and achievements outside the Geneva Palais des Nations where it held its meetings. It fell prey to those who used any possible arguments with the intention of securing the Commission's abolition. In a way, its unresponsiveness was proof of the toxic political environment curtailing its work and preventing it from presenting itself to the world media in a consensual, constructive and efficient manner.

It does not, therefore, appear as a surprise that the Council, immediately upon its establishment as a General Assembly subsidiary organ, deployed significant efforts in broadly disseminating information on its activities and avoiding the recurrence of past misrepresentations in the media.

Although these objectives are far from being achieved, it is of interest to mention the following:

- In accordance with Section G of the Council Resolution 16/21, an Office of the Council President was established, thus consolidating the practice which had emerged from the first session onwards[111] and providing a tool to support the position of the President, which has been regularly strengthened since 2006, as will be seen in the next chapter.
- A public information officer position within the OHCHR was established in 2006.

111 See also Council Decision 9/103 of 24 September 2008.

- All Council Presidents have regularly addressed media representatives and are supported in this endeavour by public information officers within the OHCHR (as from its 17th session in June 2011).[112]
- The sessions of the Council have from the very start been webcast live and the webcast archives henceforth constitute the official records of the Council in place of the old-fashioned summary records, the production of which was disrupted at the start of the Council's life.
- An SMS-alert service was set into motion, providing live practical information on the proceedings, later being replaced by resorting to the support offered by the SCHED application.[113]
- The Council website[114] was strengthened and made accessible directly. It is constantly upgraded and is complemented by an Extranet available to all and no longer needed a password.
- The use of information technology is constantly revisited with a view to refining it and facilitating access to the work of the Council,[115] and several accounts were created on social network platforms.[116]
- Special attention was devoted during the 2011 review of the Council's work and functioning to the enhancement of accessibility for persons with disabilities. One of the Council's Vice-Presidents serves as the chair of an ad-hoc task force on accessibility and reports regularly to the Council.[117]

Whether these measures were effective in addressing some of the most ill-informed reports in the traditional or social media remains to be seen. However, the Council is now in a position to react publicly to some of them through the voice of the Council President and its proceedings are far more accessible than in the past.

Even before the COVID-19 pandemic, the Council had to consider to what extent it should make use of modern technology and facilitate access to its work. In this regard, it is of interest to note that specific difficulties had often been encountered and some remained in terms of the

112 See A/HRC/DEC/17/118.
113 see for instance https://hrc57session.sched.com.
114 www.ohchr.org/HRBodies/HRC.
115 See for instance, Resolution 16/21 and Annex II of the Presidential Statement adopted on 3 December 2018.
116 Twitter: @UN_HRC; Facebook: UNHRC.
117 During the Organizational Session held in December.

use of information technology during the formal Council sessions. For instance, displaying live materials during the Council's debates or dialogues had always exacerbated tensions and had never been conceptualized fully.

The report of the Task Force on secretariat services, accessibility for persons with disabilities and use of information technology includes various provisions relating to video messaging:[118]

- In order to enhance their participation in the plenary debates of the Council, particularly during the adoption of the outcome of the review by the plenary or during interactive dialogues following the presentation of a country mission report by a Special Procedure mandate-holder, NHRIs were provided with the ability to pre-record video messages. Although this seemed rather anodyne in our post-COVID-19 contemporary world, it was actually a novelty for the Council and gave a level of prominence and visibility to the NHRIs.
- As far as non-governmental organizations are concerned, this possibility was limited to the general segment of the Council plenary sessions, interactive dialogues with Special Procedures relating to reports on country missions (particularly for organizations that contributed to the mission to that country), the plenary adoption of the UPR review outcomes (particularly for organizations involved in the national process or having sent contributions for the summary of stakeholder information), and panels/annual discussions, in order to enhance the participation of local stakeholders in plenary meetings.

The embryonic practice of pre-registered video messages did, however, not develop towards the use of more advanced technology such as videoconferencing or displaying images (pictures, videos, films) during the Council proceedings until the COVID-19 pandemic. This was largely based on the technical difficulty of organizing it in the Council's room and the fear that such means could easily be hijacked or misused, thus creating havoc and confusion during the discussion of delicate human rights situations.[119] Moreover, the possible impact of images displayed

118 See Council Resolution 16/21, paras 13 and 28, and decision 19/119, paras 46 and 47.

119 In practical terms, the Council would have no control over the origin of any material displayed on the Council's screens. Materials of

in the plenary of the Council was also taken into account. The pre-COVID-19 practice was summarized by the Bureau on 21 July 2015 and is as follows:

> The Bureau reiterated the practice established for the use of video materials over the past year, whereby guiding principles for the use of video materials were: relevance of the video material, proportionality with regard to the speaking time, and applicability of the rules of procedures of the Council. Furthermore, reference to countries may be possible if the concerned party has been consulted and had not raised objection. With regard to video materials used by Commissions of Inquiry and Special Procedures mandate-holders, the Bureau decided further that this practice should take into account the fact that such materials are to be considered as an integral part of the statements made by Commissions of Inquiry or mandate-holders and that a non-objection by concerned parties was not a requirement.[120]

In practical terms, the Bureau may approve or deny a request to display video materials in the plenary. Its decision is based on the above criteria.

2.2.10 Reaching out to the Rest of the UN System

Human rights are not isolated within the UN system. They are considered the third pillar of the Organization. It therefore goes without saying that constructive and efficient cooperation should be established between the Council and the rest of that system, particularly the New York main UN bodies.

The Commission had developed some forms of relationship with UN bodies and selected partners, mostly as a subsidiary body of the ECOSOC. At its last substantive session in 2005, it invited,[121] for instance, the following persons to participate in its meetings:

---

doubtful or fake origin could thus easily be displayed.

120 See https://extranet.ohchr.org/sites/hrc/PresidencyBureau/BureauRegionalGroupsCorrespondence/Pages/Bureau-meetings-Archives.aspx, the issue referred to during the meeting was the request of the Commission of Inquiry on the Democratic People's Republic of Korea to display a short film on the preparation of the report.

121 By virtue of decision 2005/101 of 14 March 2005, Special Representatives or Advisers of the Secretary-General on substantive thematic issues of relevance to the Commission were subjected to the same treatment as mandate-holders. Such arrangements still

- the Chairperson of the Commission on the Status of Women;
- the General Assembly independent expert to direct an in-depth study of the question of violence against children;
- the Special Rapporteur on Disability of the Commission for Social Development;
- the Chairpersons of the Committee on Economic, Social and Cultural Rights, of the Committee against Torture, of the Human Rights Committee, of the Committee on the Elimination of Discrimination against Women, of the Committee on the Rights of the Child, and of the Committee on the Protection of the Rights of All Migrants and Members of Their Families;
- and national human rights institutions were provided with the possibility to address the Commission under its agenda item 18(b) in the context of a segment specifically designed for this purpose.

However, such practices were mostly of a bureaucratic and repetitive nature, often without a Question/Answer segment or proper outcomes and quite logically, when the Council was established, they were not replicated. Some of them were mainstreamed into the normal work of the Council[122] or simply abandoned.

Sadly, as a consequence, there is no interaction today between the Council and the Commission on the Status of Women, the Commission for Social Development, or the treaty bodies. This was omitted from the institution-building package Resolution 5/1 and the significant increase in the activities of the Council has made it very difficult to envisage reinstituting such practices.

---

prevail today and are based on a generous interpretation of paras 5 (h), 6 and 11.

122 Subsequent to the adoption of Council Resolution 16/21, the summary of the information provided by other relevant stakeholders should contain, where appropriate, a separate section for contributions by the (A-status) national human rights institutions of the State under Review (para 9). The said institutions are entitled to intervene immediately after the State under review during the adoption of the outcome of the Review by the Council plenary (para 14). In practical terms, these institutions can also take the floor during the general debates after the observer States and before the non-governmental organizations and up to two national institutions may speak during any given panel.

From its inception, the Council privileged action-oriented relationships with UN departments or agencies as well as international organizations. The UPR was considered the cornerstone of this approach, with the possibility for agencies and bodies to contribute to the summaries prepared by the Secretariat. It should be borne in mind in this regard that the UPR does not start or end in the Council plenary. It is prima facie a mechanism rooted at the domestic level, with strong encouragement and expectations that States prepare meticulously their UPR. National processes are expected to involve domestic bureaucracies as well as domestic stakeholders. They should also include the contributions of international organizations' presences in the country.

The contributions of such institutions are thus expected upstream and downstream. They are encouraged to contribute to the said Secretariat's document but also to assist the authorities whenever appropriate in mapping the state of implementation of the various recommendations made during the previous UPR cycle as well as assisting them in preparing for 'their' review. During the plenary consideration of these documents, they can also participate by commenting on the review. However, the main expected achievements are downstream, with technical cooperation and advisory services to the domestic authorities.

The participation of the UN departments and agencies in the work of the Council was gauged as insufficient and inadequate when the Council's work was reviewed in 2011 since it was limited to only one of the Council's mechanisms. Ways and means were explored to extend it significantly. Hence, the Council review document introduced a provision for the organization on a yearly basis of a Mainstreaming Panel during the High-Level Segment taking place at the start of its main (spring) session.

Resolution 16/21 thus provided that the Council should henceforth 'hold a half-day panel discussion once a year to interact with heads of governing bodies and secretariats of UN agencies and funds within their respective mandates on specific human rights themes with the objective of promoting the mainstreaming of human rights throughout the UN system. The present provision does not preclude other opportunities that may arise for discussions between the Council and UN agencies and funds on the mainstreaming of human rights'. It went further in requesting States or Regional Groups to propose themes to be discussed by the panel.

In practical terms, unfortunately, the selection of such themes soon became an issue and various groups proposed topics that were at odds with each other, thus requiring a lot of effort for the President and his/her Bureau to reach a consensus.[123] Beyond the polarization exemplified by this phenomenon, it is also of interest to note that the High-Level Mainstreaming Panels held so far have sometimes also been at odds with Resolution 16/21, which emphasized the importance of interacting with the heads of governing bodies and secretariats of the UN agencies and funds. Finally, since agreement on themes for the Mainstreaming Panels proved to be difficult, proposing an 'easy' theme broad enough to agree upon progressively became an objective per se, to the detriment of identifying a subject deeply rooted in intra-UN cooperation.

- It remains that despite the efforts or steps taken to establish effective relations with other entities within the UN system, little progress has been achieved. Representatives of departments, agencies or funds are from time to time included as panelists or invited guests during high-level or enhanced interactive dialogues. There is, however, no systemic and operational relationship with the rest of the system. Successive Council Presidents have tried to overcome this issue by entertaining visits outside Geneva to increase knowledge and awareness about the Council's work, as is explained in the next chapter. Conversely, the Council's Presidents regularly invite representatives from other parts of the system to attend its sessions. The President of the General Assembly, the highest UN Official according to the Charter and representative of the Council's parent body, is always invited to deliver a speech at the start of the High-Level Segment at the Council's March Session. The Secretary-General also attends all High-Level Segments. The Deputy Secretary-General was invited to engage with the Council on 7 March 2019 on the 2030 agenda for sustainable development. Similarly, the President of ECOSOC has been regularly invited to address the Council to share information on the state of play regarding the 2030 agenda. The incoming and/or outgoing Chairpersons of the Third Committee have been invited

123 See for instance, the Bureau minutes of 4 December 2014 or 3 December 2013.

periodically since 2015[124] to address the Council either during the September Session or intersessionally.[125]

- However, it is of importance to note that the very first informal discussion between the President of the Council and some incoming or outgoing members of the Security Council only took place on 31 October 2018, 13 years after the former was established! This was followed up on 10 April 2019 by an informal breakfast meeting with the members of the Security Council. If it were not linked with the unavoidable polarization of the consideration of specific human rights issues, this would appear as quite an oddity given the complementarity of both bodies.[126] However, it is also of interest to note that it has so far been impossible to strengthen these embryonic relations between the two Councils.
- Furthermore, it is also of interest to note that, to this day, no meeting between the President of the Council and the Peacebuilding Commission could be organized and that the very simple and basic requests of the Council for the Chair of the Peacebuilding Commission to address it once per year in a purely informative manner was never implemented due to the impossibility for the latter to agree to it in a consensual manner.[127]

---

124 See minutes of the Bureau of 21 July 2015.

125 Such informal meetings took place, for instance on 7 September 2015 or 27 August 2018.

126 In a letter to the President of the Security Council dated 18 April 2019 and posted on the extranet of the Council, the President of the 13th Council Cycle proposed that the meeting be followed by informal discussions with members of the Human Rights Council on the occasion of a visit or stopover by a Security Council Member in Geneva. Two Permanent Members of the Security Council objected to that proposal.

127 See Resolution 45/31 of 7 December 2020, which includes in its OP 9 a decision to invite the Chair of the Peacebuilding Commission (PBC), commencing in 2021, to brief, on an annual basis, the Human Rights Council during one of its regular sessions under agenda item 3, on the work of the Commission, including in relation to country situations that are on the Council's agenda. The successive PBC Chairs were never in a position to get a consensual agreement on their participation in a Council meeting and accordingly declined all the invitations they received since 2021. See, for instance: https://hrcmeetings.ohchr.org/PresidencyBureau/

2.2.11 Addressing the Politicization and Polarization of the Commission/Council through Adjustments of the Working Methods

Many reasons led to the abolition of the Commission on Human Rights, but among them, the issue of the politicization of its deliberations has often been highlighted as the main one. 'Politicization' was a word used and misused in the Commission and is now, to a certain extent, in the Council.

As it is a political body, composed of the executive authorities of States, political considerations are inherent to its work. After all, great philosophers such as Aristotle – in *Politics* – or Al-Farabi – in *The Virtuous City* – have emphasized the role of politics in guiding society towards the common good and underlined the fact that humans, as political animals, live within communities and participate in governance. The latter should be a means of achieving the moral and spiritual well-being of the community.

In concrete terms, many differences exist, and have always existed, in the understanding of how this common good may be achieved and the consequent difficulties often arose in relation to societal issues. As is very clearly visible in today's societies, there are large divergences of views and competing ideologies on how such matters should be dealt with. This often results in political and social troubles at the domestic level. It would therefore be quite unrealistic and utopic to expect that the same discussions at the intergovernmental level would be deprived of any tension and that politics would not enter this terrain.

To the contrary, the author considers that politics need to be recognized as a healthy terrain for the Council to evolve in and that, if the adequate conditions of dialogue, openness, transparency and respect for others' ideas are met, it can only lead to positive results. It is the author's consideration that a body dealing with human rights issues, which gets to

---

BureauRegionalGroupsCorrespondence/Correspondence/Letter%20of%20response%20to%20the%20President%20of%20the%20Human%20Rights%20Council%20from%20H.E.%20Mr.%20Sérgio%20França%20Danese,%20Chair%20of%20the%20Peacebuilding%20Commission.pdf.

the core of any society, cannot by definition be deprived of a high level of politization.

However, what is more problematic is if polarization between various regional, political or ad hoc groups becomes the norm and pollutes the discussion to such an extent that it leads to paralysis of the concerned body. This is probably what happened to the Commission on Human Rights but fortunately not to the Human Rights Council.

Accordingly, what matters most is that the working methods and modus operandi of the Council enable it to consider any sensitive matter in depth with a minimum level of mutual understanding, respect, and trust. Or, to put it otherwise, to reach a stage of engagement where all agree to disagree.

Insofar as country issues are concerned, the recurrent problem is the balance of which politics are applied to whom. For example, many Member States have always rejected the finger-pointing or double-standard policies according to which a small minority of countries are solely scrutinized. Conversely, others have regretted the difficulties in trying to consider gross and massive violations. Terms like finger-pointing, double standards, or politicization are often used (or misused) in this connection by both sides, which thus found some common grounds of concern against the Commission.

Since the 1960s, the Commission and later the Council have considered gross and massive human rights violations starting with the setting up of specific agenda items concerning apartheid in Southern Africa and the situation of human rights in Israel and the Occupied Palestinian Territories later expanded to many other situations. Numerous resolutions were adopted, bodies and mechanisms established, and reports submitted and debated. All these included countless recommendations as to what needed to be done to overcome a terrible human rights situation which was qualified in detail in relation to international human rights and humanitarian laws. Many of those recommendations called for immediate action by the international community with a view to containing the increase in human rights violations and avoiding the existing ones degenerating into a vicious cycle of harm and destruction with terrible impacts on the human rights situation of the concerned populations.

The whole world unfortunately often watches in horror the devastating effect on humankind of conflicts with their cohort of atrocities, gross and massive human rights violations, war crimes, crimes against humanity, and other crimes as may be determined by the International Court of Justice and the International Criminal Court. Ex post facto, the latter will deliberate and advise on the matter, and this will include finger-pointing at the responsibilities of those who prompted and triggered this situation. However, by the time this is done, the dust will have settled, and scores of lives will have been lost, devastations to the highest possible level will have occurred, and atrocities and suffering inflicted on a huge number of human beings on both sides of the borders. This will also feed the vicious circle, leading to further violence in the years and decades to come.

Against this background, it is important for the Council to be involved in considering all human rights situations wherever they occur and to do so in the most energetic manner. Consequently, it is equally important to ensure that polarization does not stand in the way of the Council when it is dealing with or, trying to deal with, human rights situations.

From its inception, the Council was fully conscious of the challenges faced by its predecessor in terms of polarization and the need to find ways and means to dialogue on non-consensual issues. It was aware of the deep polarization that the consideration of human rights thematic or country-based issues would probably introduce into its work.

Accordingly, there was a genuine effort made to avoid reproducing previous mistakes. The Institution-Building Package[111] in Resolution 5/1 included a number of provisions that made the Council's working methods far more transparent and effective and thus contributed to overcoming polarization:

- Section VI of the Council's Resolution 5/1 started with the assertion that the Council's working methods should be transparent, impartial, equitable, fair and pragmatic and lead to clarity, predictability and inclusiveness.
- The practice was initiated of holding briefings on prospective resolutions or decisions during the Organizational Meetings held two weeks prior to the beginning of any session.

- The practice of holding at least one open-ended informal consultation[128] on each proposal, including those of the Presidents, was systematized and made compulsory.
- The Bureau of the Council was requested to communicate the contents of its meetings regularly through a timely summary report.
- The Institution-Building Package includes a fundamental subsection 5[129] on 'other work formats that included panel debates, seminars and round tables' that were considered tools of the Council for enhancing dialogue and mutual understanding on certain issues.
- Proposers of a country-resolution were encouraged to secure the broadest possible support for their initiatives (preferably 15 members) before action.
- There was also encouragement to bring a topic to the international community's attention in other ways than resolutions and decisions, for instance through recommendations, conclusions, summaries of discussions and President's Statements.

While a number of the measures set forth in this canvas were not implemented immediately, the imperious necessity to instil transparency and predictability into the work of the Council became a reality from the start of the Council's work and strengthened over the years, particularly in the past decade. This enabled the emergence of a working culture geared towards the promotion of discussion and cooperation rather than systemic polarization on all issues dealt with by the Council.

Although, as mentioned above, there remain, and will always remain, many areas where consensus will be very difficult, the above steps have been fruitful in ensuring that disagreements could be voiced in a manner that is constructive and respectful.

Among the features of this working culture are:

- The significant increase in the number of joint statements occurs when a group of States joins their voices to make them stronger. Joint statements are often the first step in gathering support around a thematic or country situation or a panacea when a resolution cannot be

128 Such meetings are open to all delegations.

129 See para 115 of Resolution 5/1.

adopted. In other words, joint statements serve as safety valves when sensitive issues are being discussed.

- The quasi-systematic enlarging of the community of sponsors of draft resolutions with extremely active core groups of sponsors composed of delegations from all or most regional groups contributed largely to weakening the group's logic that had prevailed during the Commission's time and the early years of the Council.
- The large number of informal negotiations held throughout any given session,[130] aiming at smoothing the main divergences between delegations.
- Panels provide the opportunity to discuss a large range of issues, mostly thematic, organized in-session or intersessionally, thus providing a lesser degree of polarization and a higher level of visibility.[131] In some instances, the issues dealt with in such a format are polarized and of a sensitive nature, for instance, sexual orientation and gender identity, the Convention on the Prevention of Genocide, the right to development, democracy, and racism, etc.
- Beyond panels, the Council is increasingly organizing intersessional seminars, meetings, or discussions, the status and nature of which are variable; some are purely expert meetings gathered by the OHCHR, while others involve the Office, the Bureau and the main sponsors. The themes studied at such meetings are varied, but some of them have touched on polarized matters where there is no consensus on their interpretation or implementation, for instance, the protection of the family, the right to peace, the prevention of human rights violations or the 2030 agenda for sustainable development. Although it is delicate to draw conclusions and identify trends based on the scarcity of data, it would seem that the format of intersessional activities, as

130 An average of 60 informal meetings are held in parallel to the Council's sessions.

131 For instance, the intersessional panel discussion on promoting international cooperation to support national human rights follow-up systems and processes held on 9 November 2016, the panel discussion on local government and human rights held on 4 September 2017, the intersessional panel discussion on human rights and climate change held on 4 October 2017, the intersessional panel on the incompatibility between democracy and racism, the intersessional seminar on the prevention of human rights violation or the intersessional meeting on human rights and the 2030 agenda held in 2019.

well as their inherent flexibility, is increasingly attractive to delegations in overcoming some of the negative aspects of polarization and upholding constructive dialogues on delicate issues.[132]

In order to deal with thematic matters of particular importance, the Council is also increasingly relying on the work of its subsidiary bodies, special procedures and the Advisory Committee.

- The Council also decided to further develop further the Commission's practice in identifying areas deserving specific interest through the establishment of relevant bodies. This practice was followed in a two-track approach.
- On the one hand, intergovernmental working groups have been established to consider substantive issues, which may or should deserve the adoption of new or complementary standards or to review and monitor the progress (or lack thereof) in the implementation of given standards. At present, the following bodies are in operation:
    - the Working Group on the Right to Development;[133]
    - the Intergovernmental Working Group on the Durban Declaration and Programme of Action;[134]
    - the Ad Hoc Committee on the Elaboration of Complementary Standards;[135]
    - the Open-ended Intergovernmental Working Group on Transnational Corporations and Other Business Enterprises with Respect to Human Rights;[136] and
    - the Open-ended Intergovernmental Working Group on the Regulatory Framework of Activities of Private Military and Security Companies.[137]

132 Number of intersessional seminars, discussions or meetings per year: 2013 (1), 2014 (0), 2015 (1), 2016 (0), 2017 (5), 2018 (3), 2019 (8).

133 Established by Commission on Human Rights Resolution 1998/72.

134 Established by Commission on Human Rights Resolution 2002/68.

135 Despite the use of the term 'Committee', the Ad Hoc Committee's composition and modus operandi are the same as any other intergovernmental working group. The Committee was established by Council Resolution 6/21.

136 Established by Council Resolution 26/9.

137 Established by Council Resolution 36/11.

- On the other hand, platforms for dialogue, cooperation and/or analysis have been established with the installation of external independent expertise. The contribution of Special Procedures is often sought in order to ensure synergies and avoid duplicative work. These bodies are as follows:
  - the Expert Mechanism on the Rights of Indigenous Peoples;[138]
  - the Expert Mechanism on the Right to Development;[139]
  - the Forum on Minority Issues;[140]
  - the Social Forum;[141]
  - the UN Forum on Business and Human Rights;[142]
  - the UN Forum on Human Rights, Democracy and the Rule of Law;[143]
  - the Permanent Forum of People of African Descent.[144]

---

138 Composed of seven independent experts appointed by the Council, it was established by Council Resolution 6/36 and its terms of reference were amended by Council Resolution 33/25.

139 Composed of five independent experts, it was established by Council Resolution 42/23.

140 Council Resolution 19/23 of 23 March 2012 specifies that the President of the Council should 'continue to appoint for each session, on the basis of regional rotation (...) a chairperson of the Forum among experts on minority issues'. It adds that the Independent Expert on minority issues 'shall continue to guide the work of the Forum and prepare its annual meetings, and invites him/her to report on the thematic recommendations of the Forum'.

141 Established by the Commission and retained by the Council through its Resolution 6/13, the Chairperson/Rapporteur of the Forum is appointed by the President of the Council from candidates nominated by regional groups. Several experts are invited to contribute to the discussions and to assist the Chairperson/Rapporteur.

142 The Forum was established by Council Resolution 17/4 and is chaired by the Working Group on Business and Human Rights. See also Council Resolution 35/7.

143 Council Resolution 28/14 specifies that the President of the Council should 'appoint for each session, on the basis of regional rotation and in consultation with regional groups a Chairperson... serving in his or her personal capacity'.

144 Established by General Assembly resolution 75/314, it is composed of ten independent experts.

These various steps have produced positive results and have helped the Council navigate the difficult geopolitical environment. Some fine-tuning and further improvements may be envisaged. As is proposed in other chapters,[145] some additional tools might be considered, such as the creation of five regional special procedures which would be entitled to consider all situations within their region (with the exception of those already dealt with by a specific country Special Rapporteur or an investigation mechanism). This would overcome the prevailing criticism about double standards and complement the universal periodic review mechanism.

Another way to broaden the landscape would be to expand the practice of requesting the High Commissioner to designate experts on specific situations as they now exist concerning Sudan, Haiti and Colombia.[146] Also, more intersessional informal dialogues with the High Commissioner would be helpful in providing a forum for delegations to interact with the High Commissioner.

Lastly, as will be considered in the next chapter, trust needs to be strengthened. In that regard the role of the Presidents and their Bureaux should be fully recognized and the contribution of many others acknowledged, such as, for instance co-facilitators or focal points appointed to deal with delicate issues in relation to the work of the Council. Additionally, informal high-level discussions on substantive or organizational issues initiated by the President may serve as new tools for the Council.

Briefly speaking, it is the author's viewpoint that the politicization of the work of the Council is absolutely normal, and that polarization between groups of countries is unavoidable, but that it should be limited in its manifestation thanks to lively, flexible and constructive working methods.

145 See the Conclusion.

146 See Resolutions S-32/1, 52/39 and 53/22 respectively.

2.3 The Council during and after the Covid-19 pandemic era

2.3.1 From March to June 2020

When the Council met in February 2020 in the context of its 43rd session, the world had entered a pandemic era which took it by surprise and the parameters of which were largely unknown. Nervousness was prevalent as from the very start of the session on 24 February, especially since the Council did not have appropriate tools to organize meetings virtually. The only available references were those contained in decision 19/119 and its Annex. Technologically and logistically speaking, it was not provided with appropriate tools to organize virtual sessions.

In practical terms, when the situation became highly problematic in organizing meetings of the Council in person, there were few precedents that could be used.

In order to fully comprehend the magnitude and impact of what would be happening a few weeks after the start of the 43rd Session, it is essential to bear in mind that the plenary meeting of the Council in beautiful room XX represents only a fraction of what the Council's galaxy is all about. Initiatives presented by States and voted on during the last days of any given Council's sessions are discussed in the context of several informal meetings per draft. This implies that should 30 draft resolutions or decisions be adopted during a given session, an average of 90 informals would have to be organized. Additionally, States, the OHCHR, NGOs, International Organizations or Specialized Agencies and other stakeholders organize side events, the number of which had grown significantly until 2020[147] (more than 500 side events had been organized in 2019).

Accordingly, arranging a session requires a huge investment by the Secretariat and the Bureau directed towards facilitating the organization of the plenary but also ensuring that all informals may proceed. Without properly held informals, the adoption of draft resolutions would become extremely difficult, if not impossible, and transform the plenary into a drafting committee, which it cannot do and certainly not in a matter

147 See section 5.5 below.

of two working days. Also, in order to sustain the *'raison d'être'* of the Council and enable stakeholders to discuss a wide range of issues in an informal manner , the ability for all concerned to organize side events without too many constraints is a sine qua non.

The first reference to measures that could be taken by the host country and mirrored by the United Nations Office at Geneva (UNOG) in relation to the COVID-19 pandemic appeared in the minutes of the Bureau on 2 March 2020. The UNOG Director-General had written to the President, inviting the Council through her to cancel all side events, encouraging representatives to refrain from travelling to Geneva for the rest of the session, and suggesting that mandate-holders who were not already in Geneva participate in the session via video-conferencing. These measures were endorsed by the Bureau and later the Council on 3 March.

Of interest, the possibility to significantly enlarge significantly the opportunities for delegates and mandate-holders to resort to video-conferencing capabilities thus extended largely beyond the scope of Decision 19/119 without being challenged. There was a de facto consensus among all delegations to preserve the well-being of all participants and common sense made it absolutely clear that video-conferencing, however it could be organized, represented the safest possible way to organize meetings in a UN context. Contrary to the United Nations in New York where the video-conferencing issues soon became politicized as they were to be linked to the issuing or non-issuing of visas by the host country, the situation was considered at the Human Rights Council in Geneva as a very technical matter having the sole health interest of delegates in mind.

Thereafter, informals were moved to a larger room to implement the host country's requirements for specific 'social distancing' to reduce the risk of infections in the Palais des Nations.[148]

The spread of COVID-19 increased rapidly over the following days and further measures were taken, such as moving the plenary of the Council to a larger room (the 'Salle des Assemblées', which was and remains the largest meeting room in Geneva). On 9 March, the Bureau recommended to the plenary that only those who absolutely needed to be there should be allowed in the meeting room (a maximum of two persons per

148 See minutes of the Bureau meeting of 6 March 2024.

delegation). As had by now become the norm in most parts of the world, delegates had to wash their hands frequently, disinfect them with hand sanitizer, abstain from attending any meeting when displaying symptoms such as fever or coughing, and refrain from shaking hands. However, the Council remained fully in operation and continued its programme of work otherwise unaltered. Other technical measures were taken by the Secretariat, such as tabling of draft resolutions in an electronic manner – something which would have been bluntly rejected by quite a number of delegations just a few weeks previously.

However, the spread of the virus continued to grow speedily and on 11 March 2024, in full coordination with the Secretariat and UNOG Conference Services, the Bureau decided to propose to the Council that it suspend its 43rd Session until further notice on 13 March 2020. However, it also recommended to the plenary that before suspending its session, it should:

> Proceed with the adoptions of the UPR outcomes scheduled for the 43rd Session on 12 and 13 March 2020 and – in case the panellists are already present in or on their way to Geneva – hold the annual debate on racial discrimination. All remaining plenary debates would be postponed to the resumption of the 43rd session; Adopt a decision extending all mandates and mandated activities which would otherwise expire until the resumption of the 43rd session; Appoint the 19 mandate holders to be appointed at the 43rd session; All resolutions that will be tabled before Friday, 13 March 2020 at 1p.m. would be acted upon at the resumed session.[149]

Other logistical measures were taken which would later on bear consequences at the Council when it resumed its work. Firstly, access to the room was limited to one person per delegation and, more importantly, only NGOs inscribed on the list of speakers would have access to the plenary.

On 13 March 2020, at the end of its morning meeting, the Council suspended its work with a great sense of anxiety given the state of the pandemic as well as the numerous challenges that it knew lay ahead. The Council was the last UN body to suspend its work... it would also be the first one to resume it a few weeks later but in a different format.

149 See minutes of the Bureau meeting of 11 March 2024.

However, immediately after this suspension, the Bureau started considering how to proceed with the COVID-19 situation and its impact on the Council's work. As the first of many precedents to follow, it started meeting via email and decided on 18 and 19 March, namely less than a week after the suspension of the Council's activities, to postpone the 36th Session of the UPR WG and rearrange the calendar of the UPR meetings. This Bureau decision was taken under the proviso that it would be formalized by the Council during its next meeting, the date of which was totally unknown – for obvious reasons.

On 1 April 2020, the Bureau started meeting online using commercially available video-conferencing capacities. It heard the representative of UNOG explaining that several options were being considered for online platforms. The Bureau also considered the document adopted by the UN General Assembly on 27 March by silent procedure, which described how the General Assembly would take decisions during the COVID-19 pandemic. Importantly, it also considered whether the Human Rights Council, as a subsidiary body of the General Assembly, could follow the procedure established in the decision of the parent body, or whether there was a need to suggest an alternative way of taking decisions for the time that the Council was not able to hold physical meetings. This was a pleonasm to state that the Bureau was contemplating measures to organize the Council and its work in a sui generis and much lighter manner than its parent body.

Understanding the importance for the Council continuing to play its role as the main human rights body during these depressing times, the Bureau also decided to hold an informal online conversation with the High Commissioner on the human rights implications of COVID-19. This was the most timely and feasible option to consider. Additionally, less than two weeks after the Council had suspended its in-person work, it decided to hold regular bureau meetings every two weeks, consider organizing further informal meetings with other stakeholders and continue examining options for resuming formal meetings and the decision-making process.

On 9 April 2020, the Bureau organized the above-mentioned informal conversation with the High Commissioner, which proved to be a success with 400 participants on a live-feed platform and over 2,000 on the UN Web TV. Interpretation in all UN languages represented a problem at the time, and more importantly, the Bureau regretted the delay and difficulties faced by UNOG in providing adequate solutions for meetings to be held virtually with full interpretation in the six UN languages.[150]

As the same meeting, the Bureau decided that it would soon organize another informal conversation with some special procedure mandate-holders and that it would try to find a way to adopt a Presidential Statement (PRST) on the human rights implications of the COVID-19 pandemic by silent procedure.

Tensions between the Bureau and UN Conference Services started to grow with the decision of the latter not to allow the use of user-friendly online platforms, which it considered as raising issues of cyber-security and confidentiality and preferred resorting to three platforms which it had identified. This bureaucratic position was and remained very hard to understand since by definition Council meetings are accessible to all and available on the UN Web TV channel.[151]

In parallel, and upon advice of the Council Secretariat, the Bureau considered that it was possible, based on precedents and on the Institution-Building Package, for the Council to adopt a Presidential Statement while not in session. The way to do this was through the silence procedure that had been agreed upon at the UNGA level.

On 30 April 2020, the Bureau organized the second informal online conversation, this time with some special procedures mandate-holders.

On 14 May, the Bureau was informed that there were hopes that meetings of both the Human Rights Council and the Conference on Disarmament could resume in June depending on the evolution of the pandemic. It

---

150 See minutes of the Bureau meeting of 18 February 2021 in which it is mentioned: Recalling the concerns expressed by many delegations in relation to the lack of real-time interpretation in all six languages on the Zoom platform, the President informed the Bureau that she would shortly be sending a letter to the Acting Assistant Secretary-General for Information and Communications Technology in order to request that the United Nations Secretariat allow the Council to use the Zoom platform with the possibility to channel interpretation in all six languages as soon as possible

151 See minutes of the Bureau meeting of 22 April and 4 May 2020.

therefore immediately decided to resume its session on 15 June 2020. However, it was obvious that serious challenges were to be faced and that attendance would be seriously reduced without any possibility for informal meetings or side events.

Discussions on the PRST continued but were marked by resistance on the part of several delegations to proceed without what they considered an adequate legal basis. Accordingly, it was decided that another PRST on the procedure to follow for the adoption of texts by silence procedure would be sent at the same time as the PRST on the human rights implications of COVID-19.

On 29 May, the Council adopted its PRST on the human rights implications of the COVID-19 pandemic (PRST/43/1).[152] However, the difficulties that had marred the adoption of the text, with many delegations asking written questions as alluded to in the minutes of the Bureau in April and May, were pivotal in providing a sense that the adoption of much less consensual documents through a silence procedure would be very disturbing and time-consuming.

It thus provided a strong incentive to the Council and its Bureau to find alternative models that would allow the Council to operate in as efficient manner as feasible in the circumstances.

While preparing for a possible resumption of the 43rd Session, the President received a letter from the Permanent Representative of Burkina Faso in his capacity as coordinator of the African Group, which conveyed a request for the Council to convene an Urgent Debate on the 'current racially inspired human rights violations, systemic racism, police brutality and the violence against peaceful protest'.[153] This followed the assassination of George Floyd on 25 May 2020 and provided an additional strong incentive for the Council to resume its work as soon as possible by any possible means. The Bureau decided to propose holding the urgent debate on 17 June, two days after the official resumption of the Council's 43rd Session.

152 See https://docs.un.org/en/A/HRC/PRST/43/1

153 See minutes of the Bureau meeting of 8 June.

As per the modalities to be followed by the Council, the virtual platform proposed by UNOG unfortunately collapsed during the holding of the Organizational Meeting preceding the resumed 43rd Session thus precluding its use during a formal meeting of the Council. Instead, the Council followed the advice of the Council's Secretariat and opted for a much lighter and user-friendly model commercially available. Given security considerations, it was considered that these arrangements would be made available exclusively during the public meetings of the Council, namely most of the meetings held by the Council with the exception of the half-hour private meeting organized in September for the consideration of the Complaints Procedure. This was also considered adequate given the fact that all the Council's procedures are transcribed live on the UN Web TV that serves as the official record of the Council. However, this was not formally blessed by the concerned United Nations departments beyond the OHCHR. The resumed 43rd Session and the following ones held in 2020 were thus organized with a certain level of uncertainty as to the technical parameters and technological tools used as well as the position of the different bureaucratic layers of the UN Conference Services in New York.

As per the specific modus operandi to be followed and which would be more or less systematically followed in the next two years with few caveats depending on physical distancing measures and the total number of persons allowed in the Palais des Nations for a given meeting, they were as follows:

- The plenary meetings of the Council took place in the Assembly Hall, while the voting process took place in Room XX. Another room was made available as an overflow room with a webcast in English.
- During the voting process, the Assembly Hall or another conference room served as an overflow room.
- Access to all meeting rooms was limited to one person per delegation (except for the voting process). A certain number of seats were reserved for representatives of NGOs, NHRIs and international organizations, as well as the press.
- State delegations not wishing to enter the plenary room physically were able to deliver their statements by pre-recorded video messages, as provided for under HRC Decision 19/119.
- Similarly, NGOs in consultative status with ECOSOC were given the opportunity to do the same insofar as interactive dialogues were

concerned, and additionally for panels and adoptions of UPR outcomes as set out in HRC decision 19/119.

- Representatives wishing to exercise their right of reply remotely were able to do so by sending a request to hrclistofspeakers@ohchr.org.
- Special procedures mandate-holders, members of investigative mechanisms and panellists unable to travel to Geneva were able to participate in the interactive dialogues and panels via video messages and video link. Those present in Geneva would address the Council in person, if they so desire.
- For action on draft proposals, all 47 Members of the Council were asked to designate two representatives to be present in the room. A Member of the Council not wishing to participate in person may opt for proxy voting by designating a representative of another State who will act on their behalf. Observer States introducing draft proposals, as well as concerned countries, were also to designate two representatives to be present in the room at the time of action on relevant resolutions. All Observer States and other Observers could follow the proceedings in an overflow room.
- Two rooms were made available for meetings of groups and informal consultations. In case informal consultations were organized virtually, these needed to be notified to the Secretariat in order to be included in the Bulletin of Informal Meetings and the online application 'Sched'.
- Side events could not take place inside the Palais des Nations during the 44th Session. If stakeholders decided to organize virtual events or events outside the Palais des Nations, these events would not be included in the Bulletin of Informal Meetings as Council side events.
- All representatives were requested to upload their oral statements through the online system for inscription on the lists of speakers before the opening of the debate or dialogue in question, or one hour before the estimated time of their delivery.

2.3.2 As from June 2020 to the End of the Pandemic

At the end of the resumed 43rd Session in June 2020, it became quite apparent that despite the numerous challenges faced, the Council had managed to proceed as closely as possible to its programme of work. The 44th Session was therefore organized immediately after the conclusion of the 43rd Session. The 45th Session proceeded according to its normal calendar of meetings.

Of importance, the Council's strong impulse to meet as normal and using all available means proved to be extremely successful. By the end of 2020, it became clear that it was the only UN body that managed to meet successfully throughout the year despite the serious disruptions posed by the successive COVID-19 waves.

The Council's tenacity in adhering to extremely flexible working methods, the strengthened role of the President and her Bureau, the trust placed in the Council's Secretariat in identifying ways and means to respond to the crises as they emerged, as well as the decision to resort to whichever safe digital tool was available, proved to be successful.

Internally, the digital platform used by the Council in a semi-confidential manner, and which had initially been disapproved by the United Nations apparatus in New York, became the norm in 2021 while the costly ad hoc platforms it had initially developed and tested were discreetly abandoned, the abherent costs of which remain as of today unknown. This came as a direct result of the successful holding of the Council sessions whereas the rest of the United Nations system had come to a quasi-standstill status. Additionally, following a strong request to that effect by the Council's President, interpretation in the six languages used by the Council for live statements on the digital platform it used were authorized and became the norm as of the 46th Session of the Council.[154]

However, it also became clear that the Council, in dealing with the organization of the resumed 43rd and 44th Sessions had to prioritize the following elements:

- Ensuring that the plenary would be in a position to meet virtually, in a hybrid manner or otherwise.
- Providing for a proper decision-making process thus focusing on the holding of informals prior to the voting in plenary.
- Ensuring the participation of all stakeholders in person (if possible), by video statements or live feed as appropriate.
- Managing the numerous interactive dialogues with special procedures and investigation bodies online or exceptionally in an in-person manner if the mandate-holders were in Geneva.
- Respecting the letter and spirit of the Institution-Building Package.

154 See minutes of the Bureau meeting of 2 March 2021.

- Reverting to in-person meetings whenever possible, thus upholding the best possible level of social and professional interaction.
- Recognizing the extremely positive added value of virtual participation for small delegations or speakers who did not have the possibility to get to Geneva in person.

Conversely, it also meant that side events – a large percentage of which are organized by and/or with civil society – could not be given the same level of priority since they were not necessary for the plenary to meet and take action on proposals which represent the core functions of the Council. Additionally, it also meant that specific attention would have to be placed on the conditions under which the live statements would be delivered. Indeed, while video statements could easily be checked prior to their delivery (regarding the identification of those making them, the environment in which they were delivered[155] and their contents), this was not the same insofar as live statements were to be delivered. This further implied that stringent measures would have to be applied to the live feed to avoid difficulties.[156] In general terms, the primary requirement was

155 See minutes of the Bureau meeting of 19 July 2024 during which the 'Bureau referred to a situation where a photograph had been displayed in the plenary next to the speaker while delivering a statement. The Bureau recalled the long-standing practice whereby any mandate holder, panellist or speaker from the floor intending to use visual materials/images in plenary debates should refer the matter to the Bureau beforehand for its consideration and approval'.

156 Issues that were discussed included, for instance the possibility of an individual not duly accredited by an ECOSOC status NGO taking the floor in lieu and place of a legitimate speaker, or a statement delivered with flags, flyers, politicized or inappropriate backgrounds, etc. At the Bureau meeting held on 18 November 2020, it was clarified that, 'in accordance with decision 19/119, the same rules that apply for visual materials used during in-person meetings also apply to virtual meetings. While delegations were welcome to display their flags and country name plates, as well as neutral backgrounds, including photographs of the head of state or government, any delegations intending to use other visual materials during their remote intervention should therefore refer the matter to the Bureau beforehand'. In a comparable manner, the summary of the Bureau meeting of 7 February 2022 indicates that,

to ensure that the same rules and practices applied for an individual to take the floor in-person would apply to online statements. This was not a minor affair.

Two additional factors became mingled into the discussions on how to organize Council sessions after the resumed 43rd Session making the matter even more complicated.

Firstly, the main building of the United Nations Office at Geneva (Palais des Nations) was being restored in the context of the Strategic Heritage Plan (SHP). This major restoration, which at the time of completion of this second edition is not completed and will not be for several years, impacted the holding of Council Sessions by drastically limiting the availability of rooms to accommodate spillover rooms, informal meetings and side events.

Secondly, the Organization faced serious liquidity and budgetary crises, which made it very difficult for it to easily absorb requests from the Council to add additional time to its sessions, either by way of lunchtime meetings, accrued meeting time in the evenings or extended meetings after the session. Additionally, these difficulties made it challenging for the Secretariat to prepare reports or organize meetings requested by the Council.[157] Consequently, the Council's Secretariat drew the Bureau's attention to these difficulties and invited the main sponsors of proposals to be in contact with it, with a view to discussing the financial implications of the outcomes of draft resolutions prior to or during the time of negotiating the texts.[158]

---

with the exception of an official representative of a UN Member State speaking in front of the national flag and/or the official picture of the Head of State, the background should be neutral without any other flag, banner, flyer, picture or symbol.

157 By its decision 45/113 of 6 October 2020, the Council, at the request of the OHCHR, decided to postpone the implementation of a number of mandated activities that could not be implemented in 2020 and to reschedule them in accordance with the timelines included in the annex to that decision.

158 See for instance minutes of the Bureau meeting of 18 February 2021.

In the months that followed the holding of the 44th Session and in view of the degradation of the health indicators, increasingly drastic measures had to be taken by the host country and echoed by the UNOG, progressively reducing the number of participants allowed in any public gathering. For instance, in November 2020, the number of delegates admitted in the UN Conference rooms was reduced from 1,000 to 50 and later to five, before being expanded to ten in April 2021 and 100 in May. Compared to hundreds of participants in the pre-COVID era, this represented a very serious backlash for the holding of the 36th UPR Working Group. However, by requesting delegations to resort to hybrid modalities (either video messages or live feed) and organizing the virtual participation of those required to be present or unable to do otherwise (delegations from the reviewed States, from troika members or from ill-equipped Permanent Missions), the session could take place with no significant alteration to the Council's work programme.[159]

In between the several COVID-19 waves, the number of participants admitted into the room varied considerably. It was reduced or expanded in a manner that made it complex to assess the practical impact on the Council's work immediately. The Bureau and the Secretariat had to analyse the situations based on technical and logistical issues, such as the number of seats available in each of the main rooms in the Palais des Nations.[160] This may at first glance be considered as relatively trivial. However, since the number of 100 participants and the number of seats available were important criteria for determining whether or not in-person voting could be held in the Council's usual meeting room XX (with its embedded voting system) or not. Similarly, this impacted who would be admitted in the room, how many individuals per delegation would be allowed in, and consequently whether NGOs or other Observers could be allowed in and under what conditions.

The same applied to the informal consultations which were held in a virtual manner – it had been concluded that the in-person meetings were by far the best way to negotiate in an appeased and constructive manner. However, the number of seats available in such rooms (39 in June 2021, for instance) impacted their modalities. On 2 June 2021, for instance, the

159 See minutes of the Bureau meeting of 29 October and 2 November 2020.

160 See for instance minutes of the Bureau meeting of 28 May 2021.

Bureau decided to recommend to the plenary that representatives of the various core groups would have a choice to either organize fully virtual informals or semi-hybrid ones allowing themselves, but not the other aprticipants, in.

On 25 May 2022, the President informed the Bureau that the Council Room XX could now be used at full capacity. However, since there remained concerns about the impact of the COVID-19 pandemic, which had not ended yet, the hybrid modalities adopted in the past years remained in place. Furthermore, the strategic heritage plan, which limited the number of rooms available to the Council aside the plenary meetings, prevented the holding of side events within Palais des Nations and thus continued to deeply affect the status and place of NGOs within the Council's architecture.

Thereafter, the restrictions would be progressively lifted over the next 12 months on par with the progressive lifting of the various COVID-19 restrictions by the host country and UNOG. It is nevertheless interesting to note that these modalities remained in place to a certain extent until September 2023, namely two and a half years after the start of the pandemic.

Two specific issues remain to be considered more comprehensively in view of their complex legal, organizational and political nature, namely the organization of a proper virtual decision-making process and finding a proper way for civil society to continue being fully involved in the work of the Council.They are described below since they may unfortunately be resorted to again as useful precedents in future should comparable circumstances arise.

2.3.3 Decision-making Process

The Election of the Council President on 15 January 2021

While it was possible to organize a session almost entirely virtually, it was obvious that should the five-person limitation that had been imposed due to the sanitary conditions remain in place, problems would be faced when decisions had to be taken. The Bureau therefore turned rapidly to the relevant IT section within the Department for General Assembly and

Conference Management (DGACM) to develop a proper e-voting system that would be easily usable.[161]

An urgent matter had, however, to be dealt with first, namely the election of the President of the 15th cycle (2021) by secret ballot. The circumstances leading to these elections are described in detail in section 6.5. At this juncture, it is sufficient to pinpoint that the Asia-Pacific Group coordinator had informed in December 2020 and early January 2021 that there was no consensus within the group and that there were three candidates for the position of President. The three Vice-Presidents who had been elected by consensus at the previous Organizational Session met in the context of the elected Bureau and considered the various issues at stake.

First, they had to ensure that the relevant provisions in the UNGA rules of procedure would be respected, namely the organization of these elections by secret ballot. Second, they had to reconcile this imperious requirement with the health and sanitary measures in place at the UNOG, which prohibited meetings with more than five participants. Third, they had to set in place a system that would ensure full transparency and generate full trust in the process.

At the Bureau meeting held on 13 January 2021, the Bureau endorsed the proposal made by the Council's Secretariat whereby the whole process would be held in the Salle des Assemblées but would be fully transparent thanks to a dual system of UN Web TV and live-feed process displaying every single aspect of the procedure to raise confidence among all viewers. These extremely detailed modalities[162] provided, inter alia, that at the elections to be held on 15 January 2021:

- One ballot paper containing the names of the candidates for election would be given to the representative of each member of the Council at the Assembly Hall;
- Only one representative per delegation would be provided brief access to the Assembly Hall in order to cast a ballot, with the exception of the two tellers and the three candidates from the Asia-Pacific Group,

161 See minutes of the Bureau meeting of 18 November 2020.
162 See minutes of the Bureau meeting of 13 January 2021

who would be able to observe the proceedings for the entire duration of the meeting, if so desired;

- The tellers would be the two Vice-Presidents who would not be presiding over the meeting;
- The arrival of delegations to the Assembly Hall would be staggered in order to comply with the five-person limit imposed by Swiss authorities to control the spread of COVID-19;
- An invitation would be sent to Council Members indicating a specific time slot of ten minutes when they would need to present themselves at the entrance of the Assembly Hall;
- The staggered arrival of the 47 delegates would be arranged in English alphabetical order of Council Members, beginning with Argentina and ending with Venezuela;
- Each group of five members of the Council would be welcomed by the Secretariat at the entrance of the Assembly Hall and called into the room when appropriate. They would have ten minutes to cast their ballots; and once they had finished, the next five Members of the Council would be invited to come into the Assembly Hall, and so forth
- If a delegate were to miss his/her allocated arrival slot, he/she would be requested to wait outside the Assembly Hall until the last group had concluded casting ballots and would be let in at the very end of the process;
- No ballots should be accepted after the last time slot had expired, and the presiding officer has suspended the meeting;
- When entering the Assembly Hall, each delegate would be provided with one ballot paper by the Secretariat and would then proceed to the Member State's seat to fill out the ballot paper;
- The presiding officer would then call the Council Members one by one in English alphabetical order, upon which each delegate would proceed to the podium, show his/her ID card to the Secretariat, sign a register and deposit his/her ballot in the ballot box that would be placed in front of the podium, where the tellers would be able to observe the casting of ballots;
- Delegates would immediately leave the Assembly Hall once they have deposited their ballots in the ballot box;
- The entire process would be broadcast live and viewers would be able to observe each delegate casting a ballot from the moment she/he arrived at the podium until the moment she/he left the podium;
- When those Members of the Council present and voting, including latecomers, had cast their ballots and left the room, then the meeting

will be suspended and the tellers will take the ballot box for counting of ballots;

- When counting is over, the presiding officer will resume the meeting to announce the results. The results would then be posted on the HRC Extranet;
- Should there be a need for a second round, this would be organized in a similar manner in the afternoon with the two candidates having obtained the largest number of votes;
- A hotline would be in operation throughout the process.

The elections were conducted to the satisfaction of all and thus provided a sound legal and political basis for setting up an electronic voting system that would be implemented at the forthcoming 46th Session. One of the most important lessons learnt during this process was that a decision-making process that would be drawn in a manner similar to these elections would take a huge amount of time, which was not commensurate with the time available during the last two days of any session for the adoption of dozens of draft resolutions or decisions. Another system, fully virtual, but transparent and trusted by all concerned, had to be built up if the Council were to operate in a quasi-normal manner.

Since there was no useful precedent in any other body or organization, this would have to be an ad hoc system able to cope with the usually high number of votes and procedural motions during a Council's session.[163]

Virtual Roll-call Vote as from the 29th Special Session

Not long after the holding of the elections and while the Bureau and the Secretariat were working very hard to set up an electronic voting system, the President received a letter from the Permanent Representative of the United Kingdom of Great Britain and Northern Ireland containing a request to hold a Special Session on the human rights implications of the crisis in Myanmar. Against the background of the provisions of the IBP, this request, which was supported by 19 Council Members, was a valid one and had to be accommodated. The conditions under which it would

---

163 It should be recalled that, at the time, the only system used in the United Nations or other Organizations required proposals to be adopted without a vote or by consensus. None of these bodies agreed to take up proposals that were not of a consensual nature.

be held would not create significant difficulties but what had to be clarified was how the voting process would be organized.

During the 10 February meeting of the Bureau, the Secretariat presented the two available options at the time and the Bureau deliberated as follows:

> On the issue of voting, the Secretariat informed the Bureau that two options would be available for the use of the Council in time for the 29th Special Session: the first option being a virtual roll-call vote via the Zoom platform; and the second option being an adjusted in-person roll-call vote that would closely follow the modalities that were used for the election of the President on 15 January, 2021. Acknowledging that the virtual roll-call vote as described by the Secretariat would be much less complex logistically and would closely resemble a roll-call vote in Room XX, the Bureau agreed to propose to the Council that the voting process for the 29th Special Session would exceptionally take place virtually via the Zoom platform.

These modalities were prepared in order to replicate as closely as possible an in-person roll-call vote with utmost attention being given to the security and transparency of the voting process.

Among the agreed steps for this first virtual roll-call voting process, were the following: (i) before taking action on the draft resolution, the Secretariat would ensure that all 47 States Members of the Council were present on the platform, that they were duly represented and in a position to take part in the voting process. If a delegation did not desire to take part in the vote, it may wish to indicate this to the Secretariat; (ii) the Secretariat would ask all Observer States (with the exception of the delegation introducing the draft text and the concerned country) and other Observers to exit the virtual meeting; (iii) each delegate who would cast the roll-call vote would have to be clearly identified; (iv) Observer States and other Observers would be able to follow the entire proceedings via the live feed on the webcast; (v) the President would then resume the meeting and proceed to action on the draft text, starting with the introduction of the text by the main sponsor, followed by general comments, a statement by the concerned country, PBI statement (if any), and explanations of vote (EOV) before the vote; (vi) if there was a request for a vote, the President would proceed with the drawing of a domino and read out the name of the Council Member to start a roll-call vote with, and the virtual roll-call vote would proceed slowly to ensure that the delegate appeared on the screen and was visible to all when registering/pronouncing his/

her vote; (vii) should any delegate fail to cast a vote for any reason during the roll-call, that delegate would be called upon a second time after the conclusion of the initial roll-call; (viii) when all Members of the Council present and voting had cast their votes, the President would close the voting and announce the results; and (ix) the results would then be posted on the HRC Extranet.[164]

E-recorded Votes Module as from the 46th Session Onwards

Virtual roll-call votes, as they were resorted to during the 29th Special Session and similar occasions, saved the day and enabled the Council to easily adopt resolutions or act on specific motions when in virtual session. However, the duration of a voting process of this nature – around 15 minutes per resolution – for the counting of the votes in favour, against, or abstentions was extremely long compared to the electronic voting system used in normal conditions – only a few seconds. Bearing in mind that no fewer than 30 draft resolutions or amendments had been acted upon during the 45th Session held in an adjusted in-person manner, when preparing for the March 2021 Session, the Bureau and the Secretariat easily concluded that a virtual roll-call vote system would be inadequate, exhausting and inefficient. Discussions were thus held between IT colleagues at the New York Headquarters and the Council Secretariat based on the system contemplated – but never used – for the General Assembly proceedings.[165] During the 46th Session, the system was tested twice with Bureau members, once with the Council Members at the experts' level and once with the Ambassadors. Thereafter, the Bureau deliberated on the matter and agreed to propose to the plenary to use the e-recorded votes modules at the 46th Session.

As per the rationale of this decision, later endorsed by the plenary, the Bureau noted the positive feedback that had been received concerning the security, reliability and user-friendliness of the platform, which had been adjusted to meet the needs of the Council and which allowed for instantaneous and sequential voting on draft resolutions.

---

164 For the full text of these modalities that were applied in a number of cases, see the minutes of the Bureau meeting of 10 February 2021, Annex II.

165 See minutes of the Bureau meetings of 16, 17 and 23 March 2021.

The Council resorted to the e-recorded votes module at the 46th Session[166] and used it in no fewer than 27 votes on amendments or draft resolutions.

---

166 The precise modalities were adopted based on 18 March 2021. They specified, inter alia, that before the Council would start taking action on draft proposals, the Secretariat would ensure that all 47 States Members of the Council are present in the Zoom meeting and that they are duly represented and in a position to take part in the voting process; Observer States introducing draft proposals and concerned countries would be allowed to remain in the Zoom meeting at which they are expected to take the floor. The proceedings will be live-streamed in all six official UN languages on the UN Web TV. A test vote using the 'e-Recorded votes' module on the e-deleGATE platform would be conducted at the beginning of each meeting before the Council starts taking action on draft proposals. The voting process would proceed via the Zoom platform in the same manner as it used to be in Room XX. Should any State Member of the Council wish to make a procedural motion as part of general comments, the representative of that State would be able to do so by (1) pressing the 'raise hand' button, (2) indicating the motion in the chat box, and (3) putting their camera on. Should there be a request for a vote on a specific draft proposal, the President would ask the Secretariat to activate the vote on that draft proposal on the e-deleGATE platform. Once the President asks the Secretariat to activate the vote, representatives would then see the specific draft proposal appear on the 'e-Recorded votes' module of the e-deleGATE platform, upon which they would be able to electronically cast their vote on that specific draft proposal. The President would proceed slowly with a vote to allow all State Members of the Council ample time to cast their vote. Should there be more than one representative from a State Member of the Council connected to the e-deleGATE platform and casting a vote for that State, the platform would reflect the last vote cast by a representative of that State. Representatives would be able to change or delete their votes as long as the vote remains open. Once all State Members of the Council present and voting have cast their votes and checked that their vote is accurately reflected on the e-deleGATE platform, the President would ask the Secretariat to close the vote on the specific draft proposal. Once the voting is closed, representatives would no longer be able to change or delete their votes. The President would announce the results, which would then be posted on the HRC Extranet. A hotline would be in operation throughout the process to address any technical issues.

This system would be used in other circumstances[167] but no other UN body, not even the UNGA for which it was initially designed, would ever make use of it, plagued as they were by their own political conundrums.

2.3.4 Participation of Civil Society at the Time of the COVID-19 Pandemic

As mentioned above, the Council's modus operandi is based on three pillars: one of a public nature, the plenary, and the other two of an informal nature, namely the informal consultations on draft proposals and the side events held in parallel with the session. Throughout the pandemic, utmost priority was logically given to the plenary and the informal consultations in order to enable the international community through the Council, to take action on human rights issues, whichever they were. Given the considerable challenges faced and the drastic measures that had to be taken to avoid the spread of the virus in UN premises, it was not possible to grant the same degree of priority to side events, which were simply set aside or limited in number at a later stage. Similarly, given the restrictions on the number of individuals that could attend a meeting in person, when limits set by the authorities and UNOG were very low (five persons for instance), priority was granted to Bureau Members and any State representative who had to be present (for instance, troika members, States under the UPR review or concerned countries). The participation of civil society representatives in person was at times simply not possible.

This situation led to the adoption of a number of measures, the traces of which are still visible at the date of completion of this second edition (for instance, the limitation in the number of NGO representatives during general debates).

Although they understood the difficulties faced, civil society representatives deeply resented, and rightly so, the depth of the measures that were affecting them since they understood that while some of these measures were not supposed to serve as a precedent they clearly would be, even if only in part.

The first issue that had to be dealt with was how to ensure that NGO participants could be given the floor during a virtual meeting. The

167 For instance, at the 30th Special Session held on 27 May 2021.

conditions under which this was anticipated in Decision 19/119 were simply overly restrictive since they were envisioned at a time when video messages or video conferences represented an oddity and were almost never resorted to.

At its 4 February 2021 meeting, the Bureau discussed this matter and considered that:

> under the proposed extraordinary modalities for the 47th session, NGOs in consultative status with the ECOSOC would be invited to submit pre-recorded video statements for a maximum of three general debates in addition to the interactive dialogues, panel discussions and UPR adoptions as they had been able to do during the 45th session. The Bureau emphasized the importance of ensuring the inclusivity of all Council members and observers in the 46th session while at the same time protecting the health and safety of all participants and staff and agreed that allowing ECOSOC-accredited NGOs to submit video messages for a limited number of general debates was a pragmatic solution to achieve that. The Bureau reiterated that the proposed modalities were extraordinary and would apply exclusively to the 46th session during the period when COVID-19 restrictions prohibit public meetings of more than five participants and should not serve as a precedent.

However, for a number of NGO representatives, the ideal way would have been to let them speak by live feed in the same manner other observers were granted the possibility to do. Accordingly, treating NGOs differently placed them in a different category, something which had always been resisted both by NGOs and the Secretariat. However, this was deemed impossible by the Bureau for obvious technical reasons: The underlying rationale for this refusal was that, while the credentials of Member States' delegates or Specialized Agencies or international organization's observers could easily be checked by the Secretariat (these were the usual handful of participants who register for the Council's sessions on a regular basis and are, for most part, well-known to their peers and all stakeholders), this did not extend to the representatives of the hundreds of NGOs allowed by ECOSOC to attend the Council's sessions.

A procedure was set up to check these credentials insofar as pre-recorded video messages were concerned (they had to be provided in advance, leaving several hours for the Secretariat to check the video and ensure that all was in good order). However, it would have been impossible in practice for the Secretariat to give immediate clearance to NGO representatives in the context of live feed statements.

This was understandable in the circumstances, but it created a rift between NGO representatives and the representatives of all other Observers, something which almost did not exist in past practices – the sole exception being the seating arrangements.[168]

The second issue that emerged at the very start of the pandemic was the necessity to limit the number of NGO speakers. This was due to the logistical and technical difficulties faced by the Council Secretariat, which was operating the Council without any additional support compared to pre-COVID-19 sessions. More importantly, since video messages did not require the speakers to be in Geneva, it was expected that their number would or could be extremely high[169] and thus place a significant burden on the ability for the Council to keep its programme of work under control.

As explained at the 10 February meeting of the Bureau, 'the Bureau reiterated the importance of NGO participation in the 29th Special Session while at the same time ensuring that the health of all participants and staff is protected. The Bureau thus agreed that NGOs in consultative status with the ECOSOC should be provided the opportunity to submit pre-recorded video statements for the Special Session, on an exceptional basis. However, recognizing the concerns raised regarding the potential for an exceptionally high number of pre-recorded video statements from NGOs, the Bureau agreed to set the list of speakers for NGOs based on the average number of NGOs that participated in the past three special sessions that were held in 2018, 2017 and 2016, respectively'. This measure would, by extension be applied to all future regular and special sessions when pre-recorded video messages from NGOs would be held admissible.

---

168 For practical reasons, Observers other than States are those listed in the blue book of the UNOG (https://www.ungeneva.org/en/blue-book), which includes 18 International Organizations and the Sovereign Order of Malta, as well as UN Departments and a limited number of other entities with which the UNGA has developed specific legal agreements. In contrast, 6,343 NGOs enjoyed active consultative status with ECOSOC as of 1 January 2023, all of them being in a position to attend or participate in a Council session if they so desire.

169 Ibid.

While fully understandable given the circumstances, it goes without saying that this added to the sense of frustration of civil society.

The third issue related to the impossibility of holding side events and the subsequent refusal by the Bureau to allow any reference in the official records of the Council of the side events organized by NGOs by virtual means outside the United Nations premises. An issue came to the forefront, namely how to refer to the side events organized by NGOs in a virtual manner. Many NGOs considered that, since they were prevented for reasons they could understand from organizing in-person side events in the Palais, they could be allowed to organize virtual side events and have them included in the Council's extranet in a separate section. This would have had the advantage of informing all concerned about such events, thus channelling viewers to the concerned events. However, throughout the whole period, successive Bureaux rejected these requests.

For instance, at the 18 February meeting, the Bureau 'regretted that once again side events cannot take place inside the Palais des Nations during the 46th session as a result of the current COVID-19-related restrictions. Recalling that in-person side events were included in the Bulletin of Informal Meetings prior to the COVID-19 pandemic, the Bureau agreed that for the sole purpose of information-sharing, virtual side events that would be organized by NGOs in parallel to the 46th session could be listed on the OHCHR civil society webpage along with a statement indicating that the events are not official Council events'.

The rationale for this position had to do with the conditions surrounding the organization of side events (see section 5.5 below). When held in person, those participating in side events must wear badges delivered by the security at the entrance of UN security based on a letter registering them by the concerned ECOSOC status NGOs. This ensures that in case of problems, such as breaches of security or non-respect of basic UN rules concerning the behaviour of meetings' participants, security or the Council's Secretariat is in a position to consider the matter and take any remedial measures that may be warranted in the circumstances. Similarly, in the case of in-person side events, the Secretariat is in a position to check that all practices are respected, including the need for the meeting to be open to all wishing to access it and for those requesting the floor to be inscribed on the list of speakers and granted the possibility to intervene – if time permits. This filtering did obviously not exist in the case of virtual side events, thus leaving the screening of the participants to the sole concerned NGO with no possibility whatsoever for any stakeholder to raise an issue regarding a problem arising in a side event. Issues which were constantly referred to were the possibility for a non-ECOSOC status NGO to 'hijack' a meeting, for participants without proper accreditation to be allowed in, for others with proper accreditation not to be allowed in, for inappropriate language or conduct being condoned or authorized by the organizers, etc.

Accordingly, the only agreed-upon practice was that a reference to the side events was made possible but only on the OHCHR civil society page – in other words on a non-HRC webpage.[170] Importantly, this webpage is not part of the Human Rights Council website, and whatever is referred to therein is the sole responsibility of the Office. A slight adjustment made to this practice was to allow for a link to be made to that page on the Council extranet from the 48th Session of the Council. One must confess that such arrangements appeared quite byzantine at the time and most confusing at present – since most of the links of the time are no longer accessible, thus making it quite hard to understand why these limitations were introduced in the first place.[171]

After more than two years of interruption, side events were authorized again on 23 August 2022 by the Bureau based on the allocation of additional rooms by the UNOG. However, the limited number of such rooms due to the Strategic Heritage Plan prevented the return to the status quo ante, and new informal guidelines were issued according to which the time slots for side events would be allocated based on availability and on a first-come, first-served basis. In order to accommodate as many requests as possible, only one side event per requesting organizer was permitted, and each side event was limited to one hour in duration. Organizers were requested to strictly respect the allotted time and to leave the room on time to ensure the smooth organization of the following side event.

2.3.5 The Post-COVID-19 Harsh Bureaucratic Reality

As early as February 2022, the Council started to consider how it would conduct its work following the eventual lifting of COVID-related

170 Seehttps://www.ohchr.org/en/resources/civil-society.

171 See https://hrcmeetings.ohchr.org/HRCSessions/RegularSessions/48session/Pages/NGO-liaison-information.aspx.

restrictions. In the two years that had elapsed since the start of the pandemic, many developments had occurred, and many delegations had become adept to the new reality that had emerged. When Decision 19/119 was adopted by the Council, it was extremely complex to organize for a speaker to address the meeting from outside Room XX. Technology was not up to expectations, and many were reluctant to use tools that were described as unreliable or considered problematic security-wise. All stakeholders, 24 months later, had become used to recording video statements or delivering live statements in a virtual manner with very few hiccups. Many statements could be registered from the field, which proved to be invaluable both for small delegations and civil society representatives. New systems had been generated even for the most complex issue of all, namely the voting process.

Against such a background, the Council began to consider how the future of its proceedings would be shaped with a view to building upon the good lessons and success stories from this period. For this reason, starting from 2022 onwards, the President appointed Ambassadors to serve as Focal Points or co-facilitators on the use of modern technology.

There was a general sense of exhilaration about the possibilities that might arise in the future, especially insofar as access to the Council and the UPR mechanisms from small delegations or from States that did not have a Permanent representation in Geneva was concerned.

Little did the Council know that the bureaucratic trends among certain parts of the United Nations, combined with the liquidity crises faced by the Organization would soon make it catch up with harsh realities.

During the first part of the pandemic period, the Council benefited from increased attention to its work due to its extreme flexibility in adjusting to the circumstances and its ability to fulfil its entire programme of work, and more. It did so without entering some of the byzantine discussions that emerged in other bodies or institutions. This was recognized by all key players and many statements made by the Secretary-General or the High Commissioner paid tribute to the Council for having met expectations in these dire circumstances. Hence, despite the serious liquidity crises faced by the Organization in those years, the Council was provided with the required support it needed under the business continuity model that had been in place since the start of the pandemic insofar as the Council was concerned.

This did not mean that the Council was left without logistical difficulties, but they mainly related to the number of lunchtime meetings which it could organize during any given session or the conditions under which remote participation models could be applied to the informal consultations or the side events.

However, in parallel with the progressively reduced impact of the COVID-19 pandemic on the work of the organization, the strong support that the Council benefited from began to crumble. From the beginning of 2022 onwards, the Bureau had to deal with requests by Conference Services to reduce the number of additional meetings or find ways and means to provide additional financial support for organizing remote participation for non-plenary meetings – despite the extremely low costs of such features. This bureaucratic pressure amplified over the subsequent months and was only slightly and very temporarily addressed by the adoption of decision 51/101 of 6 October 2022 on the need for appropriate support for at least 14 weeks of meetings per year.

Pressure amplified over the year in 2023 – see below section 3.2.1 – particularly regarding the holding of remote informals, the duration of UPR working group's meetings or the number of additional lunchtime meetings.

When the business continuity model eventually subsided by the end of 2023, the Council was informed by the Head of the Department of General Assembly and Conference Management on 18 January 2024 that live feed would no longer be made available to it[172] and that the Council had to return to the pre-COVID modalities. This came despite every possible effort deployed by the President of the 18th cycle and his Bureau and, incidentally and most importantly, despite the extremely low cost of such services which many individual laptop users take upon themselves to acquire directly on the web.

The Council adopted its Decision 55/116 on remote participation modalities for hybrid meetings of the Council on 12 April 2024, in which it (i) expressed concern at the disproportionate impact that the discontinuation of remote participation modalities had had on small delegations, in particular those of small island developing States and least developed

172 See minutes of the Bureau meeting of 19 January 2024.

countries; (ii) stressed that the continued provision of remote participation modalities for formal and informal meetings of the Human Rights Council was crucial to facilitate the participation of all its Members and observers; and (iii) decided to request the General Assembly to consider authorizing the Human Rights Council to continue its practice of using remote participation modalities for all its future formal and informal meetings.

Despite this decision, nothing changed, and the subsequent Council sessions proceeded in a pre-COVID-19 format, thereby forgetting for good the extremely positive lessons of the past few years. This was imposed upon the Council entirely against the tide of history and neglected the lessons of history.[173]

As of the date of completion of this second edition, such unilateral action by the Department of General Assembly and Conference Management stands with serious consequences for the work of small delegations, civil society and, more generally, all Council stakeholders.

At a time when the whole world is embarking on a new digital era, the Conference Services Department, which in theory is supposed to support the Council and its noble human rights work, simply wiped out several years of progress and missed out on new realities showing a strong level of disconnection from contemporaries realities and the importance of human rights.

When considering the consequences of such bureaucratic decisions, it should be reminded that the costs associated with the above-mentioned services are absolutely minimal and should not under normal circumstances even be referred to in a textbook on the Human Rights Council or in any communication to the Council or its Bureau.

173 See minutes of the Bureau meetings of 10 May and 8 July 2024. In the latter case, the USG for DGACM responded to various questions without even acknowledging the Council's efforts during the previous years and addressing matters which had been overcome by the Council several years ago, for instance, in relation to the decision-making process.

Exchanges on basic requirements for the Council to enable it to fulfil its programme of work in accordance with its mandate seem trivial and grossly irrelevant when considering the state of human rights in the world at this juncture in human rights history.[174]

Discussions as to whether the Council should meet for x number of weeks and one or two additional days, or how it should organize its meeting, whether in person or virtually, are completely inadequate and irrelevant when considering what is at stake when the Council is meeting, namely the human rights situation in the world. It is the author's firm conviction that such bean-counting is insulting to the UN institution and should be overcome rapidly. This will remain valid in the years to come as the budgetary and liquidity crises will continue to affect the United Nations. However, it will be of crucial importance to make a distinction between real and artificial problems. The former relates to the budget made available to the Office of the High Commissioner for Human Rights which are reduced in a significant manner. The latter refers to the so-called high costs of holding Council related mechanisms. Since, by definition, these costs are mostly related to interpretation, it should always been borne in mind that teams of interpreters were created further to the creation of the Council, the adoption of the Institutions-Building Package, the 2021 review process and additional decisions in the subsequent years. Hence, whether the Council interrupts its meetings one or two days before the closure of its session, this does not lead to any major saving whatsoever. It simply represents an easy way out for the NY Conference Services to make delegations understand the gravity of the liquidity crisis. If these meetings were not dealing with issues of such importance to humanity, the author would not have serious concerns about postponing them and consider it anecdotical or strategical or both. Unfortunately, depriving the Council to meet for the normal amount of time is a serious blow to the importance attached to human rights by the Organization. It undermines its raison d'être and reduce the possibility for crucial human rights issues to be considered at the highest level of the Organization with the highest possible level of visibility.

---

174 But it may also be seen as a testimony of the modest interest of some components of the international community and parts of the UN bureaucracy in providing adequate support to one of the three main pillars of the Organization (aside peace and security and development).

Maybe the best way to proceed would be to provide the Council with financial support, enabling it to meet whenever and as often it requires. If this were to imply recognizing its status as that of a de facto permanent body of the United Nations, then so be it. This would not be equivalent to recognizing it as a principal or main UN body, which would in turn require an amendment to the UN Charter. It would be a practical move, providing the Council with the budget to meet for a significant number of weeks (for instance, 20) whenever it requires during the normal UN working schedule – two meetings of three hours per day, excluding weekends and UN holidays.

2.4 The Council's success stories, its weakenesses and its role as a necessarily imperfect substitute for other organs of the UN system

In many cases, the Council and its mechanisms played a very significant role in addressing key human rights challenges and crises, some of them extending beyond the scope of its terms of reference read in a narrow manner. Often, this was the result of the combined efforts of the Council and its subsidiary bodies.

For instance, insofar as the right to food is concerned, Special Rapporteur Jean Ziegler[175] alerted the international community through his annual reports to the Council about the gravity of the situation. In his last report, he underlined that little progress had been made in reducing the number of victims of hunger and malnutrition. He mentioned that the number of people suffering from hunger had increased every year since 1996, reaching an estimated 854 million people. In a background note[176] dated 2 May 2008, the newly appointed Special Rapporteur Olivier de Schutter estimated that over 100 million more people would be food insecure as a result of the then-current crisis on the international commodities market. He added that these individuals should be given the same degree of attention as if they were arbitrarily detained by an

175 See Document A/HRC/7/5.

176 See Background Note: Analysis of the world food crisis by the UN Special Rapporteur on the right to food by Olivier de Schutter, https://www2.ohchr.org/english/issues/food/docs/srrtfnotefood-crisis. pdf.

authoritarian government or if they were being beaten by the police, and accordingly called upon the Council to convene in a Special Session in order to explore the steps which should be taken to respond to the current situation, consistent with the right to adequate food. A few days later, a request for a Special Session was transmitted to the President[177] by the required number of signatories and was held on 22 May 2008. In the ensuing Resolution S-7/1, the Council expressed grave concern at the worsening of the world food crisis, called upon States, individually and through international cooperation and assistance, relevant multilateral institutions and other relevant stakeholders, to take all necessary measures. It called upon the UN Member States to participate actively in the High-Level Conference on World Food Security and the Challenges of Climate Change and Bioenergy, held from 3 to 5 June 2008 in Rome and organized by the FAO. It also invited the latter to extend an invitation to the High Commissioner and the Special Rapporteur to help mainstream a human rights perspective in the analysis of the world food crisis, with a focus on the realization of the right to food.[178] He presented his post-Special Session report at the 9th Council Session[179] and followed it up at subsequent sessions.

Another topical example is the the human rights situation in Syria. The Council convened four Special Sessions in 2011, 2012 and 2016, and organized three urgent debates in 2012, 2013 and 2018. It requested the OHCHR to send an urgent mission in April 2011. It established a Commission of Inquiry in August 2011, the mandate of which has been extended to this date. It even created the mandate of Special Rapporteur, which will succeed the Commission at the conclusion of its mandate, and appointed the mandate-holder. It convened a panel on the human rights situation in Syria in March 2017. In the numerous resolutions[180] adopted on the matter, the Council condemned in the strongest possible terms the human rights violations and abuses as well as all violations of humanitarian law committed by all parties to the conflict. It referred to the multiple gross and massive violations that had occurred in a variety of cases,

---

177 See A/HRC/S-7/1.

178 For an account of the results of the High-Level Conference from the special rapporteur's point of view, see https://www2.ohchr.org/english/issues/food/docs/StatementOdS060608.pdf.

179 See A/HRC/9/23.

180 See for instance Council Resolution 39/15.

situations, and places, referred to multiple aspects of the Commission of Inquiry reports and recommendations, referred to the Accountability Mechanism, and called for the International Criminal Court to be used to help end impunity for applicable crimes.

In the case of South Sudan, the Special Rapporteur on IDPs reported in November 2013 on the human rights situation, calling the Council to action in March 2014. As a result, the Council required the High Commissioner to report back to the Council on these issues in March 2015. In parallel, a panel discussion on the situation of human rights in South Sudan was organized in September 2014. The High Commissioner reported back to the Council on the extent of human rights violations in March and June 2015, as a result of which the OHCHR was requested to send a mission to the country as soon as possible. Upon receipt of the report of that mission, the Council established a Commission on Human Rights in South Sudan, the mandate of which has been extended on a yearly basis ever since. In each resolution adopted on the situation,[181] the Council condemned in the strongest possible terms the ongoing violations and abuses of human rights and violations of international humanitarian law, specifying the crimes that were committed, urging all actors to put an immediate halt to the violations and abuses, calling the concerned State and all parties to end and prevent violations, recommending several steps to be taken domestically and regionally, and sharing the concerned reports with all concerned regional and universal organizations.

Such examples could be multiplied and are alluded to in the Conclusion. In brief, the Council has proven to be irreplaceable and quite fast in addressing most of the human rights challenges of the day. Since human rights are inextricably linked to peace and security and to development, debates on this matter therefore inevitably have an impact on the other two, and vice versa.

In an ideal world, this specific relation should be strongly rooted in the UN system and relations between the Geneva and New York organs should be substantive, cross-fertilizing, efficient and effective. The regular flow of information from the Council's mechanisms or the Office of the High Commissioner to the Council, leading to specific actions by the

---

181 See for instance Council Resolution 40/19.

latter, should eventually cross the Atlantic Ocean and reach the political organs of the United Nations, primarily the Security Council and the General Assembly or the ECOSOC.

However, with the crisis of multilateralism, its fragmentation and increased polarization, the increased challenges faced by the New York bodies to react to emergencies and adjust themselves to various crises, the Atlantic Ocean had proven to be more difficult to cross than the Himalaya. Combined with the quasi-paralysis of these bodies during the COVID-19 pandemic, this led the Human Rights Council to be perceived by many stakeholders as the place where things may be done and achieved.

During the various crises of the past few years, particularly after the start of the war in Ukraine, the Council proved to be a useful place where issues normally dealt with elsewhere could be addressed, although the end result would not be the same as a resolution adopted by the Charter's organs. When the 7th Urgent Debate on the situation of human rights in Ukraine stemming from the Russian aggression took place on 4 March 2022, no fewer than 3.5 million viewers were registered on the UN Web TV and the Live HRC Secretariat account on one of the major web platforms.

It remains that the Human Rights Council does not and cannot replace these other UN bodies. However, since it is sometimes perceived as filling some of their responsibilities, their failures reflect negatively on the Council. Conversely, it is also of importance to consider to what extent the Council dealt with efficiently with the numerous situations of gross and massive human rights violations which were placed directly or indirectly on its agenda in the post-Covid 19 period. While its mechanisms kept on referring to these crises, it is of relevance to note that in the years 2023 and 2024 only one Special Session (on the ongoing conflict in the Sudan) was organized, while an additional one was organized at the time of proofreading of this text (on the situation in the east of the Democraitc Republic of the Congo). Regarding the large number of conflicts resulting in massive human rigths violations, which made the headlines on a daily basis and for which the International Court of Justice and the International Criminal Court provided last recourses, it is striking and very sad to note that they were not the subject of urgent measures such as a Special Session or an urgent debate at the Council.

It might be argued that there already exists Special procedures and or investigating bodies which reported regularly on these matters. However, this argument, in the mind of the author, does not absolve the Council from being seized with the matter and pronounce itself in substance publically, swiftly and efficiently. Gross and massive human rights violations, not to mention issues relating to the breaches of the Genocide Convention, the Apartheid Convention and matters involving large scale denials of human rights or humanitarian law, require the full attention of the United Nations. Accordingly, the same existential questions raised in relation to the failures of the Commission mentioned in introduction to this Chapter are valid insofar the Council is concerned in 2025. They need to be addressed as soon as possible if the Council wishes to retain its key role in dealing with human rights crises, whichever and wherever they are.

However, when considering the efficiency and effectiveness of the Council in dealing with human rights crises as well as its possible reform, one should automatically link them with the necessary reform of the Security Council and other relevant UN bodies. Since there is no plausible expectations that this achievement may be reached soon, a sense of frustration inevitably arises insofar as the Council is concerned. The causal link which bridges human rights violations and related breaches of the international order to the Council and its mechanisms should find its natural outcome in proper implementation by the Security Council and the General Assembly. Unfortunately, since this link does not really exist, implementation and follow-up are left in disarray in many circumstances.

There exist many instances of excellent cooperation between the human rights world and the UN in the field, for instance in relation to the UPR or the Special Procedures world. However, the same cannot be stated insofar as major human rights crises or emergencies – thematic or country based – are concerned. Since the Human Rights Council is not expected to deal with peace and security issues within the framework of the UN Charter, the fact that it is considering the heavy impact of the numerous conflicts which currently exist on the human rights of so many, does however not give it the possibility to deploy the full resources of the said Charter. This is what should be done by the Security Council or to an extent the General Assembly as had been the case during the Korean crisis in the 50s. The fact that they are increasingly absent from this scene for obvious political blockages should not be considered as a blow to the efficiency or effectiveness of the Human Rights Council, it is actually a sign of their serious deficiencies and, in the case of the Security Council, its possible obsolescence.

A simple way to consider this is to check to what extent Security Council meetings, emergency sessions of the General Assembly or UN Conferences dealing with vital matters for the future of humankind involve the main human rights actors, namely the Council and its mechanisms and the High Commissioner for Human Rights. And, if and when such meetings were actually held – with or without the presence of these human rihgts key players – to what extent did they lead to meaningful outcomes or any outcome at all. The author leaves it to readers to check it for themselves, but the response seems quite obvious or as predictable as the ending of most Hollywood movies. Unless these matters are eventually overcome, there will always remain a hiatus in the full engagement of the United Nations in the field of human rights.

3 The Human Rights Council governance: the role and functions of the President and his/her Bureau

A human or animal body requires a nervous system to ensure coordination of its main components, send proper signals or instructions, ensure a high-level analysis of the tasks to be performed, some being of a repetitive nature, others being far more sophisticated, and ensure proper scrutiny of the steps to be taken to keep the body alive, and more importantly to ensure that it evolves and reproduces in a proper manner. The nervous system detects environmental changes that impact the body. Similarly, a Human Rights Council Analogy needs to consider the Council's governance, namely its President and Bureau, to determine its functions, ranging from the most usual and mundane to the most sophisticated and unusual ones.

The functions of the Council President and his/her Bureau are usually described succinctly and considered to be quite obvious and limited to issues of a procedural and organizational nature. This is, after all, what the institution-building package recalls in its paragraph 114[1] and the Council's Rule 10. It is also in line with the practice of most UN intergovernmental bodies, as described in Rules 103–107 of the General Assembly Rules of Procedure. However, reality is far from this formal description.

Since the Council's establishment, successive Presidents have held quasi-permanent functions throughout their terms, with far-reaching

1 See Council Resolution 5/1 para 114 and Rule 10 of the Council Rules of Procedure.

responsibilities. They were assisted by four Vice-Presidents,[2] who often played a significant role in advising the President on delicate matters and supporting them in presiding over the sessions.

The role and functions of the President and the Bureau must, therefore, be considered in their dual reality: first, the traditional responsibilities assumed by Bureaux, and secondly, their often unrecognized functions regarding institutional or politically sensitive matters.

3.1 The traditional roles and functions of the President and his/her Bureau

At the outset, it is of interest to recall an oddity that prevailed during the last decade of the Commission on Human Rights. Namely, the Chairpersons of the Commission were assisted by what was referred to as 'Expanded' Bureaux. There was never any form of conceptualization of how the Expanded Bureaux were composed and whether their role differed from that of the 'Inner' Bureaux. The practice arose in the 1990s for the then President to be assisted by three Vice-Chairpersons, one Rapporteur, and the coordinators of the five Regional Groups.[3] This need for collective governance became of importance when the Commission began facing considerable difficulties in reviewing its working methods and functions and adjusting them to what was becoming a fast-moving reality. It was felt that consulting directly with the regional and political groups could speed up the deliberation process and enable consensus to be reached in a closed and confidential environment.

However, this expansion complicated and rigidified the Bureau's work and its working methods. The outcomes of the Bureau meetings were

2 One of them assumed the functions of Rapporteur. At the time of the Commission, Rapporteurs were mostly Counsellors and not Ambassadors nor Permanent Representatives. With the upgrading of the Council to the level of a GA subsidiary body, it was assumed that all members of the Bureau should be Permanent Representatives (see Decision 1/101 of 19 June 2006).

3 Since this was a purely empirical edifice, at times the composition of the Expanded Bureau also included the coordinators of some of the Political Groups.

progressively limited to daily business, leaving the last Chairpersons with a limited level of support and advice. It is not anecdotal[4] that the very limited proposals of the 2003 Expanded Bureau, in response to the Commission's decision 2003/116 on steps recommended to further improve the organization of the Commission's work, were rejected by the 2004 Commission.[5]

Given the failures of the late review processes of the Commissions,[6] it was assumed that the expansion of the Bureaux members to include the regional coordinators was one of the reasons that led to a higher level of politicization and polarization. It is fair to recognize that since all decisions, even those of a purely technical nature or of absolutely no significance, had to be approved by the Groups' Coordinators, this stalled all adoption processes and made it extremely difficult to change anything, from the significant to the trivial.

By the end of its existence, there was no longer a Commission Bureau per se, and the latest documents drafted by the Bureaux[7] simply referred to the 'Expanded Bureau'. It was thus assumed that the role of the Inner Bureau had been totally superseded by that of the Expanded Bureau.

From its creation, the Council reverted to a more traditional governance structure with a President and four Vice-Presidents, among whom one played the role of Rapporteur, checking the reports of the sessions and being entrusted with the task of stewarding various procedural and organizational matters. Informal consultations with Regional and Political Groups' Coordinators may still be organized, but only in a

---

4 What may, however, be anecdotal but not insignificant is that the meetings of the Bureau at the expert level on these matters were chaired by the CHR Secretary in the absence of a consensus on who should preside over the said meetings.

5 See, E/CN.4/2004/127, para 17 according to which 'on the recommendations of its officers, the Commission endorsed the recommendations that document E/CN.4/2003/118 and Corr.1 and the agreed provisions of E/CN.4/2002/16 would continue to govern the organization of work and conduct of business of the sixtieth session'. This is to be read as a rejection for lack of consensus of the proposals put forward by the 2003 Bureau.

6 See below.

7 See E/CN.4/2003/118.

few cases—typically when the Council is addressing extremely delicate matters or at the start of a President's mandate. Nowadays, the political landscape has become far more complex. In addition to the five regional groups and political groups (such as the EU, the Organisation of Islamic Conference (OIC), the Arab Group, or the Non-aligned Movement), other groups have also been sought for advice. For instance, the Organisation Internationale de la Francophonie, the Commonwealth, the Forum of Small States, and the group of Small Islands Developing States, as well as ad hoc groups.

The President is elected at the Organisational Session, which takes place immediately before the start of a Council cycle, and, to date, this has been done by acclamation with two exceptions.[8] There is a strict geographic rotation,[9] and normally, the four Vice-Presidents are elected by acclamation at the same meeting. When difficulties arise, one of the regional groups may request that the election of the officer from within its group be made at the next Council Organisational Meeting. The quorum required for a Bureau to take action is three members according to the established practice. Of importance, elections for the position of the President of the Council took place in January 2021 and 2024, respectively.

The President, assisted by Vice-Presidents, presides over the Council's meetings and represents the Council by delivering statements at the openings of the Council's subsidiary bodies. In particular, the President oversees the adoption of various proposals during the final two days of the session, a fact which is of fundamental importance given the complexity of the Council's voting process. Similarly, the presiding officer takes a position when points of order are being raised, and given the sensitivity of certain issues, this may not be without difficulty. Both functions require specific skills, experience and knowledge. The role of the Secretariat in these matters is not negligible, given the institutional memory and procedural skills it has accumulated over the years.

The Council's yearly and three-year programmes of work, as well as its Annual Calendars, are prepared by the Bureau and the Secretariat, which

8 The Chairperson of the 2003 Commission session and those of the 2021 and 2024 Council sessions were elected by secret ballot.

9 In the following order: GRULAC, Eastern European Group, African Group, Western European and Others Group, and the Asian Group.

are also entrusted with additional organizational functions since the Council Review. In particular, new procedures were set in motion regarding the establishment of the lists of speakers for the UPR, the drawing by lot of the first speaker on a given list, and other related tasks.[10]

Other 'traditional' functions of the President and the Bureau relate to the strict respect of the speaking time limits;[11] the organization of the High-Level Segment; debriefing by the President on his/her travels as well as the incoming or outgoing correspondence; and decisions on various organizational matters relating to the timing of specific activities.

The Bureau minutes are public and are posted on the Council Extranet. These minutes include summaries of discussions, as well as details of the activities of the President and the Bureau. They also serve as a channel to circulate a number of documents or correspondence in order to formalize them.

Presidents and their Bureaux, in coordination with the Secretariat, are also entrusted with responsibilities aimed at making the Council's work more accessible. To this end, a variety of measures have been introduced to ensure that the various stakeholders, and more broadly the public at large, have easier access to the voluminous information emanating from or directed towards the Council. This task requires specific and permanent attention and updates.

Increased efforts, however, must be deployed when it comes to ensuring accessibility for persons with disabilities. This issue has been the subject of attention from the very beginning, but the most important efforts were deployed following the adoption of the Resolution 16/21 on the outcome of the 2011 Review process. Paragraph 58 of the resolution emphasized the need to enhance accessibility for persons with disabilities to the Council and the work of its mechanisms, including its information and communication technology, internet resources, and documents,

---

10 See Appendix to the Council Resolution 16/21.

11 This is a particularly delicate task since the speaking time limits are notoriously short at the Council level. At times, statements may be limited to one minute or less (during the UPR proceedings), one minute and a half (for Observer States during general debates), or two minutes (interactive dialogues and panels).

in accordance with international standards on accessibility for persons with disabilities.

Since 2012, one of the Vice-Presidents has served as the coordinator of the process on behalf of the Bureau, presenting relevant reports to the Council and engaging directly with the UN Office at Geneva, the OHCHR and various stakeholders. More importantly, quite a number of their recommendations have been translated into deeds, and despite the need for continued progress should continue to be introduced in this regard, it is now customary for some panels to be made accessible, for documents that are not accessible to be posted on the website or on the Extranet, and for the room to be organized in such a manner as to provide easier access to persons with disabilities.

Comparable efforts were engaged on issues relating to gender equality and the prevention of harassment, including sexual harassment. Focal Points were thus designated by successive Presidents, and on 3 October 2024, the Gender and Equality Focal Point announced the launch of a new website[12] on the prevention of harassment, the rationale of which was to make the Council a space free from any type of harassment. A draft informal protocol for preventing and addressing harassment, including sexual harassment, at meetings and events of the Council was also developed –the first such instrument developed within the United Nations to operationalize the Secretary-General Code of Conduct on the same topic.

3.2 The additional responsibilities of the Council President and the Bureau

The Council's architecture has evolved profoundly over the past decade, paralleling the quasi-exponential increase of its activities. Successive Presidents and their Bureaux were presented with a large number of matters, often urgent, which they had to consider in depth to make appropriate recommendations to the Council. In most circumstances, these matters required bilateral or multilateral consultations, as well as a great deal of analysis and research and the identification of viable

---

12 See https://www.ohchr.org/en/hr-bodies/hrc/conduct-of-participants.

options. Although neither the Presidents nor their Bureaux had any formal decision-making power – as this remains the exclusive responsibility of the Council in accordance with the General Assembly Rules of Procedure – they acquired substantial powers of initiative, discussion, and negotiation on behalf of the Council as a whole, a role that they often played to the limits. This was always based on the assumption that consensus among all members on issues of importance relating to the Council's work and function is the rule, thus dissipating fears that the Council would become as polarized and politicized as its predecessor. It was considered fundamental that all efforts should be deployed to avoid dissent, confusion, and even chaos entering the proceedings. The role of the President and the Bureau was therefore considered an anteroom for the Council's consideration of delicate matters. Conversely, when despite multifaceted engagements by the Presidents, consensus could not be achieved, action on their proposals was usually postponed until consensus could be reached.[13] In most circumstances, some form of agreement was eventually reached, and progress achieved, or new courses of action contemplated.

The Council's flexibility and its irresistible inventiveness owe much to the numerous initiatives and the strong commitment of successive Presidents and their Bureaux.

The following pointers may shed light on the importance of the presidential functions.

3.2.1 Leading the Institutions-building and Review Processes

From the start, the Council had to determine how to translate the General Assembly Resolution 60/251 into deeds. In particular, it had to thoroughly analyse the provisions contained in paragraphs 1–6 of said resolution to ensure their proper implementation. This involved a dual

13 Such issues concerned, inter alia measures in relation to the enhancement of the Council's efficiency and effectiveness (Bureau meetings of 21 February 2012 and 30 August 2017), the regional or political group sponsoring of resolutions (Bureau meeting of 18 September 2015), or the organization of special meetings to listen to Heads of States (Bureau meeting of 2 December 2015).

aspect, namely envisioning the functions of the newly established body[14] while considering how it would assume, review, and, where necessary, improve and rationalize all mandates, mechanisms, and responsibilities of the former Commission on Human Rights.[15]

In previous circumstances, this would have been achieved through the channel of the Expanded Bureau and an intergovernmental working group or comparable body. However, given the experience of the former Commission and its progressive paralysis in the last decade of its existence, the President and Bureau of the 1st Council Cycle opted for a more flexible approach. The President thus operated as the leader of the institution-building process, which kept the Council busy for no less than five sessions in the concerned one-year cycle.[16] The President's actions included proposing Decision 2/102 on the blanket one-year extension of all mandates, mechanisms, functions, and responsibilities of the Commission.[17]

Of particular significance were Decisions 1/103 and 1/104 of 30 June 2006 on the UPR and the implementation of paragraph 6 of the General Assembly Resolution 60/251, the wording of which underlined the move to a new era. Paragraph 1 of these decisions provided for the establishment of an intersessional intergovernmental Working Group, while paragraph 3 requested the President 'to chair the Working Group with the assistance, if necessary, of one or more facilitators[18] from among permanent missions in Geneva, to undertake open-ended, intersessional, transparent, well-scheduled, and inclusive consultations with the participation of all stakeholders'.[19] The Working Groups provided a formal setting for

14 See in particular para 5 (a)–(j) of General Assembly Resolution 60/251.
15 Ibid., para 6.
16 1st session, June 2006; 2nd session, September and November 2006; 3rd session, November and December 2006; 4th session, March 2007; and 5th session, June 2017.
17 See Council Decision 1/102 of 30 June 2006.
18 The General Assembly practice of appointing facilitators was thereby brought into the Geneva environment.
19 See also Decision 3/4 of 8 December 2006 on the implementation of General Assembly Resolution 60/251 insofar as the agenda, annual programme of work, methods of work and rules of procedure were concerned.

the expression of positions by concerned countries, but the reality of the work had actually moved to the facilitation process. A major shift with the Commission's practice had thus been set into motion, with considerable repercussions for future circumstances. The Presidents of the 4th and 5th Council Cycles followed similar arrangements for the review of the work and functioning of the Council five years after its establishment.[20] The Presidents of the 12th and subsequent Council Cycles set aside the practice of establishing a formal intergovernmental Working Group when dealing with issues of an institutional nature; they resorted exclusively to the appointment of facilitators when considering options to strengthen the efficiency and effectiveness of the Council.

The new role of the Council President was epitomized by the end of the first Council Cycle when the texts of what were to become the institutions-building package[21] were agreed upon after weeks of extremely delicate negotiations at midnight[22] on 18 June 2007.[23] These proposals had been submitted directly by the President, a practice that had not been followed beforehand and which echoed that of the General Assembly when it adopted the President's Resolution 60/251, establishing the Council.[24]

The practice for Council Presidents to lead delicate negotiations on institutional and related matters was consolidated at the Organisational Meeting that marked the start of the 2nd Cycle. On 19 June 2007, immediately after the election of the new Bureau, a point of order was raised by the Representative of Canada, arguing that no formal decision had actually been taken on the institution-building texts the previous night. His position was that the President had simply orally indicated that an agreement had been reached, with the understanding that the text would be submitted to a formal vote on 19 June 2007. The new President led intense negotiations, and a few hours later, he ruled that a decision had

20 See Council Resolution 12/1 of 1 October 2009.

21 See Council Resolutions 5/1 and 5/2 of 18 June 2007.

22 Until the review of the Council, the Annual Council Cycles ended on the anniversary day of the very first meeting of the Council (18 June 2006).

23 See A/HRC/5/21, paras 57–59.

24 In normal practice, when a text does not enjoy consensus, it is submitted by States and not the President. Presidential texts are deemed to represent the views of all members of the Council.

actually been taken and that the Council had adopted the text the previous evening. The President's ruling was put to the vote and approved by 46 votes to 1 (Canada).[25]

This ruling and the ensuing vote were of fundamental importance and enabled the Council to establish its institutions. If the question had been posed otherwise, the voting results would probably have been entirely different, and the support for the institution-building package would have been significantly weakened. They also strongly testified to the new roles that the Council Presidents, and by extension their Bureaux, would henceforth play in the UN human rights architecture.

The same practice was followed a few years later when the Council reviewed its work and functioning in accordance with the General Assembly's request contained in paragraph 16 of Resolution 60/251. The President of the 5th Council Cycle stewarded the process directly and through facilitators he appointed.[26]

Given the difficulties faced both in terms of this Council Review and the General Assembly's Review of the Council's status in accordance with paragraph 1 of the said resolution, he took the broad step of convening a Retreat of Council members in Bangkok in December 2011.[27] His intention was to gauge the multifaceted situation and identify as precisely as possible the 'red lines' that existed. This informal Retreat was considered pivotal in paving the way for an agreement on a scaled-down Presidential proposal, the negotiation of which took place during a lengthy week at the President's Permanent Mission. The agreement, which was ultimately reached, was then formally consolidated in Resolution 16/21.

---

25 See A/HRC/OM-1, paras 17–19.

26 See Chapter 7.

27 See Minutes of the Bureau of 12 January 2011 and the Statement by the President at the informal plenary meeting of the General Assembly held on 30 March 2011 on the review of the status of the Council.

The same practice was followed in 2015 (Berlin Retreat),[28] 2016 (Evian Retreat),[29] 2018 (Ljubljana Retreat),[30] 2019 (Dakar Retreat), 2023 (Prague Retreat) and 2024 (Rabat Retreat) by the Presidents of the 9th, 10th, 12th, 13th, 17th and 18th Council Cycles, respectively. In most of these instances, the Presidents considered how the Council could refine its working methods and strengthen its efficiency and effectiveness. Substantive issues were also included in discussions on various themes considered of importance. For instance, the President of the 13th Council Cycle convened the Dakar Retreat with a clear focus on pressing substantive issues.[31] In all these instances, broad and thorough exchanges of views took place in an informal setting away from Geneva with Council Member States, coordinators of regional or political groups, a representative of the Coordinating Committee of Special Procedures, and a selected number of NGOs.

Given the expansion of its activities, the Council constantly faced financial difficulties, which the President and the Bureau addressed by reaching out to the relevant UN bodies and departments.[32] The Council also encountered difficulties related to the financial and administrative support extended to it given the continuing increase of its activities. In particular, in a letter dated 9 August 2016, addressed to the President of the 10th Council Cycle, the Director-General of the UN Office at Geneva highlighted the steep increase in the number of meetings held by the Council from 2002 to 2016,[33] and the consequences in terms of budget allocations for the various United Nations Office at Geneva (UNOG) Divisions supporting its work. He informed that, in 2017, UNOG would only be able to service a total of 135 meetings, and 130 meetings in

28 21–23 May 2015.

29 1 and 2 September 2016. See President's farewell remarks at the 5 December 2016 Organizational Session.

30 Welcoming remarks by the President of the Council at the Council Retreat in Ljubljana from 10 to 12 October 2018.

31 Migration and human rights, human rights in the digital age, climate change and human rights and business and human rights against the background of growing social inequalities.

32 See for instance minutes of the Bureau of 16 January, 29 June, and 9 November 2011, and 7 January 2015.

33 From 128 to 153 meetings per year.

subsequent years. This represented a 20 per cent reduction, which had a potentially huge effect on the programme of work.

The President and his Bureau had to establish urgent mechanisms to address this matter and develop proposals to present to the Council for adoption. Almost immediate measures were taken, resulting in a significant reduction of the speaking time limits,[34] while longer-term efficiency proposals were considered by that Bureau and its successors. Ideas were explored regarding the annual number of panels,[35] the format of the general debates and that of the plenary segment of the UPR, the bi- and triennialization of initiatives, improvements in information technology to enhance the Council's working methods, and the possibility of increasing resources allocated to the Council. The format for addressing these matters evolved over the years, starting with the direct implication of the President and his Bureau (2016), followed by the participation of a Vice-President in a tripartite task force with UNOG and OHCHR representatives (2017), and later the designation of facilitators (2018 and 2019).[36] On 3 December 2018, following a year-long effort, the President of the 12th Council Cycle submitted and secured consensual approval of a revised draft Presidential Statement on enhancing the Council's efficiency, including addressing financial and time constraints. The President of the 13th Council Cycle subsequently appointed facilitators to implement the agreed conclusions outlined in the documents and revisit other matters that had proven more challenging.

However, the deepening of the financial and liquidity crises plaguing the United Nations continued to affect the Council in the years that followed. As mentioned in the previous chapter, the COVID-19 pandemic

---

34 Down to three minutes for members and one minute 30 seconds for observers during general debates. Similarly, both members' and observers' speaking times were reduced to two minutes for panels and interactive dialogues. The duration of panels was ultimately reduced to a maximum of two hours instead of three hours.

35 An issue which had already been the subject of a proposal by the President of the 6th Council Cycle (see minutes of the 21 February 2012 Bureau). This proposal did not meet consensus and could not be presented to the plenary.

36 See minutes of the Bureau meetings of 26 September 2016, 24 May and 30 August 2017, 5 February 2018, 15 and 18 January and 8 February 2019.

period did alter their impact simply because the Council, being one of the sole United Nations entities operating at its full capacity, benefited from resources that might have been affected elsewhere under normal circumstances.

Nevertheless, as early as July 2021, the Bureau noted that the provision of lunchtime meetings, which had become the standard in the past and which enabled the Council to absorb new activities, could no longer be extended to it, at least not to the extent it was in the past. Hence, on 16 July 2021, the Bureau was informed by Conference Services that only four additional lunchtime meetings would be granted to it during its September session. Accordingly, the Secretariat observed 'that even with four lunchtime meetings, the Council would still need to meet for a total of four weeks in order to complete the programme of work, due to the fact that more panel discussions and interactive dialogues had been mandated by the Council to take place during the 48th session as compared to the 45th session held in September 2020. The Bureau took note that the session would, therefore, conclude on 8 October 2021'.

This led successive Bureaux to proceed with a progressive reshaping of the Council's yearly timeline with a six-week February/March session, a four-week June/July session, and later on a five-week September/October session – far from the ten-week duration which had been the norm since 2007.

Further to intense conversations with the UN Conference Services, the Bureau decided on 23 August 2022 to present to the Council a decision for adoption at the 51st session which aimed at providing appropriate support for the Human Rights Council. This represented a revisiting of paragraph 10 of resolution 60/251 by requesting the Secretary-General to provide the Council with the support necessary to be able to meet not less than 14 weeks to fulfil its annual programme of work.[37]

This decision somewhat overcame a number of issues that had been a point of contention within the UN machinery given the heavy and increasing volume of work of the Council and its mechanisms. However, it did not settle them for good and intense discussions took place in

---

37 See decision 51/101 of 6 October 2022 and the minutes of the Bureau meeting of 23 August 2022.

subsequent sessions regarding every aspect of the Council's work. This included, for instance the provision of interpretation for the entire duration of the UPR reviews by the Working Group – namely three-and-a-half hours and a half instead of the normal three hours of a UN meeting.[38] It also involved constant negotiations regarding the number of additional lunchtime meetings to accommodate the large number of dignitaries or the voting process during the Council's sessions.[39] Or, it encompassed a refusal by the UNOG to cover the costs of virtual or hybrid informal meetings or side events in 2023 and of the Council plenary in 2024 – even though these costs were ridiculously low (a few hundred US dollars per meeting) and of no consequence to the overall UN budget.[40]

In all likelihood, given the imperious nature of addressing human rights issues regardless of their nature and occurrence, the Council will likely continue to face such challenges for a number of years, thus requiring the skilful involvement of incoming Presidents and their Bureaux.

One of the most recent initiatives by the Council President and his President in this area was the adoption of decision 55/116 of 5 April 2024, on remote participation modalities for hybrid meetings of the Council. It is rather sad, to say the least, that this decision was not implemented at the time of the completion of this second edition. It is regrettable that the responses by the Under Secretary-General for General Assembly and Conference Management to the Council's efforts were negative and reflected the position of the Organisation at the start of the COVID-19 pandemic, without taking into account the various steps taken by the Council in the subsequent years, as saluted by the international community and the UN Secretary-General.[41]

3.2.2 Dealing with Emergencies and Issues of a Political and Sensitive Nature

Special Sessions

Although it would have been expected that the nascent Council would be spared from emergencies and highly polarized matters, allowing time to

38 See for instance minutes of the Bureau meeting of 12 October 2022.
39 See for instance minutes of the Bureau meeting of 13 January 2023.
40 See for instance minutes of the Bureau meeting of 7 February 2023.
41 See minutes of the Bureau meeting of 8 July 2024.

focus on institutional matters, this proved not to be the case. On the very last day of its very first regular session, the President of the 1st Council Cycle received a letter[42] from the Permanent Representative of Tunisia, who, as Chairperson of the Arab Group, requested the President to convene a Special Session to address the latest escalation of the situation in the Palestinian and other occupied Arab Territories.

It should be borne in mind that when this letter was received, the Council was operating under vaguely defined terms of reference; Resolution 60/251 had only recently been adopted, the Council had just entered into function and so had the President, and there was no agreed-upon modus operandi for convening Special Sessions. This would be firmed up in the 12 months to come and consolidated in the institutions-building package a year later.

Given that this letter was prepared and received at the very end of the 1st session, with no luxury of time or practical possibility to refer the matter to the plenary, this was thus discussed and resolved by the President with the support of his Bureau, based on informal consultations conducted in parallel with the session.

At that time, the only reference to Special Sessions was paragraph 10 of Resolution 60/251, which states that the Council should be able to hold Special Sessions at the request of a Member of the Council, with the support of one-third of the Council's membership. The practice[43] of the former Commission regarding Special Sessions was deemed inappropriate and ineffective, and therefore not relied upon.

In a matter of a few days, the President and his Bureau proposed a number of organizational steps, which would later become precedents for the first four Special Sessions.[44] In turn, these steps were codified into

42 See document A/HRC/S-1/1.

43 Only five Special Sessions were convened by the Commission in the last 15 years of its existence.

44 First Special Session held on 5 July 2006 on the human rights situation in the Occupied Palestinian Territories; 2nd Special Session held on 11 August 2006 on the grave situation of human rights in Lebanon caused by Israeli military operations; 3rd Special Session held on 15 November 2006 on the human rights violations emanating from

paragraphs 119–128 of the institutions-building package and Rules 5 and 6 of the Council's Rules of Procedure. They covered various aspects, including the delay between the submission of the request and the holding of the Special Session, the convening of an Organizational Meeting as soon as possible after the request was received, the need for sponsors to organize informals on their draft, the specific modalities of the debate, and the procedures to be followed for the consideration and adoption of the proposal.

It became very clear that the only medium available to the Council to address in a constructive manner any emergencies or pressing matters that may present themselves would be to give the responsibility to the President and the Bureau to initiate, conduct and conclude the negotiations before securing a formal agreement at the plenary level. This was also done against the background of the imperative need to avoid any polarized and politicized discussion in the format of public meetings, which could have undermined the nascent Council in a manner similar to the defunct Commission.

The habit having been taken and seriously rooted in Council practice for the President and the Bureau to deal with urgent and delicate issues, the years that followed saw a large and increasing number of matters dealt with directly by the Council Presidents and their Bureaux.

Urgent Debates

In line with the involvement of the Council's President and Bureau in setting up the format for the first Special Sessions, successive Presidents had to cope with urgent requests for the special consideration of country-specific issues during sessions. The institution-building package did not provide specific provisions for urgent debates, and consequently the Presidents, with the support of their Bureaux, had to informally conceptualize the possibility for urgent debates to be organized during a Council session. Accordingly, they built up a sui generis practice whereby the Bureau would have to genuinely consider any request for such a

---

Israeli military incursions in the Occupied Palestinian Territory, including the recent one in Northern Gaza and the assault on Beit Hanoun; and 4th Special Session held on 12 and 13 December 2006 on the human rights situation in Darfur.

debate, consider it as a formal request to revisit the sessional programme of work, and propose to the plenary the timing as well as modalities for the general debate and subsequent adoption of the resolution.[45] However, in order for the Bureau not to be caught in political considerations of the matter at stake, it was wisely considered appropriate to limit the Bureau's role to that of a timekeeper and organizer of the debate, leaving it to the Council to decide should objections be raised against the convening of the meeting.

Other Matters Relating to Human Rights Emergencies

The Presidents and their Bureaux often hold informal exchanges of views on matters relating to human rights emergencies; however, these discussions take place in a confidential manner and cannot be reported. On at least one occasion, however, a discussion was held during a formal meeting of the Bureau (19 November 2008), and as such, was duly reported in the Minutes.

On that occasion, the Minutes, which deserve to be quoted fully, recorded the following:

> Before considering the items in the agenda, the President referred to the human rights crisis in Northern Kivu and drew attention to a letter dated 17 November from a group of 40 NGOs calling for an urgent consideration of the matter by the Council. As Council President, he considered that the Council could not remain silent in the circumstances. Human rights violations and a serious humanitarian situation have been broadly reported by many, including the UN Secretary-General. About 250.000 additional displaced persons have been reported thus bringing the total number of IDPs to about one million. Summary executions, sexual violence and looting are widespread. Lack of access to food, medication and shelter are additional constraints for civilians. The President's hope is that urgent consideration of the matter by the Council would focus on the need to strongly support the current efforts of the Secretary-General as well as those of the African Union, calling for an immediate end to the alleged human rights violations, and urging everyone to respect human rights and protect civilians in the areas in conflict.

45 Six out of the nine urgent debates organized so far were organized without any objection from the floor. As for the urgent debates on Eastern Ghouta, Belarus, and the Russian invasion of Ukraine, organized in March 2018, September 2020 and March 2022 respectively, the requests (not the Bureau proposals) were formally objected to and voted upon.

> Those responsible for the violations should be reminded that they could be held accountable for their actions. The President referred to provisions in GA Resolution 60/251 and in the HRC Resolution 5/1 concerning the convening of a Special Session. He inquired about Bureau members' opinion and advice on the matter. Members of the Bureau shared the President's concern on the seriousness of the human rights violations and the appalling humanitarian situation in Northern Kivu as well and supported the role which the Council could play in the circumstances. They also supported his efforts and indicated that consensus might easily be reached on the convening of a Special Session, provided the initiative comes from the African region. The President thanked the Bureau for its support and indicated that he would further consultations on this issue before, during and immediately after his trip to New York from 20 to 22 November.

This very rare glimpse into debates that may take place during Bureau meetings, as well as the action points referenced in that meeting, underlines the importance that Council Presidents and their Bureaux play in the substantive stewardship of the Council. It also sheds light, in an indirect manner, on the working methods of the Bureaux. It is not by pure chance that the 8th Special Session of the Council on the situation of human rights in the East of the Democratic Republic of the Congo was convened just a week after the Bureau meeting, on Friday, 28 November 2008.

Emergencies can take many forms, but they share one common feature: they always take everyone by surprise. One of the most striking examples occurred on 25 February 2011, during the 15th Special Session on the human rights situation in the Libyan Arab Jamahiriya. During the afternoon proceedings, Libya's representative delivered a statement whereby he requested the Council observe a minute of silence for the victims of the recent events in the country[46] at the end of which he indicated he was resigning from his position as Permanent Representative of the Libyan Arab Jamahiriya. Shortly afterwards, he left the room and his colleagues followed suit. The meeting proceeded without any representative from the Libyan Arab Jamahiriya. At the conclusion of the meeting, Resolution S-15/1 was adopted. The penultimate paragraph of that resolution recommended to the General Assembly that, in light of the gross and systematic violations of human rights by the Libyan authorities, the General Assembly should consider applying the measures outlined in paragraph 8 of Resolution 60/251. On 1 March 2011, the General Assembly endorsed

---

46 See A/HRC/S-15/1, para 13.

this recommendation[47] and decided to suspend the rights of membership in the Council of the Libyan Arab Jamahiriya.

The President of the 5th Council Cycle and his Bureau had to contemplate the consequences of this impromptu situation and the application for the first time ever of paragraph 8 of Resolution 60/251. Once again, the provisions of the enabling resolution were quite unclear, and a lot of discussion ensued as to what the status of the concerned country would henceforth be. In particular, the Bureau consulted the Legal Counsel and considered that having been suspended from the rights of membership, Libya would be deprived of the prerogatives of Council Members such as the right to vote, the right to participate in procedural debates privileges in the lists of speakers, etc.[48] Later, it was decided that the seat of Libya would be moved to a place in between Members and Observers. Regarding Libya's right to participate in Council proceedings, since Libya was not an Observer State but a Member State having been deprived of its rights of membership, the Bureau further deliberated whether a Libyan delegation would be in a position to address the Council at its 17th Council session. Upon advice by the UN Legal Counsel, Libya was granted the right to take the floor as a concerned State immediately after the Commission of Inquiry, established by resolution S-15/1.[49]

Other emergencies that Presidents frequently face involve alleged cases of reprisals against NGO representatives[50] participating in the Council's proceedings, either in the Council Chamber or in other premises at the Palais des Nations. Successive Presidents have progressively developed an ad hoc 'protocol' which they follow in such circumstances. In most situations, these cases require checking the facts via the various Secretariat entities, discussing the matter with the Permanent Representative of the

---

47 See General Assembly Resolution 65/265 of 1 March 2011.

48 See minutes of the Bureau meeting of 2 March 2011.

49 See minutes of the Bureau meetings of 13 and 18 May 2011 and their annexes.

50 See minutes of Bureau meetings held on 1 and 12 March, 22 and 25 June, 24 September and 9 October 2012; 23 September and 18 October 2013; 17 March and 24 October 2014; 7 and 16 January, 10 and 13 February, 13 and 19 March, 30 April, and 8, 19 and 30 June 2015; 11 March, 23 and 29 June, and 23 August 2016; 28 April 2017; 4 and 11 May 2018; and 27 April 2022.

concerned country with a view to securing the required clarification, and sharing information with the Bureau. When the matter is elevated to the plenary, references are made to the case usually in general terms without specific references to the concerned country.

However, in one case, the President felt obliged to refer the matter to the attention of the Council. This occurred during the UPR Working Group Review of Bahrain on 25 May 2012, and it was extensively referenced in the subsequent minutes of the Bureau. In this context, the President referred to her correspondence of 11 June 2012,[51] in response to a letter from the Arab Ambassador's Council dated 30 May. She emphasized that her statement dated 25 May did not contain any accusations against the concerned government but instead was an invitation or a call to the authorities to act preventively and provide adequate protection to members of civil society who had come to Geneva to attend the Review and had been intimidated through several media articles. The President underlined that she had not had time to consult the delegation and had to act quickly, as information about imminent danger had just been conveyed to her, and both the delegation and members of civil society were due to return to the country immediately after. The Bureau agreed that

---

51 In that letter, the President indicated that: 'In this context, alerted by articles in the media and social networks, the statement I delivered on 25 May 2012, following the adoption of the draft report on the Review of Bahrain, was only aimed at informing the Kingdom of Bahrain and inviting the Bahraini authorities to provide adequate protection for members of civil society who cooperated with the United Nations and its mechanisms, in the context of the UPR process. That statement did not contain any accusation against the Kingdom of Bahrain, but constituted a call to provide protection guarantees to persons facing threats allegedly from different sources, in order to prevent any problems. I also expressed my full confidence in the Bahraini authorities, given the important commitments made by its High Level delegation, which included ensuring follow-up to the UPR recommendations in cooperation with all sectors of society. Finally, I would like to highlight that previous Presidents of the Council were also very active in ensuring that the space for participation of civil society within the Council's work was safeguarded. I myself made a statement in the Council plenary on this matter on 5 March 2012, in the framework of the 19th session of the Council.'

the President's statement was intended solely as a preventive measure aiming at protecting members of the civil society and avoiding future issues and that each situation had to be considered on its own merits. The President finally reminded the Bureau that her statement was not reflected in the concerned UPR report, since it was delivered after the adoption of the report. It was also recalled that the rules applicable to official summary records – which are now replaced by webcast archives – prohibit any statements being added or removed from the records.[52]

In a later case, without referring to the concerned country, the President stated in the Council's chamber:

> I recently received allegations that during the 31st session, a member of a national delegation to this Council misused social media to deliver a message that can be construed as a serious threat against an NGO representative attending the session. As per established practice, I addressed the allegations to the Permanent Representative of the relevant delegation who conducted a prompt investigation. The Permanent Representative subsequently acknowledged that the member of the delegation committed this extremely regrettable act, but not in his professional capacity and without intentions to be a threat. I was further informed that an administrative reprimand had been issued. I assure you that I am fully seized of this matter and will continue looking into it. I cannot stress enough that this is completely unacceptable, and as such should be denunciated in the strongest of terms. I take this opportunity to call on everyone to be extremely vigilant, in all cases of potential reprisals, on-line or off-line. Social media should be used to promote and protect human rights and not the opposite.[53]

Needless to say, these interventions by the Presidents and their Bureaux may place them in delicate situations vis-à-vis the concerned countries and, by extension, their regional or political groups. The fact that this did not dissuade them from doing so shows the commitment displayed by successive Presidents and Bureaux, as well as the specific nature of the role of the Council Presidents in the UN intergovernmental system.

Instances of reprisals go well beyond civil society boundaries, as was testified by a case that occurred in July 2022. In remarkably transparent minutes, the Bureau dealt with a case of reprisal against a member of the Expert Mechanism on the Rights of Indigenous Peoples (EMRIP).

---

52 See minutes of the Bureau meetings of 22 and 25 June 2012.
53 Statement delivered on 13 June 2016.

Although such cases were raised on occasions by previous Bureaux, it was the first time the Bureau was so explicit in its deliberations and is therefore reproduced for ease of reference:

> On 15 July 2022, the President informed the Bureau that he had received a complaint containing allegations of an act of reprisal whereby a member of the Human Rights Council's Expert Mechanism on the Rights of Indigenous Peoples (EMRIP), Ms. Anexa Brendalee Alfred Cunningham, was prevented from boarding her confirmed flight to return home to Nicaragua following her participation in the 15th session of the EMRIP.
>
> The President informed that the complaint asserted that Ms. Alfred Cunningham, a Nicaraguan citizen who had been appointed by the Council as a member from Central and South America and the Caribbean of the EMRIP on 1 April 2022, had travelled to Geneva for her first official mission to participate in preparatory meetings and the 15th session of the EMRIP. Following the conclusion of the EMRIP session, when Ms. Alfred Cunningham had attempted to check-in for her return flight to Nicaragua, she was allegedly barred from boarding her flight because the airline had received an email from the Government of Nicaragua stipulating that her entry into Nicaraguan territory would be refused.
>
> The President additionally informed that the OHCHR had immediately arranged for Ms. Alfred Cunningham to return to Geneva, where she remained pending a rectification of the situation by the Government of Nicaragua.
>
> The President reported to the Bureau that he had contacted the Permanent Representative of Nicaragua and had requested clarification of the situation as well as the cooperation of the Government in rectifying the matter numerous times over the course of the past week. However, the Government had not yet provided a response to the President's request for clarification or its assurances that Ms. Alfred Cunningham would be able to return to Nicaragua without threat or fear of reprisal. The President expressed his view that Nicaragua's denial of Ms. Alfred Cunningham to return to her country without explanation indicates an act of reprisal for her participation in the EMRIP session.
>
> The Bureau expressed serious concern over the allegations and emphasized that all experts appointed by the Human Rights Council should be able to discharge their mandates without fear of retaliation or reprisals of any kind.
>
> The Bureau called on the Government of Nicaragua to cooperate with the President of the Human Rights Council to urgently clarify the situation and to give its assurances that Ms. Alfred Cunningham will not be subjected to any act of intimidation or reprisal, including impeding her return to Nicaragua, for discharging her mandate. The Bureau agreed to remain seized of this matter pending appropriate action by the concerned country.[54]

[54] From the minutes of the Bureau meeting held on 15 July 2022.

UPR

The first session of the UPR Working Group was held from 7 to 18 April 2008. It was convened and conducted in accordance with the modalities envisioned in the institution-building package. Paragraphs 18–25 were relatively precise in their formulation, but when the Working Group began its work, no agreement had yet been reached on the format of the Working Group report and that of the final outcome to be adopted by the plenary of the Council.

The usual format for such reports was to summarize the discussion and the recommendations made without specific attribution and/or clustering of the main issues. However, when the Ecuadorian and Finland Reviews took place, recommendations were made on issues relating to non-discrimination on the grounds of sexual orientation. Although both countries supported such recommendations, the issue was not consensual at the Working Group level, and it proved impossible to use terminology in the summary of the discussion and the listing of recommendations that would imply any form of endorsement by the Working Group as such. Those countries that objected to discussing issues relating to sexual orientation at the Council level preferred to leave the said recommendations out of the Working Group report.

The President of the 3rd Council Cycle initiated urgent negotiations at the end of the second day of the Working Group Session. These discussions lasted a significant period of time, and of notice it was only one hour before the formal adoption of the first Working Group report (on Bahrain) that the President was in a position to present a consensual proposal whereby the summary part would be fully attributed. Similarly, all recommendations were requested to be listed with full attribution. The Working Group report concluded with a paragraph indicating that 'all conclusions and/or recommendations contained in the present report reflect the position of the submitting State(s) and/or the State under review thereon. They should not be construed as endorsed by the Working Group as a whole'.[55]

The UPR triggered numerous challenges that required the intervention of the Council Presidents, often with the assistance of their Bureaux. On

55 See A/HRC/8/20/Corr.1

certain instances, some of the Vice-Presidents were called upon to work as de facto facilitators on a specific country review, to appease tensions and propose ways out. This often touched sensitive issues, such as territorial denominations or recommendations considered outrageous by the State under review.[56] The practice of inserting footnotes was skilfully developed. Finally, the President of the 7th Cycle was in a position to set up a proper format for the drafting of the Working Group Report or the Outcome Document[57] which is followed to this day.

By far the most delicate UPR issue dealt with by a Council President and the Bureau related to the decision by Israel to suspend its relationship with the Council. This was communicated to the President of the 6th Council Cycle on 14 May 2012. Although it was not specified in the letter, it soon appeared that this decision also included the consideration of the review of Israel under the UPR Mechanism, which was initially scheduled to take place on 29 January 2013.

The President of the 6th Cycle initiated multiple demarches, which culminated in her sending a comprehensive letter to the Permanent Representative of Israel on 28 November 2012. This remained unsuccessful

---

56 See for instance, paras 38, 72 and 73 of the Working Group Report on Cyprus (A/HRC/13/7); footnotes 2–8 and paras 34, 40, 52 and 83 of the Working Group Report on Lebanon (A/HRC/16/18); footnotes 1–4 and para 110 of the Working Group Report on Azerbaijan (A/HRC/24/13); or para 141 and footnote 1 of the Working Group Report on the Russian Federation (A/HRC/24/14).

57 See letter of 18 September 2013 in which the President of the 7th Cycle clarified the existing rules and practices by indicating that the Working Group report is of a factual nature and should reflect what was said in the room by the State under review and participating delegations, that all conclusions and/or recommendations reflect the position of the submitting State(s) and/or the State under review and should not be construed as endorsed by the Working Group as a whole; that all recommendations made during the Review should be treated equally and listed only once in the body of the report; that all recommendations should constitute a part of the outcome document and as such the State under review should clearly communicate to the Council its position on all received recommendations; and that all recommendations should focus on human rights issues and comply with the basis of the Review.

and the President of the 7th Cycle had to deal with the dire prospects of a collapse of the UPR. Following persistent mediation, the President ensured that the process would remain consensual and that the Review would take place before the end of the year. He secured an agreement by the Council on 14 January 2013 to mandate him to select the troika for Israel. Later, he drafted a proposal, which was endorsed by the Council in its decision OM/7/101 of 29 January 2013, according to which the Review would be deferred to November of the same year. He then spent several months in discrete negotiations, which enabled him to secure the return of Israel to the UPR and by extension the Council.[58]

It is of considerable importance to emphasize that thanks to strenuous efforts by the President and his Bureau, the Council took consensual steps in considering the way to deal with the matter and ensure that the UPR mechanism would remain universal. It is also of considerable importance to observe that, thanks to constant and persistent efforts by the Presidents of the 6th and 7th Council cycles, the Review of Israel eventually took place on 29 October 2013. The integrity of the UPR process was thus upheld, as well as its universal character.[59]

This particular case had a resounding impact in upholding the universal character of the UPR but also, and possibly mostly, in underlining that issues of considerable importance need to be dealt with in a consensual manner. To reach that goal, there was no other way than to delegate to the President and the Bureau a substantial level of autonomy in initiating proper responses and proposing options after adequate and multiple consultations.

Other issues relating to the UPR and by extension the work of other procedures, concerned the accreditation of States' representatives. As mentioned in other parts of this Anatomy,[60] the Council had to deal

---

58 See letters of the President dated 15 February and 14 May, and his communication of 28 October 2013. See also the letters of the Permanent Representative of Israel dated 1 March and 3 June 2013.

59 If this had not been the case, other States would have deemed it possible to defer or cancel their own review, thus undermining for good the UPR Mechanism and depriving it of its unique character.

60 See Sections 2.3 and 4.4. A rather vivid and comprehensive summary of how issues were dealt with by the Bureau concerning these

with several situations when the identification of the delegation legally entrusted with the responsibility to represent the country was somewhat complex.

3.2.3 The President's Roles and Responsibilities Regarding the Appointment of Special Procedures Mandate-holders and Members of Commissions of Inquiry or Fact-Finding Missions

Appointment of Special Procedures Mandate-holders

At the time of the establishment of the Council, there existed a vast array of mechanisms created by the Commission. Their existence and importance were recognized in paragraph 6 of Resolution 60/251, which requested the Council to assume, review, and, where necessary, improve and rationalize all mandates, mechanisms, functions and responsibilities in order to maintain a system of Special Procedures, expert advice, and a complaint procedure.

The Council completed this task in two steps.

(1) Firstly, in the context of Resolution 5/1, it established a framework for the review, rationalization, and improvements of mandates,[61] and decided, as a transitional step, that the mandates included in Appendix I[62] of the resolution would be renewed until the date on which they were considered by the Council according to its programme of work.[63]

---

matters appears in the minutes of the Bureau meetings of 1, 3 and 7 February 2022.

61 See paras 54–64 of Council Resolution 60/251.

62 All existing mandates but two were included in the list – which were thus considered abolished by their non-mention in the Appendix I (Belarus and Cuba) of Resolution 5/1.

63 See para 62, ibid., according to which 'current mandate-holders may continue serving, provided they have not exceeded the six-year term limit'. However, 'on an exceptional basis, the term of those mandate-holders who have served more than six years may be extended until the relevant mandate is considered by the Council and the selection and appointment process had concluded'. In practical terms, the mandates and mandate-holders referred to in

(2) Secondly, once Resolution 5/1 was approved, the Council initiated the review, rationalization and improvement[64] process of Special Procedures from its 5th to 9th sessions, as had been requested by the General Assembly.

A considerable amount of time was spent delineating a new manner to select and appoint mandate-holders.

During the Commission years, the selection process was quite succinct and left a wide margin of appreciation to the Commission President. Commission Decision 2000/109 of 26 April 2000, which approved the outcome of the Working Group on enhancing the effectiveness of the mechanisms of the Commission, simply mentioned that the 'selection of mandate-holders will continue to be the responsibility of the Chairperson following formal consultation with the Bureau and the regional groups through the regional coordinators. In appointing mandate-holders, the professional and personal qualities of the individual – expertise and experience in the area of the mandate, independence and impartiality – (would) be of paramount importance'.

Much criticism was raised regarding the opacity of a system that provided almost free hands to the successive Presidents without any form of oversight by the Commission. Similarly, the non-exhaustive but public list of candidates (proposed by States and all appropriate sources, including ECOSOC-status NGOs and the OHCHR) was elaborated by the Office of the High Commissioner for Human Rights. The President was expected to give priority consideration to suitable names on that list but could also consider additional nominations. The consequences, in terms of building a close network of potential candidates and the influence of politics on the selection process, were often regretted. Once again, the politicization of the Commission's processes was pinpointed and criticized. It was observed that the opacity of the system provided ample and discrete opportunities for diplomatic pressures on the President. Retrospectively, however, it is fair to recognize that Special Rapporteurs who operated during the Commission's time had, in their vast majority, been experts of exceptional independence and competence.

Appendices I and II of the resolution were extended until the process was over.

64 Which was referred to under its abbreviation, RRI.

Against this background, the Council established a complex system[65] which was conceptualized, in contrast to the previous one, as a transparent mechanism with a set of clear criteria to be followed in a four-tier approach:

- A public list of candidates is to be established by the Office of the High Commissioner.
- A Consultative Group, composed of five representatives of Member of Observer States, is established for every cycle and requested to propose to the President, in a public manner, a short-list of candidates.
- The President is called upon to consult broadly, particularly through regional coordinators, and to identify an appropriate candidate for each vacancy. As a result, the President is requested to present to Member States and Observers a list of candidates.
- If necessary, the President is requested to conduct further consultations to ensure the endorsement of the proposed candidate. The appointment of the Special Procedures mandate-holders is expected to be contemplated upon the subsequent approval of the Council before the end of the concerned session.

That procedure was fine-tuned in subsequent years, particularly at the time of the Review,[66] to provide even greater transparency as well as ensuring that short-listed candidates are interviewed. The President was also requested to justify his/her decision if they decided not to follow the order of priority proposed by the Consultative Group.

What was expected to provide objective and straightforward tools to the President and dissipate any doubts regarding the outcome of the process proved to be far more challenging than initially anticipated.

Certainly, when the names of candidates proposed by the Consultative Group were included in the President's list and approved by the Council without any difficulty, the system operated at its best and provided a gratifying level of transparency and efficiency. It should be recognized that in the vast majority of cases, this process worked out smoothly, to the satisfaction of all concerned.

---

65 See paras 54–64 of the Council Resolution 5/1.

66 See para 22 of the Council Resolution 16/21.

However, three types of difficulties may arise based on the letter and spirit of Resolution 5/1:

- It may so happen that, for a variety of reasons, the President may differ in his/her assessment of the list provided by the Consultative Group, particularly regarding the proposed order of candidates, and may disregard it partially or completely.
- It may also happen that the list prepared by the President may not suit some States in the Council.
- It may eventually happen that such disagreements transpire only at the level of the plenary when a decision is expected to be made, thus compromising or blurring the outcome of the decision-making process, leading to the postponement of the concerned decision to a later meeting of the (Organizational) Session.

In these cases, the Council Presidents have seen their responsibilities broaden considerably. Unfortunately, since nothing happening at the Council may be deemed truly confidential, such Presidential responsibilities have occasionally fallen under close scrutiny, and their holders have had to negotiate simultaneously with a multiplicity of stakeholders holding divergent views.

This uncomfortable situation has, however, strengthened the visibility and importance of the role of the President. This is particularly the case since, with the multiplication of the number of mandate-holders and the strict application of the rule limiting the mandate-holders' tenure to no more than six years, controversies regarding the choice of new candidates may occur more often than once during any Council cycle.

There is no clear rule on how to proceed when there is no consensual support in the plenary for a President's list. In cases when this happens, the practice is that the whole list of candidates proposed by the President is set aside, and a decision postponed to the next possible opportunity. This is based on the need to ensure that the special procedures are the emanation of the entire Council and not only a majority of its members. To proceed otherwise would put an end to the imperious principle of independence of the special procedures mandate-holders, or at least the perception of it. Also, postponing the decision on the entire list and not only the contested nomination is a prerequisite to ensure that there is no finger-pointing on one particular mandate, thus weakening its status and modus operandi.

At times, the postponement of a list of candidates may become very tense and complex due to the increased bilateralization of such matters. Indeed, it appears that in some circumstances, objections are made by States not only based on some elements in the candidates' backgrounds but also on their nationality, a fact which is deeply worrying.

In such delicate terrain, successive Presidents opted for different approaches. Some preferred to act in a confidential manner, accelerating and deepening their informal consultations with States or groups of States. Others opted for more open procedures with meetings of their Bureau and regional coordinators with a view to come to a clear understanding of the situation and identify a way out. The minutes of the Bureau meetings of 18 July, 22 August and 5 September 2023 shed light on how such matters are being dealt with, although in most circumstances, this is done off record or in a more informal manner.

Appointment of Members of Commissions of Inquiry or Fact-Finding Missions and Similar Mechanisms

The Council Presidents have retained a large margin of manoeuvre concerning the appointment of members of COI/FFMs. Such mechanisms were excluded from the institution-building package, as their use was considered exceptional at the time of the Commission. With the vast increase in the number of mandates and mechanisms established by the Council, successive Presidents have often been requested to appoint several members to such commissions or missions. The enabling resolutions have usually broadly defined what the President was expected to do.[67] Given that the roles and responsibilities of the President had not been envisaged in Resolution 5/1, and the establishment of these bodies presupposed that appointments had to be made as urgently as possible,[68] it was considered by default that the President should be provided with the same prerogatives as during the time of the Commission. Hence, the nominations of members to COI/FFMs often operate in a rather opaque manner, without specific rules applied. The process implicitly requires

67 Normally, three or more members are appointed based on vaguely defined criteria such as independence, impartiality, expertise, etc.

68 In almost all cases, COIs or FFMs are expected to report orally to the following Council Sessions, thus leaving only a few months for the establishment of such Commission and the creation of a core Secretariat.

the President to operate based on consultations and based on lists proposed by the Office of the High Commissioner.

The proper medium for informing the public at large of the appointment of the concerned commissions or missions is through a press release, followed by appropriate references in the context of public meetings of the Council whenever they may take place. Should there be issues – for instance, conflicts of interest – emerging either further or during the nomination process, they are dealt with directly by the President. Although the procedure is deprived of the obligation to publicize list of candidates or shed light on the rationale of the President's decision, it would be intellectually challenging not to consider that, in certain instances, some controversial matters might have reached the public domain.[69]

Complaints Against Special Procedure Mandate Holders or Members of Investigation Bodies

The Institution-building package and related texts are quite clear on how the special procedure mandate holders are appointed. The Council's practice is also very clear on how members of investigation bodies are selected. There is, however, no such clarity on how to deal with complaints against the experts' activities. Resolution 5/2, which established a Code of Conduct for Special Procedures Mandate-holders of the Human Rights Council, did not specify how any complaint in this regard should be dealt with.

Preambular paragraph 13 of the said resolution stated very clearly that one should distinguish between, on the one hand, the independence of mandate-holders, which is absolute in nature, and, on the other hand, their prerogatives, as circumscribed by their mandate, the mandate of the Human Rights Council, and the provisions of the Charter of the United Nations. However, it did not provide any assistance on how to implement this provision and related ones. This was for very good reasons linked to the impossibility of agreeing on any mechanism or tool in this regard. During the negotiations of what would become Resolution 16/21, several

69 Since the related cases were exclusively referred to in the social network or some media and certainly not in any official Council documentation, they are not mentioned here.

references were made to the possibility of setting up a body entrusted with the task of monitoring the implementation of the Code of Conduct. However, a great divergence of views emerged, and it became impossible to create such a body.[70]

As a result of the inability of the international community to agree on any specific procedure in relation to the action by special procedure mandate-holders, and by extension by members of investigation bodies, successive Presidents of the Council became recipients of complaints in this regard. It is extremely rare that such complaints are referred to in public documents.

However, in September 2020, two complaints were received by the President and discussed by the Bureau. From the minutes of the Bureau meeting of 3 September 2020, it emerged that on '31 August 2020, she had received two letters from groups of States concerning two mandate holders: the first concerns Mr. Joseph Cannataci, Special Rapporteur on the right to privacy; and the second concerns Ms. Agnes Callamard, Special Rapporteur on extrajudicial, summary or arbitrary executions. [*The letters were posted on the Extranet upon receipt and are attached to these minutes for ease of reference.*]'

The Bureau discussed the letters and agreed to formally transmit them to the Coordination Committee of the Special Procedures with the request to provide the Bureau with the Committee's assessment and recommendations, as well as any additional information it deems useful, at its earliest convenience. The Bureau further agreed to continue with the consideration of the matter once the response of the Coordination Committee is received.

A few days later,[71] the Bureau

> noted with appreciation that the Coordination Committee had taken this matter very seriously and held numerous meetings and consultations in the short period of time that was made available to them. The Bureau highlighted the relevance of the internal procedures that already exist, including the

70 See for instance, 'Hobbling the Monitors: Should UN Human Rights Monitors be Accountable' by Philip Alston (*Harvard International Law Journal*, Volume 52, Number 2, Summer 2011).

71 See minutes of the Bureau meeting of 9 September 2020.

> advisory procedure established in June 2008, to enhance the effectiveness and preserve the integrity of the system of special procedures, and that allow to address questions, concerns and complaints raised by States and other relevant stakeholders concerning the working methods and other issues related to Special Procedures mandate holders. The Bureau welcomed that with regard to the Special Rapporteur on the right to privacy, the Committee had informed in its letter that it was willing to work with the mandate holder, the States concerned and the President of the Council in the coming weeks in order to facilitate interaction and the sharing of information between all parties concerned. The President informed that she would be willing to engage in such a process with the Coordination Committee and the Special Rapporteur concerned.
>
> With regard to the question of when the members and observers of the Council may discuss this and other matters related to the working methods of special procedures, the Bureau appreciated the Committee's willingness to organise its next conversation with States and other stakeholders in the weeks to come. The Bureau additionally underscored that the General Debate under item 5 also provides a place for delegations to discuss issues related to the Special Procedures.
>
> The Bureau therefore agreed to share the letter of the Coordination Committee with all delegations and to support the use of the established internal procedures, such as the advisory procedure of the Coordination Committee to address complaints against mandate holders of the Special Procedures.

Of significant importance, the President and her Bureau filled an important vacuum in the institution-building package by underlining in a very clear manner that complaints in relation to the activities or conduct of the Special Procedure mandate-holders had to be dealt with by the Coordinating Committee of the Special Procedures. It is or was often mentioned that the Coordinating Committee or the Bureau never took any concrete measures against the action – or lack of – by a Special Procedure mandate. To counter this argument, it may be of relevance to pinpoint the following minutes of the Bureau meeting of 2 March 2021 which are self-explanatory: 'The President recalled that on 31 August 2020, the then-President had received a letter from a group of States concerning the Special Rapporteur on the right to privacy, Mr. Joseph Cannataci, and the six country visit reports that the Special Rapporteur had not yet presented to the Council. The then-Bureau had transmitted the letter to the Coordination Committee along with the request for the Committee to provide its assessment and recommendations. The Committee had informed the then-Bureau that it was willing to work with the mandate-holder, the States concerned and the President of the Council in order to facilitate interaction and the sharing of information between all parties concerned. The President additionally recalled that on 9 September 2020, the then-Bureau had agreed to support the use of established internal procedures such as the advisory procedure of the Coordination Committee to address complaints against mandate-holders of the Special Procedures.

In this regard, the President appraised the Bureau that the Chair of the Coordination Committee for Special Procedures had informed her that the Special Rapporteur had submitted only three of the six country visit reports sufficiently in advance of the scheduled presentation of those reports. The Chair had briefed the President about all of the efforts and actions taken by the Committee on this case since early 2020. However, in light of the absence of three reports and after a lengthy process, the Committee had informed the Special Rapporteur that, pursuant to the object and purpose of the Internal Advisory Procedure, it regrettably found itself in a position not to be able to support him or his decisions on this matter.

The Secretariat additionally informed the Bureau that, since his appointment in June 2016, the Special Rapporteur on the right to privacy undertook six country visits: two in 2017; two in 2018; and two in 2019, and that the reports of these visits have not been presented to the Council. The Secretariat clarified that three of these reports had been submitted and made publicly available on the reports webpage of the 46th session and informed that the Special Rapporteur's report of his country visit to the United Kingdom had been received by the Secretariat on Friday, 26 February. The Secretariat additionally recalled that the country concerned should have a minimum of four weeks to respond or comment on their country visit report before it is presented to the Council.

In light of the fact that the three outstanding reports (the United Kingdom, Republic of Korea and Germany) had not been submitted at least four weeks ahead of the scheduled date of presentation, the Bureau confirmed that those reports would not be presented to the Council for its consideration during the current session.

The Bureau expressed strong dissatisfaction with the current state of affairs, particularly with the failure of the mandate-holder to fulfil his reporting obligations to the Council. The Bureau noted that various stakeholders, including the former President of the Council, the Coordination Committee of Special Procedures, and States have repeatedly raised their concerns related to this matter with the Special Rapporteur for more than a year. Underscoring that reporting on country visits is a fundamental part and parcel of the reporting obligations of mandate holders, the Bureau reiterated that these visits are an important mandated activity of special procedures mandate-holders and that the presentation of the related reports to the Council is an integral part of this process as it provides the opportunity for engagement with the country concerned and the Council as a whole.

The Bureau further stressed the exceptional nature of this case and noted that this was the first time the Council was facing such a situation.

The President highlighted that the presentation of the reports and the interactive dialogue with the Special Rapporteur on the right to privacy was scheduled to take place on 5 March 2021 and indicated that she had been in contact with the six countries concerned with the country visit reports in order to seek their views on the situation and the way forward.

As a consequence of not having presented all of his country visit reports, and given the advice of the Coordination Committee, the Bureau decided that the presentation by the Special Rapporteur on the right to privacy of the annual thematic report and all country visit reports and the related interactive dialogue scheduled to take place during the 46th session would be cancelled. The Bureau further agreed that the Special Rapporteur would be urged to submit the outstanding country visit reports prior to 15 April 2021, and the Bureau would reconvene on this matter following that deadline to discuss and decide on next steps. .

At the time of proofreading the current edition, another matter of importance arose which was discussed by the bureau extensively. On 1 April 2025, the President informed the Bureau that he had received a letter from the Permanent Representative of Israel alleging persistent non-compliance of the Special Rapporteur on the Palestinian Territories occupied since 1967, Ms. Francesca Albanase, with the provisions of the Code of Conduct of the Special Procedures. The meticulous procedure followed by the Bureau included consultations with the Coordination Committee which in a letter dated 28 March 2025 attached to the minutes of the Bureau concluded that there had been not violations of the Code of Conduct by the concerned Special Rapporteur. During the same Bureau meeting the President referred to conversations with both the Chairs of the Coordination Committee and the Special Rapporteur regarding personal attacks faced by the Special Rapporteur and the negative consequences on her family and those working with her. The issues discussed during this meeting and summarized in the minutes referred both to the ways Special Rapporteurs should fulfil their mandates and the issue of personal attacks against mandate-holders.

As a caveat, it should be underlined that a body similar to the Coordinating Committee does not exist insofar as the members of investigation bodies are concerned. Accordingly, any complaint in this regard may only be addressed using the good offices of the President and his/her Bureau.

Also of importance, it should be noted that while the President has the authority to propose to the Council the selection of Special Procedure mandate-holders and to designate directly members of investigation bodies, s/he does not have any responsibility in dismissing them should s/he consider their actions or conduct inappropriate. This results directly from the principles of independence and impartiality of mandate-holders or members of investigation bodies. Should such a prerogative be granted to the President, this would de facto trigger an avalanche of complaints against experts, thus nullifying these two principles.

3.3 The New York - Geneva gap

The General Assembly Resolution 60/251 decided to establish the Council in replacement of the Commission as a 'subsidiary body of the General Assembly'. It did not, however, elaborate on the legal and practical consequences of this decision. In particular, from the start, the Council Presidents had to face issues regarding the interaction between the Council and the General Assembly, particularly its Third Committee.

The challenges faced by the Council in this regard have often been referred to as a so-called 'gap' between Geneva and New York, and related in particular to different perceptions about the respective responsibilities of the Council and of the General Assembly, particularly its Third Committee. This gap was, and continues to be, reinforced by the lack of coordination among diplomatic missions in both cities.

This gap has at times risked generating a complete disconnection between the two bodies. This was particularly the case when the Third Committee decided to defer consideration and action on given resolutions that were validly adopted by the Council. The General Assembly's re-opening of a resolution of the Council was considered by successive Presidents as weakening the authority and competence of the Council, as well as undermining the integrity of the whole UN human rights system.

Since the success and impact of the Council depend greatly on coordination and cooperation between Geneva and New York, successive Presidents have visited the UN Headquarters several times per year and, since 2011, after each Council session. These efforts underline the importance attached by the Presidents to strengthening efforts to enhance genuine and constructive dialogue with the Council.

At first, issues arose regarding how the Council's Annual Report should be presented at the General Assembly and/or the Third Committee. Whereas the President of the Council's First Cycle argued that the report should be presented at the plenary only, some of his New York counterparts at times considered that this should be dealt with exclusively at the Third Committee level. After several years of hesitation and exchanges between the General Assembly and the Council, through their Presidents, the Assembly, in paragraph 6 of its Resolution 65/281 of 17 June 2011 on the status of the Council, decided:

> to continue its practice of allocating the agenda item entitled 'Report of the Human Rights Council' to the plenary of the General Assembly and to the Third Committee, in accordance with its decision 65/503 A, with the additional understanding that the President of the Council will present the report in her or his capacity as President to the plenary of the General Assembly and the Third Committee and that the Third Committee will hold an interactive dialogue with the President of the Council at the time of her or his presentation of the report of the Council to the Third Committee.

Additional difficulties arose regarding the roles of the General Assembly concerning the resolutions adopted by the Council, as well as its Annual Report. While there was no difficulty regarding the Council's decisions requiring specific action by the General Assembly,[72] issues arose in relation to the possibility (or not) that the General Assembly, upon recommendation of the Third Committee, could postpone or alter the contents of a resolution[73] adopted by the Council in its own right. Successive Council Presidents have upheld the view, during their exchanges with

72 For instance, in relation to the Council's standard-setting activities.
73 This happened in the cases of Council's Resolutions 1/2 and 24/24.

the General Assembly and the Third Committee, that such texts should under no circumstances be reopened by the General Assembly. This understanding has, however, not yet been confirmed in any General Assembly resolution or decision, leaving the matter in a blurred status. It is the author's opinion that the role and status of the Council as the main UN human rights body should prevent any reopening of its deliberations – with the obvious exception of standard-setting activities, which are to be endorsed by the Assembly.

Similarly, doubts remain as to whether the Council's own Annual Report may be reopened by the Assembly. Despite significant efforts by the Council's Presidents, the General Assembly's resolutions taking note of the Council's Annual Reports have almost systematically been put to a vote, thereby testifying to the desire of some States to be in a position to reopen the matter for various reasons if they so wish.

As described in the previous chapter, successive Presidents have used the opportunity of their regular official visits to New York to establish or strengthen relationships with other UN bodies.

As far as the financial implications of the Council's resolutions – the amount of which has reached important levels commensurate with the increased activities of the Council – further significant efforts by the Council's Presidents and others put the matter to rest at the end of the Review process: in paragraph 7 of its Resolution 65/281, the Assembly decided 'to consider through its Fifth Committee all financial implications emanating from the resolutions and decisions contained in the annual report of the Human Rights Council, including those emanating from its September session'. The concrete implications of this apparently unexciting provision are of significant importance. In practical terms, all decisions and resolutions contained in the Council's Annual Reports are now channelled simultaneously to the Third and Fifth Committees (and not consecutively), a fact which strengthened the Council's status vis-à-vis the Third Committee.

The above-mentioned steps would not have been achieved without the successive Presidents embodying the Council and representing its interests to the best of their abilities during visits to the UN Headquarters and interactions with a multiplicity of actors.

3.4 Representing the Council outside Geneva

The Council was established to replace the Commission and at a higher level. Its activities and involvement expanded significantly over the years, and it is generally considered the highest UN body dealing with human rights. Consequently, the successive Presidents were approached and invited to a variety of events. Budget constraints[74] and the heavy nature of the Presidential mandate, however, have made it extremely difficult for Presidents to accommodate all invitations. Nevertheless, aside from the regular visits to New York – which are budgeted and are to be read in the context of the Geneva – New York relationship – three categories of Presidential participation in external activities may be identified:

(1) The Presidents have been invited to brief and interact with regional organizations. Successive Presidents have thus attended sessions of the Ministerial Committee of Human Rights of the Council of Europe,[75] and human rights institutions within the European Union.[76] The President of the 12th Council Cycle participated in an OHCHR Regional Workshop for small islands developing States held in Georgetown (Guyana), during which he visited CARICOM and held official meetings with senior Guyanese authorities. The President of the 13th Council Cycle participated in a similar Workshop in Nadi (Fiji). He also undertook an official mission to the Headquarters of the African Union, where he addressed the Peace and Security Council of the African Union and met the Chairperson of the African Union Commission and the Special Representative of the Secretary-General to the African Union. The Presidents of the 16th and 17th Council Cycles also extended their visits to NY headquarters by a visit to multilateral financial institutions and the OAS

74 A maximum of three annual visits to New York is budgeted.

75 February 2013, 2014, 2015, 2016, 2018, 2022, 2023 and 2024.

76 Working Party on Human Rights of the Council of the European Union (15 November 2016 and May 2018); Sub-Committee on Human Rights of the European Parliament (9 November 2009, July 2015 and 15 November 2016); and the EU Political and Security Committee (May 2018). Visits to the EU Headquarters were also organized in 2007 and 2008. Visits in 2023 and 2024 were of a broader nature and included discussions with various representatives and bodies.

Headquarters in Washington, DC. The President of the 18th Council Cycle participated in a Regional Workshop for small islands developing States held in the Maldives.

(2) Council Presidents have also participated in various external activities organized by the OHCHR or UN entities, such as an international conference in Nairobi on National Human Rights Institutions organized by the International Coordination Committee of NHRIs,[77] the 2nd World Forum on Human Rights held in Marrakech in November 2014, and a SIDS/LDCs meeting in Mauritius in July 2013.

(3) Council Presidents have also been invited to international gatherings or national visits; examples include visits to Brazil (25–30 April 2009)[78] and Bahrain (16–20 May 2009),[79] as well as participation in a cross-regional perspective on best practices and policies for promoting religious tolerance and strengthening resilience in Singapore in June 2016. Other invitations have been entertained on a more informal basis and, as such, are not accounted for in official Council documentation.

3.5 Additional responsibilities[80]

In recent years, successive Presidents have taken it upon themselves to organize or launch initiatives that were of an unexpected nature. This was linked with the considerable extension of the Council's work and the increasing role played by the President and his/her bureau since the COVID-19 pandemic. Illustrations of this role were provided in the above section 2.5 on the COVID-19 pandemic, including the intense activities deployed by the Bureaux in stewarding the Council during this difficult period of time.

---

77 3 October 2008.

78 A/HRC/11/CRP.4.

79 A/HRC/11/CRP.5.

80 Other initiatives deserve to be included therein, such as the organization of a commemorative event to celebrate the HRC 50th session on 15 June 2022; a 'bring your child to the Council' informal event held on 21 September during an informal mock Council meeting; or a segment of the Organizational Meeting of 30 August 2022 to bid farewell to High Commissioner Michele Bachelet.

Also, the Presidents intensified their efforts in dealing with the necessary rationalization of the Council's modus operandi and its consideration of thematic issues of interest by organizing informal meetings or conversations – for instance, on fostering freedom of expression through the UPR process organized with UNESCO on 5 September 2022. More recently, the President of the 18th cycle organized high-level informal Presidential discussions on the link between climate change, food security and health security on 20 June 2024 and on artificial intelligence, new technologies and the digital divide and their impact on human rights on 3 September 2024 with the active participation of several Heads of Agencies and senior officials from the UN.

Aside from his efforts concerning the efficiency and effectiveness process, the President of the 18th cycle also established the first President of the Council's Advisory Board on Gender Equality to provide guidance and suggestions on advancing gender equality and helping mainstream a gender perspective during his presidency.

In line with the principles of gender balance and fully integrating a gender perspective in the work of the Council and its mechanisms, as established in Council Resolution 5/1, as well as the Council's mandate to mainstream human rights within the United Nations system, as established in General Assembly Resolution 60/251, the Advisory Board, with both normative and operational expertise, would be an informal space for critical thinking, analysis and advice to support the President of the Human Rights Council in mainstreaming gender equality and women's empowerment throughout the Council, with the aim of accelerating and making tangible gains on the agenda and improving the lives of women and girls around the globe. The Advisory Board would also give the opportunity to UN agencies and International Organizations based in Geneva to share their good practices, achievements, and challenges towards achieving gender equality in their own institutions.[81]

---

81 See minutes of the Bureau meeting of 22 August 2024.

4 The Human Rights Council stakeholders

A body is composed of organs, which need to be described, and the role and functions of which need to be fully grasped. Two or more organs working together in the execution of specific body functions form an organ system. This chapter aims to study the various stakeholders of the Council with a view to understanding their roles and prerogatives and, consequently, grasping the level at which they interact.

In most United Nations or other international organizations, many, if not all, participants of official meetings are representatives of Member States. At times, representatives of other organizations or agencies may be provided with the right to address the gathering. However, there is usually no provision for the participation of other stakeholders or the public at large.

In stark contrast with such bodies, the Council's stakeholders are quite numerous and of a variable nature, comprising representatives of States, international organizations, NGOs, national institutions, and other stakeholders such as experts and individuals.

4.1 Member States

As a testimony to the intense discussions that preceded the establishment of the Council, General Assembly Resolution 60/251 includes several provisions relating to the quality, number, election, as well as the roles and responsibilities of the Council Members.

While some voices expressed the wish to create a body reduced to 15 Members, in manner similar to the Security Council, others pleaded for a body membership that would have remained much closer to the composition of ECOSOC[1] and, consequently, that of the Commission on Human Rights.[2] The consensus that emerged from strenuous negotiations was that the new body should be composed of 47 Members. Members were to be elected directly and individually by secret ballot, requiring a majority of the Members of the General Assembly, with a provision that the rights of membership of any Member may be suspended by the General Assembly should it commit gross and systematic violations of human rights.

The *quality of membership* was thus subjected to several provisions, their intent being to uphold the fact that being a Member of the Council bears with it rights but also responsibilities.

- According to paragraph 7 of the resolution, Members of the Council are elected directly and individually by secret ballot by the majority of the Members of the General Assembly.
- Paragraph 8 indicates that, whereas the elections are open to all States that are Members of the United Nations, their contributions to the promotion and protection of human rights, as well as their voluntary pledges and commitments, should be taken into account.
- The same paragraph provides that the General Assembly, by a two-thirds majority of the Members present and voting, may suspend the rights of membership in the Council of a Member of the Council that commits gross and systematic violations of human rights.
- Further to paragraph 9, the Members elected to the Council must uphold the highest standards in the promotion and protection of human rights, fully cooperate with the Council and be reviewed under the UPR during their term of membership.

The said resolution did not, however, provide any modus operandi for these provisions to be translated into deeds. It was mostly left to the wishes of the General Assembly's Member States.

The following elements may be mentioned in this context.

---

1 Fifty-four Members.
2 Fifty-three Members.

4.1.1 Clean Slates

At the United Nations, the normal practice when the number of candidates corresponds to the number of seats to be filled, a practice referred to as 'clean slates', is to dispense with the election by secret ballots. However, in accordance with the above-mentioned paragraph 7, as far as the Council is concerned, whatever the number of candidates and available slots, the practice of clean slates is automatically waived. This desire to eliminate the clean slates' practice contrasts with the common practice in the UN General Assembly and ECOSOC environments. Indeed, the practice normally followed by the General Assembly and most subsidiary organs[3] provides for dispensing with the secret ballot for elections to subsidiary organs when the number of candidates corresponds to the number of seats to be filled, unless a delegation specifically requests a vote on a given election. Given the letter of paragraph 7 of Resolution 60/251, elections by secret ballot are thus being held whatever the number of candidates.[4]

However, given the absence of a mechanism to avoid clean slates in practice, it remains that in most circumstances since the creation of the Council, de facto clean slates have been by far the preferred way of electing Members despite the strong but indirect inducements contained in paragraphs 8 and 9 of Resolution 60/251.

It may be argued that, in accordance with the letter and spirit of the resolution, even in cases of clean slates, it would be possible to set aside a candidate considered as not upholding the highest standards in terms of the promotion and protection of human rights. In practical terms, this situation has never arisen and in all circumstances, Members elected via a clean slate process always received a number of votes much higher than the prescribed 97 votes. This may be considered an oddity, given that the number of sponsors of Council or General Assembly

---

3 See para 16 of the General Assembly Decision 34/401 on the rationalization of the procedures and organization of the General Assembly, which appears as Annex V to the General Assembly Rules of Procedure.

4 It is of interest to note that the subsidiary bodies of the Council are not subjected to the same restrictive rule and that, for instance, Members of the Council Advisory Committee are often selected by clean slates.

resolutions on certain fundamental rights or issues often exceeds 100 States. Theoretically, one might expect these sponsors may not cast a ballot in favour of candidates they may consider problematic in terms of their human rights record. Nevertheless, it should be recalled that the General Assembly's practices concerning elections to subsidiary bodies are not conducive to a substantive assessment of the validity or opportunity of a candidate against specific criteria but respond to other, often political, imperatives.

Since the establishment of the Council and in the spirit of paragraph 7, many comments have been offered regarding the imperative need to ensure that there are more candidates than seats to be filled. This was and is often included in groups' or individual States' submissions in relation to the Council's elections. References are thus commonly made to the spirit of Resolution 60/251 as well as the intent of the negotiators, many of whom advocated strongly for the establishment of a democratic Council composed of Members fully committed to the protection and promotion of human rights. Additionally, it is also linked to the interests of transparency, fairness and quality of membership, the underlying idea being that the main UN intergovernmental body in charge of human rights should comprise States that are deploying genuine efforts to protect and promote human rights. The presence of those facing basic and grave human rights situations is thus considered by some as contrary to this wish.

Furthermore, it may be advanced that the practice of clean slates runs to an extent against the spirit of paragraphs 7–9, when read jointly. Indeed, when the number of candidates in a regional group matches the number of available seats, the outcome is, as mentioned, obvious. This deprives others of the ability to evaluate and ponder the contribution of States to the cause of human rights before electing them to the Council.

However, the data tell a story that is not in line with such wishes. Whereas 18 elections have been held since 2006, one regional group[5] proceeded with non-clean-slate elections in only one case, whereas the four other regional groups did so in between five and nine cases (out of 18)[6] only.

5 The African Group in 2013.

6 The Asian Group in 2006, 2008, 2014, 2015, 2017, 2019, 2020, 2022 and 2024; the Eastern European Group in 2006, 2007, 2008, 2011,

This is equivalent to saying that for the Western European and Others Group, there were only 25 per cent of elections (a quarter) held with a minimum level of competition against 75 per cent (three-quarters), the results of which were absolutely clear before the ballots were even cast. It is hard to refrain from noticing a bit of irony in this particular case considering that some members of this particular group often refer to the need for introducing more democracy in the choice of Council Members.

Accordingly, beyond the rhetoric, which is not without a high level of politicization, ways and means remain to be identified to translate the relevant provisions of Resolution 60/251 into deeds, which otherwise appear as wishful thinking. It is, however, fair to state that such a goal is difficult to attain. In addition to the wish of certain countries to ensure their (re)election at all costs, the main impediment to this goal is obviously the reluctance of many to be candidates in an open race and run the risk of losing an election.

Lastly, one should bear in mind that the responsibilities attached to becoming a Member of the Council and the organizational, logistical and administrative consequences attached to it are quite significant, a fact which deterred many potential candidates, particularly SIDS and LDC, from presenting themselves for election.[7] Thanks in part to the activity of the Trust Fund on SIDS and LDCs, this trend seems to be on the verge of being reversed. Indeed, the President of the 13th Council Cycle was also the first one to come from an LDC (Senegal) and at the 15th cycle, the President (Fiji) and two Vice-Presidents (Bahamas and Somalia) came from SIDS/LDC countries.

Although some would argue it is commonsense that some States should be excluded from becoming Members, the complexity of the human rights system and the realities of our contemporary world make it extremely difficult to concretize any attempt at formalizing or identifying criteria that would ban certain UN Members from acceding to the Council.

2016 and 2023; the Group of Latin America and the Caribbean in 2006, 2011, 2013, 2014, 2016, 2019, 2022 and 2023; and the Western European and Others Group in 2006, 2007, 2008, 2012 and 2015.

7 This is especially the case for those countries which either do not have a Permanent Mission in Geneva or do not have enough staff and capacity for that effect.

Human rights treaty bodies often point out that there is no human rights paradise on earth and that human rights violations occur in all countries in the world. It should also be emphasized that the key question regarding the threshold for membership to the Council is yet unresolved and consequently the criteria that may be used to determine whether a UN Member State fulfils the requirements for membership have never been clearly spelt out, nor is there is an instance assessing them.

Some of the proposed criteria – deemed to be objective – advanced during the Resolution 60/251 negotiation process or at a later stage appear quite inadequate in this regard. For instance, ratifying the main human rights instruments, not being overdue in submitting reports to treaty bodies, or extending a standing invitation to all Special Rapporteurs do not guarantee that the country is beyond reproach. It is commonly known that some countries have fulfilled these criteria while the human rights situation prevailing in their country was far from ideal. It is also very clear that others may not meet these criteria due to capacity constraints but have generally ensured a safe human rights environment.

It may be advanced that the only criterion with a semblance of objectivity would be that States under investigation or inquiry initiated by the Council may not fulfil the requirements in paragraphs 7–9 of the said resolution. This would align with the principle of not being judge and jury on its own case. The mechanism for such criteria to be set into motion is, however, particularly hard to envisage in a world mostly driven by political perceptions and would not be entirely fair since a number of acute human rights situations are not addressed by the Council whereas common sense may argue that they should. Additionally, this approach would further polarize discussions, as any State contemplating the possibility of barring another from candidacy might lobby vigorously to initiate a mechanism against it. Would this be in the spirit of the said resolution? This remains to be considered in depth.

Correlated to the above issues is the possibility for the General Assembly to deprive a Council Member State of its rights of membership. This has occurred in only one instance, as mentioned above, at the conclusion of the 15th Special Session of the Council on 'the situation of human rights in the Libyan Arab Jamahiriya', held on 25 February 2011. At the request of the delegation of Libya – whose Members had defected dramatically during the meeting – the Council recommended to the General Assembly that, 'in view of the gross and systematic violations of human rights by the Libyan authorities, consider the application of the measures foreseen in paragraph 8 of General Assembly Resolution 60/251'.[8]

Based on this precedent, when a country is deprived of its membership rights, the consequences are drastic. Contrary to common perception, the said Member State does not retain the rights attached to Observer States. This is because it remains de jure a Member but without the rights attached to it. It can therefore not be considered an Observer State. Hence, it cannot speak unless specifically invited to do so as a concerned country, cannot table an initiative, and cannot raise a procedural motion. Additionally, the delegation's seat is moved to the end of the Member's rank, before that of the Observers. This whole scenario had to be developed, as there was no precedent within the UN system.

An unexpected scenario emerged in 2018 when the United States decided to withdraw from the Council. In a Note Verbale dated 19 June 2018, the United States Mission to the United Nations conveyed an official notification that the United States had resigned its membership in the Human Rights Council, effective 5:00 p.m., 19 June 2018. Furthermore, the United States Mission revealed that the United States would not participate further in the June session or in future sessions, and would not serve out the remainder of its term. This decision translated into deeds by the absence of the United States delegations from any Council session, even as an Observer State.

As a result of this decision, Iceland was elected on 13 July 2018 to serve as a member of the Council from 13 July 2018 for the remainder of the United States' mandate.

Several years later, the General Assembly met and agreed to suspend the rights of membership of the Russian Federation. This decision was taken by way of UNGA Resolution ES/11/3 of 7 April 2022. Aware of the Libyan Arab Jamahiriya precedent, the Russian Federation informed the President of its country's decision to resign from the Council before term.[9] Many questions were raised as to the possibility for a Council Member State to resign after the withdrawal of its rights to membership by the General Assembly. Seized with the matter by the Secretariat, the

8 See para 14 of the Council Resolution A/HRC/RES/S-15/1.

9 See minutes of the Bureau meeting of 12 April 2022

Office of Legal Affairs confirmed that there was nothing in Resolutions ES/11/3 and 60/251 that would limit Russia's ability to withdraw or resign as a Member. Additionally, whether the resignation occurred before or after the adoption of the resolution withdrawing the rights of membership did not make any difference. Lastly, the Secretariat informed that whether Member States not members of the Council wished to attend future sessions of the Council appeared to be a matter for each member to decide, including the Russian Federation.

Further to the resignation of the Russian Federation, the Czech Republic was elected by the General Assembly on 10 May 2022 to fill the vacancy and complete the term of membership of the Russian Federation.

4.1.2 Apportionment of Seats

Moving from a subsidiary body of the Economic and Social Council to that of the General Assembly,[10] the methods of apportionment of seats between regional groups changed significantly, as spelt out in paragraph 7 of Resolution 60/251.[11]

Table 4.1 shows the increase or decrease in the number and percentage of allocated seats per region from the Commission to the Council. The table quantifies quite eloquently the impact of the change in the distribution of seats that resulted from moving from the ECOSOC environment to that of the General Assembly. This change became part of the political negotiations and eventually, as part of a larger package deal, led to an agreement on the number of Member States as well as the ability for Member States to call for a Special Session with the support of one-third of the Council's membership.

It is of interest to note that if the General Assembly ratio had been applied to a 15 Member Council, as had been advanced by some Western delegations, particularly the United States, in 2006, the distribution would have been four Members each for the African and Asian groups, three

---

10 Paragraph 1 of General Assembly Resolution 60/251, which established the Council as 'a subsidiary organ of the General Assembly'.

11 Group of African States, 13 seats; Group of Asian States, 13; Group of Eastern European States, six; Group of Latin American and Caribbean States, eight; and Group of Western European and Other States, seven.

Table 4.1 *Changes in the number of allocated seats per region from the Commission to the Council*

Groups	Number of Members of the Commission on Human Rights	Percentage of the total	Number of Members of the Human Rights Council	Increase or decrease in number of seats	Percentage of the total	Increase or decrease in percentage
African	15	28%	13	-2	27.5%	-0.5%
Asian	12	23%	13	+1	27.5%	+4.5%
Eastern European	5	9%	6	+1	13%	+4%
Latin American and Caribbean	11	21%	8	-3	17%	-4%
Western European and Other States	10	19%	7	-3	15%	-4%
Total	53	100%	47	-6	100%	—

for the Latin America and the Caribbean region, and two each for the Eastern European and the Western European and other States Groups. Those who advocated for a smaller Council realized late in the negotiation process that they had, in practice, no choice other than to agree with a body whose composition was larger than what they would have expected in order to secure a vital presence in the Council. Indeed, had they secured an agreement on a much smaller body, the distribution of seats between regional groups, which is based on the number of States per region, would have significantly reduced their representation. Today, out of 47 Members of the Council, seven are from the Western European and Other Group. A smaller body would have drastically reduced their number. However, their agreement with the new composition was linked to a new provision reducing the threshold for convening Special Sessions to one-third of the Members of the Council, thus enabling a minority of Members to call for a Special Session. Indeed, a simple majority would have made it far more difficult to convene such Special Sessions.[12]

4.1.3 Pledges and Commitments

Candidates for the Human Rights Council are recommended to make pledges and commitments regarding their contribution to the promotion and protection of human rights. While this elicited considerable comment and played a tremendous role in the negotiation process, it is interesting to note that, in the absence of a body or mechanism to monitor the said pledges and commitments, coupled with the clean-slate practice, making pledges and commitments has rapidly become the norm, but without any real repercussions regarding their content. Although these pledges and commitments are prominently referenced in the institution-building package as part of the legal basis for the UPR – on par with the Charter of the United Nations, the Universal Declaration of Human Rights and the human rights instruments to which a State is a party – in practical terms, pledges and commitments are rarely referred to during the review process.

Some informal channels are used to compensate for this omission, for instance, side events organized before the elections to the Council, during which interested candidates present their pledges and commitments. However, it would be difficult to draw conclusions on the practical impact

12 See para 10 of GA Resolution 60/251.

of such informal exchanges on the casting of ballots in a formal and confidential setting, tainted with a high level of politicization.

4.1.4 Roles and Privileges of Member States of the Council

Contrary to the universal bodies representing the vast majority of General Assembly subsidiary bodies, the Council, with its reduced size, had to conceptualize the roles of Members vis-à-vis those of Observer States, the latter representing three-quarters of the UN membership.

In most cases, Members are provided with prominence in terms of the timing and duration of their statements. This is particularly the case insofar as general debates are concerned, with Members being placed in the first basket of speakers, and Observers in the second with different speaking time limits.[13] However, this rule was not extended to all Council methods of work, particularly panels and interactive dialogues. There are, however, a number of privileges extended to Members only.

The President and the Bureau Members can only be Members of the Council.[14] Also, the rules relating to the quorum provide that the President may declare a meeting open and permit the debate to proceed when at least one-third of the Members are present, while the presence of a majority of Members is required for any decision to be taken.[15]

---

13 At the time of completion of this anatomy, the time limits were two minutes and 30 seconds for Members and one minute and 30 seconds for Observers.

14 See below for developments on the Council's Resolutions 37/24 of 23 March 2018 and 38/18 of 6 July 2018. Whereas it has always been considered that Council gatherings taking place intersessionally were to be considered as formal meetings of the Council, in these instances the Council decided that such meetings or seminars would be chaired by individuals designated by the President of the Council. Hence, such meetings are considered of a hybrid nature: while the meetings or seminars are arranged in a manner quasi-similar to any formal meeting of the Council, their chairing by an individual who is not a Member of the Council Bureau prevents them from being governed by the rules and practices of the Council. They are thus to be considered as hybrid meetings of the Council.

15 See rule 19 of the Human Rights Council rules of procedure replicating rule 67 of the rules of procedure of the General Assembly.

The voting process,[16] which is the culmination of the Council deliberations, is limited to Members, with Observers playing a marginal role only.[17] For procedural motions raised during other segments of the Council sessions (points of order, motion of adjournment, etc.), Members play the leading role. Although Observers may raise such motions, the ability to object to a ruling by the President or the presiding officer (a Vice-President) is strictly limited to Members.

Under the UPR, the initial Members of the Council were the first to be reviewed at the first, second, and third Working Group sessions.[18] Under paragraph 18(d) of Council Resolution 5/1, the troikas established to facilitate each review, including the preparation of the report of the Working Group, are composed of three Rapporteurs selected by drawing lots from among the Members of the Council.

The Complaint Procedure is a Member-State-driven procedure. This results from the confidentiality of the mechanism. Accordingly, the Working Group on Situations is composed of five Members appointed by their respective regional groups.[19] When the Council considers consistent patterns of gross and reliably attested violations of human rights and fundamental freedoms under this procedure,[20] this is done in a strictly confidential manner.[21]

Requests for Special Sessions are restricted to Council Members, requiring formal signatures from 16 Members before the President may take

---

16 Including the elections of the Members of the Advisory Committee.

17 Observers may introduce a resolution or written amendment and speak as a concerned country at one specific moment during the voting process.

18 See para 9 of the General Assembly Resolution 60/251. This played a crucial role in ensuring the participation of all UN Member States in that mechanism. The initial Members were eager to be perceived as cooperating with this new mechanism and when the time came for other States to be reviewed (after 47 previous reviews), it was extremely hard for any one of them to be the first to decline participating in the process.

19 See para 96 of the Council Resolution 5/1.

20 As frequently as needed but at least once per year (para 103 of Resolution 5/1).

21 See para 104 of the Council Resolution 5/1.

action.[22] Even though the practice provides for Observers to be listed in the letter convening a Special Session, this bears a political value but not a legal one.

4.2 Groups of States

In any society, individuals or entities rarely proceed in isolation, as doing so often leads to obsolescence or marginalization. The same rule applies to the intergovernmental machinery, particularly the Council.

In truth, however, there are few instances where an individual State may proceed without privileging alliances.

This may obviously happen when the concerned country is of such an overwhelming nature and power, politically speaking, that its voice does not need to be amplified by belonging to a group of States. For such a State, although it does belong nominatively speaking to one or several groups of States, it may feel free to follow whichever path it considers appropriate even if this is somewhat at odds with the common position of fellow Members of the concerned group of States.

However, this may also happen in the opposite manner, where States are not suspected of privileging their own policies and priorities as inherent parts of their extremely proactive foreign policies. In such circumstances, and insofar as the Council is concerned, if States hold a high moral or political ground and are considered moderate and constructive players in expressing their policies, they may be called upon – whatever their size – to lead discussions, bridge gaps between groups holding deeply divergent views on a given subject, launch initiatives that others may consider unlikely to succeed, or propose compromise language on delicate texts.

Nevertheless, in most cases, States are reluctant to act in isolation. They prefer to benefit from the logic of a group whereby all will join, thus making the outcome of a voting process more realistic. While individual members of the group may lose visibility and perception, this will be a

22 See para 10 of General Assembly Resolution 60/251 and rule 6 of the Human Rights Council.

small price to pay considering the advantages of securing the support of a group.

Paradoxically, the five regional groups,[23] which have a legal status within the General Assembly realm, no longer constitute leading groups, with the notable exception of the African Group, which continues to launch initiatives on its own volition. All other groups are simply operating on procedural matters, serving as a clearing house for their Members to come to terms with certain requirements. The coordinators of these groups act as focal points for sharing information and channelling requests made under the institution-building package or the General Assembly rules of procedure. This is typically the case insofar as nominations to certain bodies or functions are concerned. They do not hold positions of a substantive nature.

In turn, political groups have increasingly taken the lead in the Council's substantive work. These groups are usually the political wing of international organizations or longstanding groups sharing common views or purposes on specific thematic or country matters. The European Union, the Organization of Islamic Cooperation, the Non-Aligned Movement, and the Group of Arab States belong to this category. They do share the characteristic of regrouping Members who hold similar or comparable views on substantive or procedural matters.

Interestingly, other groupings with a lesser degree of commonality in views are increasingly playing a role in the work of the Council. This shift is driven by a desire to overcome the polarization inherent in Council proceedings. Cross-regional groups such as the Organisation Internationale de la Francophonie or the Commonwealth are playing an interesting role in certain matters, given the cross-regional nature of their membership. They provide a useful platform for testing initiatives or sharing thoughts on matters without running the risk of falling into semi-Pavlovian reactions when proposals are being made or studied by other groups.

Other recently formed groups have emerged as key players in the work of the Council, for instance, the SIDS/LDCs group or the Forum of Small

23 The African Group, the Asian Group, the Eastern European Group, the Latin American Group and the Western European and Other Countries Group.

States. They serve as catalysts for information sharing and ensure that the status of their membership is not neglected by other constituents.

More informal groups have progressively stepped into the work of the Council, with a view to regrouping States that may share comparable views on important matters. Such groups may be of a very ad hoc nature to support a set of rights (for instance, the rights of the child) or given mechanisms and thus may be active only when the relevant matters are being considered. Some informal groups address highly sensitive matters, enabling countries sharing the same point of view to express it behind the banner of an ad hoc grouping. One of the best-known ad hoc groups is the Like-Minded Group, which brings together States holding the same position on how the Council should work and, in particular, on how certain country or thematic matters should or should not be dealt with.

An interesting characteristic of these ad hoc groups is that their composition may vary from one instance to another, which means that the list of States they represent may change from one instance to another. As a result, written statements from these ad hoc groups must be accompanied by a precise list of countries on behalf of which they have been delivered.

The importance of the role played by groups, whatever their nature, should not be underestimated. Their presence is highly visible, and they have been given a number of formal and informal privileges. For instance, groups may speak before individual States, thus enabling them to speak in all circumstances, even when the number of speakers is limited (for instance, the panels). During General Debates they are automatically brought to the top of the list of Member States, provided the group includes at least one Member State. In this case, even if the delegation delivering the statement is an Observer State, it is provided with the right to speak for the duration normally reserved for Member States.

More substantively, during consultations conducted by the President, the coordinators of the relevant or concerned groups are consulted as a matter of standard practice. When obstacles arise in the Council proceedings, proposals by the President are often, if not always, informally tested with them.

Regional or political groups have been recognized with the right to launch initiatives. For instance, these groups can be identified on resolutions, even those concerning Special Sessions.

A specific issue may arise when a Member of a regional or political group does not share the view of the others. In this case, it is up to the concerned group to apply its own rules or practices, if applicable. Hence, certain groups will always consider it to be necessary that all their Members sign the initiatives or formally join in the statement delivered on their behalf.

Other groups may consider that the authority left to their coordinator to deliver a statement, launch an initiative or table a resolution does not necessarily imply that they formally agree with all of its aspects. In the latter case, it may happen that a resolution is tabled by a State acting on behalf of a specified regional or political group with a footnote added to the effect that one or more Members of the group have withdrawn their sponsorship.

Since there are almost no written or formal rules governing the activities of regional, political, or other groups, their contributions to the work of the Council have mostly been left to the concerned group. Anecdotally speaking, even though it may be perceived as an aberration by outsiders, a resolution may be tabled by a group of States, but its Members may remain totally free to disassociate themselves from the text, support amendments that significantly alter its meaning or even abstain or vote against it when they deem it appropriate. In fairness, when a course of action is not explicitly prohibited by the rules or practices, as is often the case concerning the Council, it may be proceeded with whether or not logic or common sense would argue against it.

4.3 Observer States

Observer States are Members of the United Nations that are not Members of the Human Rights Council. They enjoy rights and privileges distinct from those of the Council's Members, with the most significant difference being their exclusion from the Council's voting process.[24] Similarly,

24 They may introduce a resolution or written amendment and speak as a concerned country at one specific moment during the voting

although Observer States may raise a point of order during general debates or interactive dialogues, they may not challenge the decision of the President.

This has led to the practice of Observer States identifying a 'proxy' among the Members of the Council who would be in a position to argue in favour of the Observer's viewpoints and participate on their behalf in the ensuing decision-making process. In practical terms, when an Observer raises a point of order during a discussion, proxies may take the floor to support their arguments or position, ensuring the presiding officer hears the expression of views by some Members of the Council. Similarly, during the voting process, an Observer may introduce a resolution or decision but may not engage in a discussion at the general debate level. Hence, a proxy is de facto identified by the Observer who may represent its views, and, more generally, the community of sponsors, in responding to questions from the President.

In recent circumstances, this modus operandi has become more complex. Indeed, further to the withdrawal by the General Assembly of the rights of membership of the Russian Federation and the immediate resignation of the latter from the Council, the question arose as to how to deal with its initiatives. As mentioned, an Observer is fully entitled to table a resolution or an amendment. The UNGA rules of procedure do not provide any insight as to what would happen if a text thus submitted by an Observer would not be co-sponsored by at least one member of the Council. However, the practice of the Commission on Human Rights, which had been automatically transferred to the Council by virtue of Operative Paragraph 7 of UNGA Resolution 60/251, was based on the rules of procedure of the Functional Commissions of the ECOSOC.[25]

---

process. After the closure of the voting process, with action taken on all proposals placed before it, including the elections to the Advisory Committee, the approval of the list of mandate-holders, and the adoption ad referendum of the Sessional and/or Annual Report of the Council, the Council authorizes the Observers to deliver brief remarks on the voting process as a whole. This is done as a matter of courtesy, does not entail any legal implications and is organized only if time permits.

25 See https://www.ohchr.org/sites/default/files/Documents/HRBodies/CHR/RoP.pdf.

Rule 69, relating to the participation of non-Member States, indicated that a non-Member State did not have the right to vote but 'may submit proposals which may be put to the vote on request of any member of the Commission or of the subsidiary organ concerned'.

True to the spirit of the Council's practice, when an Observer State tabled an amendment in the past, it was sufficient to consider that if a proxy had been identified, this indicated the desire of at least one Member State of the Council to have the text considered by the Council. Since proxies had always been identified by Observer States having submitted a draft text, all such initiatives had always been acted upon.

However, in March 2023, a situation occurred which was replicated in subsequent sessions, whereby several amendments emanating from an Observer State, the Russian Federation, were not co-sponsored by a Member State and for which no Member State had been identified as proxies. In such cases, before giving the floor to the State concerned to introduce the amendments it had tabled, the President asked the room whether any Member considered that they should be considered by the Council. Since none responded in the affirmative, these texts were not considered.[26] Of course, the same question was not asked when other amendments had been tabled with at least one Member State being a co-sponsor or agreeing to act as a proxy.

Another significant distinction, often misunderstood, is that discussions regarding any decision – regardless of its nature or timing – are limited to Members only. The fact that many decisions are adopted without specific formalism[27] has led to the unfortunate consequence that Observer States may at times believe that they have the right to interject in the discussion of any issue, whereas the consideration of any action is, by definition limited to Members. In practical terms, whenever the President needs to decide upon a specific course of action by way of gavelling, the concerned discussion is limited exclusively to Member States.

---

26 See https://hrcmeetings.ohchr.org/HRCSessions/RegularSessions/52/Pages/resolutions.aspx and drafts L.46, L.55, L.63, and L.65 to L.78.

27 For instance, action on the programme of work, postponement of a discussion, or agreement on a specific course of action or modality.

The Council has, however, been very generous in granting rights and privileges to Observers that closely resemble those of Member States. For instance, Observers are allocated speaking time limits that are either similar to those of Members[28] or only slightly reduced.[29] They may initiate proposals and deliver the same number of statements as Members. When the President is appointing facilitators to assist on certain issues, he or she may appoint individuals from Observer States.[30] Participation in the High-Level Segments is open to all United Nations Member and Observer States. Panels may be moderated by representatives of Observer States.[31]

Informal consultations by the President or the Bureau are open to all UN Member and Observer States (as well as NGOs and national human rights institutions).

Participation in the UPR is open to all UN Members.[32] Given paragraph 9 of the General Assembly Resolution 60/251 which provided that Members elected to the Council were to be reviewed during their term of membership, a distinction was introduced in the order of the review, with initial Members of the Council being reviewed first. However, once

---

28 In the case of interactive dialogues or panels.

29 In the case of general debates.

30 The President of the 5th Council cycle (Sihasak PhuangKetKeow) designated five facilitators and one coordinator in the context of the review process. Four of the five facilitators and the coordinator of the process in New York were Permanent Representatives of Observer States (Morocco, Finland, Romania, India and Algeria). This practice was followed by subsequent Presidents when they started dealing with the efficiency process. In particular, the President of the 12th Council Cycle (Vojislav Suc) resumed this practice by appointing six facilitators to help him in the context of the efficiency and effectiveness process, of which two were Permanent Representatives of Observer States (Fiji and Latvia). Such practice was followed thereafter by each President.

31 In a number of circumstances, the main sponsor of a resolution, having established a panel, selects one of its nationals as a moderator. Alternatively, a representative of that country may deliver a message or a panellist may have the same nationality.

32 See para 5(e) of GA Resolution 60/251 and Sections C and D as well as para 18(b) of Council Resolution 5/1.

the first UPR cycle was completed, this provision became obsolete. The only remaining difference between Members and Observers under the UPR Mechanism is that the groups of Rapporteurs (troikas) selected by drawing lots under paragraph 18(d) are drawn from the Members of the Council.

4.4 Who is qualified to represent a UN Member State?

In most circumstances, individuals representing one of the Council's stakeholders are identified without any specific difficulties and no challenges arise. As far as Member or Observer States are concerned, those referred to in the listings relating to Permanent Missions[33] are allowed in and may sit at the seat reserved for their delegations. This is based on information communicated to the Protocol and Liaison Service.

As far as other stakeholders are concerned, entrance into the Council's room is based on a badge delivered by UNOG security, applying relevant UN and Secretariat rules and practices. Hence, an NGO representative may attend a session if they provide an official letter registering them to the session and signed by the head of the said organization. Although at times there are challenges to the accreditation – or more properly stated the registration – of an NGO representative by way of a point of order, the issue is solved by the Secretariat checking the procedure and reassuring the Council that all was done in a proper manner.

The same principles apply mutatis mutandis to all other stakeholders. This is a simple and direct implementation of the applicable rules based on security requirements, Council's rules and practices, as well as sound and safe management of UN premises. There may be some technical or other types of difficulties linked with fraud attempts or when an individual does not have an ID document emanating from one of the 193 UN Member States or two Observer States. In that case, the concerned individual is not admitted into UN premises and this is not linked to Council's but to the UNs' basic rules.

---

33 Otherwise referred to as the UNOG 'Blue Book'. See https://www.ungeneva.org/en/blue-book.

However, recently, new issues have arisen regarding the representation of States at the Council. Some are linked to bilateral issues, others to the legal quagmire or uncertainty around the legal status of States' representatives.

4.4.1 Bilateral Issues

From time to time, a State may object to the inclusion in the delegation of another State of an individual for a variety of reasons. One such reason may be linked to the fact that the said individual is considered to be representing a territory that is considered by the former as not part of the latter or not as a UN Member State. While in the past such issues arose in a discrete manner and were dealt with at the Secretariat level, increasingly such matters have been raised in the public domain and had to be dealt with by presiding officers and/or the Council's Bureau.

The constant position of the Secretariat and of OLA was based on the following principles: (i) the Council applies the rules of procedure established for committees of the General Assembly in accordance with General Assembly Resolution 60/251 and the annex of HRC Resolution 5/1; (ii) Rule 100 of the rules of procedure of committees of the General Assembly, entitled 'Representation of Members', provides that '[e]ach Member may be represented by one person on each Main Committee and on any other committee that may be established upon which all Members have the right to be represented. It may also assign to these committees advisers, technical advisers, experts or persons of similar status'. It is for each Member State to designate the members of its delegation pursuant to this rule; and (iii) as a general rule, the Secretariat does not 'accredit' members of a Member State delegation to a UN meeting. As long as the names of individual delegates of a Member State are conveyed by a Permanent Mission in due form, i.e., by a formal notification from a Permanent Mission that is duly signed or initialled, indicating that the individuals represent the State concerned in a specific session or meeting, the Secretariat's role is limited to taking the necessary administrative actions, particularly the issuance of ground passes if the delegates concerned do not have them. The Secretariat is not in a position to request the exclusion of a specific individual who is listed as part of the delegation of a Member State.

Nevertheless, given the ever-shifting nature of multilateralism in the present circumstances, delegations may dismiss such legal reasoning and raise the matter in the public domain by way of Notes Verbales and points of order.[34]

However, the outcome always remains always the same, with the reiteration of the previously mentioned rules and principles.

Issues linked to the legal uncertainties surrounding the representation of certain UN Member States after a coup d'état or comparable situations.

In the past, when dramatic changes happened in a country, those representing it stepped down and their accreditation was removed. Their name(s) were later removed from the 'blue book'. As mentioned earlier,[35] the most dramatic such case happened on 25 February 2011 when the representative of the Libyan Arab Jamahiriya took the floor, requested a minute of silence, read out a very strong statement against his government, at the end of which he formally announced his resignation from the Permanent Mission and left the room.

However, in more recent circumstances, this issue took a rather dramatic stance. From June 2021 onwards, the President started receiving conflicting information from the Permanent Mission of the Republic of the Union of Myanmar in Geneva and in New York. Both claimed to represent the government and intended to register representatives for the forthcoming Council's sessions and activities. The Geneva representatives were linked with the de facto authorities while those in New York were representatives of the authorities that had been imprisoned during the coup d'etat.

What made this case a very complex one is that both Missions had a sound legal basis to request the possibility to register a delegation. The Permanent Mission in Geneva acted based on a Note Verbale signed by the duly accredited representative, namely the Deputy Permanent Representative and Chargée d'affaires a.i.[36] The Permanent Mission in New York acted as representatives of the Head of State and the Minister

34 See, for instance minutes of the bureau meeting of 29 April 2021.

35 See Section 4.1.1 above.

36 See https://www.ungeneva.org/en/blue-book/missions/member-states/myanmar.

for Foreign Affairs as listed in the official UN list of Heads of State, Heads of Government and Ministers for Foreign Affairs.[37]

In accordance with General Assembly Resolution 396 (V) of 14 December 1950, whenever more than one authority claims to be the government entitled to represent a Member State in the United Nations, and this question becomes the subject of controversy in the United Nations, the question should be considered by the General Assembly. In this very specific set of circumstances, based on the recommendation to that effect by the Bureau, the Council noted on 21 June 2021 that, pending a decision by the General Assembly on the representation of Myanmar, the Council Secretariat would not be in a position to process requests regarding the participation of anyone as part of the delegation of Myanmar in Council meetings, including during its 47th session. Consequently, the Council decided that the consideration of the report of the UPR of Myanmar that was supposed to be adopted at the 47th session would be postponed.

Consensus could easily be achieved on the issue of the UPR, the pillar of this mechanism lying in a constructive dialogue between the representatives of the reviewed States and the Council. Additionally, immediately prior to the adoption of the report, the reviewed State is requested to express positions on recommendations made during the previous UPR Working Group review. The absence of a delegation representing the reviewed State would have negated these important principles. Additionally, the position of both parties would have been seriously at odds, thus nullifying any possibility for the report to be considered genuinely by either one or the other delegation.

The situation was very different regarding the two other instances when Myanmar was supposed to appear before the Council, namely in the context of the presentations of the oral update by the High Commissioner and the oral progress report by the Special Rapporteur which were both expected to be followed by an interactive dialogue under Council Resolution 46/21. Some States considered that the decision taken regarding the postponement of the adoption of the outcome of the UPR review should be applied mutatis mutandis to these two interactive dialogues, with a postponement of these interactions to a later stage. Others believed

---

37 See https://www.un.org/dgacm/sites/www.un.org.dgacm/files/Documents_Protocol/hspmfmlist.pdf.

that they should be conducted but with a representative of the Geneva Permanent Mission, as it represented the views of those who held de facto authority over the country and were thus best placed to respond to the reports. Still others believed that this would serve as an extremely bad precedent, which might be applied in several other cases when a country is subjected to a coup d'état. They argued that the legitimate authorities should represent the country during these interactive dialogues, or at least that the discussions should be held without a representative of the State concerned.

The deadlock could not be overcome at the Bureau level, which concluded that a question related to the holding of the interactive dialogues with the High Commissioner and with the Special Rapporteur should be put to the Council for its decision. This was done on 1 July 2021 by resorting to the e-recorded voting module. The question raised was: 'should the Council hold the two interactive dialogues at this 47th session?'[38] The Council responded in the affirmative, voting in favour of the decision by 26 votes to seven, with 14 abstentions. Since the Council had already taken note that the Council Secretariat could not take a position on the issue of which delegation represented Myanmar, this implied that the interactive dialogues would be held without a delegation.

The General Assembly did not take any position on the matter of the credentials of Myanmar as of the completion of this second edition and as a result this position still remains at that time.

In later circumstances, other issues were dealt with, creating some forms of difficulties but not to the extent faced in the case of Myanmar.

For instance, when the Council held its 32nd Special Session on the human rights implications of the ongoing situation in Sudan on 5 November 2021, an issue arose as to who from the Permanent Mission of Sudan would deliver a statement on behalf of the concerned country. This difficulty arose since the then Permanent Representative and Deputy Permanent Representative held opposite positions regarding the issues unfolding in their country. But this was solved in a practical manner in the room and also with the postponement of the UPR review of

38 See Sessional report A/HRC/47/2, paras 5–10, page 6.

Sudan, which was supposed to take place more or less at the same time, to the following UPR Working Group session.[39]

Another issue could potentially create difficulties in future circumstances, namely the representation of Afghanistan at the United Nations. It is important to underline that at the time of completion of this second edition, the Permanent Mission of Afghanistan in Geneva does not represent the Taliban. During the period under review, on 17 August 2021, the Permanent Representative of Pakistan on behalf of the OIC and the Permanent Representative of Afghanistan requested the convening of the 31st Special Session on the serious human rights concerns and situations in Afghanistan. Additionally, the Council held its eighth urgent debate on the situation of the human rights of women and girls in Afghanistan on 1 July 2022 during its 50th session. Although that urgent debate was requested by Member States of the European Union that were members of the Council, the Permanent Representative of Afghanistan made a statement as a country concerned. Lastly, the UPR review of Afghanistan took place on 29 April 2024, with the same representative leading a delegation, introducing the review, and responding to questions.

Of interest, in a letter dated 12 July 2023,[40] the Permanent Representative of Afghanistan requested a postponement of the review to allow for more productive, effective, and fruitful engagement with all relevant stakeholders. This was to be read against the background of the severe and unprecedented circumstances' since the Taliban's military takeover, which had 'severely impacted Afghanistan's ability to adequately prepare and participate in the review process for the 4th cycle'. Implicitly, one could discern a concern that a UPR review of a country based on a report and comments made by a representation not supporting the de facto authorities in Kabul would be somewhat unrealistic. At a meeting of the

39 See letter of the Permanent Representative of the Sudan to the President dated 27 October 2021 (https://hrcmeetings.ohchr.org/PresidencyBureau/BureauRegionalGroupsCorrespondence/Corresp2014DL/N.272.21.pdf) and minutes of the Bureau meeting of 2 November 2021.

40 https://hrcmeetings.ohchr.org/PresidencyBureau/BureauRegionalGroupsCorrespondence/Correspondence/Letter%20from%20Afghanistan%20requesting%20postponement%20of%20UPR%204th%20cycle%20review.pdf.

Bureau held on 15 September 2023, the Bureau rejected this request and considered that the review of Afghanistan should take place as originally scheduled.

The rationale behind this decision was that, unlike the case of Myanmar – where there existed a serious discrepancy between the political allegiances of those representing the country in Geneva and in New York, as well as with the list of Heads of State and Foreign Affairs Ministers – the UNOG Blue Book included the name of the Permanent Representative, while the aforementioned New York list did not include any name for the Head of State, Head of Government or Foreign Affairs Ministers for Afghanistan. Against the priority given by the Bureau to maintaining the order of reviews and ensuring 100 per cent participation in the process, a peer review of the human rights situation in Afghanistan was deemed important.

These three cases serve as a reminder that in a troubled world, where the legal representation of States at the United Nations may become increasingly fluid and delicate, decisions should be taken urgently by the Credentials Committee and later endorsed by the General Assembly. However, given the crisis that multilateralism faces in New York, it is becoming harder for the main UN bodies to make relevant decisions of relevance on sensitive matters. This has a snowball impact that directly affects other bodies in the system, particularly the Council.

4.5 Other observers

The General Assembly's Observers,[41] who are only two in number, are considered to have the same rights as the Council Observers, who are Members of the United Nations. This derives from General Assembly Resolutions 52/250 and 58/314[42] which conferred upon Palestine and the Holy See additional rights and privileges of participation in the sessions

41 The Holy See and the State of Palestine.

42 See also para 33 of the agreed provisions in document E/CN.4/2002/16 of the Commission on Human Rights included in the Compilation of recent documents in relation to the enhancement of the working methods of the Commission on Human Rights (1999–2005).

and work of the General Assembly and the international conferences convened under the auspices of the Assembly or other organs of the United Nations, as well as in UN Conferences.

Accordingly, the differences in treatment between Observer States and General Assembly Observers, insofar as the Council is concerned, may only derive from Council resolutions that limit certain rights or privileges to UN Member States. The only such case concerns the UPR, which is limited to the 193 Member States of the United Nations. While Palestine and the Holy See may attend and participate in all 193 reviews, they are not subject to a review themselves.

In practical terms, there is one additional difference, namely the organization of the Council room, where the seat of the Holy See is placed immediately after those of the Observer States and before the representatives of international organizations or agencies. The same was true for Palestine, until 10 September 2024 when the Council decided to follow the General Assembly's newly established practice as it emerged from the adoption of Resolution A/RES/ES-10/23 of 10 May 2024.[43] Accordingly, the State of Palestine was granted the right to be seated, as from 10 September onwards, among Observer States of the Council in (French) alphabetical order.

It is worth noting that all international organizations or entities that have entered into a formal agreement with the General Assembly have progressively been granted rights and prerogatives equivalent to those of General Assembly Observers. However, the General Assembly or the Council has not granted them the right to raise a point of order or exercise a right of reply.

4.5.1 NGOs

One of the main characteristics of the Council, as well as its predecessor, the Commission on Human Rights, is the access granted to NGOs. There is no other body within the UN System or in other organizations where

43 See minutes of the Bureau meeting of 22 August 2024. It should be noted that all other aspects of the resolution were already implemented by the Council based on its longstanding practice as well as that of the Commission.

the space granted to civil society is as important. NGOs with ECOSOC[44] status have rights and prerogatives which are comparable to those of other Observers, and their presence is palpable in almost all aspects of the work of the Council. Their representatives deliver statements across all segments of discussion and are also granted the right to organize side events. Additionally, they are also in a position to attend open-ended informal consultations organized by sponsors of resolutions. NGOs actively participate in, and have the opportunity to speak at, informal meetings organized by the President or the Bureau.

Some figures[45] may be of interest in this regard. On average, the time consumed by NGOs[46] represents 30 hours or 33 per cent of the total time used for General Debates, Interactive Dialogues and Panels at any given session. This compares favourably with the time set aside for Member States (22 hours or 25 per cent) or Observers (20 hours or 21 per cent). Moreover, taking into account that the modalities for the interactive dialogues and panels are quite restrictive for NGOs, the time used by them during the general debates – the modalities of which do not provide limits on the number of speakers – represents half of the total (15 out of 30 hours).

The total number of NGOs participating in the Council sessions is growing continuously and almost doubled from 2006 to 2018 (from 407 to 874). Additionally, the total number of side events organized by NGOs has grown significantly from 87 in 2006 to 590 in 2018, and the number of oral statements delivered by NGO representatives multiplied tenfold between 2006 and 2018 (from 276 to 2715).[47] This situation changed somewhat with the COVID-19 pandemic (see above section 2.3), and it is now

44 See ECOSOC Resolution 1996/31 of 25 July 1996.

45 Based on statistics for the pre-COVID-19 period, these figures in percentage are quite similar to those of the March or June 2018 Sessions. For additional information on the participation of NGOs during the different segments of discussion, see below.

46 The NHRIs are computed in the same category, but their participation in the work of the Council is relatively modest compared with that of NGOs. The statistics provided in this section are only marginally affected by the merging of NGOs and NHRIs.

47 It should be borne in mind that the number of Council meetings held in 2006 (72) was significantly lower than in 2018 (142).

harder to analyse the relevant data since a threshold was established as to the maximum number of NGOs participating in a given General Debate (an average of the three previous years for the same debate at the same session). Similarly, considering the limitation of rooms available to the Council as a result of the Strategic Heritage Plan, the number of side events organized by NGOs has plummeted in the past five years.

It should, however, be mentioned that there is a large variety of NGOs with ECOSOC status that attend the Council proceedings and it is hard not to allude at this stage to the existence of quite a large number of organizations, lobbies, entities and groups which rarely address the Council meetings in a topical manner or without strong political motivation, thus pursuing their own political agenda without engaging in constructive participation in the work of the Council. Their existence and presence do not, however, alter the crucial importance of the input by a vibrant civil society represented by dozens of independent organizations which alert the Council and its mechanisms to numerous issues of concern per year. The existence and disruption by the former should not overshadow the legitimacy and fundamental input by the latter.

The modalities for NGO participation follow those established at the Commission on Human Rights. In accordance with paragraph 11 of General Assembly Resolution 60/251, NGO participation is governed by arrangements outlined in ECOSOC Resolution 1996/31 and the practices observed by the Commission on Human Rights. The main difficulty in analysing these rules and/or practices is that there are almost no written materials on the matter; this is largely due to the high level of polarization existing at the Commission and later the Council, which made it impossible to encapsulate in a written document the guiding principles or sets of practices governing the participation of NGOs in the Council sessions.

As for the practices[48] inherited from the Commission and retained by the Council, they can be summarized as follows:

---

48 See the compilation of recent documents in relation to the enhancement of the working methods of the Commission on Human Rights (1999–2005), in particular, document E/CN.4/2001/CRP.1 on the main rules and practices followed by the Commission on Human Rights in the organization of its work and the conduct of business.

- NGO speakers take the floor as representatives of the accredited NGO, which assumes full responsibility for the content of the statement. All NGOs are encouraged to provide written copies of their oral statements to conference room officers.
- Written statements submitted by NGOs in advance of the session are circulated in plenary.

With regard to the accreditation of NGOs, the practice has been that, pursuant to ECOSOC Resolution 1996/31, it is up to the NGOs themselves to designate authorized representatives to participate as Observers in public meetings of the Council. The legitimacy of duly accredited NGO representatives is not challenged by the Council, and their status in and relationship with the organization they represent are not questioned. It is the responsibility of the Secretariat to ensure that NGOs are duly accredited in accordance with existing rules and procedures. Whenever any government participating in the work of the Council requests the Secretariat to verify or confirm the accreditation of any particular NGO speaker, immediate action is taken in this regard and the results of the verification are publicly reported by the Secretariat to the plenary of the Council. There has been a longstanding practice at both the Commission and later the Council of so-called 'multiple representation', where a single individual represents several NGOs. There is nothing in ECOSOC Resolution 1996/31 incompatible with one person representing two or more NGOs, as long as it is clear on behalf of which NGO or NGOs that person acts and speaks in each instance.

NGOs are not permitted to distribute documents, pamphlets or any other materials within the Conference Room.

- However, any materials that NGOs intend to put on the tables reserved for NGOs outside the Conference Room must be attributed to an ECOSOC-status NGO.

NGO representatives who are duly accredited to the session and wish to reserve a conference room for meetings related to Council agenda items must apply to the Secretariat of the Council. The request should include the subject of the meeting, the proposed time, and the name of the person responsible for organizing and conducting the meeting. These meetings are announced in the Bulletin of Informal Meetings.

Additionally, a number of cases arose (and continue to arise) where representatives of Member States requested the Commission (later the Council) Bureau, the Commission (later the Council) Secretariat, the High Commissioner, or the UNOG Director-General to consider the suitability of an individual or individuals representing the accredited NGO being granted access to the Council, on the basis that he/she posed a security risk or threat.

On occasion, these requests were based on Interpol arrest warrants. The Commission's Expanded Bureau requested its Chairperson to enquire with the Office of Legal Affairs (OLA) about the modalities for considering such matters. In response to that request dated 13 June 2005,[49] the OLA established that:

- The ECOSOC Resolution 1996/31 does not provide a basis for the Bureau, the Commission Secretariat, or the Director-General to consider the suitability of a representative of an NGO on the basis of a security risk. Rather, the resolution is directed to establish conditions for the consultative status of NGOs with ECOSOC.
- However, ECOSOC-status NGOs are required to conform to the principles governing the establishment and nature of their consultative relations with the ECOSOC. Organizations that do not meet these requirements may be suspended or excluded from participating in the work of the ECOSOC. The conduct of individuals who represent these organizations may also have an impact on their status in the ECOSOC. While it is clear that individuals authorized to represent NGOs are obliged to conform to these principles, the focus of Resolution 1996/31 is on the organization and not the individuals. The focus of the resolution is to ensure that only those NGOs whose objectives and actions are consistent with the UN Charter participate in meetings of the United Nations, rather than being directed to security concerns.
- There is no general prohibition as such to prevent individuals subject to Interpol 'red notices' from being accredited to any meeting of the United Nations. The United Nations is not obliged to act with respect to notices issued by Interpol. However, it may if it chooses. The Organization having the duty to protect its officials, visitors

[49] This legal advice was circulated to the Members of the Expanded Bureau and through them to the Commission's Members.

and assets can deny access to its premises to any individual on the grounds of security concerns.

- In particular, in each location where the United Nations has a presence, there is a 'designated official' responsible for security. The designated official for security in Geneva is the Director-General at UNOG. It is up to the judgement of the designated official to assess the risks in any given situation and take the appropriate measures. Although the Organization is not legally bound to take any action in respect of Interpol 'red notices', they may be a key element to be considered when assessing security risks.

The Council's current practices are built on the above elements. However, the modalities for the participation of NGOs have evolved on par with novelties and adjustments introduced in the Council's work and functioning. At present, they may be summarized as follows:

- Up to four civil society representatives belonging to four different NGOs may take the floor at the end of the general segment that follows the High Level Segment.
- NGO representatives may address the Council during panels or interactive dialogues. However, the amount of time set aside for this purpose is limited. In the case of panels, a maximum of four NGO representatives may address the Council. Insofar as interactive dialogues are concerned, 15 minutes are set aside for NGO representatives to engage with mandate-holders.
- The participation of NGO representatives in the general debate is not limited beyond an averaging of their numbers over a period of three years, although questions are regularly raised as to the sustainability of this engagement considering the constantly increasing number of NGO representatives' statements and the time constraints of the Council. Currently, their participation is grouped in one segment after Member States, Observer States and Others.
- The participation of NGOs in the UPR is regulated by the Council Resolution 5/1, which provides (a) that the OHCHR shall prepare a summary of credible and reliable information provided by other relevant stakeholders, i.e., NGOs, and (b) that they will be able to attend (but not participate in) the review in the Working Group. As far as the consideration of the final outcome document by the plenary of the Council is concerned, 20 minutes are set aside for NGOs to comment on the review report as already adopted by the UPR Working Group.

NGO representatives and, more generally, all individuals or groups wishing to bring to light cases of human rights violations at the international level may face direct or indirect retaliatory measures. This is particularly the case when it comes to the Council and its mechanisms. Cases of reprisals abound in the intergovernmental human rights system and the United Nations has been dealing with the matter for several decades.

The Declaration on the Rights and Responsibilities of Individuals, Groups, and Organs of Society to Promote and Protect Universally Recognized Human Rights and Fundamental Freedoms, usually referred to as the Declaration on Human Rights Defenders, adopted by the General Assembly on 9 December 1998,[50] lists a number of rights and protections accorded to human rights defenders and specifies the duties of States in this regard. Of importance, article 12, paragraph 12.2 requests States to 'take all necessary measures to ensure the protection by the competent authorities of everyone, individually and in association with others, against any violence, threats, retaliation de facto or de jure adverse discrimination, pressure or any other arbitrary action as a consequence of his or her legitimate exercise of the rights referred to in the present Declaration'. The underlying concern has amplified over the years, alongside the strengthening of the human rights architecture as well as the increased interest in such matters by the public at large. Accordingly, the Commission on Human Rights established a Special Procedure mandate on the situation of human rights defenders.[51] In parallel, in line with the priority attached to the matter by the Organization as a whole, the Assistant Secretary-General for Human Rights was designated by the Secretary-General as the senior officer to lead efforts within the UN system to address intimidation and reprisals against those cooperating with the United Nations in the field of human rights.[52]

Issues relating to acts of intimidation or reprisals have been raised since the establishment of the Council. These allegations include arrests to

---

50 See A/RES/53/144.

51 Initially the mandate was that of a Special Representative of the Secretary General on the situation of Human Rights, which was transformed into that of a Special Rapporteur. See, in particular Council Resolutions A/HRC/RES/34/5 of 23 March 2017 and 36/21 of 29 September 2017.

52 See the ASG's most recent report A/HRC/39/41.

prevent travel to Geneva, travel bans in anticipation of travel to Geneva, intimidation and threats to civil society actors or their families, the labelling of civil society representatives as 'traitors' in national/local online and print news sources, social media and public statements by government officials, intimidation and hate messages on social media by representatives of States, and the filming and photographing of defenders in Palais des Nations and in Geneva. In addition to this, reports have also been received from NGOs of pressure to cancel side events or reconsider panellists at those events or intimidation to remove speakers from NGO speakers' lists.

In its resolution adopted at the conclusion of the review of the Council's work and functioning, the Council included paragraph 30, in which it strongly rejected 'any act of intimidation or reprisals against individuals and groups who cooperate or have cooperated with the United Nations, its representatives and mechanisms in the field of human rights and (urged) States to prevent and ensure adequate protection against such acts'.

Successive Presidents have regularly referred to this matter in various instances during their terms of membership, particularly at the start and conclusion of each regular session and during Organizational Meetings or Sessions as well as in the context of the UPR. Such references may be of a general nature[53] or triggered by a specific case.[54]

---

53 For instance, the President of the 12th HRC cycle stated in concluding remarks on 28 September 2018:

> I regret that yet again I must inform you that since last session, I have received additional allegations of acts of intimidation and reprisals. I must reiterate once again that the participation of civil society in the Human Rights Council is crucial, and any act of intimidation and reprisal against an individual or group who has cooperated, is cooperating, or seeks to cooperate with the Council is completely unacceptable. Let me remind you again that this Council condemns and rejects all acts of intimidation or reprisal by Governments and non-State actors against individuals and groups who seek to cooperate or have cooperated with the United Nations, its representative and mechanisms in the field of human rights. All acts of intimidation or reprisal against these individuals and groups must end. I call on all of you to take all necessary measures to prevent and ensure adequate protection against such acts. In his statement at the 74th session of the General Assembly on 1 November 2019, the President of the 13th HRC cycle stated: Civil society plays a fundamental role in ensuring that the Council's deliberations remain relevant and close to the reality on the ground. They also have a key role to play in monitoring and capacity-building efforts in their countries of origin. It is therefore essential to maintain space for the active participation and contribution of civil society in the Council, as this makes the Council unique among other United Nations intergovernmental bodies. Following the allegations of reprisals and intimidation that were brought to my attention during the past year, I have unfortunately had to reiterate on several occasions that acts of reprisals and intimidation against those who have cooperated with United Nations human rights mechanisms are unacceptable and must stop.

54 For instance, the President of the 10th HRC cycle stated in the Council chamber on 13 June 2016:

> I wish to recall Council Resolution 12/2, in which this Council condemns all acts of intimidation or reprisal by Governments and non-State actors against individuals and groups who seek to cooperate or have cooperated with the United Nations, its representative and mechanisms in the field of human rights, and Resolution 16/21, in which the Council strongly rejects the same. In this connection, I wish to also reiterate that maintaining a safe space for the active participation of

They have also handled cases brought to their attention using their good offices through bilateral meetings and/or appropriate discussions at the Bureau level. As of 31 October 2024, dozens of minutes of Bureau meetings referred to cases of reprisals either in generic or specific terms.[55]

---

civil society representatives is not only part of the mandate of this Council but is also in our common interest. The Vice Presidents and I are convinced that a constructive atmosphere and cooperative spirit, allowing for an open exchange of views and a frank discussion while respecting the dignity inherent in this body, is essential for the credibility and effective functioning of the Human Rights Council. As President of this Council, together with my Bureau, I will continue following up on all allegations that are brought to my attention of acts of reprisal and intimidation that are carried out in connection with the Human Rights Council, its mechanism and procedures. We should all be vigilant. Acts of intimidation and reprisal are taking different shape. Nowadays, platforms of social media, including Twitter, are widely used by all concerned, including Human Rights Council participants. Unfortunately, they may also be misused as a means of attacking and threatening human rights defenders, NGOs or the Council's Special Procedures mandate-holders. Against this background, I wish to address a situation that was recently brought to my attention. I recently received allegations that during the 31st session, a member of a national delegation to this Council misused social media to deliver a message that can be construed as a serious threat against an NGO representative attending the session. As per established practice, I addressed the allegations to the Permanent Representative of the relevant delegation who conducted a prompt investigation. The Permanent Representative subsequently acknowledged that the member of the delegation committed this extremely regrettable act, but not in his professional capacity and without intentions to be a threat. I was further informed that an administrative reprimand had been issued. I assure you that I am fully seized of this matter and will continue looking into it. I cannot stress enough that this is completely unacceptable, and as such should be denunciated in the strongest of terms. I take this opportunity to call on everyone to be extremely vigilant, in all cases of potential reprisals, on-line or off-line. Social media should be used to promote and protect human rights and not the opposite.

55 https://hrcmeetings.ohchr.org/PresidencyBureau/BureauRegionalGroupsCorrespondence/Pages/Bureau-meetings.aspx. Specific cases were referred to concerning Bahrain, South Sudan, Maldives, Nicaragua and Eritrea.

In one specific case, the matter was elevated to the plenary, and at a later stage the President specified that such a statement did not contain any accusation against the concerned government but instead was an invitation or a call to the authorities to act preventively and provide adequate protection to members of civil society who had come to Geneva to attend the concerned review and had been intimidated through several media articles.[56]

Further to the adoption of Resolution 16/21, an informal internal protocol was developed for the handling by the President of allegations of reprisals in connection with Council sessions, the UPR Mechanism and Special Procedures. This protocol includes a number of steps that may be taken in cases of allegations of reprisals: (a) transmission of information by the Secretariat to the President; (b) should the information be corroborated by credible sources, the President may meet with the Permanent Representative of the concerned State; (c) this may be followed by an official letter requesting written information and explanation on the allegations; (d) the President may then inform the Bureau of the allegations; and (e) should the President not be satisfied with these explanations he/she may name the State concerned in the Minutes of the Bureau and later raise the issue in the plenary with reference to the facts and the name of the State.

Additionally, it is of interest to note that, since 2015, an average of ten cases per year have also referred to the attention of the Secretary-General in the context of his yearly report on reprisals. Possible acts of reprisals against NGO representatives are therefore dealt with by the President in a variety of ways. Despite the increase in the number of allegations received and the growing importance taken by this issue in the public domain during or in connection with the Council sessions, it is important to note that most of those participating in Council sessions[57] do so with-

---

56 Minutes of the Bureau meetings of 22 and 25 June 2015.

57 Around 300 NGOs participate and are represented by 1,200–1,500 individuals at any given session. To place these figures in perspective, at the 42nd session, out of 2,632 total registrations, 2,381 were approved and 1,895 badges were printed. Of these, 1,795 were NGOs, of which 1,665 were approved and 1,269 collected their badges. Additionally, 486 registrations were made for Member or Observer States, with 349 approved and 414 badges collected.

out any form of harassment or reprisal. The existence of safeguards and mechanisms set in place to deal with deviations from this rule testifies to the seriousness with which the Council deals with cases of reprisals.

4.5.2 National Human Rights Institutions

NHRIs play a crucial role in the UN human rights architecture. Their importance was sanctioned by the General Assembly Resolution 48/134 of 20 December 1993, which included as an Annex the Principles relating to the status of national institutions, otherwise known as the 'Paris Principles'.

At an International Conference held in Tunis in 1993, NHRIs established the International Coordinating Committee of NHRIs with the aim of coordinating the activities of the NHRI network. In 2016, the Committee changed its name to the Global Alliance of National Human Rights Institutions (GANHRI). In accordance with the Paris Principles and its own statutes, the GANHRI categorizes NHRIs into three categories as follows: A, fully compliant with the Paris Principles; B, partially compliant with the Paris Principles; and C, non-compliant with the Paris Principles. As of 8 August 2018, there were 79 NHRIs accredited with A Status by the GANHRI, i.e., in compliance with the Paris Principles.

At the time of the Commission, NHRIs had the ability to participate in the consideration of agenda item 18 (b),[58] at which time they were given the floor during one slot. This was, however, not followed by a general debate and NHRIs could not intervene under other agenda items.

For several years after the establishment of the Council, the status of NHRIs was somewhat blurred owing to the shortened nature of the

---

Intergovernmental organizations and International Organizations made 62 requests, 38 approved and 27 badges collected. Finally, 17 NHRI representatives registered, and 15 collected their badges. Regarding side events, 179 registrations were made, 144 approved, and 123 badges printed.

58 Agenda item XVIII was entitled 'Effective functioning of human rights mechanisms'. Sub-item (b) related to national institutions and regional arrangements.

Council agenda.[59] They were, however, given the floor during the general debates and interactive dialogues together with NGOs. However, the status of National Institutions was significantly strengthened at the conclusion of the Council Review in 2011 with the adoption of Resolution 16/21 of 25 March 2011.

- In accordance with paragraph 13 of that resolution, A-status NHRIs are provided with the ability to intervene immediately after the State under review during the adoption of the outcome of the UPR review by the Council plenary. Furthermore, the information provided by the NHRIs accredited in full compliance with the Paris Principles for the States where these NHRIs exist appears in a separate section at the beginning of the Summary of Stakeholders' Submissions prepared by the OHCHR in accordance with paragraph 15(c) of Resolution 5/1. Conversely, the information submitted by B- or C-status NHRIs is not individualized and is streamlined alongside all other stakeholders' submissions.
- Further to paragraph 28 of Resolution 16/21, the A-status NHRIs are also provided with the ability to intervene immediately after the country concerned during the interactive dialogue, following the presentation of a country mission report by a Special Procedure. This practice was subsequently extended to interactive dialogues with an investigation mechanism.[60]
- As a result of these provisions, the ability to record video messages was extended to NHRIs in these two situations.[61]
- Additionally, as a result of paragraph 22(a), A-status NHRIs were provided with the ability to nominate candidates as Special Procedures mandate-holders.

These privileges are in addition to the NHRIs' ability to address the Council under all agenda items in the context of panels or general debates. In the former case, two NHRIs are given the ability to address the panel, while in the latter case they are given the floor immediately before NGOs.

---

59 There is no equivalent to the Commission agenda item XXVIII in the Council's agenda.

60 See minutes of the Bureau of 17 March 2023.

61 See Council Resolution 16/21, paras 13 and 28 and decision 19/119, paras 46 and 47. See Chapter 2, Section 2.2.9.

4.6 Indigenous Peoples' representatives

The participation of Indigenous Peoples at the United Nations, particularly in the intergovernmental mechanisms and bodies, has always been considered essential by their representatives. For quite a long period of time, there was however an inherent contradiction between the extremely dense network of procedures and mechanisms established to deal with the rights of Indigenous Peoples and their representation during meetings of the Commission on Human Rights and the Human Rights Council.

The focused attention on the Indigenous Peoples by the General Assembly, the Commission on Human Rights and its Sub-Commission on the Promotion and Protection of Human Rights, and the Human Rights Council led to the establishment of the Permanent Forum on Indigenous Issues, the Special Rapporteur on the rights of Indigenous Peoples[62] and the Expert Mechanism on the Rights of Indigenous Peoples.[63] The matter was dealt with under item 15 of the Commission on Indigenous Issues and is now considered under item 5 of the Council's streamlined agenda on human rights bodies and mechanisms. Of importance, when it met for the first time in June 2006, the Council adopted the resolution which invited the General Assembly to adopt the United Nations Declaration on the Rights of Indigenous Peoples.[64]

However, none of these initiatives dealt with the very controversial topic of how the Indigenous Peoples should be represented at the Council. Operative Paragraph 11 of Resolution 60/251 contented itself with emphasizing that the participation of and consultation with Observers, including States that are not members of the Council, the specialized agencies, other intergovernmental organizations and national human rights institutions, as well as NGOs were to be based on arrangements and practices observed by the Commission on Human Rights, while ensuring the most effective contribution of these entities. It did not refer to the Indigenous

62 See Commission on Human Rights resolution 2001/57.

63 See Council Resolutions 6/36 and 33/25

64 See Council Resolution 1/2 on the Working Group of the Commission on Human Rights to elaborate a draft declaration in accordance with para 5 of General Assembly Resolution 49/214 of 23 December 1994.

Peoples simply because, at the time of the Commission, they were not recognized as Commission's stakeholders and were to be accredited by NGOs in order to be given the possibility to speak at the plenary.

This situation was obviously extremely frustrating for Indigenous Peoples since the very bodies aimed at discussing issues of direct relevance to them did not provide them with a status that would have authorized them to speak as Indigenous Peoples.

The accreditation process to the Council's subsidiary bodies of relevance to Indigenous Peoples, namely the Expert Mechanism on the Rights of Indigenous Peoples, provided that the meeting would also be open

> to indigenous peoples' organizations and non-governmental organizations, whose aims and purposes are in conformity with the spirit, purposes, and principles of the Charter of the United Nations, based on arrangements, including Economic and Social Council resolution 1996/31 of 25 July 1996, and practices observed by the Commission on Human Rights, through an open and transparent accreditation procedure in accordance with the rules of procedure of the Human Rights Council, which will provide for the timely information on participation and consultation with States concerned.[65]

This process remained largely unsatisfactory since it listed the Indigenous Peoples' organizations after a long series of other entities, which did not represent them and were not subjected to an accreditation procedure of the same nature.

This contradiction started to be debated at the Council and led to the organization of an intersessional interactive dialogue on ways to enhance the participation of indigenous peoples on 15 July 2019. Later, a round table on ways to enhance the participation of Indigenous Peoples' representatives and institutions in meetings of the Council on issues affecting them was organized on 16 July 2021.

However, a breakthrough was achieved by the adoption of Resolution 54/12 on 11 October 2013, which decided to organize a two-day intersessional meeting before the 57th session of the Council and another one before the 58th session in order to hold a dialogue on concrete ways to enhance the participation of Indigenous Peoples in the work of the Council. The

65 See Resolution 6/36, operative para 9, and 33/25 operative para 13.

listed participants were States, relevant United Nations agencies, funds and programmes, international organizations, Indigenous Peoples from the seven Indigenous sociocultural regions, national human rights institutions and civil society organizations. For the first time, Indigenous Peoples were listed immediately after the States and international organizations and before NGOs. More importantly, it did not set up an accreditation procedure.

Even more important was the fact that this meeting, which took place on 18 and 19 July 2024, was a formal intersessional Council meeting. Hence, all the rules and practices applicable to a Council meeting were in place, and a way was found to allow Indigenous Peoples to be represented in a dignified and constructive manner.

Additionally, operative paragraph 23 of the same resolution requested the President of the Human Rights Council to organize the participation of Indigenous Peoples' representatives and institutions, duly established by themselves from the seven Indigenous sociocultural regions, in consultation with the Expert Mechanism on the Rights of Indigenous Peoples and with the support of the Office of the High Commissioner, for the interactive dialogues with the Special Rapporteur on the rights of Indigenous Peoples and with the Expert Mechanism on the Rights of Indigenous Peoples at the 57th session of the Council. This actually meant that from the 57th session of the Council onwards, Indigenous Peoples' representatives were allowed to register as such and participate in the interactive dialogues of concern to them. They were thus included in the list of speakers, after States and international organizations but before NGOs.[66]

A vacuum was thus filled, and a discrepancy fixed. What remains to be considered is how the Indigenous Peoples' representatives would be able to participate in other segments of discussions not directly related to the work of the Expert Mechanism or the Special Rapporteur. Several options may be contemplated, such as equating their participation to that of NGOs but that would add a significant amount of time to the already overwhelmed Council's programme of work. Another option would be to limit the number of participants to one or two per Indigenous sociocultural region, but this would de facto set their status at a level below NGOs.

66 See minutes of the Bureau meeting of 22 August 2024.

Yet another option would be to reconsider the participation of all observers, including those who are not currently authorized to speak at the Council, such as parliamentarians or representatives of local and regional governments. This would be a Dantesque task, but if considered over a somewhat long period of time, it may assist in revisiting the current procedures that are overly complex and heavy. Geopolitics aside, this may prove to be a worthy challenge.

5 The structure of sessional and intersessional activities

The circulatory system is an organ system that permits blood to circulate and nutrients to be transported around the body. This chapter aims to aid understanding of how the Council is performing its multiple functions during sessions or in the intersessional period of time, thus enabling issues to be discussed and situations tackled.

Bodies are composed of fluids, mainly blood, which carry the necessary elements for the body to exercise its functions in a meaningful manner. Resorting to yet another unsatisfactory analogy, the structure of Council sessions and intersessional activities may be equated to the circulatory system, enabling it to perform the numerous functions and responsibilities placed on it by the international community.

The Council was established in 2006 and since then has developed its activities in a constant and comprehensive manner. The number of mandates it has created and activities it has developed have grown significantly and continuously over the years. In sharp contrast with its predecessor, the Commission on Human Rights, the Council has opted for very flexible approaches to the challenges it has faced. New responses have been explored and often agreed swiftly by oral decisions or agreements read out by the President or at times through inclusion in specific resolutions, provided they were deemed acceptable regarding General Assembly Resolution 60/251 and the Institution-Building Package. This high level of flexibility combined with an appetite to cover every possible issue of relevance to its work was and is commendable. However, it has also led to the development of many different layers of tools, mechanisms and procedures as well as different prisms through which to read them, making the Council's manifold activities, sessional or intersessional, hard to grasp.

This chapter aims to decrypt each one of these activities, underlining the framework upon which they were built, their modus operandi, the challenges they may still face and the potential changes that are being or may be contemplated to overcome them. What the chapter does not contain is an examination of the Agenda of the Council. Given the methodology followed by the author, namely referring to and focusing exclusively on available documents and well-known practices, it would have been inappropriate to refer to a matter that is highly politicized and for which few public references exist. The Agenda is included in Resolution 5/1, but most documents relating to how and why it was developed in this manner are not accessible. The fact that there is a fundamental rift between those who would like items 4 and 7 and possibly 10[1] to be merged and others who are absolutely opposed to this is well known. The arguments put forward by both sides are mostly or exclusively of a political nature, their rationale being discussed in section 2.2.11 above.

At the outset, it is important to quantify the Council's work by referring simply to the number of meetings held every year and comparing them over time, including with its predecessor, the Commission on Human Rights. This should be considered against the background of a variety of increasingly stringent measures adopted over the years, particularly in terms of strict time-saving measures – leading to speaking time limits of one minute and 30 seconds for regular Council activities and even reduced speaking time limits during the UPR WG sessions – to monitor and somewhat control the overall amount of time used by the Council on a yearly basis..

The constant increase in the number of meetings between 2006 and 2024 is striking. The number stabilized in recent years, but an average Spring session totals more than the yearly meetings of the Commission. Overall, the number of yearly meetings of the Council more than doubled between 2006 and 2024 despite the reduction in the number of meetings during the COVID pandemic.

1 Item 4, Human rights situations that require the Council's attention; item 7, Human rights situation in Palestine and other occupied Arab territories; item 10, Technical assistance and capacity-building.

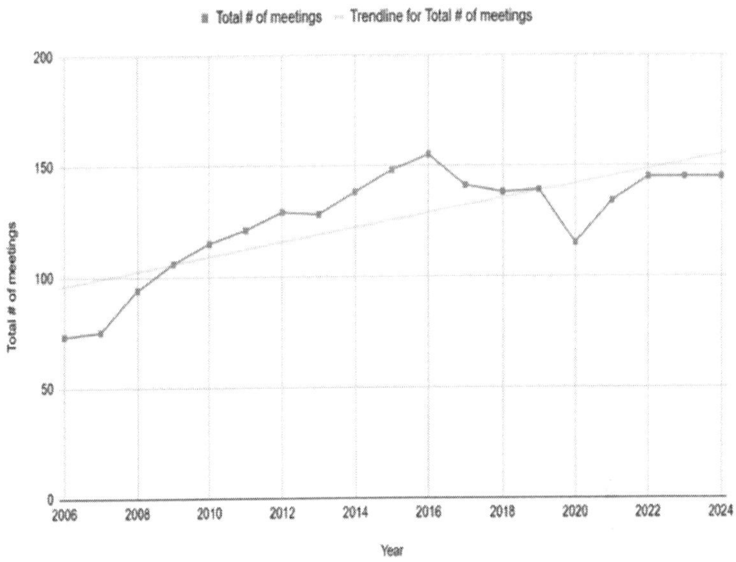

Figure 5.1 *Total number of meetings from 2006 to 2024*

Figure 5.1 gives an account of this constant increase:

The Council has thus seen a marked increase in its workload, resulting in a record number of meetings held,[2] a fact which should be linked with a continued increase in the number of resolutions adopted and, more importantly, the mandates generated by such texts.

It should however be pointed out that the analysis of the number of meetings should be complemented with a decryption of how these meetings are being held. Initially, and for quite a number of years, the number of weeks of meetings remained the same (four weeks in February/March and three weeks each in June/July and September). However, whenever

2 The Council's 'normal' working day is constituted of three consecutive meetings from 9:00 a.m. to 6:00 p.m. At the March 2016 session, this was complemented by eight evening meetings from 6:00 to 09:00 p.m.

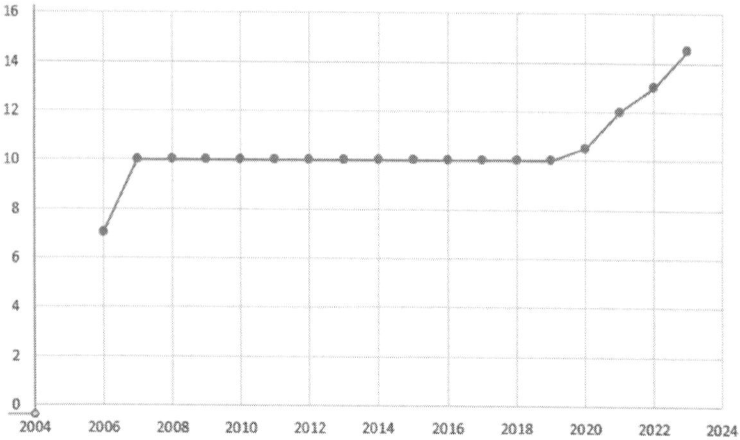

Figure 5.2 *Number of Council weeks of meetings per year*

the need arose, the UNOG Conference Services provided additional interpretation time via extended or lunchtime meetings.

However, as of the middle of the 2010s and with the emergence of successive financial crises, the costs of such extra daily meetings became such that it was felt easier and better to simply extend the Council's sessions rather than adding extra hours every day. Accordingly, while the number of meetings have increased slightly or at a reduced pace since 2016, the number of weeks of sessions increased significantly, from ten to 15 weeks, thus adding to the perception that the Council was and is constantly increasing its activities and overburdening stakeholders – which, for a number of them, also cover the activities of the other Geneva-based UN meetings, including those of specialized agencies.[3]

Figure 5.2 gives a good sense of how this phenomenon is translated into deeds and how this may affect the perception by delegations that the pressure upon them increases dramatically year after year, whereas the number of meetings does not necessarily increase; to the contrary:

3 See above section 3.2.1 and minutes of the Bureau, for instance those of the meeting of 16 July 2021.

The urgent need to revisit the Council modus operandi emerged from the UNOG DG letter of 9 October, combined with the clear perception by delegations since 2015 that the Council was operating at a pace that was not sustainable by most, if not all, delegations. Hence, there have been a variety of initiatives led by successive Presidents and their Bureaux to enhance the Council's working methods and efficiency, or, to put it otherwise, deal with more substantive issues in less time.

These efforts have led to some meaningful results in terms of time management, mostly by reducing proportionately all speaking time limits and applying them rigorously. However, other more substantive proposals faced resistance for various reasons, mostly because any change in the Council modus operandi automatically impacts, legally in reference to Resolution 5/1, or politically regarding the Council's ability to deal with emergencies or human rights, insofar as the implementation of the Council's work at the domestic level is concerned. At present, the Council still operates above the threshold proposed by Conference Services.

However, this situation will inevitably be affected by measures taken by Conference Services as a result of the liquidity and budgetary crises. Whether or not these are steps taken as the objective results of the said crisis or a political desire to make States feel the harshness of the current circumstances is described in Chapter 2.3.5. Whatever the conclusions one may drawn for oneself, it is hard not consider these moves as self-defeating for the UN.

5.1 The sessional activities

The Council's sessions' framework has evolved significantly since its establishment. It is usually considered that the main features of any given session are the high-level and general segments (at the main session), the dialogue or general debates with the High Commissioner, the interactive dialogues with mandate-holders and investigation bodies, the panels, the consideration of the UPR outcomes and the voting process. Whereas this remains largely true to date, many nuances have been introduced over time. A number of new tools and mechanisms have been introduced, for instance, urgent debates, different types of interactive dialogues referred to as 'clustered' or 'enhanced' dialogues, specific general debates following the presentation of a specific report, high-level panels and several other features.

At the outset it may once again be useful to provide some general facts and figures regarding the structure of a Council session.

An important element that should not be underestimated is the sheer number of segments of discussion per session. Excluding the voting process, which follows its own rules and procedures, there are 60-80 segments of discussion during any given session. This implies that should a delegation be willing to participate in all such segments, it would have to be prepared to deliver the same number of statements, something which is obviously out of reach for most, if not all, delegations participating in the work of the Council.

The high number of segments of discussion, which has grown continuously since the Council's establishment, explains why the Council has been obliged over recent years to take harsh measures in terms of time management, reducing them to the bare minimum, namely one minute 30 seconds for Observer States. Additionally, stringent measures have been taken regarding the duration of the panels and the clustered interactive dialogues. However, even with such drastic measures, much remains to be done to reduce the Council's heavy workload to a manageable number, both for the United Nations Secretariat and for all stakeholders.

Lastly, it is of interest to note a lack of understanding regarding the amount of time each segment of discussion represents in reality, thus implying an over- or under-representation of certain features in the context of the rationalization of the Council's working methods and the introduction of time-saving measures. This is also linked to the level of politicization that a segment of discussion may represent: the higher the polarization is, the lower the expectation of engaging in a constructive discussion of possible time-saving measures. Accordingly, there may be a heavy focus on trying to find new ways to deal with panels, whereas the expected gains may be only a few hours. Conversely, since agreement may not be forthcoming for political reasons, the discussion on how to distribute the general debates and interactive dialogues between the three annual sessions in a rational manner was often left aside unless there was an emergency attached to its consideration, whereas the expected gains would be considerable.

Of all the efficiency efforts initiated since 2016, the most significant onecame out of the Presidential Statement adopted on 6 December 2019.[4] Given the delicate financial situation and the continuous increase of the workload of the Council and thanks to the efforts of the Bureau, a major and balanced revisiting of the Council's programme of work was approved. It included three major changes, namely (i) deleting all general debates from the June session, (ii) conducting the annual interactive dialogue on the annual report of the High Commissioner at the June session, and (iii) de-clustering all interactive dialogues. Further measures will be taken in the years to come in relation with the looming budgetary and liquidity crisis faced by the Organization.

Additionally, the rationalization process aiming at bi- or tri-annualizing resolutions and interactive dialogues was given a major boost.

5.1.1 High-Level Segment

The practice of grouping dignitaries in a distinct category at the beginning of the main session of the Council is comparable with the practice of many organizations, particularly its parent body, the General Assembly.

Until 2003, dignitaries addressed the Commission whenever they wanted and spoke from their delegation's seats. This situation resulted in major disruptions in the programme of work of the Commission while not giving appropriate recognition to the status of the speakers. In March 2003, at the start of the 59th session, new arrangements as anticipated in document E/CN.4/2003/118 were set in motion and the very first High-Level Segment was organized.[5] The main features of this segment were that

---

4 See PRST OS/13/1 on the Efficiency of the Human Rights Council – addressing financial and time constraints.

5 See para 6 of document E/CN.4/2003/118, 'Enhancement of the working methods of the Commission Reform of the working methods of the Commission on Human Rights with a view to strengthening the promotion and protection roles of the Commission: report containing a set of recommendations addressed by the Expanded Bureau of the fifty-eighth session to the Expanded Bureau of the fifty-ninth session of the Commission on Human Rights, submitted pursuant to Commission decision 2002/115.'

it was organized in the UNOG Salle des Assemblées,[6] during the first week of the session and provided a higher level of protocol by having dignitaries speaking from the rostrum, discouraging dignitaries from speaking outside the segment[7] and preventing parallel activities being programmed during the segment.[8]

The modalities for the Council's High-Level Segments followed the main principles spelled out by the Commission,[9] it being understood that such meetings now take place in the Council Chamber (Room XX). Additionally, ad hoc rules were progressively identified clarifying from the very first session the process to be followed in organizing the list of speakers. These practices specified that each dignitary would be entitled to a 10 minute segment but this duration was reduced at a later stage to seven minutes.

It was decided that the list would be established by the Secretariat on a first-come first-served basis with several caveats as follows:

- The High-Level Segment is preceded by the Opening Segment to which the President of the General Assembly, the Secretary-General,

---

6 The Salle des Assemblées is the largest room in Palais des Nations – but not the most convenient one since it lacks an electronic voting system and its arrangement is not conducive to interaction between delegations. This remained the location of the HRC High-Level Segment until the Council was moved to the current Room XX.

7 When speaking outside the High-Level Segment, dignitaries – below the level of heads of States – address the Commission, now the Council, from the seat of their delegation and are not escorted into the room by UN officials.

8 A parallel event is expected to generate attention on the part of delegations thus distracting them from the High-Level Segment. This provision was applied extremely strictly for several sessions but with more flexibility in recent circumstances to the point that it can well be said that it is now obsolete.

9 As summarized by para 116 of the HRC Resolution 5/1 according to which 'the HLS shall be held once a year during the main session of the Council. It shall be followed by a general segment wherein delegations that did not participate in the HLS may deliver general statements'.

the High Commissioner and the representative of the host country are invited to address the Council, in this specific order.

- The first-come first-served principle is applicable at the same dignitary level. Heads of States and Governments form the first category, followed by Deputy Prime-Ministers, full-fledged Ministers, Vice-Ministers and Heads of International Organizations. This implies that the chronological order is valid for the same category of dignitaries. Should a Minister withdraw from the list and be replaced by a Vice-Minister he or she will be moved down the list at the first available opportunity to his or her level.
- The first-come first-served principle is applied on a meeting-by-meeting basis. This means that the level of dignitaries is taken into account for one meeting at a time only. A Head of State or Government may speak whenever they deem it appropriate. Other dignitaries may select whatever day they prefer, it being understood that a Deputy Prime Minister will normally be accommodated at the start of any meeting or whenever they wish, while, given their much higher number, Foreign Affairs Ministers will be listed in the first-come first-served order for the meeting which they have expressed a preference for. Vice-Ministers have little chance of addressing the Council on the first day of the High-Level Segment and they will always speak after the level of Ministers and above.
- The definition of 'dignitary' being someone in a position to address the Council at the High-Level Segment was questioned in various instances but solved by considering that any representatives below the level of Vice-Minister but above that of the Permanent Representative in Geneva may address the Council. In order to provide States with the ability to deliver statements without a representative from the capital, a general segment, which takes place immediately after the completion of the High-Level Segment, was established from the very beginning. Their speaking time limit was reduced to five minutes and they address the meeting from the floor.
- The participation of representatives of entities other than States which have a legal status with the General Assembly follows a slightly different procedure. They intervene after all other dignitaries or when an opportunity arises. The heads of a limited number of international organizations which have a long-standing relationship with the Council and the former Commission of Human Rights are thus allowed to participate. Other entities interested are encouraged to

address the Council at its general segment following the High-Level Segment.[10]

- Lastly, it is of special interest to note that, in view of the special relationship between the Council and civil society, four speakers designated by NGOs are given the floor at the end of the general segment. They are not representing any specific NGO but civil society as a whole.[11]

The number of dignitaries attending the Council's High-Level Segments increased in the last decade to stabilize at around 90 to 100 immediately before the COVID-19 pandemic with a percentage of participants at the rank of full-fledged Minister or above in a range of 60–67 per cent.

When the COVID-19 measures were fully in place and the sessions operated in a virtual manner, dignitaries addressed the High-Level Segment by way of pre-recorded video-messages or live feed.[12] This boosted the number of statements (130 at the February 2021 session) as well as their level (81 per cent of participants at the level of Ministers and above[13]). It is of interest to note that despite the end of the pandemic and the encouragement for dignitaries to attend in person the number of participants attending the High-Level Segment remains at a very high level (126 in February 2024) while the level slightly reduced (67 per cent at the full-fledge ministerial level or above).

The level of attendance at the High-Level Segment of the Council has by now reached a comparable level to that of the UN General Assembly although the level of attendance remains obviously lower.

10 See minutes of the Bureau Meeting of 25 February 2015.

11 This implies that the individuals are listed by name (see for instance para 14 of the first Annual Report of the Council contained in document A/61/53) rather than by institution. This also implies that they may or may not represent any specific NGO – for instance a Nobel Laureate or a prominent human rights activist with no particular affiliation.

12 Live-feed was never encouraged for dignitaries' statements since technical hiccups may interrupt the delivering of the message and create confusion and ensuing embarrassment.

13 The February 2021 HLS was attended by six heads of State, three Prime Ministers, 12 Deputy Prime-Ministers, 84 Ministers, 16 Vice-Ministers and nine representatives of observer organizations.

In comparison, the number of dignitaries who addressed the Commission at its last substantive session was 90 and the percentage of speakers at the ranking of full-fledged Ministers or above was only 54 per cent.

Outside the High-Level Segments, at the March, June or September Sessions, dignitaries may address the Council. However, the level of formalism is significantly reduced: the dignitary speaks from the floor of his/her delegation and at a time that is decided by the podium based on the Council's programme of work. The level of visibility is thus significantly reduced with dignitaries addressing a room that is somewhat preoccupied by other issues. However, given a recent trend for dignitaries to express the wish to address the Council outside its main session and given the disruption this may cause, the Bureau of the 13th Council Cycle clarified that in such sessions only full-fledge Cabinet Ministers could do so.[14]

5.1.2 Interaction with the High Commissioner for Human Rights

As previously mentioned, the relationship between the High Commissioner and her Office with the Council is crucial. The complementarity of the two mandates established under General Assembly Resolutions 48/141 and 60/251, respectively, is striking. Methods were thus developed with a view to establishing constructive lines of communications between the two institutions.

---

14 This was discussed at the Bureau meetings of 18 July and 11 October 2019. During the latter meeting, the Bureau agreed that dignitaries may address the Council at the coming September 2020 Session provided that this is at the highest possible level (i.e., head of State or government, Minister for Foreign Affairs, or another Minister of equal rank), the Bureau clarified that 'another minister of equal rank' should be another Cabinet Minister who is a member of the government and whose name is listed as such in the official gazette or on the official webpage of the government. The Bureau reiterated once again that the modalities of participation of dignitaries of various ranks, including at the level of a vice-minister, remain unchanged during the High-Level Segment at the March Session. This position has become a precedent and is often referred to in Bureau minutes – see for instance minutes of the Bureau Meeting of 6 September 2021 or 10 February 2023.

The High Commissioner and her Office are often referred to in the Council resolutions as the enabler or implementer of Council requests. This is perfectly natural since the Council is invested with powers that could be referred to as of a declaratory or parliamentary nature while the Office of the High Commissioner, being an essential part of the UN Secretariat, may be considered as the implementer of the Council pronouncements while supporting fully *and* in priority the High Commissioner independent mandate as it derives from the Assembly Resolution 48/141.

Incidentally, it may be noted that requests to conduct a study, organize a seminar or collect information are sometimes addressed to the Secretary-General of the United Nations In such a case, the Secretary-General normally refers the matter back to the OHCHR since it is the leading department in charge of human rights.

Three times per year, the High Commissioner presents either an Annual Report in March or Updates in June and September to the Council. The Commissioner also presents an annual report to the Third Committee of the General Assembly.

The modalities of the formal interaction of the High Commissioner with the Council were consolidated over a period of several years. The High Commissioner Annual report is currently presented at the June session of the Council and this is followed one day later by a comprehensive interactive dialogue. This enables him/her to take into consideration the discussion held in the context of his/her numerous bilaterals organized in parallel to the High-Level Segment.

The updates at the March and September sessions are considered by the Council in the format of a general debate (namely without a questions and answers modus operandi).

The presentation of the High Commissioner Annual Report or Updates constitutes one of the milestones of any given session. It is in the context of such a statement that the High Commissioner takes a position on thematic or country-based human rights issues and/or priorities as well as on matters relevant to the United Nations human rights architecture and his/her activities as well as that of the Office.

It should however be pointed out that the interactions with the High Commissioner in this context have often been considered as springboards for discussing a number of country issues and from time to time sensitive or delicate thematic issues but quire rarely substantive issues stemming out from the update or the report.

This is complemented by the presentation of numerous reports submitted at the request of the Council under its different agenda items. Their presentation precedes the start of the general debates which conclude the consideration of the item. Owing to time constraints, it is not possible for these reports to be subjected to individual channels of discussion. Accordingly they are normally presented by the High Commissioner or his/her representative immediately before the general debates on the substantive item which is the closest to its subject.[15] Given a recent increase in the number of mandates established under its agenda item 2, the Council has slightly amended its procedure by expanding the scope of the general debate under that item to all matters relating to that item including the High Commissioner update.

An issue which will require serious consideration in the years to come is how to reconcile the increase in the number of mandates given to the High Commissioner's office and the financial and liquidity crises faced by the Organization.

5.1.3 General Debates

The general format for the expression of position at the United Nations is through prepared statements delivered by the various stakeholders during what is commonly referred to as a general debate.[16] At the Council, general debates take place under all substantive items of the agenda, from item 3 to 10.

As per agenda item 2 which relates to the 'Annual report of the United Nations High Commissioner for Human Rights and reports of the Office

15 The same applies to reports of Intergovernmental Working Groups, of the various Forums established by the Council as well as of the Coordinating Committee of the Special Procedures.

16 Although the term 'debate' implies that a form of discussion takes place, this is certainly not the case in the vast majority of cases. In normal circumstances, the General Debates are a mere juxtaposition of statements with no response, if only by way of a right of reply.

of the High Commissioner and the Secretary-General', the dynamics are as outlined above.

All stakeholders have the right to deliver a statement during a general debate.[17] Most governmental and non-governmental representatives consider the general debates as extremely important opportunities to share their position on a multiplicity of issues and listen to other stakeholders. From a lay person's point of view, the succession of hundreds of statements, the duration of which does not exceed two minutes and 30 seconds for Members and one minute and 30 seconds for Observers, may appear prohibitive and quite wearying to grasp fully their sense and importance.

Speakers are grouped into three categories, namely Council Members, Observers (States and International Organizations) and civil society (NHRIs and NGOs) and their order in each category follows a first-come first-served principle. The coordinators of Groups of States (regional, political or ad hoc groups) are placed at the top of the Member States' category.[18]

The number of participants in the general debates tripled from the early years of the Council to the start of the pandemic[19] and has constantly evolved since the establishment of the Council. With the pandemic and the measures adopted to allow virtual statements to be made as well as the cancelling of the general debates at the June session, this number has by now been reduced. As for NGOs, given the increase in the number of expected statements delivered by video-messages, measures were taken to contain a possible out-of-hand increase by limiting the number of statements which an organization can deliver during general debates

---

17 Following the practice of the Commission, in contrast with States which can deliver a statement under each general debate, NGOs may deliver statements under five general debates only.

18 Provided there is at least one Member State in the Group of States on behalf of which the statement is being delivered. Should this not be the case, the Group of State's statement will be moved on top of the Observers' list.

19 There were for instance 355 statements delivered at the 10th session compared to 1,000 at the 42nd.

held during a session and limiting the number of NGO statements to an average of those delivered by NGOs in the three previous sessions.

As far as States are concerned, those delivering statements usually come a few minutes before their allotted time and leave almost immediately afterwards. Additionally, the statements quite often include expressions of position which are a reiteration of what has been said in previous similar circumstances.

In view of the foregoing, the level of attention during the general debates is at its peak during the statements by coordinators of regional, political or ad hoc groups – particularly joint statements on issues of policy or on country situations – and declines afterwards.

The participation of civil society in the work of the Council is quite impressive. Their contribution to the general debates often exceeded that of Member or Observer States. However, a closer reading of these figures shows – without any possibility of corroborating quantities in an objective manner – that the number of statements delivered by lobbies or various groups having an ECOSOC status has grown significantly and now represents a large majority of all statements pronounced by civil society. Often the same lobby, group and/or government-oriented NGO (called GONGOs in opposition to independent, 'real' NGOs) uses consecutive general debates, interactive dialogue and panels to address the same issues or country situations in a repetitive manner. Also, few individuals, mostly from GONGOS, manage to be registered by different ECOSOC status NGOs and deliver more or less the same statements but under a different name.

Whereas the opportunity to deliver statements by civil society representatives is unique and of immeasurable value to the Council and the international community, it is hard to argue that the same is true for the ever-increasing number of lobbies/GONGOs inscribed on the list of speakers. The increase in the number of such entities has had a negative impact on the contribution by 'real' NGOs.

It would be of significance both for the civil society and for the Council and its mechanisms for the above-mentioned 'real' NGOs be identified and provided with some additional prerogatives, thus preventing the hijacking of the debates by lobbies, GONGOs, illiberal groups and similar entities. For a variety of reasons this cannot be done by the Council or its Secretariat. However, in theory, should a third party be in a position to 'certify' NGOs according to objective, fair and equitable criteria, this would represent a step forward. Such criteria may, inter alia, include the independence and impartiality of the organization, transparency in terms of its sources of funding, clarity in terms of both programmes and structure, conformity of the organization's aims and purposes with those of the major United Nations human rights instruments and alignment of the action at the UN level with the organization's announced objectives and priorities.

5.1.4 Urgent Debates

Urgent debates represent a sub-category of the general debates. The modus operandi is similar but the circumstances under which they are conducted and the outcomes are significantly different. These debates are triggered by an emergency situation arising during a session. They are to be considered as specific general debates taking place during a Council regular session based on the request by one or more Member States. They are concluded by a resolution adopted at the end of the discussion.

There is no clearly defined set of rules defining the urgent debates and spelling out their modalities. As historical and political background, it is of interest to recall that the Commission had developed a tool entitled 'Special Sittings' which provided for specific modalities to be followed in such circumstances. The special sitting was to follow specific ad hoc modalities and detailed innovative speaking-time arrangements.[20] The practice of special sittings by the Commission was complex and required heavy negotiations on specific texts, voting in a formal setting.[21]

---

20 See E/CN.4/2004/127, para 25: ten minutes for the concerned parties and 150 minutes for Member and Observer States which were distributed among the regional groups as follows: 36 minutes for the African Group, 29 minutes for the Asian Group, 26 minutes for the GRULAC, 24 minutes for WEOG and 12 minutes for the EEG. The NGOs were not given the floor.

21 However, the requirements for the holding of special sittings were simpler than for a Special Session: such motions simply required a simple majority of the Commission's members present and voting. On 2 April 2002, the High Commissioner delivered a statement on the deteriorating human rights situation in the Occupied Palestinian Territories calling for a Special Sitting to be organized

When the Council faced its first emergency during a regular session, it decided to opt for a lighter procedure which it entitled 'urgent debate'. This was deliberately conceived as significantly less tainted with formalism than the 'special sittings' held during the Commission era. It was conceived as a mere adjustment of its work programme which does not require a written decision. As with any other change to the Council programme of work, a Member State simply addresses the Bureau of the Council with a request to organize an urgent debate. The Bureau then proposes a date. Tthe request to agree to a change in the programme of work may be subjected to a vote, as happened in response to the request to hold an urgent debate on the Eastern Ghouta on 2 March 2018.[22] While none of the previous requests had been subjected to a vote there would be few votes held thereafter.[23]

As per the modalities of the urgent debate, they are simplified to the extreme in that they follow strictly those of any other general debate held by the Council with the caveat that they begin with introductions by invited speakers. These speakers are usually the High Commissioner and a representative of the Coordinating Committee of Special Procedures. Additionally other speakers may be invited to attend as proposed by

by the Commission on this topic. This was followed by Resolution 2002/1 adopted at the conclusion of the Special Sitting whereby the Commission requested the High Commissioner to head a visiting mission to travel to the area and return expeditiously with a view to reporting to the Commission. By its Decision 2002/103 of 16 April 2002, the Commission regretted that the High Commissioner had been prevented from travelling to the area and required the High Commissioner to report urgently to the Commission on the deteriorating situation. By its Resolution 2002/90 of 26 April 2002, the Commission regretted the lack of cooperation from Israel and requested the High Commissioner that the matter be monitored closely. On 23 March 2004, Pakistan, on behalf of OIC, tabled a decision calling for a Special Sitting of the Commission on an urgent basis 'to consider the situation in the OPT resulting from the assassination of Sheikh Ahmed Yassin on the morning of 22 March 2004'. At the end of the said special sitting the Commission adopted a Resolution 2004/1 of 24 March 2004 on the said matter.

22 See HRC 37th session, 2 March 2018.

23 Votes were held at the 4th (Eastern Ghouta), 6th (Belarus), and 7th (Russian invasion of Ukraine) urgent debates.

the main sponsors of the request for an urgent debate to be held. In this regard, an important issue emerged during the sixth urgent debate held during the 45th Session of the Council on the Situation of Human rights in Belarus. The concerned country supported by others vehemently objected to the choice of an invited speaker who was expected to represent civil society. In this particular case the absence of any written materials describing who should select the invited speakers became a problem and led to a long series of points of order.

After the urgent debate, the Bureau discussed the matter and made the following recommendation[24] which may be considered as the literation of a practice for any forthcoming urgent debate:

1. As per established practice, the High Commissioner for Human Rights as well as a Special Procedures mandate holder speaking on behalf of the Coordination Committee should be invited to make introductory remarks during the opening segment;
2. Additionally, the initiators of the urgent debate should be given the opportunity to propose a limited number of speakers for the opening segment. In the case of a country-specific urgent debate, the country concerned should equally be provided the opportunity to propose a speaker to participate in the opening segment;
3. In order to ensure maximum transparency, the names of invited speakers for the opening segment should be announced to all delegations at least 24 hours in advance of the start of the urgent debate

    - The urgent debates held since the establishment of the Council are as follows: The first urgent debate was held during the 14th regular session of the Council in June 2010, on the Flotilla incident.
    - The second was held during the 19th regular session of the Council in March 2012, on the human rights situation in Syria.
    - The third was held during the 23rd regular session of the Council in May 2013, on the situation of human rights in Syria.
    - The fourth was held during the 37th regular session of the Council in March 2018, on the situation in Eastern Ghouta.
    - The fifth was held during the resumed 43rd regular session of the Council in June 2020, on current racially inspired human

24 See minutes of the Bureau meeting of 14 October 2020.

rights violations, systemic racism, police brutality against people of African descent and violence against peaceful protests.
- The sixth was held during the 45th session in September 2020, on the situation of human rights in Belarus.
- The seventh was held during the 49th session in February 2022 on the situation of human rights in Ukraine stemming out of the Russian Aggression.
- The eighth was held during the 50th session in July 2022 on the situation of the human rights of women and girls in Afghanistan.
- And the ninth urgent debate held during the 53rd session in July 2023 on the 'alarming rise in premeditated and public acts of religious hatred as manifested by recurrent desecration of the Holy Quran in some European and other countries'.

If there were any lessons to learn from this, one could observe that out of nine urgent debates held so far, two were of a thematic nature or, at least, did not pinpoint specifically to the human rights situation in one State or a Group of States. This is in contrast with two thematic Special Sessions out of 36.

Until the COVID-19 period of time, there was a sharp contrast in the number of Special Sessions[25] and urgent debates. The convening of Special Sessions by the Council is relatively easy with the sponsorship of only one-third of the membership (16) required[26] and attracts considerable attention from the media during a period of time when the Council is, by definition, not in session. Calling for an urgent debate during a session is an additional strain on the already heavy Council programme of work while triggering moderate media attention loss as they may be in the middle of dense sessions. Lastly, any regular session provides for ample opportunities to discuss any type of human rights issue that may arise anywhere in the world. However, in the past few years, the situation changed. The intersessional period has become far heavier than before and there is consequently less visibility than before on a Special Session. Urgent debates are easier to organize with only one Member State being in a position to trigger such a debate without the hassle of having to gather a sufficient number of signatures. They are more flexible with the

25 Thirty-six Special Sessions compared with nine urgent debates.
26 Thirty-six Special Sessions have been organized by the Council in 18 years of activities.

possibility to postpone the consideration of a given resolution to the end of the session or even not to propose any document for adoption. And, lastly, they also provide more possibility to organize debates on non-country issues or meetings touching both thematic and country matters as the last one on the alarming rise in premeditated and public acts of religious hatred as manifested by recurrent desecration of the Holy Quran in some European and other countries.

Contrary to the Special Sessions which, once 16 Member States' signatures have been collected, must be convened, the convening of an urgent debate may be challenged by the Council. Indeed, being conceived as a mere change in the programme of work, implies that any Member State may actually refuse to alter the said programme of work. In other words, objections may be made in which case the Council may be called upon by one Member State to reject the call for an urgent debate and a vote takes place. As far as the adoption of a resolution at the end of an urgent debate is concerned, the voting process follows exactly the same procedure as the standard voting process.

As far as which tool to prefer in case of a human rights emergency arising close to or doing a Council's session, it should be recalled that there are three regular sessions per year for a total period of more than 15 weeks per year. Additionally, for situations arising less than three weeks before any given session, it may theoretically be considered by interested parties that it could be the subject of either a Special Session before or of an urgent debate during the forthcoming session. Henceforth, for almost half of the year, should an emergency arise, sponsors may opt for an urgent debate instead of a Special Session. The advantage of an urgent debate is certainly that of an easier modus operandi with no need for signatures to be collected. This is somewhat balanced by the risk of a call for a vote on the request and the reduced level of visibility – although the urgent debate on the situation of human rights in Ukraine stemming out of the Russian Aggression attracted a considerable level of attention the web with millions watching live the proceedings.

5.1.5 Interactive Dialogues

The interactive dialogues represent the backbone of a Council session. It is always delicate to share statistics concerning the organization of a Council session. However, one way which the author found of use in assessing the Council's work is to structure sessions according to the various segments of discussion. The word 'segment' regroups every instance when a delegation may deliver a statement. When computing the number of such segments for one given session and distributing them according to categories of discussion, one may gain a good overview of the work distribution as well as the perception that delegates may have of that particular session.

At the 57th Session, the Council's programme of work included 70 segments of discussion representing as many opportunities for States' delegations to deliver a statement. Out of these segments, 14 segments related to the UPR, there were nine general debates, six panels and 42 interactive dialogues. As a comparison, ten years earlier, at the 27th Session, the number of segments for the UPR and for the general debates were obviously the same but there were nine panels and 16 interactive dialogues. During that period, the proportion of interactive dialogues thus increased from 32 to 60 per cent. Conversely all others reduced proportionately.

These statistics are useful in taking stock of a major shift in the working methods of the Council. Interactive dialogues have become the norm whereas at the time of the Commission, they were the exception. Indeed, and this is often forgotten, for the most part of the Commission's history there was no interactive dialogue at all.[27] Considering the importance which interactive dialogues now represent at the Council, it is of interest to note that their considerable share of the Council's time was achieved progressively but rapidly over a period of less than 15 years.

---

27 The Report of the Inter-sessional Open-ended Working Group on enhancing the effectiveness of the mechanisms of the Commission annexed to Decision 2000/109 or 26 April 2000 indicated in its para 30 (xii): 'there would be important benefits in having more interactive debate on the reports of rapporteurs. It recommends that time be made available for such debate in the course of the Commission session, immediately following presentation of the report by the mandate holder'. This was conceptualized and implemented at a later stage following paras 16–19 of document E/CN.4/2002/16 according to which: 'Question-and-answer sessions or briefings may be organized for mandate-holders (to be held parallel to the plenary or during the lunch hours, avoiding to the extent possible the proliferation of informal meetings and the holding of various meetings simultaneously). These meetings are designed to allow for a fuller discussion between Special Procedures, States and NGOs.'

The rationale for such interactive dialogues is linked to the growing understanding that Special Procedures are the jewel in the crown of the Council because of their direct connection with the ground and the richness of the mandates. Therefore, the yearly work of such a large number of experts cannot just be the subject of a short presentation and vague references in the context of a general debate as was the case before.

Additionally, the deficiencies of the general debates should not be underestimated. As previously mentioned, with the proliferation of the number of stakeholders, the debates have progressively become the mere juxtaposition of a large number of statements with no 'debate' nor any form of interaction.

The interactive dialogues have therefore become the normal way for a Special Procedure, commission of inquiry or fact-finding mission, as well as for the High Commissioner reports, oral or written, general or specific, to be examined and commented on by the Council in a substantive manner. Also of interest, the nature of these interactive dialogues has profoundly changed over the same period of time. Whereas ten years ago most of the interactive dialogues concerned special procedures, the situation has significantly changed with the addition of a number of dialogues with investigation mechanisms and a very steady increase of the dialogues with the High Commissioner.

Figure 5.3 shows quite clearly the trends both in terms of the increase of interactive dialogues and their distribution among their three main components:

Their interactive modalities have been adjusted to circumstances but are now quite firmly grounded in the Council's procedures.

The interactive dialogues are structured in two main parts, the presentation of a report followed by a question-and-answer segment. With the exception of the yearly interactive dialogue with the High Commissioner for which there is no speaking time limit set up for either his/her presentation or his/her responses, strict time limits have been imposed on the various participants in the interactive dialogues.

Since the adoption of the Presidential Statement PRST OS/13/1 of 19 December 2019 mandate-holders are provided with a total of 20 minutes, with two additional minutes allocated for every Council visit report and/

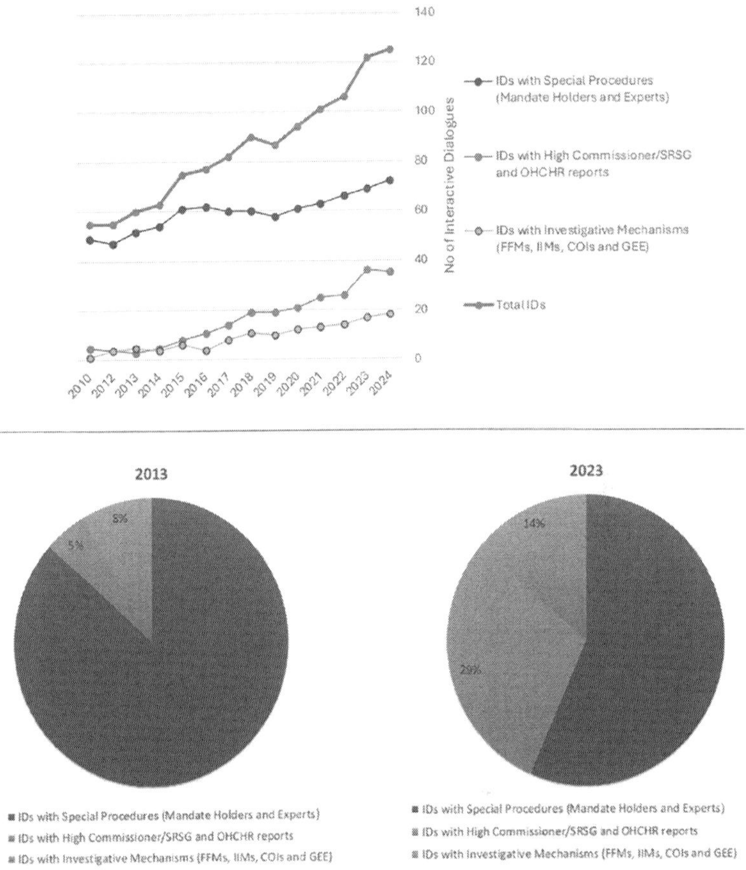

Figure 5.3 *Evolution of the number and type of interactive dialogues from 2013 to 2023*

or other mandated report it being understood that the bulk of their presentation should not exceed ten minutes. This distribution of time is now likely going to be adjusted given pressures from the Conference Services and should be checked regularly with the Secretariat.

Until that date, thematic mandate-holders were, grouped in so-called 'clusters' of two experts, However, this arrangement was not deemed satisfactory since delegations had to squeeze two statements into a very short one and often the issues discussed were fundamentally different and therefore not conducive to a fruitful and coherent discussion.

Concerned Countries

Concerned countries speak for up to five minutes, immediately after the presentation of the reports by the mandate-holders or investigation mechanisms provided they cooperated with them.[28] These are privileges which are of significant importance since the speaking time has been reduced to one and a half minutes across the board and the list of speakers are increasing in volume session after session. Being considered a concerned country thus provides a higher level of visibility as well as a longer period of time to comment on the situation. However, this privilege is not an obligation, and a State may prefer for political or other reasons not to use them, mostly in order to underline its opposition to the enabling resolution or the concerned report.

Quite a number of questions and comments were referred to the author on issues relating to the definition of a 'concerned country' in the practice of the Council since the release of the first edition of this book. In order to square away this notion it should be borne in mind that two distinct situations may be referred to as follows:

- As per country situations, concerned countries are those which are listed in the enabling resolution(s). This appears self-evident but is not necessarily so and is challenged at time, either by States that do not want to be identified as concerned countries for political reasons or conversely by States which desire more time to develop their arguments.
- A reference to the concerned country in the resolution is essential. For instance, insofar resolutions tabled concern Palestine, if the title or body of the resolution refer to Palestine and to the occupied Syrian Golan then the latter would also be considered as a concerned country, otherwise not.

---

28 Of interest, the speaking time limits of these countries remain what they were at the Commission and have not been altered since the establishment of the Council.

However, this reference must be of a substantive nature. Generally, this relates to preambular or operative paragraphs of a given resolution which should refer directly or indirectly to a country in relation to human rights violations. For instance, a country resolution concerning the situation of human rights in one particular country may also draw attention to the situation of human rights in another one in an explicit manner. In such a case, both countries will be considered as concerned countries.[29]

Should a country be referred simply because it was the location where a conference took place or a document, whichever its status, was adopted does not make it for the country to be considered as concerned by the resolution. For instance, The United States were referred twice in a preambular paragraph of Resolution 43/1 of 19 June 2020 on the promotion and protection of the human rights and fundamental freedoms of Africans and of people of African descent against excessive use of force and other human rights violations by law enforcement officers. However, this was done in reference to a resolution and a statement made in other institutions and which quoted the country. The resolution itself did not refer to the situation of human rights in the United States and therefore the United States was not considered as concerned country.

Another issue may arise if a resolution may be considered as implicitly concerning a country without mentioning it explicitly. This was for instance the case for resolutions adopted under item 10 on the cooperation with and assistance to Ukraine in the field of human rights until 2023. Since Resolution 47/22 of 13 July 2021 did not refer to the Russian Federation, that country was within its right in refusing to be referred to as a concerned country by the President. However, as from Resolution 53/30 which included for the first time a reference to the Russian Federation, that country is now systematically invited to speak as a concerned country even if it does not desire to do so and is therefore called upon by the President when the time comes. Also, Resolution 51/35[30] on the technical assistance and capacity-building to address the human rights implications of the nuclear legacy in the Marshall Islands did not

---

29 See for instance the references to Eritrea in the resolutions concerning the situation of human rights in Ethiopia (e.g., inter alia, Resolution S-33/1 of 17 December 2021).

30 Adopted on 13 October 2022.

mention the United States of America and was therefore not recognized as a concerned country.

As per thematic reports, contrary to missions' reports, countries referred to in a report of a generic nature, in a follow-up report, in a table or chart, or in a statement are never considered to be 'concerned' countries. Similarly, none of the countries which may be referred to by the High Commissioner in her/his introduction may be considered as a 'concerned' country. This is simply due to the fact that there is a large number of such countries at any given session and giving them the right to speak for five minutes instead of one and a half minutes would alter significantly the time used for interactive dialogues and general debates at each Council's session.

Exceptions are however being made when thematic Special Rapporteurs undertook field visits and reported back to the Council via specific mission reports. In such cases, the countries having invited the special procedures to visit them are granted the privileges of concerned countries and granted additional time to speak. This was agreed to underline the importance of a sound cooperation between States and the system of special rapporteurs.

National Institutions and NGOs

Further to the Review of the Council in 2011, a special status was granted to A-status national human rights institutions which are entitled 'to intervene immediately after the country concerned during the interactive dialogue, following the presentation of a country mission report by a Special Procedure mandate holder'.

Representatives of NGOs are given the floor at the end of the interaction. They are regrouped in slots of 15 minutes. In practical terms this enables a maximum number of ten NGO representatives, respectively, to address the Council. These numbers have not changed whereas that of States' representatives taking the floor during interactive dialogues has grown constantly over the years which is very different from general debates when the number of civil society speakers is much larger. This explains partly why NGOs remains very hostile to the PRST OS/13/1 which decided that general debates would only be organized in March and September.

5.1.6 Panels

Upon its establishment, the Council's Members expressed a desire to break away from the over-politicization and polarization of the Commission on Human Rights and instil into its working arrangements new formats which would authorize constructive discussions and debates around issues of a thematic nature with the participation of external experts. This was perceived as a complement to the UPR, the modalities of which were being worked out at the specific request of the General Assembly and the purpose of which was to deal with the situation of human rights in all UN Member States in the same constructive, universal and transparent spirit.

Hence, paragraph 115 of Resolution 5/1[31] stipulates: 'Other work formats may include panel debates, seminars and roundtables.' It provides that the 'utilization of these other work formats, including topics and modalities would be decided by the Council on a case-by-case basis. They may serve as tools of the Council for enhancing dialogue and mutual understanding on certain issues. They should be utilized in the context of the Council's agenda and annual programme of work, and reinforce and/or complement its intergovernmental nature. They shall not be used to substitute or replace existing human rights mechanisms and established methods of work'. Of the various tools envisioned in this paragraph, the organization of panels proved to be by far the most successful one.

The typology of panels includes three categories, namely the Annual High-Level Panel on mainstreaming of human rights throughout the United Nations system,[32] the annual or biennial days or panels and the ad hoc panels, the convening of which is limited in time and scope.

---

31 Section VI, A, 5 of the Annex to the HRC Resolution A/HRC/RES/5/1.

32 A/HRC/RES/16/21 provides in its paras 42–44 that:

> 42. The Council shall hold a half-day panel discussion once a year to interact with heads of governing bodies and Secretariats of United Nations agencies and funds within their respective mandates on specific human rights themes with the objective of promoting the mainstreaming of human rights throughout the United Nations system. The present provision does not preclude other opportunities that may arise for discussions between the Council and United

The Annual High Level Panel on Mainstreaming

The Annual High-Level Panel on Mainstreaming takes place during the High-Level Segment, preferably on its very first day to enable the participation of the Secretary-General, the President of the General Assembly and other high-level dignitaries. It is the only panel which is referred *ad nominem* in the Resolution 5/1. Given its very precise scope, it is expected to include high-profile panellists from the UN system with 'heads of governing bodies and Secretariats of United Nations agencies and funds'. However, from the very start, the choice of a topic agreeable to all groups proved to be a major challenge postponing an agreement to very late during the year, usually at the Organizational Session held at the beginning of December.[33]

Annual, Biennial or Quadrennial Panels or Days of Discussion

From the start, some panels were considered by the Council as dealing with topics of such importance that they required periodic consideration by the Council. They are usually referred to as 'annual or biennial panels'. Their periodicity varies (biennial or annual) as well as their duration (half day or full day). They have been established by successive Council resolutions or, in the case of the annual commemorative meeting (or debate) of the International Day for the Elimination of Racial Discrimination and debate on the state of racial discrimination worldwide, by a General Assembly resolution. It should be noted that, apart from their recurrence, their modalities are similar to those of ad hoc panels. The specific

---

Nations agencies and funds on the mainstreaming of human rights. 43. State or regional groups may propose issues to be discussed by the panel. On the basis of such proposals and consultation with all regional groups, the President of the Council will propose the theme of the panel discussion for the upcoming year for approval by the Council at its relevant Organizational Session. 44. The Office of High Commissioner, in its capacity as Secretariat of the Council, shall coordinate the preparation of the documentation required for the panel discussion.

33 The late agreement by the Council on the topic to be selected, makes it, in practice, quite difficult to gather the said heads of agency, bodies or funds as well as other dignitaries given their prior commitments. See for instance the Bureau minutes of 7 September, 9 October and 6 December (Annex) 2012.

themes for the discussion are identified in the yearly resolutions adopted on the said topic. The following is a list of such panels:[34]

- the annual full day meeting on the rights of the child (March);[35]
- the annual interactive debate on the rights of persons with disabilities (March);[36]
- the biennial high-level discussion on the death penalty (March);[37]
- the annual commemorative meeting of the International Day for the Elimination of Racial Discrimination and Debate on the state of racial discrimination worldwide (March);[38]
- the annual full day discussion on women's rights (June);[39]
- the annual thematic panel discussion on technical cooperation (June);[40]
- the quadrennial panel on promoting human rights through sport and the Olympic ideal (June);[41]
- the annual panel on adverse impacts of climate change (June);[42]
- the annual discussion on integration of a gender perspective (September);[43]
- the biennial panel discussion on youth and human rights (September);[44]
- the annual half-day panel discussion on the rights of indigenous peoples (September);[45]

---

34 The resourcefulness of the co-sponsors in referring to these activities is once again quite striking. Indeed, the resolutions identify such panels as 'debate', 'meeting', 'discussion' or 'interactive debate'.

35 HRC Resolutions 7/29, 19/37and 39/20.

36 HRC Resolutions 7/9 and 49/12.

37 HRC Resolutions 26/2 and 48/9.

38 There is lack of clarity as to the status of this meeting given the varying nature and language of the concerned General Assembly resolutions. See General Assembly Resolutions 70/140, 71/181, 72/157, 77/205 and 78/234.

39 HRC Resolutions 6/30 and 53/27.

40 HRC Resolutions 18/18 and 54/28.

41 HRC Resolution 37/18.

42 HRC Resolution 50/9 and 53/6.

43 HRC Resolution 6/30.

44 HRC Resolution 51/17.

45 HRC Resolutions 18/8 and 33/13.

- the biennial panel on the right to development (September);[46]
- the biennial panel on unilateral coercive measures (September).[47]

Non-recurrent Panels

Non-recurrent panels are organized as a result of Council's resolutions adopted to that effect. These are one-time only panels and constitute the largest number of panels organized every year. Their importance should not be underestimated since in quite a number of cases they enable the Council to dwell on novel human rights issues or matters that are somewhat hard to conceptualize. They are also part of a process that may lead at a later stage to the establishment of a new mandate or mechanism. Indeed, any new human rights issues dealt with by the Council start by a new resolution which may be of a declaratory nature and may include a request for a report by the High Commissioner or the Advisory Council. Usually, the second iteration of the resolution a year of two later may include the convening of a panel which will then open the door for the consideration of other avenues for considering the matter at stake – this may be part of a standard setting effort or the establishment of a new mechanism. Also, should a panel on a specific topic be held several times in a short timespan, this will creative an incentive for it to become a recurrent one.

As an illustration of the above, the following are non-recurrent panels organized since the start of the COVID-19 pandemic:

i. panels commemorating a particular event or conference:
   - 25th Anniversary of the Beijing Conference (February 2020);
   - 10th Anniversary of the Guiding Principles on Business and Human Rights (July 2021);
   - 10th Anniversary of the UN Declaration on Human Rights Education and Training (September 2021);

ii. ad hoc panels:
   - New digital technologies (July 2020);
   - Prevention of and response to female genital mutilation (June 2021);

46 HRC Resolutions 42/23 and 54/18.
47 HRC Resolutions 27/21 and 52/13.

- Deepening inequalities exacerbated by the COVID-19 pandemic (September 2021);
- Promotion and protection of human rights in the context of peaceful protests (September 2021);
- Public policies on COVID-19 (March 2022);
- Access to COVID-19 vaccines;
- Menstrual hygiene management, human rights and gender equality (June 2022);
- Countering negative impact of disinformation on the enjoyment of human rights (June 2022);
- Human rights violations against Rohingya and other minorities in Myanmar (June 2022 and June 2023);
- Good governance in protecting human rights during and after COVID-19 pandemic (June 2022);
- Right to work in connection with climate change actions (September 2022);
- Negative impact of colonialism and human rights (September 2022);
- Voluntary funds for the UPR (March 2023);
- Role of media literacy in achieving freedom of expression (July 2023);
- Cyberbullying against children (September 2023);
- Countering religious hatred (March 2024);
- Right to social security (March 2023);
- Quality education for peace and tolerance for every child (September 2023);
- States' obligations on the role of the family in supporting human rights of its members (September 2024);
- Economic, social and cultural rights within the context of addressing inequalities (September 2024).

Of interest from this list, is certainly the predominance of panels linked to high-profile thematic issues of concern insofar as human rights are concerned such as the COVID-19 pandemic, climate change or digital age. There is also a striking echo to the societal issues dividing the international community in the establishment of specific panels such as on the role of the family, economic, social and cultural rights or religious hatred.

Panels' Modalities

The panels' modalities follow an empirical model: although each one stems from a specific resolution, taken together they are progressively geared towards harmonization and consistency. Some elements always derive from the resolutions, particularly the description of the topics to be discussed and at times listing some of the experts to be invited to attend the panel discussion. However, the general thrust of the panels is to enable a presentation of topics by a variety of specialists, experts, invited guests and other contributors which are expected to elicit a constructive discussion with the Council. This two-pronged approach represents the backbone of all panels. This is elaborated and specified further by the concept papers by the main sponsors in coordination with the Secretariat. They are normally introduced at the Organizational Meeting preceding the session at which the panel takes place. Panellists and moderators are listed therein as well as invited guests who may deliver a statement at the start of the panel. The High Commissioner or his/her representative always delivers a speech at the start of the panel followed by statements of panellists. Should there be a moderator it is understood that the moderator 'moderates the panellists' while the President remains in charge of the meeting, giving the floor to delegations inscribed on the list of speakers and dealing with any procedural motions that may arise. The speakers from the floor are arranged in chronological order and divided in two slots and a spill-over list. Each slot includes 12 States, one national institution and two NGOs. Should there be dignitaries they speak first, followed by coordinators or groups of States and individual States or organizations that manage to be included in the list which is drawn up directly in the room via an electronic registry system.[48] The civil society representatives are drawn up and listed using a separate electronic system.

The panels' modalities were thus standardized in a progressive and empirical manner over the years and their duration, as from the Council

48 In practical terms, this implies that most of the individual States' delegations inscribed on the list of speakers cannot address the Council and their statements are posted on the Extranet if they so desire.

37th Session onwards, reduced to two hours. The Presidential Statement adopted on 3 December 2018 based on the Bureau's proposal stipulates:[49]

> The duration of the panel discussion will be strictly limited to two hours. A maximum of one hour will be set aside for the podium, including opening statement(s), moderator comments, if any, panellist presentations, and their responses to questions and concluding remarks. Speaking time limits for the panellists and guests, if any, will be calculated based on the maximum one hour limit for the podium.
>
> States and observers, including national human rights institutions (NHRIs) and non-governmental organizations (NGOs), intervening from the floor will also have a maximum of one hour. Each speaker will have two minutes to raise issues and to ask panellists questions. The list of speakers for the discussion will be established at the beginning of the panel and, as per practice, statements by high-level dignitaries and groups will be moved to the beginning of the list.
>
> The practice of having two slots for Member and observer States (2×12), NHRIs (2×1) and NGOs (2×2) will be maintained but the possibility for panellists to intervene in-between will depend entirely on the time used at the start of the panel.

The number of panellists is thereby limited to a maximum of four including one moderator – it being understood that the one-hour segment set aside for the podium is to be strictly complied with. Hence, should there be more speakers from the podium, their speaking time limits will be reduced in proportion.

The enabling resolutions may or may not provide for a summary to be prepared at the end of the panels and transmitted at the next session of the Council. Whereas the usefulness of such summaries may not be easily grasped and quite at odds with the philosophy underlying the convening of panels, namely that of flexibility, constructive and flexible engagement on the part of all participants, it remains that most of the panels held in recent circumstances provided for a request for the OHCHR to prepare such a summary. At times, sponsors may be tempted to include a reference to a later interactive dialogue on the said summary. Such attempts are extremely far fetched and discouraged since these summaries are nowhere close to a substantive analysis of the issues at stake but a simple UN general compilation of views expressed and the process followed with not much interest substantively speaking.

---

49 See PRST/OS/12/1 of 3 December 2018.

There is strong encouragement for those drafting the concept papers to select panellists and moderators with a proper gender and geographic distribution. This imperious need progressively emerged from an empirical lessons-learned process. Indeed, there is an over-representation of women panellists in women- or children-related panels. Conversely, there is a marked over-representation of male panellists in the other panels. Despite considerable efforts on the part of the organizers, the Presidency and the Secretariat, the situation unfortunately continues to display an over-representation of male panellists across the board.

A broader assessment reveals that the panels' features have had a tremendous appeal for Council's members and consequently their number has grown significantly over the years. This trend became, however, less predictable recently.

The variation in the number of panels per year may be the result of three factors – which could be summarized by a common-sense assessment that 'too many panels kill the panels'.

- The first consideration is that the multiplication of segments of discussion and in particular of panels does not trigger a similar expansion of the interest on the part of the various stakeholders, the media, social network and consequently the public at large. On the contrary, experience shows that it is considerably more difficult to attract interest to panels when there is a large number of them during a particular session.
- The second relates to the time-management impact of the holding of panels. Given the fact that a panel (until the Council 37th Session) lasted three hours, holding 20 of them per year represented 20 meetings per year to be 'squeezed' in the regular Council schedule. Consequently, this led to serious pressure from consecutive Bureaux to discourage the holding of too many panels and to reduce their number.
- The third remark is that the lighter and more innovative the panel is, the greater the likelihood of interest being generated among the participants and the public at large.
- On the other hand, one may also concede that, if well conceived and nicely programmed – for instance one should always avoid a panel on the day when resolutions are being tabled which implies that there will be chatter in the room and almost no one will display any focus on what is being discussed in the room or at the podium – a panel

may serve as a very stimulating springboard for the consideration of neglected or new issues.

Consequently, the future of Council panels may require the introduction of innovative tools such as video-clips or short films, the transformation into question/answers narratives instead of a juxtaposition of statements and an increased attention to organizational matters such as placing the panellists closer to the public, rather than the typical and rigid 'podium' format.

The organization of intersessional panels is increasingly in demand since they serve the purpose of enabling discussions of thematic matters outside the very heavy regular session programmes of work.

5.1.7 Other Work Formats Deriving from the Interactive Dialogues

The Council differs from the Commission in many aspects emanating from the General Assembly Resolution 60/251 and spelled out in the Institution-building Package. However, as mentioned several times before, the main difference in terms of work and functioning between the two bodies resides in the ability of the Council to adjust its procedures more easily to the reality of the world.

From its establishment, the Council opted for a far more flexible approach according to which what is not explicitly rejected or disregarded by Resolution 5/1 should be deemed feasible, once it has been encapsulated in an oral or written decision or pronouncement by the President on behalf of the Council.

As a case in point, as from March 2010 onwards, the Council set up new working methods which were the result of an accumulation of practices. The rationale of this move lay in the unsuitability or inappropriateness of the classical forms of work (interactive dialogues, panels or general debates) to situations requiring a dialogue to be established with a group of experts, UN representatives and concerned countries. The legal background was found in paragraph 115 of Resolution 5/1.[50]

---

50 Section VI, A, 5 of the Annex to the HRC Resolution A/HRC/RES/5/1.

The terminology used in this regard was developed hastily, and lacks coherence and consistence. This comes as a result of the Council's decision-making process, where different stakeholders (core group of sponsors) work on different proposals and after lengthy and strenuous negotiations reach a deal on a text which they cannot reopen once agreed.

The typology of such an ad hoc format is hard to grasp. Various resolutions may refer to stand-alone interactive dialogues, stand-alone high-level interactive dialogues, discussions, enhanced interactive dialogues or enhanced dialogues whereas there never was any attempt at delineating the differences between each one of them. Hence a level of vagueness in their presentation which is commensurate to the vagueness of the enabling resolutions

Even if the terminology varies from one activity to another, a few common elements may be highlighted:

- There is more than one external entity (or panellist) at the podium. Usually a relevant mandate-holder or representative of the Coordinating Committee of Special Procedures is joined at the podium by representatives of the United Nations and regional organizations as well as experts.
- The concerned country is invited to join panellists at the podium if it so wishes and provide its viewpoints on the issues being discussed.
- Other stakeholders such as representatives of civil society may be invited to address the meeting from the podium should this be stemming from the explicit terms of the resolution.
- Whenever the word 'dialogue' or 'debate' is used in the title of the activity or implicit from the resolution, the interactive dialogues modalities or those of the general debates apply.[51]
- It is striking to note that since 2015, there has been a significant growth in the number of such segments. Whereas there were almost no such dialogues previously, the number suddenly rose to three to five per session.

---

51 A discussion is for instance considered as a form of a general debate. However, this term was used at the 37th Session in lieu of the interactive dialogue with the Special Rapporteur on the situation of human rights in the Islamic Republic of Iran who passed away a few days before the start of the session.

The plausible reasons for such a growth may be explained by the following factors:

- The main co-sponsors may wish to enhance cooperation with the concerned country as well as relevant regional organizations and United Nations representatives.
- Given the significant increase in the number of interactive dialogues, the main sponsors concerned about a specific human rights (mostly country) situation, may also be tempted to resort to a tool which departs from the normal terminology (ID, panels or debates) to trigger greater cooperation and visibility and be perceived as being at a level higher than other comparable tools.
- The recent acceleration may also be linked to the introduction of time-saving measures regarding interactive dialogues and panels. The stand-alone or enhanced interactive dialogues are indeed organized in such a manner that a number of 'panellists' address the Council from the podium – thus diverging from the normal ID.

5.1.8 The Universal Periodic Review Mechanism

As often mentioned, the Universal Periodic Review Mechanism – mostly referred to as the 'UPR' – is generally considered the jewel in the crown of the Council, together with the Special Procedures, its main achievement and by all accounts the main difference from the Council's predecessor, the Commission on Human Rights. Its structure, as envisioned in the General Assembly Resolution 60/251 and codified in the Council's Resolutions 5/1 and 16/21, is a rather complex one. After an initial first cycle[52] which saw several issues of importance introduced in its modus operandi or clarified by practice, the procedures of the second[53] third[54] and fourth cycles appear cast in stone and to a large extent quite rigid in their articulation.[55]

---

52 2008/2011.

53 2012/2017.

54 2017/2021.

55 Whereas the negotiations of what would become Resolution 16/21 led to few changes in the Council's working methods introduced before the start of the second cycle, there was no discussion on changes that could be introduced before the third cycle.

The plenary consideration of the UPR outcomes takes place several months after the Working Group's sessions at which the Review took place. The one-hour segment set aside for the plenary consideration of the UPR outcome is divided into three equal parts of 20 minutes duration, the first one allotted to the State under review, the second to the Member and Observer States as well as relevant stakeholders (i.e., international organizations and subsidiary bodies) and the third to civil society. Should one category of speakers consume less than the allocated 20 minutes, the time saved is generally not granted to the two other categories, a practice which enables the Council to deal with 14 reviews in less than 12 hours.

One of the few substantive changes introduced at the time of the Review of the work and functioning of the Council in 2011 relates to the role played by A-status[56] national human rights institutions of the State under review which are entitled to intervene immediately after the State under review during the adoption of the outcome of the Review by the Council plenary.[57]

The modalities for the establishment of the list of speakers during the plenary Review were adopted by the Council on 12 September 2012 at the start of the Council's 21st Session.

As far as Member and Observer States as well as relevant stakeholders are concerned, the time allocated to them (20 minutes) is divided between all those inscribed in the list, it being understood that a minimum amount of one minute and 30 seconds is kept for each speaker. This implies that should there be more than 14 speakers inscribed on the list; those not in a position to speak are provided with the opportunity to post their statement on the Extranet. In order to avoid difficulties in selecting the concerned speakers, all concerned are expected to register the week before the start of the plenary consideration of the UPR, listed in alphabetical

---

56 Namely those NHRIs consistent with the principles relating to the status of national institutions for the promotion and protection of human rights annexed to General Assembly Resolution 48/134 (the Paris Principles).

57 See para 13 of HRC Resolution 16/21.

order with the Bureau drawing by lot the State called upon to deliver the first statement.[58]

The previous system operated on a first-come first-served basis with only a limited number of speakers taking the floor. This led to the unfortunate practice of State representatives[59] lining up for hours on the eve of the Review with a view to ensuring their participation in the discussion.

With regard to civil society, the speaking time limits remains two minutes for all within a segment of 20 minutes maximum.

5.1.9 The Complaints Procedure

The Complaints Procedure which succeeded the former 1503 procedure is something of an oddity and certainly a challenge for the researcher. Indeed, although it is framed in a very comprehensive manner in Section IV of Resolution 5/1,[60] the requirement for confidentiality of the procedure prevents an exhaustive presentation and consideration of the matter. A description of the procedure is included in above section 1.4.2.

The consideration of the various cases referred to the Council by its Working Groups is organized under item 5 of the Council agenda in two successive sequences replicating the Commission's practice:

> At the first (meeting), each country concerned would be invited to make opening presentations. A discussion would then follow between members of the Commission and the country concerned, based on the contents of confidential files and the report of the WGs [Working Groups]. In the interim between the first and second meetings, any member or members of the Commission could submit an alternative or an amendment to any texts forwarded by the WGs. Any such draft texts would be circulated confidentially by the Secretariat in accordance with the rules of procedure in advance of

58 This diverges from the modalities followed by the UPR working group according to which the total amount of time available to Member and Observer States, namely two hours and 20 minutes, is divided equally between all speakers. Consequently, when numerous speakers are inscribed on a list, the amount of time available to them may be reduced to one minute or less.

59 With the intent to either denounce or support the State under Review.

60 See paras 85–109 of the HRC Resolution 5/1.

> the second meeting. At the second (meeting), members of the Commission would discuss and take action on the draft resolutions or decisions.[61]

Delegations from the States concerned, whether they are representing a Member or an Observer State, are invited to attend the first confidential meeting when they can present their position and respond to questions raised by the Council. They also share their general comments on the resolution moved to action during the second meeting.

Further to paragraph 103: 'The Council shall consider consistent patterns of gross and reliably attested violations of human rights and fundamental freedoms brought to its attention by the Working Group on Situations as frequently as needed, but at least once a year'. In practical terms, this implies that when cases are submitted by the Working Group on Situations to the Council plenary, they are automatically discussed on two occasions at the next session. When no case is submitted by the Working Groups during a specific Council cycle, the plenary will nevertheless organize one general debate per year in closed session on the Working Groups report.[62]

At the end of the process, the Council may decide: (a) to discontinue considering the situation; (b) to keep the situation under review; (c) to appoint an independent expert under the confidential procedure; (d) to discontinue reviewing the matter under the confidential complaint procedure in order to take up public consideration of the same; or (e) to recommend to the OHCHR to provide technical cooperation, capacity-building assistance or advisory services to the State concerned.[63] Although the procedure seems to attract less attention today, it is of interest to note that the Council has adopted 25 decisions since its inception. Whereas most cases eventually led to discontinuing review of the situations, one of them included a request to the OHCHR to provide technical cooperation (DRC – 2011) without specifying how this would be monitored.

61 See Decision 2000/109 of 26 April 2000, para 4 (ii).

62 At its September Session.

63 Ibid., para 109. A complete list of the Council action under the Complaint Procedure is available at https://www.ohchr.org/Documents/HRBodies/ComplaintProcedure/SituationsConsideredUnderComplaintProcedures.pdf.

As mentioned in above section 1.4.2 there is a downward trend in terms of the number of cases dealt with by the plenary of the Council. The average number of cases considered by the Commission on Human Rights was significantly higher (4 per year) than that of the Council. While at the start of the Council, a number of cases were considered which was in line with the average of the Commission; no case has been considered by the plenary of the Council since 2014 which questions the very nature of the procedure and its future.

Given the confidential nature of the procedure, it is difficult to explain this downward trend. However, it may be possible to advance an interpretation according to which those States or Groups that had been supportive of the 1503 procedure altered their position when the Complaints Procedure was set in motion out of frustration about its outcome or working methods. In the absence of strong support, the momentum to move cases up from the Working Group on Situations to the plenary may have been undermined. Also, the significant increase in the number of urgent responses to human rights violations by the Special Procedures has probably overshadowed the importance of the Complaints Procedure – which is by nature much slower – and diverted the submission of complaints from the Complaints Procedure to other mechanisms.

5.2 Organizational meeting and sessions

In accordance with Rule 8 of the Council's supplementary rules of procedure as included in Resolution 5/1, the Council is expected to hold one Organizational Meeting (now called Organizational Session) at the beginning of each cycle to elect the Bureau and adopt the agenda, programme of work and calendar of regular sessions for the Council year indicating, if possible, a target date for the conclusion of its work, the approximate dates for the consideration of items and the number of meetings to be allocated to each item. In addition, Organizational Meetings are held two weeks before the beginning of each session and, if necessary, during the Council sessions to discuss organization and procedure. Lastly, in order for the Council to select the troikas under the UPR procedure, the Council is also required to organize an Organizational Meeting two weeks prior to the holding of the first UPR Working Group of the year.

An Organizational Meeting (or Session) of the Council is an official meeting of the Council at which proposals may be discussed and approved by the Council. The contents of such decisions are expected to be in line with Rule 8 of the Council's rules of procedure. However, whenever the Council is in session, it may take decision on any pertinent issue whatever the envisaged scope or programme of work. This was agreed by virtue of the adoption of Decision 5/102 of 18 June 2007 on the 'postponement of consideration of all pending draft resolutions and decisions and of the draft report' which was made necessary by the adoption of the Institution-Building Package at midnight on 18 June 2007.

Since at the very session at which the Institution-Building Package was adopted the Council agreed to defer the consideration of a number of resolutions to the next possible opportunity, namely the ensuing Organizational Meeting, it is thus to be considered that the adoption of any type of decision, resolution or statement is in full agreement with the said Institution-Building Package.

In practice, the Council has also used the opportunity of the holding of Organizational Meetings to take decisions on issues such as the appointment of mandate-holders or the selection of topics for the High-Level Mainstreaming Panel when no agreement could be reached at the previous plenary session. When issues arise in connection with the resignation of a Bureau Member, the Council may also decide to hold a brief Organizational Meeting at the start of the UPR Working Group to elect a new officer. This is done to take advantage of the interpretation services extended to the Working Group which are similar to those extended to any given plenary session.

More importantly, one of the most delicate issues ever dealt with by the Council was partly solved by convening ad hoc Organizational Meetings during UPR sessions. It resorted to a procedural artifice by suspending (instead of concluding) its Organizational Meeting to resume the meeting at a later stage to allow for some form of agreement to emerge. Indeed, when Israel informed it on 14 May 2012 that it would not participate in its UPR, the Council President faced a complex and unprecedented situation at the start of the second UPR cycle. He had to deal with it by resorting to several key procedural decisions, in particular a decision not to conclude the Organizational Meeting on 14 January 2013 and to resume it on 29 January 2013 thus leaving time for him and his Bureau to consult broadly and find a solution. As a result of this process, the Council was in a position to adopt consensually its Decision OM/7/101 on 29 January

2013, which set the course for the holding of the UPR Review of Israel on 29 October 2013.

When the Council is meeting in the context of an Organizational Meeting its membership remains the same as for the regular sessions. However, when the General Assembly decided,[64] upon the suggestion of the Council, to synchronize the Council cycles with its own, this generated some difficulties in terms of the election of its Bureau. From 2013 onwards, the Council cycle started on 1 January at a time when most delegations were not available owing to the end of year break. It was thus felt that the Organizational Session should henceforth be held much earlier, namely in December of the previous year, to avoid a vacuum in the Council's direction.[65] This generated a legal difficulty since the election of any Bureau has to be organized by the body in the corresponding composition. To avoid a catch-22 situation, it was considered that the Bureau members could henceforth be elected by the Council in its previous year composition provided that no member of the Council in its next year composition would raise an objection. Should a difficulty arise, this would have to be dealt with at a later stage in full conformity with the rules of procedure.

5.3 Special sessions

During the negotiations of what would become the Council in replacement of the former Commission on Human Rights, one of the most debated and contentious issues related to the possibility for the Council to meet between regular sessions to debate issues deemed of importance. The General Assembly Resolution 60/251 thus stipulates in its paragraph 10 that the Council should be able to hold Special Sessions, when needed, at the request of a member of the Council with the support of one-third of the membership of the Council. This provision was later clarified and

---

64 From its inception the Council cycles were running from the 18 June to 17 June of the following year. The Council's cycles were aligned with those of the General Assembly by virtue of para 4 of the General Assembly Resolution 65/281 of 20 July 2011.

65 The fear was that should a Special Session need to be organized at the very start of the year, there would be no presiding officer to convene and steer the meeting.

complemented in the context of the adoption by the Council of Resolution 5/1 with the insertion of a Section D and two specific rules governing the convening of such sessions.[66]

The ability of the Council to react to emergencies in the field of human rights represents one of the most distinctive features with its predecessor the Commission on Human Rights. While the Commission organized only five Special Sessions in its long existence, the Council has organized 37 of them since its establishment in 2006. More remarkably, it managed to organize five of them, namely as many as the Commission in several decades, during the year when it was brutally hit by the COVID-19 restrictions, namely 2021.

The Special Session should be held, in principle, not earlier than two working days, and not later than five working days, after the formal receipt of the request.[67]

This rule has suffered few exceptions only:

- Special Sessions held more than five working days after the formal receipt of the request:
    - The 4th Special Session on the situation of human rights in Darfur was held on 12 and 13 December 2006 further to a request dated 30 November 2006. In this case, it should be pointed out that the request was made during the 3rd regular session of the Council which took place from 29 November to 8 December 2011. It set up a precedent according to which when an emergency issue arises during a session it may be dealt with in the context of an urgent debate during the session or a Special Session immediately after the closure of that session.
    - The 7th Special Session on the negative impact on the realization of the right to food of the worsening of the world food crisis caused, inter alia, by the soaring food prices took place on 23 May 2008, while the request was dated 8 May 2008.
    - The 35th Special Session on the deteriorating situation of human rights in the Islamic Republic of Iran, especially with respect to

66 See paras 119–128 and Rules 5 and 6 in HRC Resolution 5/1.
67 See para 122 of the HRC Resolution 5/1.

women and children took place on 24 November 2022, being requested on 14 November 2022.
- Special Sessions held less than two working days before the formal receipt of the request:
  - The 14th Special Session on the situation of human rights in Côte d'Ivoire since the elections on 28 November 2010 took place on 23 December 2010 whereas the request was received on 21 December 2010. This was due to the proximity of the end of the year break.

It is however clear from the above that those requesting the convening of a Special Session are complying in most circumstances with the letter of paragraph 122 of the Council Resolution 5/1. Whereas the Council has often shown flexibility in its work, this rather unexpected self-restraint by the authors may be explained by the following:

- Those seeking to convene a Special Session in non-consensual cases, i.e., in most circumstances when a country situation is raised, may fear that their request for an exception to be made under paragraph 122 of Resolution 5/1 might be objected to by one or more Member States.
- There is an element of contradiction in stipulating that a matter requiring the urgent attention of the Council should be held more than a week after the receipt of the request.
- Convening a Special Session earlier than two days after the receipt generates difficulties in organizing the informal consultations and the Organizational Meeting requested by Resolution 5/1.

Should an objection be made as to the timing of the Special Session, the Council would have to take a decision on the matter during a formal meeting, the first possibility being the start of the Special Session itself.

Between the receipt of the request and the holding of the Special Session, open-ended informative consultations (usually (wrongly) referred to as an Organizational Meeting) should be held and the sponsors of the draft resolution should hold at least one open-ended consultation on the text and table it less than 24 hours before its consideration.

The modalities of the Special Session are those of a 'general debate' followed by the adoption of a resolution - although it would be conceivable in theory to hold a special session without an outcome. While the initial Special Sessions lasted more than three meetings, those held more recently have been shortened to an average of two meetings – although it may happen that given lack of time at the end of the second meeting the Council may decide to postpone the adoption of the resolution to the next possible opportunity. However, the 'general debate' format applicable to most aspects of the Special Session is slightly adjusted in terms of the opening segment. Since the Special Session operates in a context marked by a high level of emergency or urgency, and given the fact that by definition such a session is nothing but a shortened Council session limited to one topic of discussion and possible outcome, there is a need to frame the discussion by providing relevant information at the start of the meeting. The inputs by the High Commissioner, other UN representatives, and independent experts, directly or through the representative of the Coordination Committee, are of particular importance and take place at the start of the Special Session.

The topics considered during a Special Session may be distributed in two categories, namely the consideration (a) of a human rights situation in a country(ies) or territory or (b) of a thematic issue or set of issues. However, the practice of holding Special Sessions to discuss the former far exceeds that for the latter.[68]

Given the use of the term 'special' and the fact that the meeting is held in-between two regular sessions, it should be construed that the matter to be dealt with by the Council in the context of a Special Session should be deemed to be so urgent that it cannot be left aside until the next session. Also, the magnitude of the human rights violations registered or observed would need to be such as to require an immediate consideration, hence the recurrent use of such terms as 'crisis' or 'deteriorating situations' in the title or rationale for the convening of the session.

68 Two sessions were organized on thematic issues, the 7th Special Session on the food crisis held on 23 May 2008 and the 9th Special Session on the economic and financial crisis held on 20 February 2009. It may be too hasty to propose an assessment on this matter, but it would seem that the practice of holding such sessions has dwindled.

As far as the 35 Special Sessions held on country issues or situations are concerned, it is of importance to analyse three Special Sessions, the subjects of which went beyond the usual practice.

The 13th Special Session held on 27 January 2010 was held to address the 'support of the Council to the recovery process in Haiti after the earthquake of 12 January 2010: a human rights approach'. Contrary to all the other 'country' Special Sessions which are convened to deal with serious human rights violations, the 13th Special Session contemplated an approach whereby the Council expressed support to a country in dire need of assistance, including in the area of human rights.

Most Special Sessions are held on human rights situations in a specific country, it being understood or assumed that the concerned country is held responsible, at least partly, for the violations occurring or having occurred. However, given the devastation and atrocities committed by non-State actors, the Council briefed itself of the matter in two Special Sessions. The Council held its 22nd Special Session on 1 September 2014 on the 'human rights situation in Iraq in the light of abuses committed by the Islamic State in Iraq and the Levant and associated groups'. Its 23rd Special Session held on 1 April 2015 related to the 'terrorist attacks and human rights abuses and violations committed by the terrorist group Boko Haram'.

As per the thematic special sessions, it is somewhat surprising that only two of them were held since the creation of the Council, namely the 7th special session held on 22 May 2008 on the negative impact of the world food crisis and the 10th held on 23 February 2009 on the impact of the global economic and financial crises on the universal realization and effective enjoyment of human rights. Indeed, at the time of the establishment of the Council it was felt that such special sessions could or should be held on thematic or hybrid issues (for instance a thematic matter concerning a group of countries). This did not materialize after the holding of the 1st special session on the human rights situation in the Occupied Palestinian Territory and the idea was somewhat lost in the subsequent years.

In the current circumstances when the Council is dealing with so many issues, it may be conceivable to revisit the issue and hold thematic special sessions in between regular sessions to deal with pressing matters in this area (climate change, artificial intelligence, social inequalities, discrimination of any kind, etc.). This would by the way overcome objections by Conference Services since such meetings were generously covered by adequate financial implications at the time of the establishment of the Council.

5.4 Intersessional activities and other Council work formats

From its inception, the Council encouraged a proactive and flexible approach with a view to strengthen constructive cooperation and dialogue between the Council Members. This should be read in conjunction with some of the provisions included in General Assembly Resolution 60/251, particularly its paragraph 5(b) stipulating that the Council should 'serve as a forum for dialogue on thematic issues on all human rights' and (f) that the Council should 'contribute through dialogue and cooperation, towards the prevention of human rights violations and respond promptly to human rights emergencies'.

Additionally, according to paragraph 10 of General Assembly Resolution 60/251, the Council should 'meet regularly throughout the year and schedule no fewer than three sessions per year, including a main session, for a total duration of no less than ten weeks'. The drafting of this particular provision pinpoints clearly the diverging views between those who argued that the Council should be a permanent body able to convene at any time and under any circumstance, and those who held the view that the Council should operate as any other General Assembly subsidiary body. The compromise found in paragraph 10 allowed for some form of convergence of these apparently opposing views by fixing minimum thresholds relating to the number, duration and frequency of the Council regular sessions, it being understood that the Council should be in a position to hold Special Sessions.

Consequently, when discussing the various elements that should be included in the chapter on the working methods of the Council in the Resolution 5/1, the Council came to an agreement on what would become paragraph 115 which was entitled 'Other work formats may include panel debates, seminars and roundtables.' The underlying thinking behind this provision was to enable the Council to meet almost continuously but in formats which were not necessary those of a formal Council regular or Special Session.

However, the compromise which was found was rather opaque with paragraph 115 specifying that 'utilization of these other work formats, including topics and modalities would be decided by the Council on a case-by-case basis. They may serve as tools for the Council for enhancing dialogue and mutual understanding on certain issues. They should be utilized in the context of the Council's agenda and annual programme of work, and reinforce and/or complement its intergovernmental nature. They shall not be used to replace existing human rights mechanisms and established methods of work'. Both the title and the narrative of paragraph 115 hint at possible formats or modalities (see in particular the use of the term 'may' or 'would') other than panels, seminars or roundtables but provides no light as to their modus operandi.

Also, the paragraph does not shed light on the legal nature of such other work formats. In particular, while it is somewhat clear that an intersessional panel takes the form of a Council meeting between regular sessions, there is no absolute clarity as to the status of intersessional seminars not to mention meetings or round tables.

Regarding intersessional seminars, a distinction used to be made between those seminars organized by the Council and those which the Council requested the Office of the High Commissioner to organize. A new category was, however, established further to the adoption of Resolution 38/18 on the prevention of human rights violations.[69] Indeed, the Council decided to convene two intersessional seminars by virtue of operative paragraph 2 of this resolution whereas it required the President to appoint a Chairperson-Rapporteur based on certain prerequisites. Since a formal meeting of the Council may only be presided over by a member of the Council Bureau, the fact that this resolution required the President to appoint a chair implied that the said seminar could not be construed as a formal meeting of the Council but rather as a hybrid meeting between a formal Council and an informal seminar. However, this rather awkward arrangement was reiterated in several instances and was never challenged thus upgrading these seminars in de facto HRC meetings.

69 HRC Resolution 38/18 of 6 July 2018 on the contribution of the HRC to the prevention of human rights violations.

Another precedent had been established earlier by Resolution 37/24 on the promotion and protection of human rights and the implementation of the 2030 Agenda for Sustainable Development.[70] By virtue of OP1 of this resolution, the Council decided to organize two one-day intersessional meetings for dialogue and cooperation on human rights and the 2030 agenda. Using the word 'meeting' made it clear that this was an official gathering of the Council with all Council rules and practices applicable. However, OP6 complexified this interpretation by requesting the President to appoint for each meeting a Chairperson from candidates nominated by Members and Observers of the Council. Hence a new category of Council meetings was established, namely a meeting convened by the Council but not under the chairpersonship of the Council President of or one of the Vice-Presidents

It remains that when the word 'meeting' is used in reference to an intersessional activity of the Council, this means in legal terms that it is a formal meeting of the Council, and it should be counted as such. Participation in such meetings is governed by the same rules as any meeting of the Council during its regular or Special Session.

At times participants may not see the difference between these various intersessional activities but politically and legally speaking these are meetings of a totally different nature. For instance, when an intersessional seminar is being organized, the invitees and the modus operandi lie mainly with the group of sponsors and the OHCHR. Whereas, when an intersessional Council meeting is convened, whether or not chaired by the President of the Council, the latter is fully involved. In such a case, the Bureau operates as a guardian of the Council's rules and practices, including – and particularly – when it comes to those participating in the meeting. The resolution based on which the meeting is convened serves as a guiding tool on how to organize the meeting and, since the resolution was adopted by the Council, this presupposes that rules and practices stemming out of the Institutions Building Package are fully respected.

As with other types of activities which the Council could engage between sessions, efforts were deployed in the context of the negotiations of what would ultimately become the Council Resolution 16/21. However, these efforts did not bear fruit given the continuing divide between those

70 HRC Resolution 37/24 of 23 March 2018.

wanting to expand the Council's work relating to country situations to the intersessional period of time and those against it. While some States were satisfied with the Council meeting more frequently and being briefed on matters throughout the year by resorting to less formal mechanisms or tools than regular or Special Sessions, others feared that such opportunities would lead to additional scrutiny on country situations. The latter believed that this represented 'finger-pointing' and 'double-standards', considered as deficiencies of the intergovernmental machinery. In view of this standstill, only a limited number of intersessional activities could be agreed upon, on a case-by-case basis.

In addition to the above-described political blockage, which prevented the expansion of the Council activities beyond their 'normal' boundaries, organizational challenges played a non-negligible role. To put it simply, the already long list of meetings and their duration leaves only meagre possibilities for other intersessional activity to be held concomitantly:

- Council Organizational Meetings or Sessions – four meetings per year;
- UPR Working Group – six weeks per year;
- Complaints' Procedure Working Group on Situations – two weeks per year;
- Council Advisory Committee – two weeks per year;
- Forums – Forum on Minority Issues, Social Forum, Forum on Business and Human Rights, Forum on Human Rights, Democracy and the Rule of Law and Permanent Forum of People of African Descent – half a week each for a total of two and a half weeks per year;
- Intergovernmental Working Groups – Intergovernmental Working Group on the Right to Development, Intergovernmental Working Group on the Effective Implementation of the Durban Declaration and Programme of Action; Open-ended Intergovernmental Working Group to Consider the Possibility of Elaborating an International Regulatory Framework on the Regulation, Monitoring and Oversight of the Activities of Private Military and Security Companies; and the Open-ended Intergovernmental Working Group on Transnational Corporations and Other Business Enterprises With Respect to Human Rights for a total of four weeks per year;
- Other meetings, which although not of an intergovernmental character are nevertheless attended to by many delegations – the Ad hoc Committee on the Elaboration of Complementary Standards; Working Group on the Issue of Human Rights and Transnational

Corporations and Other Business Enterprises; the Working Group of Experts on People of African Descent the Expert Mechanism on the Rights of Indigenous Peoples and the Expert Mechanism on the Right to Development for a total of six weeks per year.

This brings the total number of weeks of Council and Council related meetings to 33 weeks per year, excluding possible Special Sessions – the duration of which is short but requires significant engagement by States, including various informal consultations and negotiations. If one is to deduct the periods of time when the level of activity is low given the proximity of the end of the year or mid-Summer break, or high given the holding of major Conferences in Geneva, this reduces the possibility of holding intersessional activities to very few weeks.

Accordingly, given the extremely heavy nature of the Council annual programme of work, the vast number of sessions held by the Council's subsidiary bodies and a number of important but unrelated meetings held in Geneva which need to be attended by delegations in Geneva throughout the year,[71] the opportunities offered to delegations to propose intersessional activities are necessarily very limited despite their attractiveness or the potential they may represent.

Nonetheless, suggestions were regularly made to organize an increasing number panels or other formats of discussion outside the regular sessions while retaining the format of formal Council meetings. Initially, further to the 2011 Review, such proposals have been regularly made at the Bureau level in order to privilege intersessional activities, the arguments being that in proceeding with this manner this would (a) alleviate the pressure from the Conference Services to reduce the number of Council meetings held per year and (b) increase the level of attention by international media given the lack of 'competition' from other Council activities during the concerned periods of time.

There is therefore an inherent contradiction between the desire to lighten the Council sessions' programmes of work by moving some of their

71 Conference on Disarmament, HCR Executive Committee, World Health Organization and International Labor Organization Annual Assemblies.

intrinsic components to the intersessional period of time and the serious difficulties faced in planning and organizing them.

As a result, until the end of the 2010s, only a few formal or informal activities of the Council were organized outside the regular or Special Sessions or Organizational Meetings or Sessions. However, with the increase in the visibility, relevance and efficiency of the Council since the start of the COVID-19 period, the number of these intersessional activities has grown significantly. The rationale of such a trend is the impossibility for the Council to absorb all the new activities within the parameters of three sessions per year and the increasing difficulties faced by the Council in organizing its sessions against the background of the United Nations liquidity crises.

5.4.1 Intersessional Meetings

As mentioned previously, the Council may decide to meet intersessionally in the context of a formal meeting but without the President of one of his/her Vice-Presidents chairing. With this caveat, the modalities for such meetings remain those of a formal meeting of the Council. It is to be understood that such meetings given their specificities can exclusively deal with the matters that were listed in the underlying resolution. The meeting not being chaired by the President, there would be no possibility for the meeting to deal with any matter other than those clearly spelled out in the given resolution – thus assuaging those fearing that any such meetings could be used to discuss extraneous matters relating to a human rights situation not envisioned in the said resolution.

5.4.2 Intersessional Panels

The only examples of panels having been organized outside sessions are: (a) the intersessional panel discussion on promoting international cooperation to support national human rights follow-up systems and processes held on 8 November 2016;[72] (b) the panel discussion on the role of local government in the promotion and protection of human rights[73] held on 4 September 2017; (c) the intersessional panel discussion on human rights, climate change, migrants and persons displaced across

72 HRC Resolution 30/25.

73 HRC Resolution 33/8.

international borders[74] held on 6 October 2017; and (d) the high-level intersessional discussion celebrating the centenary of Nelson Mandela held on 27 April 2018.[75] Such meetings are formal meetings of the Council and the Council rules of procedure as well as work modalities are applied as if the Council was in session.

5.4.3 Intersessional Seminars

Intersessional seminars on thematic issues proved to be somewhat easier to organize given their less formal degree and status as well as the fact that they are organized based on specific programme budget implications, meaning that they are not counted as formal Council meetings. Such seminars cannot be considered formal Council activities although they derive from Council resolutions. Indeed, a seminar is of an academic nature which has no pretence of equating or resembling a Council session. As mentioned, these seminars should be distinguished from those organized by the Office at the request of the Council. This is not a simple nuance. What is implied is that a seminar convened by the Council with the assistance of the OHCHR remains under the full authority and thus control of the Council. Its modalities and modus operandi must follow those agreed for such events and the President and his/her Bureau are informed about them. Seminars organized by the OHCHR at the request of the Council are fully within the authority of the High Commissioner and there is usually no exhaustive information about the modalities or participants with the President. Accordingly while the former seminars are under the responsibility of the Council, the latter are the exclusive responsibility of the High Commissioner and his/her Office.

A list of all intersessional meetings, panels and seminars organized by the Council[76] as of December 2024 is as follows:

- Second intersessional meeting of the Human Rights Council on concrete ways to enhance the participation of Indigenous Peoples in the work of the Council – 17 October 2024;

---

74 HRC Resolution 35/20.

75 HRC Resolution 37/15.

76 This listing excludes any activity organized by the High Commissioner or his/her Office at the request of the Council or on his/her own volition.

- First intersessional meeting of the Human Rights Council on concrete ways to enhance the participation of Indigenous Peoples in the work of the Council – 18 July 2024;
- Intersessional panel discussion on human rights challenges in addressing and countering all aspects of the world drug problem – 05 February 2024;
- Sixth Intersessional Meeting on human rights and the 2030 Agenda – 18 January 2024;
- HRC interactive dialogue on the oral update by the High Commissioner on the findings of the OHCHR report on the situation of human rights in Ukraine – 19 December 2023;
- HRC interactive dialogue on the oral update by the High Commissioner on the situation of human rights in Nicaragua – 18 December 2023;
- Intersessional meeting to mark the 75th anniversary of the Convention on the Prevention and Punishment of the Crime of Genocide and to discuss the role of social media – 4 December 2023;
- Intersessional Meeting – Technical cooperation and capacity-building in the Human Rights Council: taking stock of the past for a better discharge of this mission in the future – 20 April 2023;
- Fifth intersessional meeting on human rights and the 2030 Agenda – 19 January 2023;
- Intersessional panel discussion on the challenges and good practices in the prevention of corruption, and the impact of corruption on the enjoyment of human rights in the context of the COVID-19 pandemic – 15 February 2022;
- Intersessional seminar on the negative impact of the non-repatriation of funds of illicit origin to the countries of origin on the enjoyment of human rights – 08 February 2022;
- Fourth intersessional meeting on human rights and the 2030 Agenda – 18 January 2022;
- Intersessional panel discussion on the right to social security in the changing world of work – 1 November 2021;
- Intersessional round table on ways to enhance the participation of indigenous peoples' representatives and institutions in meetings of the Human Rights Council on issues affecting them – 16 July 2021;
- Intersessional Panel Discussion on the 15th Anniversary of the Responsibility to Protect – 11 May 2021;
- Third intersessional meeting on human rights and the 2030 Agenda – 14 January 2021;

- Second intersessional meeting on human rights and the 2030 Agenda – 3 December 2019;
- Second intersessional meeting on human rights and the 2030 Agenda – 3 December 2019;
- Intersessional seminar on the prevention of human rights violations – 8 October 2019;
- Intersessional interactive dialogue on ways to enhance the participation of Indigenous peoples – 15 July 2019;
- Intersessional seminars on the prevention of human rights violations – 9 April 2019;
- Intersessional high-level panel discussion on the incompatibility between democracy and racism – 2 April 2019;
- Intersessional meeting on human rights and the 2030 Agenda – 16 January 2019;
- Intersessional seminar on the protection of the family and human rights of older persons – 18 June 2018;
- Intersessional workshop on the right to peace – 14 June 2018;

- High-level intersessional discussion celebrating the centenary of Nelson Mandela – 27 April 2018;
- Panel discussion on human rights, climate change and migrants – 6 October 2017;
- Panel discussion on role of local government – 4 September 2017;
- Seminar on protection of family and disability – 23 February 2017;
- Panel on national human rights follow-up systems – 9 November 2016.

It is interesting to note that while no intersessional activity was organized during the first decade of the Council, 30 were organized in the second decade. It is legitimate to consider that intersessional activities of the Council have by now become standing features of the Council and should be studied or analysed in the same manner Sessional activities are.

5.4.4 Informal Conversations with the High Commissioner for Human Rights

General Assembly Resolution 48/141 conferred upon the High Commissioner and her/his Office a general mandate over human rights matters from a UN Secretariat viewpoint. However, the General Assembly also conferred on the Council a general mandate to oversee human rights matters but from an intergovernmental viewpoint, hence the need to refine the relationship between these two entities. The need to ensure a constructive and positive relationship between them has from the very start been considered pivotal but it has always been delicate to firm it up given the potential for oversight of one over the other.

Successive Council Presidents and High Commissioners have strived to ensure a constant flow of information and constructive cooperation and complementarity between them. Initially, certain issues relating to exchange of information on the OHCHR programmes and budget exacerbated tension and triggered discussion about possible conflicts between the OHCHR governance and the role which the Council could play taking into account the mandates of the General Mandate and of the Secretary-General[77] in this regard. This was solved by the adoption of three Presidential Statements requesting the Office to organize informal meetings to share information.[78] More topical to the present section was the discussion on the possibility for the High Commissioner to brief the Council intersessionally on country or thematic matters.

The rationale behind this initiative was that the High Commissioner should be granted the ability to address the Council Member States whenever he/she decides to do so. Should this fall between sessions, this needs to take an informal nature, with a broader margin left to all concerned in terms of the scope of the remarks and the nature of the ensuing discussion.

As a result, 'informal conversations'[79] started to be organized from 2015 onwards to give the opportunity to the High Commissioner to brief

---

77 Contrary to the High Commissioner for Refugees, the OHCHR is a United Nations Department which is subjected to the monitoring of the Secretary-General, the Controller, the CPC, the ACABQ and the Fifth Committee.

78 See PRST/15/2 adopted on 1 October 2010 with no title which referred to the Secretary-General proposed a strategic framework for programme 19; PRST/18/2 of 30 September 2011 with no title which referred to various elements relating to the OHCHR budget and funding; PRST/19/1 of 23 March 2012 with no title following up PRST/18/2.

79 Seven informal conversations with the High Commissioner have so far been held on 26 May and 15 December 2015, 30 November

Members and Observers intersessionally as he/she decides but in an informal setting and not necessarily in the Council's Chamber (Room XX).

Accordingly, the informal conversations with the High Commissioner are not, by definition, formal sessions of the Council. They are considered briefings by the High Commissioner and they complement the sessional interactive dialogue (March Sessions) or general debates (June and September Sessions) on the High Commissioner updates. The informal conversations are convened at the request of the High Commissioner and chaired by the President of the Council. The Council Chamber is not arranged with a formal Council setting and there is no webcast. However, delegations are free to ask questions of the High Commissioner on his oral presentation.

Despite their informal and ad hoc nature, these briefings generated some impact on Council activities. For instance, the first informal conversation triggered the organization of an Enhanced Interactive Dialogue on 15 June 2015 on the human rights of migrants. Similarly, it is widely considered that the convening of the 24th Special Session on the deteriorating human rights situation in Burundi on 17 December 2015 was the result of the second informal conversation.

Nevertheless, successive High Commissioners have found it increasingly difficult in recent years to request the convening of such informal conversations. This can easily be explained since it requires the High Commissioner formally writing to the President requesting that a meeting of this nature is convened. The letter being circulated to all Council Members and other stakeholders, it also needs to include some form of justification as to the rationale for the meeting. It thus involves the High Commissioner in some formsof justification or at least explanation as to why a meeting is needed and conversely exposes him/her to discrete requests by States to do the same in other circumstances. In a geopolitical environment which is already pretty charged, it is never considered an easy option to proceed with the convening of informal conversations, hence the relatively modest number of such meetings.

2016, 28 August 2018, 4 February, 6 September 2019 (COVID-19 pandemic), 9 April 2020 and 22 February 2023 (75th Anniversary of the UDHR).

Instead, the High Commissioner, based on the sole General Assembly Resolution 48/141 that established his/her mandate, may easily convene an informal meeting open to all to discuss any issues that may be considered topical. This may include references to budgetary, programmatic or administrative matters. But it may also concern human rights thematic or country issues considered appropriate by the High Commissioner. Since such informal meetings are organized directly by the OHCHR without any link with the Council President or Bureau, there is no way for anyone to exert pressure on what or why the High Commissioner may convene or not such a meeting.

Lastly, it is worthwhile mentioning that the President of the 18th cycle convened to high-level informal Presidential discussions on the link between climate change, food security and health security and on artificial intelligence, new technologies and the digital divide, on 20 June and 3 September 2024, respectively.

5.4.5 Oral Presentation of Specific OHCHR Reports

In addition to the above-mentioned activities, the Council also created a new modus operandi according to which certain reports prepared by the Office may be presented to the Council based on ad hoc requirements outside the boundaries of regular Council sessions.

In prelude to these new developments, the Council adopted its Resolution 29/23 entitled 'cooperation and assistance to Ukraine in the field of human rights' on 3 July 2015 which in its only operative paragraph invited the High Commissioner to present orally to the State Members of the Council and Observers the findings of each of the periodic reports of the OHCHR on the situation of human rights in Ukraine, as part of the interactive dialogues and through the modalities of the Council in accordance with its Resolution 5/1. This opaque request presented some challenges in terms of interpreting and implementing it. Since the OHCHR issues quarterly reports on the situation of human rights, solutions had to be found on how to proceed with the oral presentations. As per the three first reports of the year, it was easy to include them in the programme of work of the regular March, June and September Sessions. However, the presentation of the fourth report could not be included in any particular session. Hence, it was proposed by the Bureau that the OHCHR would present its fourth quarterly report orally in the context of a meeting of the State Members of the Council and Observers. This meeting is not to be considered as a formal Council meeting but an informal gathering of the participants to the Council sessions to enable the OHCHR to present the report and engage with all Council stakeholders. In practical terms, while the meetings are organized in the Council Chamber, the modalities are different from those of a Council session with no seating arrangement, no webcast, and obviously no possibility to take any decision on whatever matter. This precedent was followed by the Council in its Resolution 42/4 and 42/25 on the Bolivarian Republic of Venezuela.

Further to the convening of these ad hoc meetings, the Council also decided to organize the consideration of HC or OHCHR reports by the end of the year in the formal context of a Council meeting. In these cases, the Council is gathering in a formal manner and follows all the relevant rules and practices.

It is, however, painfully true that it is somewhat awkward for all stakeholders to understand how and why the consideration of certain reports may take place in an informal manner in the morning while the consideration of other similar reports may require the convening of a formal meeting of the Council in the afternoon. Topically, a recurrent difficulty occurred with some delegations being properly annoyed – to say the least – of being denied the right to a point of order or a right of reply during an informal meeting of the Council while these possibilities were offered to them when the Council considered a report but in the context of a formal meeting. The rationale for the refusal to granting the right to exercise a right of reply or relevant procedural motions is simply that allowing them in an informal meeting would de jure upgrade that gathering to a formal Council meeting thus re-interpreting the contents of a resolution without the Council blessing.

In view of this additional – and unnecessary – layer of complexity the argument has been made regularly for the Council to consider all these reports in the same manner. In order to achieve this goal, the co-sponsors of the concerned resolutions are approached on a regular basis to streamline the language used and avoid any difficulty as the above-mentioned one relating to procedural motions.

5.4.6 Special Meetings Convened to Listen to Heads of States Outside Regular Sessions

Dignitaries are invited to attend the Council's High-Level Segment held at the start of the March Session. However, on rare occasions, very high-level dignitaries may address the Council outside the High-Level Segment A question arose in 2007 as to the possibility of dignitaries addressing the Council between sessions. Given the number of potential instances when Ministers would be in a position to request to address the Council and the fact that the Council is not a permanent body, it was not deemed appropriate to accommodate such requests. However, the question arose as to whether heads of States or governments could ask to address the Council between sessions. Given their level and the importance of their speeches in terms of human rights and their repercussions at domestic and international levels, it was considered important for the Council to accept those on an exceptional basis.[80]

In 2015, a discussion took place at Bureau level as to the format and nature of special meetings convened to host heads of States or governments. The Bureau indicated on 9 October 2015[81] that: 'a special meeting held for protocol reasons should not be misunderstood as a Special Session of the Human Rights Council... it will be a formal meeting of the Council, to listen to the address of... which will be held in Room XX with interpretation. There will be no possibility to make statements after the address. In line with previous practice, the presence of the High Commissioner for Human Rights is envisaged to make brief remarks'.

At its 6 November 2015 meeting,[82] in view of difficulties that had arisen in relation to the visit of a dignitary 'and with a view to the systemic aspects of possible future requests, the Bureau agreed to have, in the near future,

80 Special Meetings held intersessionally by the Council to listen to heads of States or governments took place in June 2007 (President of Chile), October 2015 (President of Palestine), November 2015 (President of the Bolivarian Republic of Venezuela) and March 2017 (President of Chile).

81 In relation with the request by the Permanent Mission of Palestine to hold a Special Meeting on 28 October 2015 to listen to the address by H.E. President Mahmoud Abbas.

82 In relation with the request by the Permanent Mission of Venezuela (Bolivarian Republic of) to hold a Special Meeting on 12 November

an in-depth discussion of the modalities for special meetings, taking into consideration all concerns expressed, including resource implications'.

At its 2 December 2015 meeting, the Bureau considered the matter thoroughly and came to the conclusion that the convening of 'special meetings' outside regular Council sessions should be strongly discouraged.

Importantly, the recommendations contained in these minutes were not put forward for endorsement by the Council thus remaining a mere summary of a discussion by the Bureau.

As per the modalities of such meetings, it should be noted that when heads of States or governments request addressing the Council intersessionally, this is accommodated in the context of a 'special meeting' held for the sole purpose of listening to him/her. Since such a meeting is not a formal Council session, the rules of procedure are not applicable per se and no statement apart from the podium and that of the dignitary may be admissible. In conformity with the rules and practices relating to the High-Level Segment, no point of order may be made to interrupt the high-level dignitary. Additionally, no right of reply or any motion may be authorized.[83]

5.5 Informal and parallel meetings or activities

The plenary activities of the Council are often represented as the tip of the iceberg with many other formal and informal events organized in parallel. This use – or misuse – of a sui generis terminology should, however, not blur the clear differences between Council activities and

---

2015 to listen to the address by H.E. President Nicolas Maduro Moros.

83 This peculiarity of the Special Meetings held to listen to heads of States or governments is often misunderstood. This comes from the fact that when heads of States address the Council during a regular session, the rules of procedure apply and any delegation may request to exercise fully its right of reply under Rule 115 of the General Assembly Rules of Procedure. This is, however, not possible during a special meeting which is not to be assimilated to a full-fledged Council's session or meeting.

the events held in parallel to it, the responsibility for which is solely that of their conveners. Indeed, parallel events are purely informal and cannot be construed as direct or indirect Council activities. They are the sole responsibility of whichever institution or stakeholder organizes them and have no bearing on the Council's work. The only commonality between such events is their concomitance with the plenary session of the Council. For those visiting the Palais des Nations during the regular sessions, the distinction is quite easy to draw: the formal meetings of the Council take place in Room XX whereas the informals and side events take place two floors below in a constant hubbub, with multiple individuals and groups striding in all directions, talking, exchanging, but sometimes not much, before getting into crowded rooms where undetermined meetings take place.

At the outset, a distinction should be made between informal consultations and side events.

Informal consultations (usually referred to as 'informals'), are meetings held at the invitation of State or a Group of States, who are the main authors of draft resolutions. These meetings are envisioned by Resolution 5/1 as necessary tools in the working culture of the Council.[84] Their convening is the sole responsibility of the main authors. Their objective is to secure transparency and cooperation between delegations. They are also perceived as essential in reducing the level of polarization. In view of the language used in paragraph 113 of Resolution 5/1, should no informal consultation be held prior to the action on a resolution or a decision,[85] this could be construed as a violation of Resolution 5/1, at least in its spirit, and the basis for a challenge during the adoption process.

84 See para 113 of the HRC Resolution 5/1.

85 Given the letter of para 113, it may be considered that Presidential Statements may be exempted from such requirements. However, given its spirit, it is generally considered that action on a PRST should also be preceded by at least one informal consultation convened by the President. The only exception to this principle concerns purely technical texts where the discussion process at the Bureau level was inclusive and transparent and convening a consultation would not be necessary.

The importance of the informal consultations was underlined by the significant efforts deployed during the COVID-19 period of time when successive Bureaus deployed considerable efforts with a view to organize them at all costs, even if this implied holding them in a purely virtual manner. Given the wording of the Institution-Building Package it is quite obvious that despite the fact they are being held outside Room XX they are nevertheless an important part of the formal decision-making process at the Council.

Side events are also meetings held within United Nations premises during a Council session. They are convened by a Member State, an ECOSOC-status NGO, an A-status NHRI or the OHCHR. In a number of cases, meetings may be convened by a plurality of stakeholders (for instance States, NGOs and the OHCHR).

The side events, particularly those organized by NGOs, represent the main bulk of parallel events. It is not rare for individuals to travel to Geneva during a Council Session for the sole purpose of contributing to or participating in such meetings. More importantly, the political and media impact of such meetings – which are sometimes the rationale for their convening – cannot be underestimated as well as the divergences of view between States and Groups of States as per their topicality and modalities.[86] However, side events are of a very uneven nature. Some of

---

86 As an illustration to the sensitivity of this issue, it is of interest to analyse how the modalities for parallel events were envisaged by the Commission on Human Rights: paras 48 and 49 of a note prepared by the Secretariat and included in document E/CN.4/2001/CRP1 referred to the parallel events and provided that:

> 48. NGO representatives duly accredited to the session of the Commission who wish to reserve a conference room for the holding of meetings focused on items dealt with by the Commission should apply to the Secretariat of the Commission. The request should give the subject of the meeting, the time and the name of the person responsible for the organization and conduct of the meeting. These meetings are announced on a notice board outside the conference room. 49. Persons not accredited to the Commission who are invited to take part in parallel meetings should go, with their passport, to the 'Pregny' gate of the Palais des Nations where they will be issued with a 'Visitor' badge. A list of such persons should be drawn up by

these meetings are well attended by a multiplicity of stakeholders and resemble in many respects panels or seminars either on country or thematic issues. Others, which are often organized by lobbies or GONGOs, attract far fewer participants and their link with human rights may be at times be hard to identify.

Given the practical importance of such parallel events, it may be of interest to clarify some of their main features.[87] Whatever their nature and format, side events fall outside the scope and scrutiny of the Council.

> the responsible organization and sent to the Secretariat, if possible 48 hours prior to the date of the meeting.

However, only para. 48 could be reproduced in the list of provisions agreed by the Commission in document E/CN.4/2002/16. The matter was revisited by the Expanded Bureau of the 58th session as a result of which the Commission, on 17 March 2003, endorsed the recommendations by the Expanded Bureau as contained in document E/CN.4/2003/118 and which referred to parallel events as follows:

> The usefulness of parallel events, activities and meetings is generally affirmed and encouraged, as is the need for the existing rules and practices to be enforced. These include the following: All NGOs in consultative status accredited to the Commission should have the right to organize parallel events and should receive adequate space and support; identity badges and passes for persons invited to attend parallel events, activities and meetings should be limited in duration; Where possible, not more than one activity (e.g. seminars, briefings, press conferences, etc.) should be programmed to run in parallel with the plenary and notice of their being held should be given orally in the plenary and posted outside the conference room not less than three days beforehand. Organizers should be encouraged to hold these activities after 6.00 p.m.; In order to ensure transparency and visibility, a schedule of parallel events, activities and meetings should be kept and updated by the Secretariat; Delegations should have access to a list of persons not accredited to the Commission who are invited to participate in parallel events.

The HRC has not ventured into discussions of this nature and the practice followed to this date is as described above.

[87] Resulting from the Commission on Human Rights' practices in this regard.

Since they are organized during a Council session, they are listed in the Bulletin of Informal Meetings. The only applicable rules are those relating to the reservation of rooms within UNOG premises, namely that (a) the conveners of the meeting must be duly accredited representatives, (b) the convener must act either as a moderator or chair of the meeting, (c) the topics of discussion as they appear on the screens and in the Bulletin of Informal Meetings must respect UN terminology, and (d) all rules and practices applicable to the holding of meetings on UN premises must be respected fully. Any dispute regarding the holding of a meeting should be settled with the NGO Committee of ECOSOC. As far as the behaviour of the organizers and/or participants is concerned, this should be addressed on a case-by-case basis with the involvement of the Secretariat and the UN Director-General, as appropriate.

There is no involvement of the President of the Council and of his/her Bureau in the organization and holding of the side events. This principle suffers one major exception: should there be allegations of reprisals in the context of the organization of, holding of and/or follow-up to a side event, they are dealt with in accordance with the prevailing protocols.

The aforementioned requirements for the organization of side events explain why the Council could not agree with their organization in a virtual manner during the COVID-19 pandemic since no one would have been in a position to monitor their implementation by the concerned NGO (see above section 2.3).

6 The Human Rights Council voting procedure and procedural motions

The digestive system involves the breakdown of food into components which can be absorbed and assimilated by the body. This chapter describes how the Council proceeds with the absorption of many types of situations and crises with a view to assimilating them in the format of efficient outcomes. The way the Council takes action on proposals – usually referred to as resolutions or decisions – or motions may somewhat be compared with the way an organism absorbs nutriments to enable the body to operate over time and select priorities. This quasi digestive system, another odd analogy, is studied in the current chapter.

By virtue of the first Operational Paragraph of the General Assembly (UNGA) Resolution 60/251 establishing the Human Rights Council, the Council is 'a subsidiary organ of the General Assembly'.[1] In concrete terms, this implies that the Rules of Procedure applicable to the UNGA are the same in the Council (see Section XIII of the Rules of Procedures of the General Assembly, from Rule 96 to Rule 133).[2]

In Rule 1 of its own Rules of Procedure included in the Council's Resolution 5/1, the Council confirmed this by indicating that it 'shall apply the rules of procedures established for the Main Committees of the General Assembly, as applicable, unless subsequently otherwise

1 A/RES/60/251, 72nd plenary meeting, 15 March 2006, operative para 1.

2 Rules of procedure of the General Assembly, A/520/Rev.17.

decided by the Assembly or the Council'.[3] However, the Council's voting procedure has been significantly adjusted as a result of its own practice from its 1st Session onwards making them sui generis and somewhat distinct from those applied by the UNGA and its Committees.

Several factors contributed to this fact. Firstly, the Council is a body with a limited membership (47). Whereas the UNGA Rules of Procedure have been developed for a 'universal' body with little interest in Observers, those which apply to the Council need to take into account the preponderant role played by Observers. Indeed, almost all proposals put forward for adoption by the Council are sponsored by a mixture of Member and Observer States. In most circumstances, the groups of sponsors include Observer States and it is not unusual for one of them to be leading the negotiation of a given resolution. Hence, some space had to be made for the Observers at the time of the adoption process, although this was strictly limited by the letter and spirit of the UNGA Rules of Procedures. Accordingly, the Observer States are provided with de facto opportunities to address the Council at the very start of the adoption process and after its conclusion.

Observer States may thus propose a draft resolution or decision for adoption by the Council. They may propose, either by themselves, or in combination with Member or Observer States, written amendments.[4] As mentioned in the above Section 4.3, in such cases, they have to get at least one additional co-sponsor additional that is a Member State or if not identify a proxy that may represent their position during the process and/or indicate that it requests the text to be considered by the Council.

---

3 A/HRC/RES/5/1, 9th meeting, 18 June 2007.

4 See inter alia, rule 69(3) of the rules of procedure of the functional commissions of the Economic and Social Council which provides that an Observer State 'shall not have the right to vote, but may submit proposals which be put to the vote on request of any member of the Commission or of the subsidiary organ concerned'. From this provision it follows that if an amendment or a draft resolution is tabled by an Observer State alone, the Council must be asked whether there is at least one member agreeing to have it discussed. This may be superseded by the Observer State identifying a proxy among the Member States to represent it during the discussion, although this proxy may not be a co-sponsor.

Observer States may introduce the proposals for which they serve as one of the main sponsors. They may present these proposals by themselves or in combination with Member States. However, when the time comes for the community of sponsors to respond to procedural motions, such as written or oral amendments, this may only be made by Member States – either one of the main sponsors or a Member State acting as a 'proxy' for the main sponsor(s). Additionally, they may not interfere with the voting procedure or raise points of order in connection with the actual conduct of voting.[5]

Given the role played by Observer States during the negotiation of proposals, they may feel bound to react after the voting process. Since general comments and explanations of vote may only be made by Council Member States, a space was identified for this purpose. Indeed, at the end of the action on all proposals put forward during a Council session, including the selection of mandate-holders, the election of members of the Council Advisory Committee and the adoption of the Council sessional and/or Annual Report, the President declares closed the voting process and when time permits opens the floor to Observer States for some courtesy remarks on all proposals acted upon during the session. This is often equated by Observer States to explanation of votes or general comments after the vote but this is merely a courtesy and sometimes lack of time prevents the President giving them the floor.[6]

Secondly, the Council often adopts country- and territory-related resolutions. Here again, some space had to be found in the procedure to enable these countries to react to the proposals whether they are Member or Observer States. In practical terms, the Observer States that are concerned countries[7] can speak at the Council after all Member States have

---

5 See UNGA Resolutions 52/250 of 13 July 1998 and 58/314 of 1 July 2002 and the subsequent notes of the Secretary-General contained in document A/58/871 of 16 August 2004 according to which Palestine and the Holy See are entitled to raise points of order under rule 113 but cannot do so in connection with the actual conduct of voting.

6 For instance at the HRC 36th Session.

7 Concerned countries are those which are named in the title or the body of a given proposal. There are no concerned countries for a thematic resolution even though it may be deemed as addressing a specific situation which prevails in one or a few countries only.

made their 'general comments' and before the explanations of the vote before it occurs.[8] When the concerned country is also one of the main sponsors of a resolution, it may opt to provide comments at the very start of the discussion at the stage of the introduction of the proposals and thereby voluntarily relinquish its right to do so at a later stage.[9]

Thirdly, as the Council is operating under strict time management, out of an average of 60 meetings in March, 42 in June and 48 in September, the Council can only devote up to five meetings in March and four in June/September to the adoption of resolutions or decisions. Therefore speaking time limits have been reduced to three minutes for any given statement, including for the introduction of the proposals, which takes place at the very start of the process and not a few days previously as may be the practice in other UNGA subsidiary bodies. Also, explanations of the vote and general comments after the vote are postponed to the end of the consideration of all proposals under any given agenda item. This is time-wise particularly efficient when the Council considers proposals under agenda items 3, 4 and 10 which usually attract the largest numbers of proposals.

Lastly, the Council inherited many voting practices from the Commission. These are as follows: when rules or practices existed at the time of the Commission on Human Rights – which was an ECOSOC subsidiary body with its own Rules of Procedures – but were not foreseen under the UNGA Rules, the Council found ways and means of replicating them. This is particularly the case for the 'no action motions',[10] implying a sort of a veto of a resolution which was very commonly used at the time of the Commission.[11] The Council, following the practice of the UNGA Third

8 The voting process starts with the explanation of the vote. Thereafter, the proceedings cannot be interrupted and have to conclude before the end of the day.

9 A Member State that is a concerned country may speak in several instances during the process, during the general comments phase, at the end of it and during the explanations of vote.

10 The no-action motion, when resorted to, halts the procedure immediately and, if it is carried on, the text is deemed rejected. It is often referred to as the 'nuclear' option by those objecting to a proposal.

11 Rule 65, para 2 of the Rules of Procedures of the Functional Commissions of the Economic and Social Council provides that 'a motion requiring that no decision be taken on a proposal shall have priority over that proposal'.

Committee, interpreted Rule 116 of the UNGA Rules of Procedure as providing a potential substitute for the no-action motion. Hence, when a delegation intends to call for a no-action motion, it suffices for it to refer to Rule 116 without specifying a time when the debate is deemed to be adjourned. Should the motion pass, it is considered as adjourning the consideration of the resolution sine die.[12]

The deficiencies of the Commission also had a more insidious impact on the way the Council operates. During the long history of the Commission and in particular in its later years, it was not uncommon for proposals to be subjected to numerous procedural motions such as no-action motions, closure of the debate motions, written and oral amendments and sub-amendments, requests for separate votes, points of order and other motions.

As an example, the draft resolution on 'human rights and sexual orientation' (E/CN.4/2003/L.92) and the five amendments attached to it (E/CN.4/2003/L.106 to L.110) were considered by the Commission at the 61st and 63rd meetings of its 59th Session held on 24 and 25 April 2003 respectively. The following motions were considered and acted upon: (a) a no-action motion on L.92 rejected by 24 votes to 22 with six abstentions; (b) a procedural discussion as to the applicability of Rule 41, para 1, of the Commission's Rules of Procedure (equivalent to Rule 106 of the UNGA Rules of procedure); (c) a vote on the Chairperson's proposal to adjourn consideration of the draft resolution and the amendments proposed thereto which was adopted by 26 votes to 11 with six abstentions; (d) a procedural motion according to which L.106 to L.110 could not be considered as amendments in the sense defined by Rule 63 of the Commission's rules of procedure (equivalent to the last sentence in Rule 130 of the UNGA rules of procedure); (e) another procedural motion invoking Rule 65 of the Commission's rules of procedure (equivalent to Rule 131 of the UNGA rules of procedure) according to which if two or more proposals related to the same question, they should be voted on in the order in which they

12 Incidentally, this explains why the President, in case of doubt, always asks a delegation proposing that action on a proposal be adjourned until when it does wish to postpone the consideration of the text. Should it be until the afternoon or the following day as this has a different impact on the procedure than an adjournment sine die.

were submitted; (f) a procedural discussion according to which the issue of sexual orientation should not be raised before the Commission; (g) another motion under Rule 50 of the Commission's rules of procedure (equivalent to Rule 117 of the UNGA rules of procedure) moving that the previous discussion (f) should be closed immediately; and eventually a vote on a motion (adopted by 24 votes to 17 with ten abstentions) put forward by the Chairperson under Rule 50 according to which the debate on the procedural aspects relating to the draft resolution and the proposed amendments thereto should be closed with the understanding that should the motion be adopted the consideration of the said texts would be postponed until the 60th Session of the Commission. The summary records of the 61st and 63rd meetings of the Commission (E/CN.4/2003/SR.61 and SR.63) record 14 points of order made following the motions under Rule 65 and Rule 50. Dozens of other delegations which wanted to express themselves by way of points of order were not given the floor. The amendments to the draft L.92 were never introduced and the general comments on both the proposed resolution and the amendments never started. The meeting ended at 7:15 p.m.

This was at times considered as a leniency towards filibustering. The Council, being very sensitive not to reproduce these practices, opted for a transparent, clear and strict voting process. It thus resorted to a very stringent division of the voting process in two phases. During the general remarks segment, Member States may raise any procedural motions they wish. However, during the second segment, namely that of the explanations of the vote, this is not possible.

The Commission faced difficulties in adjusting its working methods to the pressure of circumstances. One of the main reasons for this was a longstanding practice of spelling out any change in its practices – from the benign or mundane[13] to the substantive and in-depth ones[14] – in a written proposal, generally a presidential statement, a decision or a resolution. Given the political tension,[15] such an outcome was extremely

13 For instance speaking time limits.

14 For instance the merging or discontinuation of mandates.

15 As a telling example of the politicization of the Commission in regard to the work undertaken in connection with its working methods, it is of interest to note that the 2003 meetings of the Expanded Bureau that envisaged various innovative measures were

delicate and painful, if not impossible to secure.[16] In contrast, the Council opted for a very flexible working process adjusting at times its practices and working modalities in an oral manner, the flipside being a level of opacity in its functioning.

This background had an important impact on some aspects of the voting procedure which were progressively adjusted to suit the needs of the Council. They are as follows:

- Should an amendment be adopted, there is no possibility of requesting an adjournment of the debate. Action on the next amendment or on the main text must take place immediately.
- Should an amendment be rejected, it is not possible for its sponsor to call for a separate vote on a paragraph at the explanation of vote level. This has to be announced during the general comments segment.
- These elements are extremely important but may lead to confusion. Since procedural motions are not accepted after the end of the general comments segment it is imperative that a Member State that may have the idea of raising one depending on the results of a vote to announce it while not having entered formally this segment. It is counterintuitive but needs to be forcefully applied by the Council to avoid reverting to the difficulties of the Commission.
- The management of points of order by the President under Rule 128 which specifies that 'no representative shall interrupt the voting except on a point of order in connection with the actual conduct of the voting' is handled with extreme rigour. For instance, a Member State cannot object through a point of order to the explanation of vote made by another Member State. The only way to express such a disagreement would be through another explanation of vote.[17]

---

chaired by the Secretary of the Commission. See E/CN.4/2003/118 and Corr.1.

16 The 'Compilation of recent documents in relation to the enhancement of the working methods of the Commission on Human Rights (1994–2004)' which serves as a useful tool describing the Commission's working modalities in its last five years contains not less than 12 documents and five annexes.

17 Given the fact that sponsors may not explain their vote, the only possibility for a Member State to express its disagreement against another Member's explanation of a vote is through a general

6.1 Influence of politics, history and psychology on the voting process

Decrypting the Council rules and practices in dealing with procedural motions or the voting process requires an understanding of the influence of politics and history on the overall human rights system.

Firstly, understanding the voting process requires acknowledgement that human rights are by definition politicized and polarized. Opposing a text in substance in a public manner is not always possible. While it may not be a problem for a State to express its opposition to a resolution on the death penalty or sexual orientation, it may be far more problematic to do so when it concerns, for instance, civil society, the rights of women or the rights of the child. In such a case, a State or group of States may be tempted to resort to an artifice of procedural motions, from no-action motions to the tabling of oral or written amendments and requests for separate votes. What may not be achieved by a substantive discussion may thus be secured by resorting to procedural motions. This has a lesser political cost for the concerned delegations. Whereas it is of importance to adopt measures and adjust the Council's working methods to minimize the impact of the politicization and polarization of human rights on its work, it would be naive to believe that these elements can be expurgated from the Council's activities.

Societal issues[18] are commonly dealt with by the Council. They are often the subject of intense debates and confrontations at the domestic level, during electoral processes, debates at the parliamentary level and tension over the activities of the judiciary in this regard, as well as, at times, huge demonstrations on the streets. The Council representing the views and

---

comment made after the vote, namely at the end of the consideration of the agenda item.

18 It is sufficient to mention discussions around the notion of family, sexual orientation, the impact of anti-terrorist legislations, the role of civil society, the activities of human rights defenders, the possible abolishment of the death penalty, the activities of transnational corporations, the right to freedom of expression, the right to privacy in a digital era, the implementation of economic, social and cultural rights, the struggle against xenophobia and racism, the impact of migration, etc.

opinions of 47 Member States, 146 Observer States, hundreds of NGOs, dozens of national institutions and the media representatives, the tension prevailing at the domestic level is multiplied significantly at international level. The Council represents the only UN body where all of these actors are in direct relation to or confrontation with each other. When texts relating to these matters are being discussed they obviously lead to serious but tense discussions and their outcomes can only be controversial. A consensus on such matters is all but unreachable. The fact that, in contrast to the Commission, discussions on such matters as sexual orientation, the death penalty or human rights defenders are dealt with in a tense but dignified matter, whatever the number of amendments or procedural matters, is often at odds with the vocalization of objections and the exacerbation of tensions at the domestic level. This is unfortunately rarely recognized or even understood.

Country situations – for centuries, the Gordian knot of international law was the intangibility and sublimation of the notion of national sovereignty and of the nation-state. In the face of the insufferable human tragedies of the Second World War and of subsequent genocides and global conflicts with unsustainable repercussions for the civilian population, the concept of national sovereignty has increasingly been interpreted, and rightly so, in a much narrower manner. However, the work of the Council, although slightly less tainted than in the past with remarks on the supremacy of the notions of national sovereignty and domestic law over anything else, remains extremely divisive when country situations are being discussed.

Secondly, the human rights architecture of today is the result of more than 75 years of intense activity at the UN level, each generation adding its layer of new norms, instruments or mechanisms.

The oddity of such a system is that most of these layers continue to be operational. The Council continues to adopt new norms as the Commission did in the first decades of its activities; it continues to set up country or thematic special procedures as the Commission did from the mid-1970s onwards; it continues to consider Complaints Procedures (previously referred to as the 1503 procedure) and it organizes Special Sessions or urgent debates, as anticipated in the 1990s.

In addition, the Council has added to these a vast number of new procedures and mechanisms such as the UPR, a number of investigation processes, many different panels and expanded forms of interactive dialogues. It has maximized the interaction with the High Commissioner for Human Rights, and created sui generis and ad hoc tools.[19] With the exception of the Commission, which was abolished, none of these systems have been abolished or set aside.

This juxtaposition of layers[20] linked to the multiplication of actors has created a structure that is hard to decipher and apprehend by most of the stakeholders with a multiplicity of procedures and tools, none of which is easily understood. This opacity has been seriously reinforced by efforts made to be as flexible as possible, thus avoiding the codification of procedures and working methods which led the Commission to paralysis in the early years of the twenty-first century. To describe it otherwise, the Council, in order to avoid the paralysis of the past, is adjusting its methods on a regular basis by resorting to precedents which are of a public nature but at times hard to identify in the plethora of documents emanating from it.

There is no official or comprehensive text or manual describing the ways and means for the Council to deal with its work, particularly regarding its modus operandi, procedural motions or the operation of the voting process. Some delegations may be tempted to resort to some imaginative procedural tactics based on the uncertain or unwritten nature of some of these rules and procedures. To counter this plausible course of action, successive Presidents, their Bureaux and the Secretariat strictly framed the various motions that might have, if handled differently, seriously discredited the Council.[21]

Thirdly, nowhere else in the United Nations or other international organizations systems does the civil society (NGOs and to a lesser degree

---

19 Joint statements, enhanced interactive dialogues, expanded panels, etc.

20 See Section 2.2, Chapter 2.

21 The strict handling of procedural motions as well as the voting process comes in sharp contrast with the large flexibility in regard to the creation and handling of new mechanisms and tools which is usually based on practices and common law rather than on their written conceptualization, which would be hard, if not impossible, to achieve.

NHRIs) participate in the work of these bodies. For all practical purposes they are provided with the same prerogatives as Observer States with the sole exception of the possibility of moving procedural motions and participating in the vote. They sit in the room next to international organizations, intervene in a significant number of cases in interactive dialogues and panels, and in unlimited manner during the general debates, organize numerous side events and may even participate in informals. The number of organizations and individuals is increasing almost exponentially, making them a prominent stakeholder and placing the Council in a unique position compared with the rest of the UN system, where civil society is not or is hardly, recognized. Their overwhelming presence and the fact that they may touch on a vast number of thematic issues or country situations have generated a number of procedural motions against them.

Additionally, while NGOs do not have a say when it comes to procedural matters, their mere presence and the potential loudspeakers, symbolically speaking, which they represent shed light on contradictions or anomalies in the States' position on specific thematic or country issues. This has an influence on how States position themselves during a voting process. In order to avoid a direct confrontation with civil society based, for instance, on values adhered to or not by the concerned countries, they may be tempted to resort to artificial procedural discussion rather than discussing issues of substance in a public manner.

Fourthly, while the Council voting process is often read out against the background of the political or legal prisms, the importance of psychology should not be overlooked. While it can certainly not be considered that the Council or the States that compose it are influenced by subjective considerations of this nature, this does not extend to the humans who compose the delegations. Surely, there is primary consideration as to whether a country may or may not support a certain resolution or part of it. There is, however, a certain leeway in considering the methodology that is used in opposing a certain move. If a country or group of countries considers that a certain matter or language should simply not be included in a formal text adopted by the Council, the way it/they object to it may vary considerably depending on the circumstances.

If, for instance, the matter at hand is extremely controversial in nature, the concerned delegation(s) will deploy every possible means to counter it, even if it has no hope of obtaining the minimum support behind its stand. This strategy will have the advantage of displaying publicly in the Council room, vis-à-vis other delegations, and beyond it vis-à-vis the authorities at home or the public at large via the webcast, its total and intangible rejection of a text or specific language. Here, the objective will be to express in the most vocal manner the rejection of the initiative for any future reference. Whether or not the motions will be rejected by an overwhelming number of votes will have no impact on the posture of the delegation. This political stand reinforced by psychological considerations has often been observed when matters relating to the Middle-East or to sensitive societal issues such as sexual orientation were considered by the Council.

In a number of circumstances, however, the position of a delegation may evolve from that of a total rejection by all possible means, ranging from an avalanche of procedural motions to that of a polite and courteous series of statements followed by one single request for a vote on the text as a whole. A text may thus be adopted over a period of 30 minutes or four hours based on a mixture of political and psychological considerations.

In this regard, the way the text is negotiated plays a leading role. If the concerned country or group of countries is given the opportunity to propose language, to be heard in the informals, to be approached for bilateral informal discussions, to be shown a certain level of 'respect', this may lead to a significant reduction of the number of motions and at times this may even incite the concerned delegations to disassociate themselves from the text without calling for a vote. By opposition, if the sponsors of the initiatives are utterly convinced that their text will be adopted by a broad majority and neglect or disregard any constructive engagement with those opposed to it, then there is a high risk that the concerned delegations will engage in a futile process marred with psychologically unequivocal objection.

In a very limited number of cases this may also be read in conjunction with the hope that the text may be rejected in New York at the UNGA level – in which case the succession of votes may give an indication that the text is highly controversial and far from being consensual. However, in most cases, this struggle will have no aim other than flagging in the most obvious and public manner the resolute rejection of both the text and the way it was moved to adoption. This will have no practical implication but serves as a painful reminder that procedural motions may serve as a weapon in a quasi-psychological 'warfare'.

Fifthly, countries belong to various groupings based on geographic or political proximity. A State may be member of one of the five regional groups as well as political or other groups. For instance, an Asian State may obviously be member of the Asian Group but may also be member of the Non-Aligned Movement, the Organization of the Islamic Conference, ASEAN, the Organization Internationale de la Francophonie or the Commonwealth, the LDCs and of what is referred to in Geneva as the 'Like-Minded Group' – an informal group of States which was established during the Commission era to oppose the views supported by the European Union and other countries sharing comparable values. Similarly, a European State may belong to the Western European and Others Group or Eastern European Group as well as the European Union, the Organization Internationale de la Francophonie, the Commonwealth, the Community of Spanish or Portuguese Speaking countries or the group of Nordic countries, or the Organization of the Islamic Conference.

Belonging to most of these groups does not require a formal adherence to a specific strategy when the consideration of procedural motion or of the voting process is concerned. It is usually limited to delivering joint statements, co-sponsoring various initiatives or adhering in a broad manner to common values. However, in certain specific cases, this goes much deeper and encourages adherence to certain tactics or strategies. This may lead a country that has absolutely no interest in a certain issue to strongly object to or support it, based on the importance of solidarity with fellow members of the same group expecting that the favour will be reciprocated in situations of direct interest to it.

In certain very specific cases, a State may belong to groups which hold opposite views on the same topic. This places it in a very uncomfortable situation and obliges it to build up strategies enabling it to accommodate this 'quasi-schizophrenic' condition. The Council has been very flexible in accommodating these predicaments. For instance, it is perfectly possible for a State to table a text as a co-sponsor but abstain or even vote against it when it comes to a vote, or vote in favour of a text amending it. This may or may not be formalized by adding a footnote to the draft resolution which says that a certain country belonging to the submitting group has withdrawn from the text. Other means used to overcome this problematic situation are disassociating from a text or part of it or not participating in a vote. Also, a State may simply give up in its efforts at explaining what cannot really be explained and instead decline to participate in the vote – in which it will be considered as absent.

The explanations of votes which may be offered in such cases are at times quite interesting.

Lastly, it should be remembered that whatever the success of the Council in the years that succeeded the start of the COVID-19 period, it remains a mirror of international society. If multilateralism is in crisis as it is at the time of writing of this second edition, it would be quite unrealistic to expect the Council to remain unaffected by such turmoil and deprived of political acrimony and the subsequent erosion of trust between delegations. In such periods of time, more than ever, the Council needs to adhere to strict decision-making rules and practices, thus enabling it to implement its programme of work without unnecessary troubles. And, this is precisely what the Council did...

6.2 When does the Council adopt formal decisions or resolutions?

In what would seem tautology, the Council can only adopt proposals or deal with procedural motions when it is officially in session. When it is not in session, it cannot by definition convene a session or meeting.

This may have important repercussions when the Council President, normally supported by his/her Bureau and the whole membership of the Council, considers that a certain decision, resolution or Presidential Statements (PRST) should be adopted.[22]

22 When Israel decided by way of a letter dated 14 May 2012 not to participate in the UPR mechanism, the Council President had to face an unprecedented situation at the start of the 2013 cycle. He dealt with it by resorting to several key procedural decisions, in particular a decision not to conclude the Organizational Meeting on 14 January 2013 and resume it on 29 January 2013, thus leaving time for him and his Bureau to consult broadly and suggest a proper course of action. As a result of this process, the Council was eventually in a position to adopt consensually its decision OM/7/101

When the Council is not in a position to conclude its work at a given ordinary session it must therefore identify new dates to resume and conclude the session,[23] hence the importance of identifying clearly when a formal Council session starts and ends.

- Ordinary Sessions of the Council are held three times per year in March, June and September.[24]
- Special Sessions of the Council are convened at the request of a member of the Council with the support of one-third of the membership of the Council.
- The annual Organizational Session is convened each December to elect the Council Bureau and to consider and adopt the agenda,

on 29 January 2013 which set the course for the holding of the UPR Review of Israel on 29 October 2013.

23 The Council 2nd Session was held from 18 September to 6 October and from 27 to 29 November 2006. The Council 6th Session was held from 10 to 28 September and from 10 to 14 December 2007, respectively.

24 In accordance with OP10 of A/RES/60/251. When the Council first met in June 2006, given the prescription in that paragraph that it should hold 'no fewer' than three sessions per year, the schedule of these sessions was to include a session in the latter part of the year. Hence, the 3rd Session was scheduled from 29 November to 8 December 2006. The timing of these three sessions had to be changed in subsequent years to synchronize the sequence of the Council sessions with those of the 3rd Committee and Plenary of the General Assembly at which the President of the Council is deemed to present the Council Annual Report and engage in an interactive dialogue.

programme of work and calendar of regular session for the Council year.[25,26]

- The Organizational Meetings are held two weeks before the beginning of each session.[27]
- An Organizational Meeting is held prior to the first UPR Working Group session of the year to select the 'troikas'.[28]

Outside these sessions, the Council cannot adopt any decision or deal with procedural motions. However, since the Council is increasingly resorting to the convening of formal intersessional panels or meetings, the possibility may be contemplated that in future decisions may also be adopted on these occasions if deemed appropriate or necessary.

This cannot be extended to the 'other formats' referred to in OP115 of HRC Resolution 5/1 which may include debates, seminars and round tables when the Council's rules of procedure do not apply. The same thinking extends to the informal conversations which were recently added to the toolbox of mechanisms. These are informal dialogues held between the High Commissioner for Human Rights and the Members and Observers outside the parameters of a formal session or meeting of the Council.

---

25 The scope of Organizational Meetings or Sessions was extended very early to include the adoption of substantive proposals. This was done by virtue of the adoption of Decision 5/102 of 18 June 2007 on the 'postponement of consideration of all pending draft resolutions and decisions and of the draft report' which was made necessary by the adoption of the IBP at midnight on 18 June 2007. Since at the very session at which the IBP was adopted, the Council agreed to defer the consideration to the next possible opportunity, namely the ensuing Organizational Meeting, it is to be considered that the adoption of any type of decisions, resolutions or statements is in full agreement with the said IBP.

26 In accordance with rule 8(a) of the Council's rules of procedures as contained in Section VII of the HRC Resolution A/HRC/5/1. Although this paragraph refers to a 'meeting' the term 'session' was preferred to operate a distinction with the Organizational Meetings held at different periods of time during the year.

27 Ibid., rule 8(b).

28 Ibid., OP 18(d). See also, PRST A/HRC/OM/L.1 adopted on 28 February 2008.

A discussion arose in 2015 as to the format and nature of special meetings convened to host heads of States or governments on an intersessional basis. The Council Bureau, considering such a request on 19 October 2015, indicated that: 'a special meeting held for protocol reasons should not be misunderstood as a Special Session of the Human Rights Council… it will be a formal meeting of the Council, to listen to the address of… which will be held in Room XX with interpretation. There will be no possibility to make statements after the address. In line with previous practice, the presence of the High Commissioner for Human Rights is envisaged to make brief remarks'. Further, at its 6 November 2015 meeting, in view of difficulties that had arisen in relation with the visit of a dignitary 'and with a view to the systemic aspects of possible future requests, the Bureau agreed to have, in the near future, an in-depth discussion of the modalities for special meetings, taking into consideration all concerns expressed, including resource implications'. At its 2 December 2015 Meeting, the Bureau

> upon thorough reflection on this matter and with a view to possible future requests, the Bureau agreed that 'special meetings' outside of regular Council sessions should be strongly discouraged in the future for the following reasons: The Bureau noted that HRC resolutions 5/1 and 16/21 do not provide for the Council to hold 'special meetings'. The possibility to convene Special Sessions is however foreseen, if the Human Rights Council was to meet outside of regular sessions. It was noted that Special Sessions of the Council should 'be results-oriented and geared to achieving practical outcomes' (paragraph 128 of HRC Resolution 5/1); The Human Rights Council, when in session, is open to receive high-level dignitaries, including Heads of State or Government, particularly during its High-Level Segment pursuant to paragraph 116 of HRC Resolution 5/1, while such dignitaries may also address the Council at its regular sessions on an ad-hoc basis. 'Special meetings' could have a negative impact on these opportunities presented equally to all Member States and could possibly undermine the existing Council procedure and practice foreseen for such visits; The Bureau also recalled that the principles guiding the Council's work, as outlined in HRC Resolution 5/1, stressed the need for constructive dialogue with members and observers of the Council, upholding the Council's institutional integrity. In this context, 'special meetings' were considered as not conducive to dialogue as statements and rights of reply may be considered inappropriate. Perceptions of politicization may also arise. The Bureau agreed that, whenever the Council meets, the broader human rights context is always of great importance, including contextualization, in particular through the High Commissioner; The Bureau also noted the unforeseen financial implications of 'special meetings' of the Human Rights Council.

This matter was not revisited and this Bureau interpretation was not extended to subsequent special meetings held in response to request may by heads of States or governments.

An excellent knowledge of the rules of procedures and the voting process is essential to the sound processing of a resolution, decision or amendment. Given the fact that procedural discussions may be used as a substitute to a substantive discussion, any participant in such discussions must be fully aware of what is being considered. Any mistake may have devastating consequences since a motion may be rejected simply because it was submitted too late or a vote on a given resolution may be lost because a specific motion was not anticipated.

The fact that the Council procedures are public and largely webcast adds a dramatic feature to what would otherwise look excessively technical. Often a very technical vote, for instance on a no-action motion, or a motion for or against an NGO speaker - often a representative of a GONGO, a lobby or an illiberal group - to be granted the right to conclude his/her statement, may trigger numerous comments or posts on the social network. This may also make headlines in news outlets. A substantive statement may be of a deep and thorough nature but be lost in an avalanche of other statements and remain largely unnoticed. A procedural discussion on the context of a point of order or during a vote often involves fewer countries and is watched by a large numbers of viewers, on the internet or social networks. Media representatives will refer to such discussions and the participants will be largely publicized. This underlines how crucial it is for anyone taking part in or leading the debate to be fully aware of the basic processes of the voting process.

The main weakness of this statement of fact is that when procedural discussions become a substitute to substantive exchanges this is to the detriment of the human rights victims, the conceptualization of human rights norms and the consideration of country or thematic issues. It is surely very demotivating for anyone interested in human rights to consider that one of the main focuses of attention at any given session relates to the interpretation and implementation of a given rule of procedure rather than the substance of a human rights provision as it was applied or implemented in a given case. At the same time, it is fair to acknowledge that the same conclusion may be reached regarding the work of any parliament in the world. Such is our world that details and technicalities often prevail over basic principles.

In view of the foregoing, it is of importance to study the rules and practices of the Council in the main phases of its activities. Obviously the voting process (a) is the cornerstone of the work of the Council and requires a fully and comprehensive consideration of its main steps – rigidly interpreted by its President and the Secretariat. Despite its considerable importance, the voting process does, however, represent time-wise only a fraction of the Council's activity.[29] The various substantive segments[30] (b) of the Council's programme of work are also conducive to various motions which may be moved and for which clarification by the President and the Secretariat, based on the rules and practices of the Council, may be required. Lastly, it is of interest to study briefly the other marginal opportunities[31] (c) when the Council's deliberations may lead to motions, decisions or elections.

6.3 The Human Rights Council voting procedure[32]

The Council voting procedure is divided into very distinct phases during which Member States, and to a much lesser degree Observer States, have specific roles to play.

6.3.1 Submission of Proposals

An Imperfect Attempt at Defining a Resolution, a Decision or a PRST

For many Council practitioners, including the author, there is an obvious blind spot when it comes to defining what a resolution is. They are the soul of a session, its outcome and purpose. However, little effort has been made at defining what is obvious and taken for granted. The documents, being at the core of any session and after years of practice, have become a

---

29 An average of 2.5 per cent of the total number of meetings held during a session.

30 High-Level Segment, interactive dialogues, general debates, urgent debates, panels, etc.

31 Election of members of the Advisory Committee and nomination of mandate-holders.

32 A description of the Commission on human rights' voting procedure appears in Section VIII, para 40 of the agreed provisions in document E/CN.4/2002/16 on 'Main rules and practices followed by the Commission on Human Rights in the organization of its work and the conduct of business'.

leitmotif which is referred to on multiple occasions without any attempt at clarifying the meaning.

In the context of the present analysis, it may be of interest to recall some basic elements relating to resolutions for the benefit of those who may not have spent that much time pacing up and down the Council corridors, halls or meetings rooms.

The Council, as any other UN body, adopts resolutions and other outcome documents as a result of often lengthy and complex negotiation processes. At the end, after their adoption with or without a vote, they become official decisions of the Council and are expected to bind all members of the Council whatever their position on the text. Whether a resolution was the basis of a strong consensus, the subject of numerous disassociations or voted for with a tiny majority does not change the status and validity of the resolutions, they remain documents that, depending on their phrasing, are binding on all members of the Council. When, for instance, the report of the Council is noted by the UNGA this extends to the whole UN membership.

In legal terms, a resolution is a written text adopted by a deliberative body. The substance of the resolution can be anything that can normally be proposed as a motion in reference to a situation, a theme, a mandate or any other steps envisaged by the Council. Hence it may be of a fundamental importance (new standards, setting up a Commission of Inquiry, briefing the UNGA and other bodies through it of urgent matters, creating new parameters for specific thematic issues, etc.) or of a very technical nature (speaking time limits for the UPR, drawing up list of speakers, extending the submission of a report from March to June, etc.). It includes requests addressed to States, the UN system, various bodies and other stakeholders. It may generate obligations and create, extend or abolish mandates.

The drafts of the resolutions and the ensuing negotiations are always initiated by States which are referred to indifferently as authors or sponsors. They are often tabled by a State on behalf of a number of States which identify themselves as a 'core group' behind the resolution – this has, however, no legal implications for the Council, but often represents cross-regional support to a given initiative. Their content may be long and rich in substance or short and of a purely technical or administrative nature; they can be 'country specific' or 'thematic'; they can be annual, biennial or triennial.

Politically, the meaning of a resolution is to establish or reiterate a policy which a country or a group of countries considers of importance for the Council to adopt.

It is worth mentioning that the initial idea may come from any Council stakeholder, including NGOs. However, this idea must match a concurring idea of a State, and/or a State policy or priority, in order for one or more States to embrace it and carry it as a draft resolution.

Despite common perception, the words 'resolutions', 'decisions' or 'Presidential Statements' do not appear in Section XIII of the UNGA rules of procedure, in contrast to 'proposals' and 'amendments', which are clearly defined and described (see above). According to Rule 120:

> proposals and amendments shall normally be submitted in writing to the Secretary-General, who shall circulate copies to the delegations. As a general rule, no proposal shall be discussed or put to the vote at any meeting of the (Council) unless copies of it have been circulated to all delegations not later than the day preceding the meeting. The (President) may, however, permit the discussion and consideration of amendments or of motions as to the procedure, even though such amendments and motions have not been circulated or have only been circulated the same day.

This Rule has been subjected to intense speculation or interpretation by delegations but it is mainly guided by the UNGA or Council precedents, common sense and the practice. The salient points are as follows:

- Although there is no clear definition of the terms 'resolutions', 'decisions' or 'Presidential Statements', it is commonly considered that the way in which the Council is encapsulating its work is mainly through the adoption of resolutions. They contain a number of preliminary remarks and backgrounds, referred to as Preambular Paragraphs (PP), and Operative Paragraphs (OP), which develop the position of the Council on a variety of issues under a certain agenda item and with reference to a matter briefly described in the title.
- Decisions are, in principle, much more succinct and to the fact, with few PPs and OPs limited to an action or outcome clearly determined

and linked to a previous set of actions by the Council.[33] Such decisions were commonly adopted in the initial years of the Council when, for instance, its work could not be completed and certain items or matters had to be postponed to the next session[34] or when mandates had to be extended without the benefit of a full consideration of the substance at stake.[35]

---

33 Typical of such decisions are the outcomes of the universal periodic review process.

34 See Decision 2/116 of 29 November 2006 on the 'Postponement of considerations of draft proposals'; Decision 3/101 on the postponement of 'the consideration of the draft decision on the rights of indigenous peoples'; Decision 4/105 of 30 March 2007 on the 'postponement of consideration of draft proposals'; Decision 5/102 of 18 June 2007 on the 'postponement of consideration of all pending draft resolutions and decisions and of the draft report' which was made necessary by the adoption of the IBP at midnight on 18 June 2007; and decision OM/1/101 of 20 June 2007 on the 'postponement of consideration of pending draft resolutions and decisions'.

35 Decision 1/102 of 30 June 2006 extended 'exceptionally for one year, subject to the review to be undertaken by the Council in conformity with General Assembly Resolution 60/251, the mandates and the mandate-holders of all the Special Procedures of the Commission on Human Rights, of the Sub-Commission on the Promotion and Protection of Human Rights as well as the procedure established in accordance with Economic and Social Resolution 1503 (XLVIII) of 27 May 1970, as listed in the annex to the present decision'. Of interest, the said annex did not include two mandates (on Belarus and Cuba) which had the effect of abolishing them. By virtue of the Decision 1/106 of 30 June 2006 (adopted by a recorded vote of 29 votes to 12 with five abstentions) on the 'Human rights situation in Palestine and other occupied Arab territories' the 'substantive consideration of the human rights violations and implications of the Israeli occupation of Palestine and other occupied Arab territories' was deferred to the Council next session and incorporated in following sessions. Decision 6/103 of 28 September 2007 deferred the review of the 'mandate of the Special Rapporteur on the situation of human rights in the Sudan' to the second part of the HRC 6th Session. Decision 16/118 of 25 March 2011 postponed 'the renewal of the mandate of the independent expert on human rights and international solidarity to its seventeenth session, and for that reason (decided) to extend the mandate of the independent expert until June 2011'. PRST/18/1 of 30 September 2011 extended the mandate

- It is of importance to mention that, politics having taken its toll, certain substantive texts are at times to be presented as decisions and thus of a purely 'technical' and not 'substantive' nature, so their adoption represents less of a problem than the adoption of a full-fledged resolution. The opposite may be true, and certain technical texts are referred to as resolutions even if they are merely reiterating a given action or position.
- Additionally, as confirmed in a letter of the Council President to the Arab Group dated 24 March 2015, an oral decision, if adopted in accordance with the rule 125 of UNGA rules of procedure, is to be considered as a formal decision.[36]
- PRSTs have acquired a status within the Council which is at odds with those adopted at the UNGA level.[37]

---

of the independent expert on Haiti until the Council 19th Session. Decision 24/115 of 26 September 2013 concerned the 'postponement of renewal of the mandate of the Special Rapporteur on adequate housing (. . .)'. Decision 25/116 of 27 March 2014 concerned the 'postponement of the renewal of the mandate of the Working Group on Enforced or Involuntary Disappearances'. Decision 30/115 of 1 October 2016 was on the 'follow up to PRST/29/1' extending on a one time and exceptional basis the term of mandate holders listed in the annex to the decision. Decision 36/115 of 29 September 2017 extended the 'mandate of the international fact-finding mission on Myanmar'. Such an extension may also be made via an oral decision, as confirmed by the President in a letter dated 24 March 2015.

36 The rationale of the President's letter was that 'on 16 March 2015, the (Council) took a decision by consensus. . . The OHCHR provided an update on the financial implications of the prolongation of the mandate (PBI) and stated that funds were available to cover the extension of the Commission of Inquiry for the period until June 2015'.

37 This includes the HRC Resolution 5/1 which stipulates in its OP118 on 'outcomes other than resolutions and decisions' that 'this may include recommendations, conclusions, summaries of discussions and President's Statements. As such outcomes would have different legal implications, they should supplement and not replace resolutions and decisions'. The reference in this provision to PRSTs should be interpreted as statements by the President which it was assumed would be delivered outside the Council's Room by the President in the same manner as at the Security Council.

- Given the experience of the formative years of the Council when the level of politicization was at its highest point, the PRSTs acquired a high level of recognition as they were perceived as the quintessence of what the Council could be doing using all means at its disposal based on the unanimity of its Members. PRSTs are by definition consensual texts deemed to be presented by the President on behalf of all. Although they have exactly the same effect and may be subjected to the same programme budget implications (PBI), their status entail privileges not extended to resolutions or decisions: they do not need to be tabled at the same time as other proposals – and are often submitted on the same day as their adoption, are thus often not translated and are subjected to a summarized voting process (no introduction, few general comments and no explanations of vote).[38]

---

38 For non technical PRSTs (such as the ritual text taking note of the Advisory Committee's work) see PRST/1/1 of 20 June 2006 on the 'entry into force of the Optional Protocol to the Convention against Torture and Other Cruel, Inhuman or Degrading Treatment of Punishment'; PRTS1/2 of 20 June 2006 on 'hostage-taking'; PRST/6/1 of 28 September 2007 on 'the situation of human rights in Haiti'; PRST/6/2 of 28 September 2007 on 'the Twentieth anniversary of the entry into force of the Convention against Torture and Other Cruel, Inhuman or Degrading Treatment of Punishment'; PRST/8/1 of 9 April 2008 on the 'modalities and practices for the universal review periodic process'; PRST/8/2 of 18 June 2008 on the 'terms of office of Special Procedures mandate holders'; PRST/9/1 of 24 September 2008 on the 'situation of human rights in Haiti'; PRST/9/2 of 24 September 2008 on the 'follow up to PRST/8/1'; PRST/15/1 on the 'situation of human rights in Haiti'; PRST/18/1 of 30 September 2011 on 'technical assistance and capacity-building for Haiti'; PRST/19/2 of 23 March 2012 on the 'situation of human rights in Haiti'; PRST/20/1 of 6 July 2012 on the 'reports of the Working Group on the Universal Periodic Review'; PRST/22/1 on 'mainstreaming human rights throughout the United Nations system'; PRST/22/2 of 22 March 2013 on 'technical assistance and capacity building in Haiti'; PRST/23/1 of 14 June 2013 on the 'situation of human rights in Myanmar as regards Rohingya Muslims in Rakhine State and other Muslims'; PRST/25/1 of 28 March 2014 on 'the situation of human rights in Haiti'; PRST/25/2 of 28 March 2014 on the 'situation of human rights in South Sudan'; PRST/27/1 of 26 September 2014 on the 25th anniversary of 'the adoption of the Convention on the Rights of the Child'; PRST/27/3 of 26 September 2014 on the 'protection of

- It should be mentioned that as a remnant of the Commission past, the Council adopted for a number of years a number of PRSTs which related to the human rights situation in specific countries or situations, for instance on the situation of human rights in Haiti. These replaced the elaboration of resolutions or decisions. It should also be mentioned that contrary to the practice of the Security Council or other UN bodies, there is no practice of statements by the President in front of the Council room. In various circumstances, particularly in the first few sessions, informal discussions took place and proposals were made which could have led to the President reading out declarations or statements of a general nature without attribution or with a lesser degree of constraints than pro-forma decisions or PRSTs. This would have been for the benefit of the media in the same manner as is done by the Security Council. It was, however, never translated into deeds.

---

human rights of migrants at sea'; PRST/27/4 of 26 September 2014 on the 'Ebola epidemic'; PRST/28/1 of 25 March 2015 on the 20th anniversary of 'the Fourth World Conference on Women and of the adoption of the Beijing Declaration and Platform for Action'; PRST/28/2 of 26 March 2015 on the 70th anniversary of the 'end of the Second World War'; PRST/28/3 of 27 March 2015 on the 'situation of human rights in Haiti'; PRST/29/1 of 3 July 2015 on 'enhancing the efficiency of the Human Rights Council'; PRST/30/2 of 2 October 2015 on 'promoting the right to everyone to the enjoyment of the highest attainable standard of physical and mental health by enhancing capacity-building in public health against pandemics'; PRST/31/1 of 24 March 2016 on 'the situation of human rights in Haiti'; PRST/34/1 of 24 March 2017 on the 'situation of human rights in Haiti'; PRST/35/1 of 23 June 2017 on the 'situation of human rights in Côte d'Ivoire'; PRST/OS/12/1 of 3 December 2018 on 'enhancing the efficiency of the Human Rights Council, including by addressing financial and time constraints'; PRST/OS/13/1 of 6 December 2019, PRST/OS/14/1 of 7 December 2020, PRST/OS/15/1 adopted on 6 December 2021, PRST/OS/16/1 adopted on 9 December 2022 and PRST/OS/17/1 adopted on 8 December 2023 on 'Efficiency of the Human Rights Council – addressing financial and time constraints'; PRST/43/1 adopted on 29 May 2020 on the 'human rights implications of the COVID-19 pandemic'; and PRST/OS/14/2 of 16 December 2020 on 'Methods of work of the Consultative Group of the Human Rights Council'.

- The key point is that ways and means are explored – without much success – with a view to envisaging new outcomes to a Council discussion. Going beyond resolutions, decisions or PRST would be helpful in ensuring that the Council is heard even when a resolution is impossible to consider, politically speaking. To an extent, joint statements by a number of countries may be seen as fulfilling part of this goal but with the important caveat that the views expressed are those of the signatories only. Hence the temptation at an early stage of the Council existence to find new avenues to refer to a discussion on an issue deemed urgent or of significant importance. This discussion remained embryonic and has so far not led to any meaningful outcome.
- Finally, mention should also be made of few PRSTs which were adopted 'by default' on issues deemed of a sensitive nature for which agreement was quite difficult despite the consensual nature of PRSTs. The absence of any title testifies to the sensitivity of such texts.[39]

6.3.2 Tabling of Proposals by Member and Observer States

The Council, following the longstanding and well-established practice of the Commission on Human Rights, allows for proposals to be tabled by Member and Observer States. Observer States are, however, not allowed to submit any oral amendments during the voting procedure, by definition a Council Members-driven process. Also, if they are the only sponsor of a proposal or of an amendment, the Council President needs to ascertain that the sponsor is supported by a Member State serving as a its 'proxy' or, should this not be the case, they would have to ask the room whether at least one Member of the Council would agree to consider the text.[40]

39 See PRST/15/2 adopted on 1 October 2010 with no title which referred to the SG proposed strategic framework for programme 19; PRST/18/2 of 30 September 2011 with no title which referred to various elements relating to the OHCHR budget and funding; PRST/19/1 of 23 March 2012 with no title following up PRST/18/2.

40 See, inter alia, rule 69(3) of the rules of procedure of the functional commission of the Economic and Social Council which provides that an Observer State 'shall not have the right to vote, but may submit proposals which be put to the vote on request of any member of the Commission or of the subsidiary organ concerned'. This was done in recent circumstances concerning amendments tabled

Tabling of Proposals by Groups of States

Following the practice of the Commission on Human Rights, the Council accepts that a group of States tables a text, including requests to hold Special Sessions.[41] The matter is problematic when at least one State Member of a given group is not in agreement with the tabling or co-sponsoring of the proposal. This controversial issue was intensively discussed by the Council Bureau throughout 2015. A request was made by one particular State that the practice followed in the UNGA is also applied in the Council, namely that when a Member State objects to a group tabling or sponsoring a proposal, all the members of the supporting group should be listed individually and the group should not be mentioned as a collective entity. Further to intense deliberation, no Council decision could be

---

by the Russian Federation without co-sponsors or declared proxies (see above Section 4.3).

41 On the holding of Special Sessions at the request of Groups of States see the date and signatories of convening letters reproduced or referred to in: A/HRC/S-1/1 of 30 June 2006 (OIC); A/HRC/S-2/1 of 7 August 2006 (OIC and the Group of Arab States); A/HRC/S-3/1 (OIC and the Group of Arab States); A/HRC/S-6/1 of 18 January 2008 (OIC and the Group of Arab States); A/HRC/S-7/1 of 8 May 2008 (NAM, African Group, OIC, Group of Arab States as well as a number of individual States); A/HRC/S-9/1 of 6 January 2009 (Arab Group, African Group, OIC and NAM); A/HRC/S-10/1 of 16 February 2009 (African Group and Brazil); A/HRC/S-14/1 of 21 December 2010 (African Group and the USA); A/HRC/S-15/1 of 23 February 2011 (European Union); A/HRC/S-17/2 of 17 August 2011 (Poland and the Permanent Observer of the EU); A/HRC/S-18/2 (Poland and the Permanent Observer of the EU); A/HRC/S-19/1 of 31 May 2012 (Denmark, Kuwait, Qatar, Saudi Arabia, Turkey, the USA and the Permanent Observer of the EU); A/HRC/S-21/1 of 18 July 2014 (Group of Arab States, Group of African States (Botswana withdrew its sponsorship on the same date), OIC, NAM, and the State of Palestine); A/HRC/S-22/1, 2 and 3 of 26 August 2014 (Iraq joined by the Group of Arab States, NAM, OIC, the Permanent Representative of the EU and Costa Rica); and A/HRC/S-23/2 of 26 March 2015 (African Group). As may be noted, the practice is far from being a consistent and unified one, a fact which explains the difficulties of the Council in reaching a common position on the issue of Group sponsoring, particularly insofar as requests for Special Sessions are concerned.

taken and the practice remained the same. In such a circumstance the concerned country is referred to in a footnote as disassociating from or disagreeing with the groups' tabling or sponsoring.[42]

In a letter which the Council President sent to all Member and Observer States on 22 September 2015, he noted that there was no mention of group sponsoring in the 'guidelines for submission of draft proposals' available on the Extranet. He recalled that the practice of 'double sponsoring' had developed, resulting in a 'hybrid status quo' where State and group sponsoring often coincided owing to the overlap in the membership of various regional and political groups. He noted that a number of delegations had deplored a specific lack of transparency and clarity that could easily

42 At its 21 July 2015 meeting, the Bureau 'discussed the complaints received by States on the issue of texts being tabled by group co-ordinators without the consent of one or more members of the concerned Group. Two options were considered: to allow tabling by individual members only, following the practice of the General Assembly, i.e. implying that each State would have to sign individually; or to allow group co-ordinators to continue to table on behalf of a group. In the latter case, group co-ordinators would however be responsible to inform the Secretariat about possible dissociations or withdrawals which could then be either reflected by a footnote (Group X without State X) or by individually naming all remaining States of that specific group, i.e. not reflecting the sponsorship as a "group position". It was agreed that the Bureau would inform co-ordinators and encourage them to discuss the matter within their respective groups'. At its 24 August meeting, 'in the context of discussions thereon at the last Bureau meeting, the President informed the Bureau on the response provided by one regional group as well as a letter received from a group of NGOs. The Bureau decided to conduct further consultations on this matter. The President announced that he intended to use in particular the meetings with Regional Groups prior to the session to consult further on the matter'. At its 18 September meeting, 'the President informed the Bureau of ongoing consultations on this issue'. At its 22 September 2015 meeting, 'the President debriefed the Bureau on his consultations with Regional Groups, held from 3 to 9 September 2015. The Bureau then discussed different options with regard to addressing the issue of sponsoring within the Human Rights Council. The Bureau supported the President's decision to send out a President's letter to all Permanent Delegations on this matter'.

lead to serious procedural problems. At the same time he also noted that other delegations expressed a strong preference for maintaining the current practice, stressing first and foremost reasons of practicability, given that not all delegations of UN Member States were represented in Geneva and that the current regime respected internal group proceedings which differed from group to group.

Accordingly, he concluded by proposing that States and groups engage in an informal dialogue on the issue of group sponsoring and that the Secretariat keep the Bureau informed about a pilot project underway at the 3rd Committee.[43] This issue was however not revisited, even when an electronic tool developed for the UN General Assembly enabled delegations to sponsor a text electronically was introduced in Geneva.[44] This exemplifies the difficulties faced by the Council in overcoming the groups logic, which remains prevalent.

Deadlines for the Submission of Proposals

There is an element of contradiction in rule 120 which regulates the submission of proposals. On the one hand it requires circulation of all proposals to delegations not later than the day preceding the meeting whereas the same rules of procedure (rules 55 and 153) require that all official documents should be available in all languages and all resolutions should be accompanied by an estimate of the expenditures which the adoption of a text would have on the Budget of the Organization. Indeed, translating, circulating and estimating the budget implications of any text takes much more than one day. It is usually considered that this would require three to five working days.

Accordingly, in most circumstances, practice altered the interpretation of this rule[45] and nowadays draft resolutions or decisions have to be submitted before 1:00 p.m. on the Wednesday of the penultimate week of any given Council session, namely one week at least before the start of

---

43 The matter was not revisited by subsequent Bureaux. For the full text of the letter, see the Council Extranet, Communications to and from the President, 1 January to 31 December 2015.

44 This tool is referred to as the e-delegate system.

45 Translation of documents takes a significant period of time which is generally evaluated at a very minimum of 72 hours. A little more time is required to provide financial implications (PBI).

the voting. Since delegations may require some additional time for their consultations, an extension is permitted but only once and for a maximum period of 24 hours. Should a delegation miss this deadline it may either negotiate a draft PRST – which requires securing the support of all delegations – or seek an extension directly in the room at a time set aside by the President based on a substantive justification.[46] This request

46 Until 2015, the deadlines for the submission of draft were often extended without particular justification. Anecdotally, in a well-known case, a delegation having failed to remember tabling a resolution with a view to renew a specific mandate, it did so by way of a decision tabled after the deadline (Decision 16/118 of 25 March 2011 postponing the renewal of the mandate of the independent expert on human rights and international solidarity to the Council 37th Session). At the 19 March 2019 Bureau meeting, 'the President expressed his concern about the many requests for extending the deadline of tabling draft proposals, as they would create difficulty for delegations as well as for Conference services for processing and translation. He reminded that, while under exceptional circumstances an extension may be granted by the Council, it should not become the rule. The President invited the Bureau to remind their respective regions to respect the deadlines at future sessions'. At the 30 June 2015 meeting of the Bureau, 'Many requests for extending the tabling deadline were made, which, it was reiterated, should not become the rule. The Bureau agreed to revisit this issue with a view to forthcoming sessions'. At its 21 July 2015 Meeting, the Bureau 'discussed the issue of a continuous high number of requests over the past sessions for extending the deadlines for submission of draft resolutions and revisions. The Bureau agreed that justifications for requesting an extension should be provided in each case. The Bureau also discussed the case of tabling of a draft text after the deadline. The Bureau suggested that, in order to enhance predictability and discourage such late tabling, prior agreement by the Council should be secured by the sponsor before the text is registered by the Secretariat'. At the 24 August Bureau meeting, the 'Bureau further discussed tabling of a draft text after the tabling deadline. The Bureau decided that, in order to enhance transparency and ensure predictability, a decision by the Council was needed. In the future, the sponsor would have to secure agreement by the Council before the text could be registered by the Secretariat. In cases of (merely) extending the tabling deadline, the Bureau decided that sponsors should provide justifications'. This Bureau's

becomes a proposal which by itself may be subjected to immediate action if another delegation rejects the request. Revisions must be tabled by Monday 11:00 a.m. and written amendments by 1:00 p.m. of the last week of any Council given session, respectively.

However, during Special Sessions or urgent debates, this deadline is different. Given the predicaments of both procedures based on a sense of urgency, it would simply not be possible – and indeed contradictory to the sense and purpose of these tools – to require delegations to submit their text 72 hours in advance since by definition the request to hold such meetings may come extremely late.[47] The Council practice has developed to require delegations to respect a strictly interpreted '24 hour rule' whereby all texts which are scheduled to be acted upon by the Council must be tabled and made available to all delegations by way of Extranet and other comparable means[48] at the latest 24 hours before the probable start of the adoption process. The said proposals are then circulated in an unedited version in one language only.

Languages

Proposals submitted for action to the Council should in normal circumstances be circulated in all official UN languages. However, circumstances may prevent the full availability of documents in all six languages. In most cases the draft resolutions and amendments tabled in accordance with the deadlines are available in all languages, but this may not be possible in all circumstances especially for delicate and complex texts subjected to numerous adjustments during the informals. The Council has always agreed to consider these texts in the available language although this might have been challenged at times.

---

proposal was submitted and agreed at the Organizational Meeting of the Council 30th Session (see A/HRC/30/2, para. 10).

47 The request to hold an urgent debate on the Eastern Ghouta at the Council 37th Session was submitted on 1 March 2018 and the decision to respond favourably to this request was adopted the following day. The urgent debate took place in the afternoon of 2 March 2018 and the adoption of the resolution began at the end of that afternoon – although lack of time made it necessary to postpone action on the text to Monday, 5 March 2018.

48 For instance, electronic *notes verbales*.

Oral Amendments

Oral revisions or amendments are deemed admissible by the letter and spirit of rule 120. But again the Council practice developed over time and made it possible to do so while setting up some safeguards to the transparency inherent to the Council's proceedings. Hence, it is generally considered admissible to revise a text at the last moment but delegations sponsoring the texts should endeavour to submit their revisions or amendments in written form as soon as possible to enable the Secretariat circulating an unedited text in one language only in the room prior to the adoption process. In the rare cases when this proves impossible, the President requires the concerned delegation to read at dictating speed the contents of their oral revisions or amendments. In one case, a challenge was made concerning the late introduction of an oral amendment but was defeated.[49]

It is of importance to note that since 2020, only two oral amendments have been tabled, underlining the relative decline of this type of procedural motions.

Order of Voting

Further to rule 131 of the UNGA rules of procedure, 'if two or more proposals relate to the same question, the (Council) shall, unless it decides otherwise, vote on the proposals in the order in which they have been submitted. The (Council) may after each vote on a proposal decide whether to vote on the next proposal'. Proposals are therefore considered in chronological order of the agenda items and within each item, in the chronological order of their submission.

In practical terms, this has no real bearing on the procedure in most cases considered by the Council since most draft resolutions or decisions

---

49 An oral amendment introduced by Cuba to the draft resolution on the freedom of expression mandate at the Council 7th Session in March 2008 was challenged by Canada on the assumption that proposals and amendments should normally be submitted in writing 24 hours before the meeting and that accordingly the oral amendment could not be considered at this point. The amendment was nevertheless adopted by 29 votes in favour and 15 against with three abstentions.

touch on very different matters and, consequently, the President normally announces the proposals which are ready for action without meddling with the order of submission.

However, the order is key when exacerbated political situations are considered with two drafts dealing with the same countries or subjects tabled either in the context of the same agenda item or under different items.[50]

When two texts touch on comparable matters under the same agenda item, they are considered in the chronological order of their submission. Further to the provisions of rule 131, the Council may however decide to consider the texts in a different order. However, this requires a simple majority which may be hard to get on procedural matters when several Member States may, without clear instructions from their Capitals, abstain from the vote.

More recently, the matter was revisited in a more innovative manner with States tabling drafts concerning similar or comparable situations under different agenda items. Given the unofficial and informal gradation of the seriousness of a situation from agenda item 10,[51] to item 2[52] with item 4[53] on top of this unwritten scale, those envisaging tabling a resolution on a given country and suspicious of the action of others may

50 The most striking example of the impact that rule 131 may have on the procedure happened during the 11th Special Session on the situation of human rights in Sri Lanka held on 26 May 2009. The first country which tabled a proposal for action was the very same country subjected to the Special Session, thus neutralizing the consideration of the text which the main sponsors that had called for a Special Session were negotiating. Draft resolution L.1 on 'Assistance to Sri Lanka in the Promotion and Protection of Human Rights' was submitted by Sri Lanka immediately after the call for a Special Session was made by Germany. Draft resolution L.2 on 'The Human Rights Situation in Sri Lanka' was tabled by Germany on the day of the Special Session. Action was taken in the order of submission of the draft proposals.

51 Technical assistance and capacity-building.

52 Annual report of the UN High Commissioner for Human Rights and reports of the Office of the High Commissioner and the Secretary-General.

53 Human rights situation that requires the Council's attention.

devote particular attention to the item under which they act. The political reading of such legal matter may thus induce those preferring action under items 4 or 10 to act, reluctantly, under item 2, a practice which has rapidly expanded in recent circumstances despite the absence of a strong link between the text and the action by the High Commissioner for Human Rights which is the very topic of agenda item 2. By tabling a text under agenda item 2, a delegation is thus certain that it will be acted before any text submitted under any subsequent agenda items.[54]

Since its establishment, the Council has rarely voted as to whether a vote should be conducted on a subsequent but comparable or similar text. Generally, it has considered that the adoption of the first text supersedes the consideration of the second one.[55] The logic is that two texts on the same matter may have a different if not completely contradictory effect which cannot happen.[56] However, if there is no contradiction between two texts which relate to a comparable matter, there is no reason to exclude action on the second text.[57] The drafting of the texts are therefore

---

54 Of interest, Resolutions 14/1 of 2 June 2010 and 15/1 of 29 September 2010 on the incident of the humanitarian flotilla... were tabled under agenda item 1, a precedent which was not followed subsequently.

55 After the adoption of the resolution number one (i.e., L.1) during the 11th Special Session on the human rights situation in Sri Lanka, the President indicated that the competing resolution number two (i.e., L.2) on the same matter would not be considered.

56 An example of such contradiction would be a text extending a mandate and another one abolishing it.

57 This is typically the case for all texts tabled under agenda item 7 which refer to the same geographic area but differ in nature and substance. But this has also happened in the following instances. (a) At the Council 26th Session in June 2014, two resolutions were tabled on the issue of business and human rights by Norway and Ecuador respectively. It was, however, considered that the draft submitted by the latter sought to establish a new Intergovernmental Working Group and did not therefore deal with the same question as the draft submitted by the former. (b) At the Council 36th Session in September 2017, when considering the situation of human rights in Burundi, the Council adopted two texts tabled under items 2 and 4 respectively, but this was made possible because the latter text was expurgated of any reference to what appeared in the former by way of an oral revision and that the operationalization of the texts induced two very distinctive and not contradictory action. (c) At

of crucial importance especially when a delegation believes that another text on the same topic may be adopted before its own.

Deeply connected to rule 131, but rarely invoked is rule 123 according to which 'when a proposal has been adopted or rejected, it may not be reconsidered at the same session unless the (Council) by a two-thirds majority of the members present and voting, so decides. Permission to speak on a motion to reconsider shall be accorded only to two speakers opposing the motion, after which it shall be immediately put to the vote'. The only situation when a reference was made to this rule was during the selection of mandate-holders on 1 July 2016 at the 32nd Session when difficulties emerged concerning the appointment of one special rapporteur. The Council had to postpone the approval of the President's proposed list of candidates to the resumed 32nd Session some days later on 8 July 2016. Since the Council had already adopted the President's list on 1 July 2016, and despite subsequent objections or comments by Member States, when the meeting resumed the President inquired whether any State was willing to invoke rule 123, and since none did so, it concluded the Session immediately with the list remaining as it was.[58]

6.3.3 Consideration of Proposals

The format followed by the Council in adopting resolutions or decisions is summarized in Box 6.1 and explained in details in the following sections:

---

the Council 39th Session in September 2018, the Council adopted Resolutions 38/16 and 38/21 on the situation of human rights in Yemen, submitted under agenda items 2 and 10 respectively. Once again this was possible given the lack of contradiction between the envisaged activities in both texts. (d) Similarly at the 42nd Session in September 2019 the Council adopted Resolutions 42/2 and 42/31 on the situation of human rights in Yemen (items 2 and 10) and Resolutions 42/4 and 42/25 on the situation of human rights in the Bolivarian Republic of Venezuela (items 2 and 4).

58 See A/HRC/32/2, paras 28–34.

BOX 6.1 STANDARD VOTING PROCEDURE

Draft proposals are normally considered in the numerical order of the agenda items and within each item, in the chronological order of their submission.

The general speaking time limit during voting is 3 minutes.

Voting is a member's process. Observer States may only intervene up to the stage of introduction of draft proposals.

1. Introduction of draft resolution/decision by one of the co-sponsors.
2. Additional co-sponsors, if any: delegations are invited to record their co-sponsorships in the Council e-Sponsorship platform in e-deleGATE.
3. General comments, if any *(by members of the Council only)*, including amendments, procedural proposals (such as requests for a separate vote and other motions).
4. Statements by State(s) concerned, if any and if requested.
5. Financial implications (PBIs), if any: statements of programme budget implications are published on the Extranet.

Voting

6. Explanations of vote *before the vote*, if any (co-sponsors will not be allowed to explain their vote, unless the draft resolution has been amended).
7. Any request for a vote?
8. Vote, if requested, or adoption of a draft proposal without a vote.
9. Next draft proposal under the same agenda item, if any (following the same order as above).

or, if it was *the only or the last* proposal acted upon under a particular agenda item:

10. Explanations of vote *after the vote and general comments*, if any (at the end of an agenda item).

Observer States will however be given the opportunity to make interventions following the voting process, once all proposals have been considered, at the end of the session, if time permits.

Pre-voting Stage

During the last two days of each session all proposals and amendments thereto are being acted upon[59] in the order of the agenda items and within each item in the chronological order of their submission.

(1) *Introduction of the draft*: the draft proposal is introduced by one or more co-sponsors (Member and/or Observer States) which lead the negotiation process and are referred to as the main sponsors. Should there be amendments to the main proposal, they are introduced immediately afterwards. As per the standard practice, should there be more than one amendment by the same delegation, the President proposes, to save time, that they are introduced all together, it being understood that action on each one of them will be taken separately. After the introduction of all amendments, the President gives the floor to the representative of the community of sponsors of the main proposal[60] to seek its position on the amendments. Should one or more of them be agreed upon by the sponsors they become oral revisions to the main proposal and are automatically inserted into the text and consequently the amendments will be deemed withdrawn by their authors. If the amendments are rejected by the community of sponsors, the President moves the discussion to the general comments phase of the discussion.
(2) *Additional co-sponsors*: Contrary to the practice at the Commission or in other UNGA subsidiary bodies, the practice of reading out the names of all additional sponsors has been dispensed with by the Council to save time. However, the full list is available at the podium and used by the President and the Secretariat. This is of importance since under the last sentence of rule 128 of the UNGA rules of procedure, 'The (President) shall not permit the proposer of a proposal or of an amendment to explain his vote on his own proposal or amendment'. The sponsors of a proposal may participate in the general comments segment of the voting process but not during the explanations of vote. An electronic system was introduced at the

59 Adopted or rejected by vote or without a vote.
60 When proposals are introduced by Observer States, the response to the question by the President must be answered by a Member State which will act as a 'proxy' for the main sponsor and therefore as a representative of the community of sponsors.

Council 41st Session which allows for the delegations to share the drafts which they are considering tabling and allow States to sponsor them. This is based on a system developed by the UNGA (e-delegate system).

(3) An interesting but rather puzzling practice[61] has emerged at the Council level in continuation of the Commission's practice according to which a delegation may become a sponsor or withdraw sponsorship to a proposal or an amendment thereto even after the text is adopted and up to a maximum period of 10 working days after the closure of the session. If the withdrawal is made very close to the consideration of the draft, the President would have to inform the room about it to avoid any confusion as to why a State listed in the written documentation as a sponsor is actually given the floor.

(4) *General comments*: Immediately after the introduction of a proposal a general comments segment is opened to which all Council Members may participate whether or not they are sponsors of the main proposal.

(5) This segment is often considered as a 'mini-debate' opened at the stage of the adoption of a resolution or decision. Whereas in most circumstances, very few delegations participate in this segment, when issues exacerbating a certain level of controversy or when matters are deemed of political or legal importance by those concerned, it is not unusual to register a high number of statements made at this point.

(6) At this stage, it is of crucial importance to note that, when a proposal is subjected to amendments, the general comments will concern both the proposal and the amendments thereto. When the voting starts, the amendments and the proposals will be voted separately and not subjected to general comments anymore.[62]

(7) The general comments represent the last opportunity before voting (which includes explanations of vote) for delegations to raise

61 It would appear normal that States supporting a resolution and wishing to become one of its sponsors indicate this before adoption. However, politics taking its toll, it may happen that for a variety of reasons a country may join as a sponsor after the session. Readers of the Sessional Report will, however, not see any difference on this account.

62 This is often a source of misunderstanding and is therefore recalled at the start of the meeting by the President.

procedural motions or make oral amendments. Accordingly, when the President and/or the Secretariat are made aware by the concerned delegations of their intention to use this opportunity, the floor is granted to them irrespective of the order in which the delegations are registered in the list of speakers maintained by the Secretariat.

(8) Under Rule 116 of the UNGA rules of procedure, a representative may thus move 'the adjournment of the debate on the item under discussion. In addition to the proposer of the motion, two representatives may speak in favour of, and two against the motion, after which the motion shall be immediately put to the vote'.

(9) *Adjournment of the debate*: As previously mentioned, if a delegation specifies, spontaneously or at the request of the President, a timing when the discussion should resume,[63] this is considered as an adjournment of the debate. In such circumstances, the President will inquire with the representative of the community of sponsors whether it agrees with the motion. If yes, then the debate is postponed. If not, the provisions in rule 116 applies and there is a vote.[64]

(10) *No-action motion*: Such motions are not frequently moved. This happens only when the topic of the resolution is exacerbating an extremely high level of polarization and politicization and when informal discussions have proven to be fruitless and deeply antagonistic. When introducing such motion, a delegation is raising a point of order immediately after the introduction of the proposal. It is also not uncommon for it to refer squarely to the terms 'no-action', thus clarifying immediately the intention. In such a case, the opinion of the representative of the community of sponsors is not sought since

63 For instance 'in an hour', 'at the start of the following meeting', or 'the following day'.

64 At the Council 2nd Session in October 2006, Bahrain on behalf of the Group of Arab States moved a motion for the adjournment of the consideration of the draft resolutions on impunity, on the effective implementation of international instruments on human rights and on the freedom of opinion and expression to the next day. That motion was adopted by 25 in favour, 20 against and two abstentions. Similarly, after the introduction of the draft resolution on preventable mortality and morbidity at the Council 15th Session in September 2010, Pakistan moved the adjournment of the debate on the draft until the afternoon. Since the motion was objected to, a vote was carried and the motion was defeated by 32 against, 14 in favour and no abstentions.

by definition a no-action motion is deemed to be antagonistic with the purpose of interrupting the discussion with immediate effect. A vote is carried out after up to two delegations in favour and up to two against have expressed themselves. The consideration of no-action motions – although referred to in the respective Council sessional reports as motions for adjournment – are considered as extremely sensitive and politicized as they testify to the deep polarization of delegations on a given proposal. They are however not often used (only seven times since the Council's establishment) since a number of delegations vote against them as a matter of principle – based on the rationale that their adoption would prevent the Council from voting on the substance of the text. The prospect for their adoption is therefore extremely thin (twice in 12 years), thereby reinforcing their political and tactical nature, the proponents of such motions having often no hope whatsoever that they may be carried.[65]

---

65 No-action motions have been less often resorted to at the Council than at the Commission on Human Rights. However, the following examples might be quoted: (a) the amendments proposed by Germany to the draft resolution adopted at the conclusion of the 11th Special Session on the situation of human rights in Sri Lanka held in May 2009 were subjected to a no-action motion called by Cuba which was carried by 22 votes in favour, 17 against and seven abstentions; (b) the draft resolution entitled 'Promoting reconciliation, accountability, and human rights in Sri Lanka' tabled at the Council 25th Session in March 2014 was subjected to a no-action motion called by Pakistan which was defeated by 16 votes in favour, 25 against and six abstentions; (c) an amendment to the draft resolution on the 'protection of the family' submitted at the Council 26th Session in June 2014 was subjected to a no-action motion called by the Russian Federation which was carried by 22 votes in favour, 20 against and four abstentions; (d) the draft resolution entitled 'Effects of terrorism on the enjoyment of human rights' tabled at the Council 28th Session in March 2015, was subjected to a no-action motion called by Mexico which was defeated by 14 votes in favour, 23 against and ten abstentions; (e) an amendment proposed by South Africa to the draft resolution on the 'protection of the family: contribution of the family to the realization of the right to an adequate standard of living for its members, particularly through its role in poverty eradication and achieving sustainable development' tabled at the Council 29th Session was subjected to a no-action motion by the Russian Federation which was carried by

(11) *Rules 117 and 118*: Under rule 117, a representative may at any time move the closure of the debate on the item under discussion. Permission to speak on the closure of the debate is accorded only to two speakers opposing the closure, after which the motion is immediately put to a vote. Under rule 118, a representative may move the suspension of adjournment of the meeting. Such motions are acted upon immediately. These rules have not yet been resorted to at the Council level. Rule 117 should not be confused with rule 116. The closure of debate under rule 117 if invoked would interrupt abruptly the general comments segment and move the procedure to the voting phase with immediate effect.

(12) *Oral amendments*: As previously mentioned, delegations have ample opportunities to table written amendments to a proposal until Tuesday, 1:00 p.m. of the last week of the session. Circumstances may nevertheless compel some delegations[66] to introduce oral amendments at a later stage. This is limited by the 24-hour rule referred to in the second sentence of rule 120. However, given the fact that the last sentence of the same rule provides an opportunity for the President to permit the discussion of oral amendments, even though they may not have been submitted beforehand, since there is no limitation to the number of speakers the representative of the community of sponsors does not generally object to the consideration of amendments to avoid lengthy procedural discussions.

(13) *Challenging the amendments*: Theoretically, it may be possible to invoke the last sentence in rule 130 of the UNGA rules of procedure and challenge an amendment based on the fact that it does not 'merely adds to, deletes from or revises part of the proposal'. Although it may be argued that quite a number of amendments are

---

22 votes in favour, 21 against and three abstentions; (f) the draft resolution entitled 'Situation of human rights in the Islamic Republic of Iran' tabled at the Council 31st Session in March 2016 was subjected to a no-action motion moved by (the Bolivarian Republic of) Venezuela, which was rejected by 14 votes in favour, 23 against with nine abstentions; and (g) the draft resolution on the 'protection against violence and discrimination based on sexual orientation and gender identity' tabled at the Council 32nd Session in June 2016 was subjected to a no-action motion by Saudi Arabia which was rejected by 15 votes in favour, 22 against with nine abstentions.

66 Member States only.

not aligned with this definition, the fact that a procedural discussion of this nature is not limited to a specified number of speakers[67] means that there is a general reluctance of the community of sponsors of the main proposal to engage in what may otherwise become a very tortuous and lengthy discussion.[68]

(14) *Separate votes (or votes on separate paragraphs)*: Rule 129 of the UNGA rules of procedure provides that 'a representative may move that parts of a proposal or if an amendment should be voted on separately. If objection is made to the request for division, the motion for division shall be voted upon. Permission to speak on the motion for division shall be given only to two speakers in favour and two speakers against it'. This rule is often used by delegations calling for separate votes on specific PP or OP of the main proposal or of the amendments thereto either in block or separately.[69] They have to do that in the general comment segment, namely before the amendment is acted upon. This implies that a paragraph may be the subject of an amendment purporting at nullifying it and, if the amendment is rejected, it may be subjected to a separate vote.

(15) It is interesting to note the counterintuitive aspect of this practice since it would appear quite logical to allow for such requests to be made after amendments were rejected. However, to ensure clarity, predictability and transparency, it is required that all procedural motions, including this one, be made at the general comments stage. Hence when amendments are introduced, their author might indicate that should its amendment be rejected, it will call for a separate

---

67 For instance two against and two in favour.

68 Such a discussion may take a very long period of time and may lead to points of order and additional votes. This is why it is generally not considered suitable to get into this argument and there is a preference for a straight vote on the amendment per se.

69 The practice of the Council evolved to simplify the terminology used in rule 129. Instead of voting on a motion for division, which is a rather opaque concept, the Council President calls for delegations which agree with the contents of the separate parts of a proposal or an amendment to vote in favour of the motion. Those who disagree with them will be asked to vote against. This simplification of the process although at odds with the letter of the rules is certainly on a par with its spirit and the need to ensure transparency of the voting and a proper conduct of the proceedings.

vote on specified paragraphs of the initial proposals which are the subject of the amendments.

(16) The last part of rule 129 stipulates that 'if the motion for division is carried, those parts of the proposal or of the amendment which are approved shall then be put to the vote as a whole'. In the early years of the Council, this provision was at times invoked by a delegation which considered that once an amendment has been adopted this should trigger an automatic vote on the proposal.[70] This is no longer raised.

(17) *Merging of amendments*: Although the UNGA rules of procedure are very detailed on the question of division of proposals and amendments, they do not refer to the opposite situation, namely the possible merging of various amendments with a view to acting on some or all of them 'en bloc'. Accordingly, should such a motion be advanced, it will not be limited to a specified number of speakers and its outcome will thus be very uncertain and quite clearly time-consuming.[71]

(18) *Withdrawal of motions*: Rule 122 of the UNGA rules of procedure provides that 'a motion may be withdrawn by its proposer at any time before voting on it has commenced, provided that the motion

---

70 At the Council 7th Session, on 27 March 2008 the President ruled on the matter as follows: 'When votes have been requested on separate paragraphs or when amendments have been adopted, we should proceed with the adoption of the text as a whole or of the amended text in the usual manner: we should proceed with the explanations of vote before the vote and when this is done the President will ask whether there is a request for a vote on the text as a whole or the amended text. If there is not such request, I will take it that the text as a whole or the amended text is adopted without a vote'. This is in line with the Office of Legal Affairs' advice on the matter, according to which unless there is a specific request for a vote the application of rule 129 does not automatically trigger a vote on an amended proposal.

71 This is the main reason why the authors of some of the Council draft proposals subjected to a large number of amendments did not advance such a procedural motion. Although some sponsors envisioned doing so, they had eventually to balance the probable significant amount of time required to consider all amendments separately with the time needed to discuss a procedural motion aiming at merging the amendments and the uncertainty attached to a probable vote on the matter.

has not been amended'. It is indeed considered that when a proposal has been amended the Council becomes the owner of the revised text. Since the voting starts at the stage of the explanation of vote, it is not possible for the author of a proposal to raise to a point of order and withdraw its proposal after an amendment has been adopted.[72]

(19) It is of interest to note that a significant number of amendments tabled at any given session are withdrawn by their authors based on the outcome of informals and late discussions in the room.

(20) *Concerned countries*: The Council adopts proposals that in a number of instances refer specifically to certain States or territories. Accordingly, after the completion of the general comments segment, concerned parties are provided with the opportunity to deliver a statement as a 'concerned country'. This is of particular importance for Observer States which do not have the possibility of addressing the Council during the voting process.

(21) When several draft proposals concern the situation of human rights in the same geographical area, and should these texts be adopted consecutively, concerned countries may opt for addressing the Council once only. They may be provided with an amount of time exceeding the prescribed three minutes but limited to the cumulated amount of time that would be available to it should it speak as a concerned country under all resolutions.[73]

(22) *Financial implications of resolutions*: In accordance with rule 153 of the UNGA rules of procedure, 'no resolution involving expenditure shall be recommended by (the Council) for approval by the General Assembly unless it is accompanied by an estimate of expenditures prepared by the Secretary-General'. Accordingly, before engaging into the voting process, the Council is informed by the Secretariat about the PBI of the concerned proposal or amendment thereto. This is generally done by a circulation of the PBIs in advance of the meetings via electronic means or during the meeting. Finally, an oral statement can be made alerting delegations on the financial

---

72 Similarly, the community of sponsors of the main proposal may not call for a brief adjournment of the meeting once the voting process has started, namely after the first explanation of vote.

73 For instance, under item 7, it is quite often the case that two concerned countries address the Council once only on all texts of concern to it.

implications if only in a general manner.[74] It should however be acknowledged that there is extremely little time, if not at all, for delegations to appraise themselves of the content of the PBI. This unfortunately deprives them of the possibility to react in a meaningful manner. Hence, delegations need to contact the secretariat much in advance to get a sense of what may be included in the said PBI by the UN Controller. This system leaves much to desire and runs counter to the spirit and probably the letter of rule 153. In an ideal world, a representative of the UN Controller should be available to respond to delegates' questions at least one week before the end of the session.

Voting Stage

(1) The voting as envisaged in rule 128 of the UNGA rules of procedure begins with the first explanation of vote before the vote. The conduct of the vote proceeds as follows:
  (a) Since the voting may not be interrupted after the President has announced its beginning, it is of crucial importance for the President with the assistance of the Secretariat to ponder whether there will be sufficient time for the process to be concluded before the end of the last meeting of the day. Should he/she anticipate that this may not be the case, he/she would have

74 As a lapse in the strict delineation of the general comments and the voting segments, should a financial statement be read out in the room without having been circulated in the room beforehand, this would enable a Member State to request the floor and move a procedural motion such as an adjournment of the meeting to consider the said PBIs. This would, however, have to be made before the first explanation of vote which is considered as the formal start of the voting process. The only precedent which may be referred to is that of the above-mentioned no-action motion called by Pakistan on the draft resolution on the situation of human rights in Sri Lanka at the Council 25th Session. This was made after a clarification made by the Secretariat on the absence of regular budget funding of the mechanism proposed in the draft resolution.

no other choice than to interrupt the process at this stage and resume it at the first possible opportunity.[75, 76]

(b) *Explanations of vote before the vote*: Whereas the general comments are opened to all Council members, in accordance with rule 128 of the UNGA rules of procedure, the explanations of vote are not permitted by the proposers (sponsors) of a proposal or amendment under discussion.[77] The representative of a Member sponsoring a proposal or a motion may however speak in explanation of vote thereon if, and only if, it has been amended. This is in accordance with rule 60 of the rules of

---

75 This requires a delicate extrapolation of the potential number of explanations of votes and votes to ponder the time necessary to conclude the voting and balancing it with the probable timing when interpreters will leave the room. It is unclear what the situation would be should the Council not have concluded its voting process in time and thus have no other solution than conducting it without interpretation or resuming it at the next opportunity, particularly should all members of the Council not be favourable to any of these proposals. The author only remembers one case when the Council opted for the consideration of a proposal without interpretation during the consideration of the Complaint Procedure in closed session.

76 During the urgent debate on the human rights situation in the Eastern Ghouta, in the Syrian Arab Republic, the Council adopted its Resolution 37/1 in two phases: the main proposal and the amendments thereto were introduced and commented upon (general comments) on 2 March 2018. However the proceedings were interrupted at around 5:30 p.m. – given the lengthy adoption process that was anticipated and the explanations of vote and subsequent votes deferred to 5 March 2018 in the morning.

77 Given this provision, the practice has emerged for some delegations to withdraw their co-sponsorship of a given proposal in order to be in a position to participate in the explanations of vote segment, thus providing the possibility for those supporting the text to provide an explanation as to why the comments made by those against the main proposals are invalid or inadmissible and therefore to be rejected. Those delegations usually join as sponsors immediately after delivering their explanations of vote. This is against the spirit of the rules of procedure but not its letter. It should be noted that this may also be done by not joining as a sponsor immediately but waiting until after the adoption of the text to do so.

procedure of the functional Commissions of the Economic and Social Council. It also derives from rule 122 of the UNGA rules of procedure on withdrawal of motions.

(c) *Proposals without amendments*: Should there be no amendment to the proposal, the Council President will ask whether there is a request for a vote. He/she may also take note that such a request was made either during the stage of general comments or more commonly during an explanation of vote.[78]

(d) *Proposals with amendments*: When one or more amendments have been moved to a proposal, they will be acted upon first.

(2) The voting on the amendments follow the prescription of rule 130 of the UNGA rules of procedure according to which: 'When an amendment is moved to a proposal, the amendment shall be voted on first. When two or more amendments are moved to a proposal, the (Council) shall first vote on the amendment furthest remove in substance from the original proposal and then on the amendment next furthest removed therefrom, and so on until all the amendments have been put to the vote.' In practice, and further to the need for the voting process to be predictable, easily understood and transparent, the order of consideration follows the chronological order in which the amendments were submitted. Should oral amendments have been moved to a proposal they would be considered in the chronological order of their submission after action on the written amendments. It is only when various amendments are submitted to the same paragraph that the provisions contained in the second sentence of rule 130 will come into effect.

(3) When two or more amendments have been moved to a proposal, the explanations of vote before the vote on the first amendment will be listened to first, followed by a vote if so requested. Explanations of vote before the vote on the subsequent amendments will proceed in the same manner until all amendments are exhausted.

(4) When a representative has requested – during the general comments segment – that parts of the proposal or the amendment should be voted on separately, this should take place before the vote on the said

78 The requests for a vote must be made in an unequivocal manner. It is not sufficient for instance for a delegation to state that it would vote against, oppose, reject, despise (or whichever term it may deem appropriate to use at this stage) a draft, it must use the proper terminology and call for a vote in an explicit manner.

proposal or amendment.[79] This is preceded by explanations of vote before the vote on the separate paragraphs. If there is more than one separate vote, explanations of vote before the vote will be listened to before each vote.

(5) Once all amendments have been acted upon, the Council will move immediately and without interruption to the action on the proposal as a whole, as revised or amended. As mentioned above, there is no interruption to the procedure and no delegation can move a motion for the suspension of the meeting or adjournment of the debate at this stage.

(6) *Points of order*: As prescribed by rule 128 of the UNGA rules of procedure, points of order are not entertained during the voting process with the sole exception of a point of clarification in connection with the actual conduct of voting. This usually refers to a question to the matter being voted upon or to a technical difficulty that may be faced in connection with the process of voting.[80] When such points

---

79 In theory, there may also be a call for a vote on separate paragraphs of a proposal that has not been subjected to a proposed amendment but this does not happen in practical terms. Should this be the case, the separate votes would proceed as described in this paragraph.

80 When considering L.24 on the mandate of the Special Rapporteur on the promotion and protection of the right to freedom of opinion and expression held on 28 March 2008 at the Council 7th Session, one delegation called for a suspension of the meeting in accordance with rule 118 of the rules of procedure during the explanation of vote before the vote on an oral amendment. The President, referring to rule 128 which limits points of order during a vote to the 'actual conduct of the voting' declined the request on that basis arguing that the point of order was on the 'content and not the conduct' of the vote. The voting process on the amendment resumed accordingly. In a comparable manner, during the consideration of the draft resolution L.34 on human rights and coercive measures at the Council 37th Session held in September 2017, the representative of Brazil, when explaining its vote, referred to Venezuela. Since the resolution had been tabled by the (Bolivarian Republic of) Venezuela on behalf of the Non-Aligned Movement, its representative could not take the floor on an explanation of vote before the vote. It therefore decided to interrupt the speaker by way of a point of order and argued that the explanation of vote by Brazil was inadmissible. The Council President reminded the room about the very restrictive nature of rule 128. When a further point of order was

of order arise, they are immediately decided by the President in accordance with the provision of rule 128.[81] This comes in sharp contrast with the normal handling of the points of order outside the voting process which are interpreted in a much more flexible manner.

(7) *Request for a vote*: Any Member State may request for a vote either on a draft decision, resolution or amendment. Presidential Statements being agreed by all – making them the only texts considered as unanimous – they cannot be the subject of a vote. The majority of proposals are adopted without a vote and may thus be considered as consensual, although this does not prevent Council Members for disagreeing with parts or the whole of the text. In the latter case, concerned Member States in explaining their votes indicate that they disassociate from some or all parts of the proposals.

(8) *Electronic votes*: As a rule, the Council votes by electronic means. The President asks the Secretariat to 'open the voting machine' and consequently the Member States to cast their votes. They leave the necessary amount of time for delegations to ascertain that the vote as displayed on the screen corresponds to their intention and when they are satisfied that this is the case the vote is closed and the results displayed on the screen are announced by the President. Should a delegation notice after the conclusion of the vote that it voted contrary to its own intention for technical reasons, it raises a motion of order and indicates what its original intent was. Nevertheless, this does not alter the result of the vote which remains as formally announced by the President. This information is however recorded

---

made by the same country, the President did not entertain it until the conclusion of the statement by Brazil, at which point he provided the floor to Venezuela on a point of order. Several other delegations moved points of order but the President, having listened to the first one and noted that this was not in any way related to the conduct of voting, decided not to entertain any further ones and came back to the speakers that had expressed the wish to explain their vote before the vote on L.34.

81 This relates to the experience of the voting process at the Commission on Human Rights which was on occasion marked by many interruptions of the voting process by way of points of order clearly unrelated to the conduct of voting. Hence the rigidity of the procedure and the refusal to grant the floor to several speakers raising successively points of order during the voting process.

in the Council sessional report.[82, 83] During the COVID-19 period, a virtual electronic voting system was introduced which is detailed in above section 2.3.3.

(9) *Roll-call votes*: There may be technical difficulties preventing the holding of an electronic vote – as had been the case during the COVID-19 period or when a vote takes place at the early stage of a session when the electronic voting system is not yet fully in place. In such a case, a roll-call vote is organized in conformity with the provisions of rule 127 of the UNGA rules of procedure.[84]

(10) *Results of the vote*: Rule 125 of the UNGA rules of procedure provides that the 'decisions of the Council shall be made by a majority

---

82 This Commission on Human Rights' practice was spelt out in document E/CN.4/2003/118, para 4.1 letter (c) according to which 'should a situation arise where a delegate would ask for the floor after the voting and state that the vote as recorded does not reflect what he/she had intended, this would be noted by the Chairperson and duly reflected in the official records of the meeting. However, the vote would not be carried out again and the official records of the vote would remain as they appeared on the screen, unless the Commission decides to reconsider the proposal in accordance with rule 55 of the rules of procedures. A footnote would be inserted in the report of the session after the name of the Member State concerned indicating that the delegation had intended to vote differently'.

83 No-action motions were often moved at the time of the Commission on Human Rights. At its 58th Session held from 18 March to 26 April 2002, a no-action motion on the draft resolution L.30 on the situation of human rights in Cuba failed by a roll-call vote of 23 in favour, 24 against and six abstentions. A series of points of order were made subsequent to the statement by the Democratic Republic of Congo that its intention had been to vote in favour of the motion rather than abstaining. The emotional discussion that followed only subsided when it was clarified that even if the results had been altered the motion would have been deemed as rejected given the equally divided vote on the matter (24 in favour and 24 against).

84 Rule 127 of the UNGA rules of procedure indicates that 'the roll-call shall be taken in the English alphabetical order of the names of the members, beginning with the member whose name is drawn by lot by the (President). The name of each member shall be called in any roll-call, and its representative shall reply "yes", "no" or "abstention".'

of the members present and voting'. Rule 126 complements rule 125 by indicating that 'the phrase "members present and voting" means members casting an affirmative or negative vote. Members which abstain from voting are considered as not voting'.[85] Pursuant to rule 133, 'if a vote is equally divided on matters other than elections, the proposal shall be regarded as rejected'.

(11) *Explanations of vote and general comments after the vote*: In accordance with rule 126 of the UNGA rules of procedure, the President may 'permit members to explain their votes, either before or after the voting'. As previously mentioned, the Council has dispensed with the practice of allowing explanations of vote after the vote to be made immediately after the adoption (or rejection) of a proposal. Similarly, sponsors of the texts are provided with the opportunity to make general comments after the vote. All explanations of vote and general comments after the vote are regrouped at the end of the concerned agenda item in order to save as much time as possible.[86]

(12) *Observers*: As previously indicated, after the closure of the voting process, with action taken on all proposals placed before it, including the elections to the Advisory Committee, the approval of the President's list of mandate-holders and the adoption of the Sessional and/or Annual Report of the Council,[87] the Council authorizes the Observers to deliver brief remarks on the voting process as a whole. This is done as a matter of courtesy, does not entail any legal implications and is organized only if time permits.

---

85 Members absent during the vote or not participating in the vote are obviously considered as not voting.

86 This is the source of misunderstanding by a number of delegates having attended the voting process in other UN bodies where explanations of vote may be recorded immediately after the vote.

87 These reports are adopted ad referendum which means that the comments by delegations are forwarded to the Vice-President Rapporteur in the two weeks that follow the conclusion of the session.

6.3.4 Examples of Complex Adoption Processes

BOX 6.2

1. Resolutions 5/1 and 5/2 of 18 June 2007

These two resolutions are generally referred to as the 'institution-building package' (IBP) of the Council – later on complemented by Resolution 16/21 on the 'review of the work and functioning of the Human Rights Council'. The process of negotiations of the iconic IBP was difficult and tainted with a high-level of politicization and polarization. The end result was the joint adoption of the two resolutions on 18 June 2007 at midnight. However, the overall process was subjected to various conflicting interpretations.

Many delegations had expressed strong issues of concern relating to several key aspects of one or the other document, particularly insofar the agenda of the Council or the Code of Conduct for mandate-holders was concerned. The main principle which guided the negotiations in 2006 and 2007 was that nothing is adopted until everything is adopted. A delicate balance was achieved and the President submitted the two texts for a joint adoption on 18 June 2007.

Further to an intense day (and night) of negotiations, the clock was stopped at midnight and shortly afterwards the President indicated that an agreement had been reached which was followed by a standing ovation. As referred to in the Sessional Report,[88] 'at its 9th meeting, on 18 June 2007, the Human Rights Council decided, without a vote, to agree on the text introduced by the President entitled "United Nations Human Rights Council: institution-building" (A/HRC/5/L.2) considered jointly with the draft code of conduct for special procedures mandate-holders of the Human Rights Council (A/HRC/5/L.3/Rev.1)'. The term 'agreement' was nevertheless vague and ambiguous, particularly in view of the fact that the President had mentioned that the necessary follow-up concerning that agreement would be deferred to the Organizational Meeting.

88 A/HRC/5/21, page 45, Decision 5/101 and paras 60–63.

At the Organizational Meeting held on 19 June 2017 (which coincided with a change in Presidents and Bureaux of the Council at the end of the first Council cycle, with President Alfonso De Alba from Mexico being succeeded by President Doru Romulus Costea from Romania) a point of order was raised by the representative of Canada, contending that no 'decision' had been taken at the 9th meeting of the 5th Session, on 18 June and that a vote still needed to take place. The President ruled that a decision had been taken and that the Council needed to proceed with the necessary follow-up. The President's ruling was put to the vote and approved by 46 votes to 1 (Canada) with no abstention.[89]

2. Resolution S-11/1 of 27 May 2009

This resolution entitled 'Assistance to Sri Lanka in the promotion and protection of human rights' was adopted at the end of the 11th Special Session on the 'Human rights situation in Sri Lanka' held on 26 and 27 May 2009.

The Special Session had been convened at the request of Germany supported by more than one-third of the membership. The request was included in a letter dated 19 May and tabled at 4:30 p.m.

Subsequently, Sri Lanka tabled its own draft resolution on 22 May at 10:25 a.m. which bore the symbol number L.1. The sponsors of the Special Session tabled their own draft resolution on 25 May at 9:59 a.m. which bore the symbol number L.2.

In accordance with the above-mentioned procedure, when action took place on 27 May 2009, this took place in the order of the submission of draft proposals.

Germany tabled several amendments aiming at incorporating into L.1 several of the main provisions in L2. Cuba tabled a motion of closure of the debate under rule 117[90] which was carried by 22 in favour and

89 A/HRC/OM/1/1 paras 17–22.

90 Since this was the first time ever the Council dealt with a no-action motion, there was hesitation as to which provision was equivalent to it. Rule 117 on closure of the debate was eventually opted for but

17 against with seven abstentions. The L.1 resolution as revised was adopted by 29 in favour, 12 against and six abstentions.

In subsequent years, the events as they unfolded at the 11th Session served as lessons learned. It has now become a practice that when a Special Session touches upon a country or situation which is particularly tense or complex, those requesting it are attaching to their request a preliminary draft proposal. Thus they ensure that whatever the circumstances their text will be acted upon first in accordance with the provisions of Rule 131 of the UNGA rules of procedure.

3. Resolution 24/24 of 27 September 2013[91]

This resolution, formally referred to as 'Cooperation with the United Nations, its representatives and mechanisms in the field of human rights' – or in more simple terms as 'Resolution 24/24 on reprisals' – was adopted on 27 September 2013 after a lengthy process of consideration of various amendments. Its topic, which has become a delicate one over the last decade, touched on issues relating to human rights defenders and reprisals. Those who were strongly against the text proposed a large number of motions as follows:

(1) The main text (L.17/Rev.1) was introduced and orally revised by Hungary on behalf of a large group of sponsors.
(2) A series of written amendments had been proposed but only two of them were eventually withdrawn (L.42 and L.45).
(3) The remaining seven amendments as tabled by the Russian Federation (L.40), (Bolivarian Republic of) Venezuela (L.41 and L.43), China (L.44), India (L.46 and L.48) and Pakistan (L.47) were acted upon separately as the rules and practices imposed it. All were rejected by a voting pattern of up to 16 States in favour of the amendments and up to 30 against with few amendments.

---

it should have been rule 116 on adjournment of the debate. In subsequent cases, the appropriate rule (116) was referred to.

91 The webcast archives are available at: http://webtv.un.org/search/ahrc24l.17-vote-item5-37th-meeting-24th-regular-session-human-rights-council/2700338025001/?term=&lan=english&cat=Regular%2024th%20session&sort=date&page=2.

Also at the same meeting, at the request of the representative of India, a separate vote on the deletion of operative paragraph 8[92] of the draft resolution A/HRC/24/L.24 as orally revised was taken. The motion to delete operative paragraph 8 from the draft resolution A/HRC/24/L.17 as orally revised was rejected by 30 votes to 15 against, with two abstentions.

Also at the same meeting, at the request of the representative of (Bolivarian Republic of) Venezuela, a recorded vote was taken on the draft resolution as orally revised. The draft resolution, as orally revised, was adopted by 31 votes to one, with 15 abstentions.

It is of interest to note that from this vote onwards, the most controversial issues in particularly sensitive proposals were subjected to amendments aimed at withdrawing the concerned paragraphs to be followed in case of rejection by a separate vote on the said paragraphs. This implies in concrete terms that two motions having the exact goal are put to a vote. Since challenging such a situation would probably take much more time than going through the motions, the main sponsors allow it to proceed.

The voting pattern showed a clear majority of delegations in favour of the text as is, and against the amendments. However, the polarization of the Council (very few amendments), the number of votes on the amendments, the separate paragraph and the text as a whole foreshadowed the high level of polarization that would be replicated and would not subside at the UNGA. Given the universal composition of the UNGA, the procedural efforts which were inconclusive in Geneva led to a different result in New York. The African Group proposed a text entitled 'Report of the Human Rights Council' which purported to defer consideration of and action on the HRC Resolution 24/24 to allow time for further consultations. In a series of tense votes at the 3rd Committee and at the plenary of the UNGA, the European-led counterproposal was rejected (83 votes against to 80 in favour with 18 abstentions). The deadlock proved to be insurmountable over the next

92 Paragraph 7 of Resolution 24/24 (previously para 7 of L.17) requested the Secretary-General to designate a UN-wide senior focal point to engage with all stakeholders on issues relating to reprisals.

two UNGA cycles and the status of Resolution 24/24 remains to this date unclear.[93]

4. Resolution 31/32 of 24 March 2016[94]

This resolution entitled 'Protecting human rights defenders, whether individuals, groups or organs of society addressing economic, social and cultural rights', otherwise referred to as the 'Human rights defenders resolution', was adopted on 24 March 2016. The text was subjected to 31 amendments which, apart from four amendments which their sponsors proposed to act upon en bloc, were all voted upon individually. Hence, 27 votes were carried and none of the amendments passed. The proponents of the amendments gathered between 11 and 14 votes in support and their opponents between 20 and 23. The draft as orally revised was adopted by 33 votes in favour and six against, with eight abstentions.

Of interest is obviously the sheer number of amendments tabled and the fact that the vote, despite its duration (more than three hours), proceeded without disruption or major tension. Also, it is noteworthy that the sponsors of the main draft preferred to act on all amendments separately as requested by their sponsors rather than seeking a motion to group them all together with a view to rejecting them en bloc. The controversies surrounding the consideration of the draft resolution on 'human rights and sexual orientation' and the five amendments attached to it by the Commission on Human Rights at its 61st and 63rd meetings in April 2003 served as a reminder of difficulties

93 The request by the Secretary-General to the ASG on Human Rights to act on issues relating to reprisals made this controversy quite obsolete. On 4 October 2016, the Secretary-General issued a statement informing that he had decided 'in consultation with the High Commissioner for Human Rights, to designate my new Assistant Secretary-General for Human Rights, to lead our efforts within the UN system to put a stop to all intimidation and reprisals against those cooperating with the United Nations on human rights'.

94 See webcast archives at the following link: http://webtv.un.org/meetings-events/human-rights-council/regular-sessions/31st-session/watch/ahrc31l.28-vote-item3-65th-meeting-31st-regular-session-human-rights-council/4815520399001.

that may arise when many points of order or other procedural motions are raised.

5. Resolution 32/2 of 30 June 2016[95]

This resolution entitled 'Protection against violence and discrimination based on sexual orientation and gender identity' – often referred to as the 'SOGI resolution' – was adopted at the Council 32nd Session on 30 June 2016. It was subjected to a no-action motion, 11 amendments (none of which was withdrawn), four votes on separate paragraphs and a vote on the text as a whole as revised and amended.

The no-action motion (motion to adjourn the consideration of the draft resolution) was rejected by 15 votes to 22, with nine abstentions.

Four of the amendments were rejected while seven were adopted. Of interest, three votes rejecting amendments L.71 (17 in favour, 18 against with nine abstentions), L.72 (17 in favour, 18 against with nine abstentions) and L.81 (17 in favour, 19 against with eight abstentions) and one approving amendment L.78 (18 in favour, 17 against with nine abstentions) were extremely tight.[96] Depending on the circumstances or the composition of the Council, the results may have gone in different directions.

In addition to the references to the words 'sexual orientation and gender identity' the most controversial provision related to the decision by the Council 'to appoint, for a period of three years, an Independent Expert on protection against violence and discrimination based on sexual orientation and gender identity'.

The title of the resolution (22 in favour, 15 against with eight abstentions), preambular paragraph 4 (21 in favour, 14 against with nine

95 For the webcast archives see: http://webtv.un.org/search/ahrc32l.2rev.1-vote-item3-41st-meeting-32nd-regularsession-of-human-rights-council/5009164455001/?term=&lan=english&cat=Regular%2032nd%20session&sort=date&page=4.

96 In accordance with rule 133 of the UNGA rules of procedure, if any of these votes had been equally divided, the amendment would have been rejected.

abstentions), operative paragraph 2 (23 in favour, 14 against with eight abstentions) and operative paragraphs 3–7 (21 in favour, 17 against with seven abstentions) were all retained with a larger majority than the vote on the corresponding amendments.

Subsequently, the draft proposal L.2/Rev.1 that was to become Resolution 32/2 was submitted to a vote and was carried by 23 votes in favour to 18 against with six abstentions.

It is noteworthy that, despite the extremely lengthy and complicated process, the voting was courteous and dignified and led to an extremely significant result. This came in sharp contrast with the consideration of the draft resolution on 'human rights and sexual orientation' (E/CN.4/2003/L.92) and the five amendments attached to it (E/CN.4/2003/L.106 to L.110) at the Commission on Human Rights 59th Session on 24 and 25 April 2003. In accordance with the IBP, the first Independent Expert, Mr Vitit Muntarbhorn, was appointed by the Council at its 33rd Session on 30 September 2016. This had an impact on the ensuing deliberations at the Third Committee level since it would have been rather problematic for the UNGA not only to reverse, alter or postpone the consideration of a HRC resolution but also to disregard the appointment of the relevant mandate-holder.

6. In Summary: Main Stages of a Complex Adoption Process

(1) Introduction of draft Lx by its sponsors.
(2) A delegation may make a point of order and raise a no-action motion. Up to two speakers in favour of the motion and two against will be given the floor. Vote will take place immediately on the no-action motion. If approved, the action on Lx is interrupted and the President moves to the next resolution. If rejected, the consideration of Lx resumes.
(3) Introduction of written amendments A1, A2, A3, etc. by their sponsors. The sponsors should indicate at this stage that, if the amendments are to be rejected, they are calling for a separate vote on, for instance, paragraphs a–c.
(4) The President seeks the views of the sponsors of Lx on each of the proposed amendments.

(a) If endorsed by the Lx sponsors an amendment becomes a revision and is inserted into document Lx.
(b) If rejected by the Lx sponsors an amendment will have to be discussed and acted upon. If a separate vote has been requested it will be acted upon after the action on the amendments.

(5) The President summarizes the state of play and indicates that general comments will be on Lx and the amendments not agreed by the Lx sponsors.
(6) The general comments segment is opened by the President. Member States should comment on both the draft Lx and the Amendments not accepted by the sponsors of the resolution (for instance A1, A3 and A5).
(7) A delegation may make an oral amendment in which case the President seeks once again the views of the Lx sponsors. If rejected it will be part of the general comments discussion.
(8) In the course of the general comments section other motions may be advanced such as for instance an adjournment of the debate, which may be voted upon if the Lx sponsors do not agree with it.
(9) When all general comments are made, the President moves to the explanations of vote before the vote segment. At that moment, no procedural motion is acceptable with the sole exception of a point of clarification from a delegation about the conduct of the vote (for instance about the text being voted upon or a request to fix the voting system).
(10) Explanations of vote before the vote on A1 are being made. Only those Members which are not sponsors of A1 may speak. This is followed by a vote on A1. If A1 is adopted it becomes part of Lx. At that moment, the text Lx as amended does not belong to the sponsors anymore and becomes the property of the Council as a whole. If rejected, the Lx sponsors remain the owners of the text.
(11) Immediately after the vote, the President moves to the EOV on A3, A5 and later the oral amendment. The same rules apply.
(12) When all amendments are acted upon, the President moves to the votes on separate paragraphs a–c.
(13) Delegations may explain their vote. This is followed by a vote on each one of these paragraphs which may be retained or not. Each paragraph for which a separate vote has been requested is subjected to a vote.
(14) The President then moves to the vote of the text as a whole as it may have been revised and/or amended. This is preceded by explanations of vote.

(15) After the vote, explanations of vote and general comments may be made but this takes place when all texts under the same item have been adopted.
(16) Complex voting process of this nature may take several hours.

6.3.5 Facts and Figures as well as Proposed Interpretation

Resolutions

Statistics relating to the number of resolutions adopted by the Council are at times interpreted as underlining a continuous growth which may lead to around 180–200 texts being adopted by 2025. This is based on the trends noticeable since the establishment of the Council and leads to a number of conclusions as to the prolific output of the Council and conversely its lack of efficiency or effectiveness. It also serves the purpose of calling Members and Observers of the Council to restrain themselves as much as possible in submitting new proposals and when they need to table a text to do that on a bi- or triennial basis.

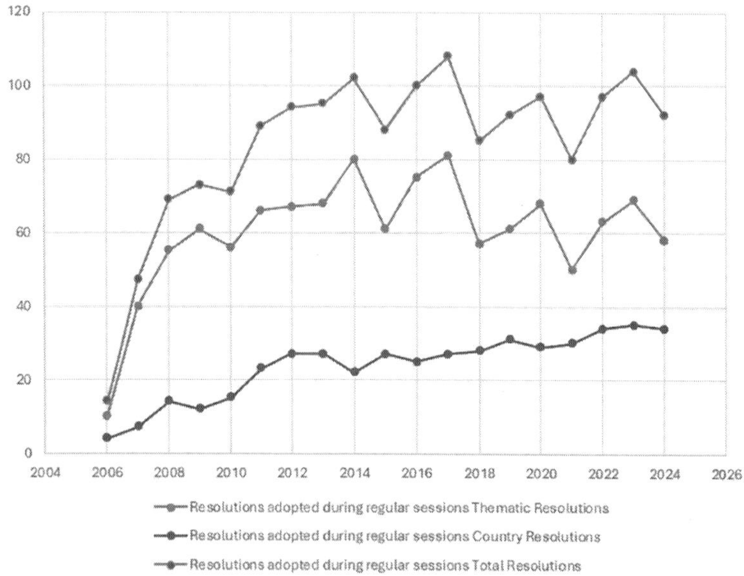

Figure 6.1 *Resolutions adopted during regular sessions*

However, when put into perspective, these figures may be subjected to a different interpretation. Indeed, the available data on the number of resolutions adopted by the HRC in the past 19 years[97] are shown in Figure 6.1.

It is of interest to note that the number of resolutions adopted by the Commission on Human Rights during its final decade, although variable depending on circumstances, remained stable, oscillating between 90 and 125. When the Council was established, there was a sharp decline in that number, and it took the Council five years to get back to figures that were in line with those of its predecessor. However, since 2011, the Council seems to have reached its 'cruising speed' of around 90–110 texts per year. The 2017/2019 and 2024 relative decreases should be interpreted as the consequence of the efficiency and effectiveness process, which advocated in a concrete manner the bi- or tri-ennialization of resolutions, while the 2020/2021 decline is linked with the COVID-pandemic.

The exception is therefore not the sharp increase in the number of proposals adopted every year between 2006 and 2011 but rather the brutal reduction of their number at the time the Commission was abolished and the Council established. This does not represent a judgemental posturing but the recognition of the impact the abolishment of a major UN body may have on any of its successors, whatever its strengths and failures.[98]

As far voting pattern of the Council is concerned, it is of crucial importance to recall that despite the common reference, the number of requests for a vote on draft resolutions remains surprisingly stable at around 32 per cent over a period of five years marked by the adoption of significant texts on both country and societal issues.

Additionally, an more importantly, although there might have been a large number of votes actually carried out at any given session, the prospects of a draft resolution being rejected are very small. From the start of

97 The exact figures are as follows: 107 (2003); 121 (2004); 111 (2005); 41 (2006); 60 (2007); 71 (2008); 77 (2009); 77 (2010); 101 (2011); 95 (2012); 98 (2015); 108 (2016); 113 (2017); 86 (2018); 92 (2019); 80 (2021); 97 (2022); 104 (2023) and 92 (2024)..

98 It should be remembered that when the Commission was abolished and the Council established, the crucial work of Special Rapporteurs was set aside for a period of almost two years.

the COVID-19 pandemic in March 2020 to the end of 2024, a period of five years during which 15 regular sessions were held, a total of 500 draft resolutions were tabled, out of which only two were rejected.[99] This represents a ratio of 99.6 per cent of resolutions adopted against 0.4 per cent rejected. Additionally, only one draft resolution was withdrawn before action in circumstances that will be described in the next section.[100]

This rather overwhelming situation comes from the reluctance of sponsors of resolutions to keep a text on the agenda when they understand that the chances of getting it adopted are getting close to the 50 per cent threshold. No delegation in such a situation would insist on putting it to a vote if there is no quasi-certainty or at least a sound level of confidence of it being adopted. The only situation when a sponsor would nevertheless push for their initiative to a vote is when this is sustained for political reasons, in order to make a point vis-a-vis other States, the media or civil society.

At the time of the Commission on Human Rights, the situation was slightly different with delegations showing more intent in tabling texts that they knew could or would be defeated. In several instances, the Commission's members tabled proposals concerning certain countries' situations, which were later rejected.[101] This happened in eight cases over

99 See draft resolution A/HRC/48/L.11 on the situation of human rights in Yemen which was rejected on 7 October 2021 by a vote of 18 in favour, 21 against and seven abstentions. Draft decision A/HRC/51/L.6 on the human rights situation in the Xinjiang Uyghur Autonomous Region of China which was rejected on 26 September 2022 by 17 in favour, 19 against and 11 abstentions.

100 See draft resolution A/HRC/48/L.14 on realizing a better life for everyone which was withdrawn by its sponsor on 8 October 2021.

101 The following texts or requests were rejected by the Commission: in 2005, a draft resolution on the 'question of detainees in the area of the US naval base in Guantanamo'; in 2004, three draft resolutions on 'the situation of human rights in the Republic of Chechnya of the Russian Federation', on 'the human rights situation in Zimbabwe' and on 'the human rights situation in China'; in 2003, a request for a Special Sitting on the 'effect of the war on the Iraqi people and their humanitarian situation' and four draft resolutions on 'the human rights situation in the Republic of Chechnya of the Russian Federation', on the 'human rights situation in Sudan', on

three years. This practice has not been followed through and there has never been any text tabled and later rejected by the Council. This may be the subject of at least two distinct interpretations. Since causality is never a straight line, it may be the case that both are valid and should be read together:

- The Commission was extremely politicized and its Members did not hesitate to propose controversial texts which they well knew would not be adopted, whereas the Council's Members are extremely aware of how important it is that the Council is not over-politicized and thus avoid tabling such texts unless they have an assurance that they stand a pretty good chance of being adopted.
- Conversely, it may be argued that the Commission's Members did not let politics blind their judgement and human rights standing and thus did not hesitate to table controversial texts, whereas the Council's Members are so eager to avoid confrontation that they do not table texts which they know would not be adopted, even if such texts would be of importance for the protection of human rights worldwide.

As will be seen in the following section, even though the results of the voting process are highly predictable, the strategy has shifted towards an increasing number of requests for a vote as well as tabling of amendments. To put it otherwise, the Council's polarization or politicization resides in deeper and sometimes quasi-invisible layers. It should not be interpreted based on results but on the means or strategies being developed.

Stepping aside from these remarks, nothing in the previous paragraphs should be construed as implying that the Council should not review its working methods or that the adoption of around 100 texts per year is an efficient way to deal with the human rights situation in the world. It simply means that these trends should be quantified and qualified over a longer period of time to serve as objective indicators.

The reiteration of similar or comparable texts every year does not necessarily serve any objective interest for the global human rights community and in certain instances, it may very well serve the sponsors' own purposes or domestic policies. However, the importance of the Council

---

'the human rights situation in Zimbabwe' and on 'human rights and sexual orientation'.

looking into as many human rights situations as possible should never be neglected as well as the need to not disregard the priorities that others may have in terms of promotion and protection of human rights. Whatever its major weaknesses and the difficulties which may be faced by stakeholders in understanding the need for a given text to be tabled and adopted, it would be far more problematic for the Council if it were to neglect some grave human rights situations.[102] In that case, the Council's very existence would be in jeopardy, and rightly so.

Procedural Motions

Once again, a comparison of the Council and the Commission practices is particularly telling. Although it is often advanced that the Council is as 'politicized' and 'polarized' as its predecessor, a careful analysis of the work of these bodies tells a somewhat different story. The picture is far more complicated than it may look at first sight and the oversimplification advanced by some should not be considered as a clear depiction of the truth. On the contrary, the situation appears, as usual, nuanced and as is well known, there is never a simple response to a complex question.

The Council does not operate in a vacuum or in total isolation from the rest of the world. As was stated in previous sections, the controversies which mar the public debate at the domestic level on societal issues find an echo in the Council deliberations. Similarly the difficulties faced by the UN intergovernmental machinery in dealing with serious situations also affect the Council's work. Hence, delegations, whatever they are and wherever they may come from, may raise procedural motions of many kinds aimed at rejecting texts which they do not adhere to or may even reject utterly. Procedural motions are to be seen in the bigger political scheme as a tool to ensure that a given aim is reached, or if this is not possible, to make it as difficult as possible for the proponents of a certain course of action to see them easily agreed upon by the Council – whether or not this aim is in sync with the advancement of human rights at the domestic and/or international levels. Over the years, the various

102 As mentioned in an earlier chapter, the failure of the Commission on Human Rights to address the genocide and massive violations perpetrated in such countries as Cambodia, the former Yugoslavia or Rwanda serves as a cruel reminder of this statement.

procedural motions described in the previous sections were used but not necessarily in the same manner and with the same level of consistency.

No-action motions are often considered as the most disruptive tools available to delegations wishing to 'kill' a text since a motion to defer action on a proposal sine die, if it passes, ensures that there is no substantive consideration of the matter. As mentioned above, since the establishment of the Council, seven no-action motions have been moved by delegations and only three were carried. This comes in sharp contrast with the practice at the Commission where not less than eight no-actions or adjournments of debate were moved by delegations during its last three sessions only.

Over the years, several moderate delegations have adopted a principled position on this issue and consider it impossible to vote in favour of such motion. They believe that any human rights issue deserves a substantive discussion and not only a procedural one. This fact enabled the Council to move away from the practice of its predecessor in terms of no-action motions.

However, just as nature abhors a vacuum, delegations may find opportunities when and where they did not exist before. At the time of the Commission, motions for separate votes and oral amendments were commonly resorted to. Since its creation, the Council practice has evolved differently,. Procedural motions are rarely used, particularly no-action motions that have almost disappeared from the radar screen, with the exception of the tabling of amendments. Increasingly, amendments are tabled on many provisions of a single text and a vote is called on every single one of them as mentioned in a previous section. However, there is no clear pattern in this regard and the situation may vary considerably from one session to another depending on the texts being discussed or the general political environment. There is accordingly a striking difference between the practice of the Commission in its last three years of existence and that of the Council over the recent years.[103]

---

103 It should be pointed out that the practice of the Commission privileged the tabling of oral amendments whereas that of the Council privileges written amendments. The comparison is therefore somewhat to be tainted with some necessary nuances. Nevertheless, the number of amendments per year considered were: 14 (2003); 36

The fluctuation in the number of amendments tabled every year may depend on different factors which are hard to qualify. Firstly, a single text may attract a large number of amendments such as HRC Resolution 31/32 which attracted not less than 31 amendments in 2016. Secondly, it should be borne in mind that many important thematic texts have by now been bi- or tri-ennialized. Accordingly, there may be gap years when the number of amendments is relatively low and conversely others when the number is relatively high, thus aiming at an average which is, in any case, significantly higher than at the Commission. Thirdly, the working atmosphere may differ from one year to the other. Paradoxically, when geopolitics are in turmoil, there may be a tendency for Geneva delegations to avoid disrupting further the work of the Council and work towards less votes and frictions and simplifying texts or reducing the prospects for amendments to be tabled.

Lastly, it should be borne in mind that some texts may attract more attention than others, especially when they include elements concerning societal issues which are challenged by a number of countries. Such issues relate to the death penalty, human rights defenders, the rights of women, particularly sexual reproductive rights, and sexual orientation and gender identity.

Figure 6.2 is therefore quite symptomatic of a complex pattern: whereas the prospects of amendments being adopted are quite dim, their numbers have grown haphazardly and have become an inherent part of the voting process and a symptom of a new form of polarization of the Council.

There is no predictability as to whether a text may or may not be submitted to amendments and if so how many of them may be acted upon. The atmosphere of the informal discussions, the efforts made by the sponsors of the text to take on board some of the proposals, the goodwill displayed by all concerned in discussing these matters and the nature of the text itself have an influence on the amendments that may or may not be tabled. Amendments have by their nature become a tool used in the negotiation process since they may encourage core sponsors to be more amenable to requests from other sides if they consider that the voting

(2004); 21 (2005); 40 (2013); 44 (2014); 31 (2015); 116 (2016); 51 (2017); 46 (2018); 29 (2019); 58 (2020); 103 (2021); 86 (2022); 69 (2023) and 45 (2024).

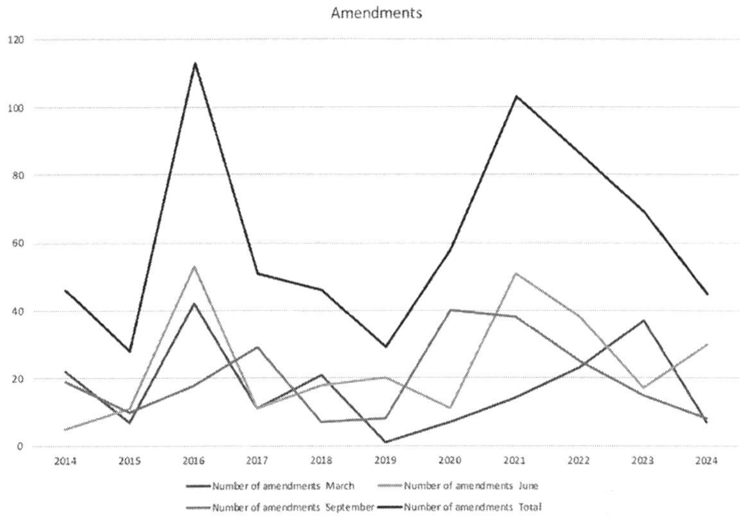

Figure 6.2 Number of amendments tabled at every session since 2014

pattern may be very tight. It is therefore awkward but perfectly logical that the topic of a given resolution may trigger the tabling of dozens of amendments or none, depending entirely on circumstances

A brief review of the situation over the last five years (2020–2024) will be probably more enlightening. During this period of time, 363 amendments were tabled representing more than two-thirds of the resolutions tabled at the same time. The following may be deducted from the facts and figures available in the Council reports and website:

- Out of these 363 amendments, only four were adopted thus representing a meagre 1.1 per cent, a fact which clearly underlines that amendments are rarely tabled with a prospect of them being adopted.
- However, it should be underlined that 24 amendments were rejected by a narrow margin. The author usually refers to texts, whichever their nature, for which the difference in votes is expected to be less than five votes as being within the 'margin of error'. As far as amendments are concerned, it is fair to state that their number is not insignificant. 24 amendments falling in this category during a five-year period represents 6 per cent of the overall number of amendments

but more importantly 15 per cent of those eventually acted upon. This is not negligible. Given the fact that these situations arose when certain societal texts were being considered, explains the tension that prevails during the last segment of any given session.

- 181 tabled amendments were withdrawn before action was taken. This represents half of the total number of amendments and emphasizes their nature as tools in the negotiation process culminating in the last 48 hours of any given session.
- 26 amendments were not acted upon because their sponsor did not find a Member State willing to act as a proxy or agree with them being discussed.
- In most situations, the amendments were therefore withdrawn, not acted upon or rejected very easily. However, certain situations deserve a closer attention since they reveal what it often not accessible to the laypersons.
- At the 48th Session, in September 2021, for instance, a draft resolution on the situation of human rights in Yemen was defeated. As mentioned earlier the rejection of a draft resolution is extremely rare and this created confusion in the room. Accordingly, the tension was at its highest in the Council. Additionally, at the same session, two amendments were adopted, for the first time in more than a decade. These concerned amendments on the draft resolution on the negative impact of legacies of colonialism on the enjoyment of human rights.[104] Despite their adoption, the text was nevertheless put to a vote and adopted with 20 in favour, no one voting against and 20 abstentions. Thereafter, given this very particular background, the sponsor of another unrelated text, draft resolution L.14 on realizing a better life for everyone, decided to withdraw its text considering probably that the margin of error might have been reached. Still at the same session, four amendments on the draft resolution concerning the death penalty were rejected but fell squarely within the margin of error.
- At the 50th Session, in June 2021, Resolution 50/10 on the mandate of the independent expert on the protection against violence and discrimination based on sexual orientation and gender identity was subjected to a large number of amendments, with 12 of them falling within the margin of error. Two of these latter texts were rejected

104 See Resolution A/HRC/48/7 adopted on 8 October 2021 and amendments L.59 and L.60.

despite having the same number of delegations voting in favour and against – based on rule 133 of the UNGA rules of procedure which specifies that if a vote is equally divided the proposal shall be regarded as rejected.

- At the 52nd Session held on March 2023, two amendments to Resolution 52/24 on the contribution of the Council with regard to the human rights implications of drug policy were adopted and another one rejected although falling within the margin of error. At the same session two other amendments were rejected with a narrow margin.

A thorough analysis of the amendments is certainly the best way to get close to the polarization that exists at the Council level. Whereas studies are often undertaken on the voting patter of Council resolutions – something which is obviously interesting but often misleading and certainly incomplete – it is the author's consideration that studying the amendments and the policy surrounding them is one of the few tools which may highlight the deep points of friction between delegations as well as the degree of polarization on certain societal issues. As far as country issues are concerned, the situation is usually easier to decipher since amendments are rarely tabled on such texts[105] and the position of many States well-known and clearly expressed.

6.4 Procedural motions in the context of the substantive work of the Council

6.4.1 The Structure of the Council's Sessions

As mentioned above, the Council meets three times per year, its main session taking place in February/March, and the two other sessions in June/July and September/October, respectively.

The Council's sessions' programmes of work include standard segments which are as follows: (a) High-Level Segment followed by a

105 There are some notable exceptions such as for instance the resolution which was adopted after the urgent debate on the human rights situation in Belarus in the run-up to the 2020 presidential election and its aftermath in September 2020 which was subjected to not least than 17 amendments.

General Segment (at the main session only); (b) interactive dialogue[106] on the Annual Report or general debates[107] on the oral update by the High Commissioner for human rights; (c) interactive dialogues with the mandate-holders of the Council; (d) panels; (e) consideration of the UPR outcomes; (f) Complaints Procedure in closed session;[108] and (g) ad hoc segments[109] and the voting process which was considered in the previous section.

Should a delegation wish to participate in all of the activities scheduled under all these segments, it would have to prepare not least than 80 statements – making it an extremely heavy burden for delegations, particularly those without a mission as well as small delegations.

Given the large number of issues dealt with under each one of these quite numerous segments of discussions, it is no surprise that a number of procedural motions may be advanced at any point. The following section sheds lights on which they are and how they can be moved.

6.4.2 Rules and Practices Relating to Points of Order

(1) *Legal background*: In accordance with rule 113 of the UNGA rules of procedure, 'during the discussion of any matter, a representative may rise to a point of order, and the point of order shall be immediately decided by the (President) in accordance with the rules of procedure. A representative may appeal against the ruling of the (President). The appeal shall be immediately put to the vote, and the (President's) ruling shall stand unless overruled by a majority of the members present and voting. A representative rising to a point of order may not speak on the substance of the matter under discussion'.

(2) As mentioned above, the requirements in rule 113 have been adhered to very strictly by the Council and their successive Presidents during the voting process. This strict application finds its origin in the rather chaotic situation that emerged at the Commission on Human Rights during the consideration of the draft resolution submitted by

---

106 In March.

107 In June and September.

108 At least once per year.

109 Such as urgent debates.

Brazil on human rights and orientation in 2003.[110] From the very beginning of the Council work, procedural challenges and motions have always been dealt with in a strict respect for the letter and spirit of the rules of procedure.

(3) However, during the general course of the discussion, the clarification provided for in Annex IV,[111] paragraph 79, of the rules of procedure has been followed. This provision indicates that 'in addition the presiding officer may, if he considers it necessary, request an expression of views from delegations on a point of order before giving his ruling; in the exceptional cases in which this practice is resorted to, the presiding officer should terminate the exchange of views and give his ruling as soon as he is ready to announce that ruling'.

(4) The practice of listening to a number of delegations in favour or against the views expressed by the delegation having risen to a point of order is being followed by the Council, particularly during the general debates or the interactive dialogues. This allows the President to clarify the situation and propose a motion which is in almost all circumstances not challenged nor subjected to a vote. It should be noted that the presiding officer is not expected to listen to all points of order made and may very well listen to some of the points of order requested, as long as s/he considers having had a chance to listen to all viewpoints. This is not always well-understood by delegations not given the floor but it is the mere application of the aforementioned rule as well as in the interest of a good time management.

(5) *High-Level Segment*: It should be pointed out that points of order are not admissible during the High-Level Segment. This follows a procedure which was initiated by the Commission on human rights when it established its own procedures in relation with the statements by guest speakers.[112] The aim of preventing any delegation

---

110 See introduction to Chapter 6.

111 Conclusions of the Special Committee on the Rationalization of the Procedures and Organization of the General Assembly.

112 Paragraph 35 of the Agreed provisions in document E/CN.4/2002/16 on 'Main rules and practices followed by the Commission on Human Rights in the organization of its work and the conduct of business' states that 'the Commission shall also continue to apply the ruling made by the Chairperson of its fifty-fourth session that recourse to points of order as a means of interrupting guest speakers would not be allowed'. The footnote to para 20 of

from disturbing a dignitary by way of a point of order is obvious: it is to set up an atmosphere which is commensurate with the necessary level of dignity inherent to the Council's work. Hence, delegations wishing to express disagreements with a dignitary's statement during the High-Level Segment (or at a later stage during the session) may only do so by way of a right of reply or of a statement in the corresponding general debate. It needs to be pointed out that the special meeting organized by the Council to hear a head of State or government does not provide for the possibility for any right of reply or any other statement. This Council's procedure is in line with the UNGA practice.

(6) *Panels*: It should further be highlighted that points of order are deemed inappropriate during panels. The rationale behind this factor relates to the nature of panels which are normally of a consensual nature with a number of panellists invited to share their views and opinions on a number of topics. It is thus expected that participants interact with the panellists by referring to the comments they made and asking questions to them. Raising points of order against a panellist's statement or any contribution to the discussion would thus be deemed contrary to the spirit of the interaction during panels. However, since it is possible for speakers to address specific human rights issues by way of example or illustration and within the context of the topic being discussed, concerned countries may feel compelled

---

the same document adds that an understanding was reached in the Commission on the following: statements by guest speakers are part of the general debate of the Commission. The only difference from other statements is that guest speakers are not bound by the items under consideration (or even by the agenda of the Commission). In practice, this means that guest speakers may address any human rights issue. Since their statements are part of the general debate, the same procedural rules apply, including the possibility for any State to disagree with the statement. The normal channels for such disagreement are (a) to express it in the course of the general debate (as a regular statement) or (b) to exercise the right of reply at the end of the meeting. Rule 42 of the rules of procedure prohibits speaking on the substance of the matter in raising a point of order. Consequently, the Chair would not admit the use of 'points of order' to express disagreement with or provide any arguments in favour of or against questions of substance raised by guest speakers.

to respond. In such cases, the speakers will be requested to express their disagreement during the discussion rather than resorting to a right of reply. This practice may be difficult to implement. Indeed, the duration of panels being very short, and the list of speakers reduced to the minimum, it may very well be that countries referred to in statements are simply not in a position to deliver statements during the panel. In such cases, the presiding officer, in coordination with the Secretariat, tries to identify the best possible and appropriate way for a disagreement to be expressed without interfering too much with the smooth running of the panel. Usually, a way out may be to give a delegation the right to make a point of clarification if it deems absolutely necessary.

(7) *Points of order and rights of reply*: Rules 113 and 115 of the UNGA rules of procedure cannot be used concomitantly. Of significant importance, it is not possible to interrupt a right of reply by a point of order since the latter cannot be considered as the 'discussion' of a matter in the sense of rule 113. Additionally, should this be tolerated, it would provide opportunities for delegations having already exhausted their two rights of reply to exercise de facto a third one, a possibility which is prohibited strictly by the Council's rules and practices.

6.4.3 Typology of Points of Order and/or Corresponding Rulings by the Presidents

(1) It is extremely difficult to quantify the points of order or the rulings by the presiding officer at any given session. Their occurrence may vary from none to more than 100. A variety of factors may influence this extreme variation, noticeably the level of politicization, the nature of the discussion, the heavy nature of the negotiation process outside the Council's Room, the time constraints and the general political atmosphere. In most cases, the points of order are raised in the context of interventions by NGOs and this may be based on issues relating to the topic of the statement, the language used and the speaker delivering it.

(2) However the qualification of points of order or rulings by the President is much easier and generally relates to the following matters:

   (a) *Respect and dignity*: Presiding officers will always insist on the need for everyone to adhere to a language that is commensurate with the dignity inherent to the discussion of human rights issues. Should a point of order be made, the President reminds that everyone has the right to express his/her views but that this should remain within the accepted framework, tolerance and respect being the keywords of the work of the Council.

(b) *UN standards and terminology*: Presidents may at the end of a given statement or in response to a point of order request all delegations to adhere and uphold UN standards when referring to countries or territories.

(c) *Contextualisation*: As mentioned, there is quite a large number of segments of discussion during any Council's session, and many of them relate to the consideration of oral and/or written reports by the High Commissioner, mandate-holders, commissions of inquiry or fact-finding missions, and other ad hoc mechanisms or procedures. In these contexts reference to one or several countries is appropriate if it is contextualized and considered to be an example or illustration of the matter under discussion. The handling of related points of order requires a high dose of diplomatic skills.[113]

(d) *Insulting language and personal attacks against the High Commissioner, independent experts or dignitaries*: Given the tension which characterizes the discussions of some matters, it may happen that the High Commissioner and more commonly the mandate-holders or members of a commission of inquiry or fact-finding mission[114] are subjected to derogatory and inflammatory remarks which are of a purely personal nature.[115] With the current multilateralism crisis and the increasing number

---

113 Concerned delegations may feel compelled to consider that the references to their countries were far too specific and/or deprived of any meaningful link with the topic under discussion and raise a point of order. It is up to the President with the assistance of the Secretariat to ponder to what extent this is indeed the case and give back the floor to the speaker with recommendations on how to proceed in delivering the remainder of the challenged statement.

114 Such remarks may also be directed against a dignitary or high-level officer and be subject to the same ruling.

115 Several instances may be mentioned, for instance harsh statements delivered against High Commissioner Louise Arbour or Commission of Inquiry Chairperson Richard Goldstone or Commissioner Doudou Diene, and current and former Special Rapporteurs, for instance Philip Alston, Agnès Callamard,

of illiberal groups and NGOs at the Council, such insulting, defamatory or intimidating language is unfortunately on the rise. In such cases, the President calls the speaker to order and reminds him or her to refrain from any personal attacks against the speakers. As to how to draw the line between what is acceptable or not, it is often mentioned in an informal and obviously too succinct manner that stating that a report, or its content, is a lie is unwelcome but deemed acceptable but saying that the special rapporteur is a liar is totally prohibited.

(3) *NGOs*: The vast majority of the points of order are made by States in relation to the statements by NGOs.[116] In addition to the abovementioned matters, the following elements may be referred to:

(a) *Accreditation*: Points of order are often delivered on the suspicion that the speaker is not duly accredited by an ECOSOC status NGO, in which case it is up to the Secretariat to clarify the matter immediately.[117]

(b) *Security threat*: Delegations may interrupt a speaker based on the assumption that he or she represents a security risk. In normal circumstances, the concerned delegation should have raised this matter prior to the discussion. In such cases it is up

---

Christine Chanet, Sheila Keetharuth, Yanghee Lee, Richard Falk, Idriss Jazairi, Alfred de Zayas or Jean Ziegler.

116 It should be pointed out that the content of any given statement is the sole and exclusive responsibility of the NGO having accredited the speaker. Should a delegation consider that the matter raised or the manner in which it was spelt out are against the ECOSOC rules, it is up to this delegation to raise the matter directly with the NGO Committee of ECOSOC which is the sole body within the UN system in a position to deal with the matter. The Council Secretariat may only deal with behaviour within the UN premises with the conduct of individuals that may be deemed inadmissible (disturbances in the room, verbal insults or physical assaults on persons, etc.), in which case the normal rules applying to the proper conduct of individuals within the UN premises would apply strictly.

117 Since the setting up of electronic means of registering NGO participants to the session, such instances are become increasingly rare given the electronic filters and firewalls which have been set in place as well as the close monitoring of the accreditation documents by the Secretariat.

to the Council Secretariat to alert the designated UN Senior Officer (the UNOG Director General) in charge of security and initiate proper investigations.[118]

(c) *Reprisals*: Conversely, remarks may be made either by governmental or non-governmental delegations that reprisals against those participation with the United Nations may have occurred in relation with the holding of the session. As repeatedly mentioned by Presidents,[119] the 'Council strongly rejects any act of intimidation or reprisal against individuals and groups who cooperate or have cooperated with the United Nations, its representatives and mechanisms in the field of human rights, and urges States to prevent and ensure adequate protection against such acts'. There is a protocol in place which needs to be followed when such allegations are made.

(4) *The impact of the webcast on the raising of points of order and their handling by the President*: All Council's proceedings are webcast and the webcast archives represent the official records of the Council's sessions. The advent of social networking has generated a large influx of comments and attacks based on images or statements from the Council that were taken out of context from the normal proceedings or without necessary explanations as to their rationale. This is particularly the case when points of order or rulings are concerned. This is a rather unfortunate situation which has at times generated a trend towards the delivery of remarks which could be construed as provocative either for domestic consumption or aimed solely at generating what is now commonly referred to as a 'buzz' on the social network. In this context, it is regrettable but fair to state that a one minute 30 second statement during a three-hour segment may not generate a lot of attention whereas a succession of points of order and/or rulings may be usable and extremely successful in such a distorted context. For this reason, and based on precedents, the

118 All such investigations have to this date concluded that the concerned individual did not raise any security threat and was thus authorized to participate in the Council's sessions.

119 See HRC Resolution 16/21 para 30.

Presidents do not generally interrupt any speaker on their own initiative but make remarks about their statements immediately after their delivery.[120]

(5) Several GONGOs and other similar illiberal groups or lobbies have followed the practice of inserting on purpose in their statements insulting languages, defamatory remarks and violent attacks against the United Nations, the Council and its mechanisms for the sole purpose of being interrupted by the presiding officer or by points of order. Thereafter, they use such interruptions as a mean to state that their freedom of speech was violated at the Council. This is obviously an aberration but there is not much that can be done at this stage given that the sole body that could be looking into the matter is the NGO Committee of ECOSOC which is too rarely seized with matters of this nature and does not have a strong history of struggling against the activities of GONGOs and similar groups.

6.4.4 Challenges against the President's Rulings

In accordance with rule 113, when points of order have been raised, particularly when there are a number of them, rulings are expected to be made by the Presidents. In most circumstances, such rulings take into account both sides of the discussion and after they are delivered the floor is given back to the speaker who has been interrupted. Occasionally the floor is moved to the next speaker. Challenges to the presiding officers' rulings are rare since on the one hand the rulings are balanced and at times relatively cryptic and on the other hand challenging the presiding officer is a gesture which is not deprived of a high level of politicization. Since such challenges are considered hostile and aggressive they are therefore rarely risen to in the room but rather in follow-up informal conversations. Nevertheless, there have been cases when rulings were challenged:

(1) During the consideration of the universal periodic review of China by the plenary of the NRC, on 22 October 2013,[121] one stakeholder, the

---

120 A controversy arose on 6 March 2009 when a representative of an NGO was interrupted by the presiding officer because his statement was clearly out of order. This led the concerned NGO to post the webcast images on its website and initiate a virulent campaign by affiliated lobbyists.

121 See A/HRC/25/2, paras 826–830.

International Service for Human Rights, referred to the death of a 'human rights defender, Cao Shunli' and before concluding its statement said that it would use its remaining speaking time to observe a moment of silence. At that juncture, China raised a point of order. China referred to HRC Resolution 5/1 and paragraph 31 of its Annex, in which it was stated that 'other relevant stakeholders will have the opportunity to make general comments before the adoption of the outcome by the plenary'. China stated that the time allocated for stakeholders to speak must only be used for making general comments and statements, in order to correspond to the Council's rules of procedure: any other use of speaking time would countermand those rules. Twelve delegations took the floor to support China's point of order. Nine delegations spoke against the point of order. Having listened to the various speakers, the President recalled that in accordance with NRC Resolution 16/21 it was crucial that individuals or groups wishing to cooperate with the Council and its mechanisms were able to do so. With regard to the issue of the use of speaking time, the President ruled that as this matter was of a procedural nature, he would take it to the Bureau for its consideration. China objected to the President's ruling, which was put to a vote. Of the 47 members of the Council called to vote, 45 were present and two absent; 13 voted in favour, 12 abstained and 20 voted against the President's ruling. The matter was not referred to the Bureau and the discussion continued with the next speaker.

(2) During the interactive dialogue with the Special Rapporteur on the independence of judges and lawyers, Mónica Pinto, on 25 June 2016,[122] the delegate of (the Bolivarian Republic of) Venezuela raised a point of order in relation to the statement made by the USA, opposing the reference to Venezuela which had not been mentioned in the report of the Special Rapporteur. Four delegations supported the point of order[123] while three delegations spoke against it.[124] Under rules 113 and 127 of the UNGA rules of procedure, the Council conducted a roll-call vote on the question of whether a reference in the statement to a country not mentioned in the report of the Special Rapporteur was in order. The result of the vote was affirmative with

---

122 See A/HRC/32/2 paras 76–81.

123 (Plurinational State of) Bolivia, Cuba, Ecuador and the Russian Federation.

124 Germany, the UK and the USA.

13 in favour and 12 against with 11 abstentions. Of interest, the vote was not conducted on the President's ruling which had expressed the usual position in relation to the contextualization of the statements and the possibility for delegations to refer to countries as way of examples. The vote which took place was phrased, on purpose, on the substance of the objection by Venezuela.

6.4.5 Observers and Procedural Motions

Contrary to the voting process, Observer States may rise to a point of order. However, their rights are limited by the provisions in the UNGA Resolutions 52/250 of 13 July 1998 and 58/314 of 1 July 2002 and the subsequent notes of the Secretary-General contained in document A/58/871 of 16 August 2004. Further to these documents, UN Member States which are non-members of the Council may raise points of order under rule 113 but not make other procedural motions, including appealing the ruling of the rules of the presiding officer.[125]

---

125 This was detailed in a Note by the Secretariat circulated to the members of the Council's Bureau on 3 December 2007 which attached an advice shared by the Office of Legal Affairs. This advice had been requested on 27 September 2007 by Egypt on behalf of the African Group which had sought clarification on the 'right of non-members of the Council to make a point of order in the work of the Council'. The advice read as follows: '9. Palestine and the Holy See, by virtue of (UNGA) resolutions 52/250 and 58/314 quoted above are entitled to raise points of order Rule 113 in the Council. Pursuant to those resolutions, these entities are not permitted to challenge the decision of the presiding officer or to raise points of order in connection with the actual conduct of voting. 10. With respect to Member States which are non-members of the Council pursuant to HRC Resolution 60/251, they may raise points of order Rule 113 but not make other procedural motions, including appealing the ruling of the presiding officer'. See also paras 33 and 34 of Agreed provisions in document E/CN.4/2002/16 on 'Main rules and practices followed by the Commission on Human Rights in the organization of its work and the conduct of business'. This procedure is obviously applied to NGOs which may not challenge a presiding officer's ruling either during a meeting or in any document circulated with a UN logo.

6.4.6 Rights of Reply

In accordance with rule 115 of the UNGA rules of procedure, 'During the course of a debate, the (President) may announce the list of speakers and, with the consent of the (Council), declare the list closed. He may, however, accord the right to reply to any member if a speech delivered after he has declared the list closed makes this desirable'.

A right of reply is to be considered as a disagreement to a speech or statement pronounced during any segment of discussion – with the below exceptions and for which the concerned delegation was not in a position to respond during its own speech. In this sense, rights of reply are to be considered as 'exceptions' to the normal conduct of business.

In the annexes to the UNGA rules of procedure, it is specified that 'delegations should use restraint in the exercise of their right of reply… and that their statements in exercise of that right should be as succinct as possible'.[126] It is further stated that 'statements made in the exercise of the right of reply, should be delivered, as a general rule, at the end of meetings'.[127] It is further specified that 'the number of interventions in the exercise of the right of reply for any delegation at a given meeting should be limited to two per item'.[128]

The implementation of these provisions – similar in nature to those contained in the rules of procedure of the functional commissions of the Economic and Social Council – was clarified by the Commission on Human rights which limited the number of rights of reply to two per delegation and per segment of discussion or items.[129]

---

126 See para 77 of the Annex IV to the UNGA rules of procedure entitled 'Conclusions of the Special Committee on the Rationalization of the Procedures and Organization of the General Assembly'.

127 Ibid., para 78.

128 See paras 8–11 of the Annex V to the UNGA rules of procedure entitled 'Decision 34/104 on the rationalization of the procedures and organization of the General Assembly'.

129 See the 'Compilation of recent documents in relation to the enhancement of the working methods of the Commission on Human Rights'. For instance, para 21 of document E/CN.4/2002/16 states that 'Rights of reply will be limited to two replies, of three minutes for the first and two minutes for the second. All rights of

The current practice of the Council derives from the UNGA rules of procedure, the Commission's practice and its own consideration of the matter. Two rights of reply are authorized per delegation at the end of the day or alternatively at the end of the general debate on any given agenda item if it concludes before the end of the day. The first right of reply is limited to three minutes and the second to two minutes.

It should be pointed out that the first right of reply should refer to all issues that might have arisen during the discussion of any matter during the day or general debate. Hence, it is not possible for a delegation to exercise several rights of reply concerning statements made by several speakers during the day.[130] The first right of reply must refer to all issues raised by all speakers during their daily statements which the concerned delegation considers as requiring its response. Delegations can therefore not exercise multiple rights of reply on the pretence that they are replying to different statements.

The second right of reply is limited strictly to responses to statements that may have been delivered during the right of reply segment.[131]

---

reply will be exercised at the end of the meeting, at the end of the day (6 p.m.) or at the end of the general debate on any particular item' or para. 33 of document E/2003/23 which stated that 'At its 40th meeting, on 9 April 2003, the Commission also accepted the recommendation of its officers that for the remaining agenda items two rights of reply should be exercised per item, 3 minutes for the first and 2 minutes for the second. The timing of the rights of replies would be at the discretion of the countries concerned.'

130 Delegations are sometimes arguing that they should be entitled to one right of reply in response to statements by Member and Observer States and one in response to NGO speakers. This obviously goes against the above-mentioned rules of procedure and practices and is not entertained by presiding officers. The rules and practices impose that a delegation may only exercise one right of reply against all statements that it feels obliged to respond to.

131 There again it is not possible for a delegation to use the second right of reply to respond to statements made during the day or the general debate. The second right of reply comes exclusively in response to another right of reply.

Since time constraints are increasingly impacting on the work of the Council, it may be that a right of reply segment starts late in the day and that several speakers add themselves to the list. When giving the floor to all of them would prevent all concerned delegations from speaking, the presiding officers privileges the first right of reply and does not entertain the second ones, since this would lead to some delegations not being in a position to respond and thus break the fairness with which this matter should be dealt. It is important to note that the rights of reply are not postponed to the following morning, they are simply deemed exhausted for the day. The presiding officer may also propose to listen to rights of reply without interpretation and with the agreement of the room proceeds accordingly.

The sole exception to this rule is when the closure of the debate under an item coincides with the end of the day, in which case it is possible and normal to resume the exercise of the rights of reply before moving to the next item.

Some segments of discussion may not be subjected to rights of reply:

- Delegations may not exercise a right of reply in relation to the speech of a head of State or government delivered in the context of an intersessional meeting convened for this exclusive purpose.
- Delegations may not exercise a right of reply against a statement made from the podium by the High Commissioner and/or his/her representative, a mandate-holder or any other expert or representative of a Council subsidiary body. The normal channel for expressing disagreement with a statement from the podium is in the context of a delegation's statement pronounced during the debate or dialogue.
- As far as panels are concerned, organizational constraints prevent all delegations from taking the floor. Indeed, the presiding officer can only entertain statements by 30 group's coordinators, Council Members or Observers distributed in two slots. Should a delegation not be in a position to express its disagreement owing to its place in the list of speakers, its only recourse would be to submit its statement to the Secretariat for posting wherever appropriate.

Adjournment of the debate and no-action motions

While there is no formal prohibition to resort to the procedural motions contained in rules 116–118 of the UNGA rules of procedure, in practical terms they are only raised in conjunction with action on proposals – interpreted in the broadest sense of the term.[132]

Urgent Debates

Since such meetings are convened in response to an emergency situation and given the role played by other UN bodies, particularly the Security Council, it may theoretically be argued that the debate supporting the deferral of the holding of the urgent debate should be deferred based on article 12, paragraph 1 of the UN Charter. It writes that 'while the Security Council is exercising in respect of any dispute or situation the functions assigned to it in the present Charter, the General Assembly shall not make any recommendation with regard to that dispute or situation unless the Security Council so requests'.

The advice given by the UN Legal Counsel on 26 March 2003[133] with regard to the call for a Special Sitting on the 'human rights and humanitarian situation in Iraq as a consequence of the war' made on the very same date settled the matter. In his response, the Legal Counsel reminded Office of Legal Affairs (OLA) constant position that 'article 12 of the Charter is directed to the General Assembly and not to any other organ. Article 12 of the Charter thus does not place a *legal* bar on the Commission discussing the proposal or making any recommendations or decisions within its competence. Should it make a recommendation to ECOSOC that body would have to decide on the appropriate course of action'. This advice as shared with the members of the Commission on the following day applies mutatis mutandis to the Council either in the context of a call for a Special Session or for an Urgent Debate.

132 See Section 6.3.

133 Shared with the Expanded Bureau of the Commission on the same date and with the whole membership the following day.

6.5 Elections of the HRC President of the HRC Advisory Committee members

6.5.1 President of the Council

Under rule 103 of the UNGA rules of procedure,[134] the Council must proceed with the election of its President and Vice-Presidents by secret ballot unless it decides otherwise in an election where only one candidate is standing.

The practice had almost always prevailed at the Commission on Human Rights (with the exception of the election of its 2003 Chairperson) and in the first decade of the Council's existence of electing that the Bureau members were elected by acclamation. When the Council cycle was changed to align with that of the General Assembly, the Council decided that to ensure that the Council's Bureau would be up and running as from 1 January onwards, the elections would take place at an Organizational Session to be held at the beginning of December. This was meant to enable the incoming President and Bureau to get acquainted with the Council rules and practices and be prepared for the first UPR meetings which customarily take place early in January.

The principle of elections by acclamation did not mean that there was never any difficulty in the selection process. But, usually, these difficulties however serious, were dealt directly between the two concerned countries which were proposing the name of a candidate or at the regional group level. These matters never reached the level of the plenary and were therefore never discussed in a formal manner at Council or Bureau level. Notice of it appeared in the context of postponement of the election of the concerned Vice-President to a later Organizational Meeting in January.[135] This simply meant that no agreement was reached

---

134 Rule 9 of the Council's own rules of procedure reproduces this specific rule but without a reference to the possibility of elections by secret ballot. This was done bearing in mind the wish that such elections should be consensual to avoid frictions in the Bureau and the Council. It remains that, should a difficulty arise, the UNGA rules apply.

135 In practical terms, it is known that difficulties arose among groups such as the Eastern European Group or the Group of Latin America

at the regional group level which deserved further deliberation. As long as there were at least three Members of the Council elected as Bureau Members, this meant that the Bureau could meet and take appropriate action and organize Council sessions. As far as how issues were settled at the group level there is not much information to share since the activities of these groups are outside the realm of formal United Nations activities and are not supported by public minutes. In one instance, the pre-selection of a candidate for the position of President of the Council at the Western European and Others Group level was achieved by quasi-election at group level according to information that reached the Bureau in an informal manner in December 2019.

Nevertheless, in recent circumstances the Council was informed by the concerned regional groups coordinators that no consensus could be reached at their level and that the matter had to be settled at the Council plenary level.

In December 2020, the President was informed by the regional coordinator of the Asia-Pacific Group that more time was needed to nominate a candidate for President thus triggering the postponement of the elections to January 2021. In the meantime, upon a proposal to that effect from the President, an Organizational Meeting took place on 16 December 2020 – in a hybrid manner given the COVID-19 pandemic situation – to elect the three Vice-Presidents who were supported in a consensual manner by their respective regional groups.[136] Their task was to constitute a three-person Bureau and prepare both the UPR meetings and the election of the President. The incoming Bureau was once again informed on 13 January 2021 that no consensus had been reached within the Asia-Pacific Group and that there were three candidates for the elections for the 15th Council cycle.[137]

---

and Caribbean Countries in several instances. See for instance the minutes of the Bureau Meeting of 15 December 2020.

136 Vice-Presidents from the African Group, the Group of Latin America and Caribbean Countries and the Western European and Others Groups. See minutes of the Bureau meeting of 15 December 2020.

137 His Excellency Mr. Yusuf Abdulkarim BUCHEERI, Permanent Representative of Bahrain; Her Excellency Ms. Nazhat Shameem

The modalities for the elections were somewhat difficult to set in motion given the COVID-19 circumstances and the restrictions to five delegates in a position to accede the room and are described in section 2.3. The basic tenants of these modalities were that they should follow very strictly the UNGA rules of procedure and relevant practices and that transparency should be ensured with all proceedings displayed live both on the UN Web TV and the Council live feed.[138] UNGA rules 125 and 132 provide that the decision should be made by a majority of the Members present and voting and that where no candidate would obtain in the first ballot the majority required, a second ballot would be taken. If in the second ballot the votes remain equally divided the President would decide between the candidates by drawing lots. Given the circumstances, the first and only ballot took place on 13 January 2021 proceeded slowly but well as a result of which the new President for the 15th cycle was elected and the Bureau established in full.

Thereafter, at the start of the Organizational Session which took place on 8 December 2023, the Coordinator for the Group of African States informed the Council that there were two candidates[139] for the position of President of the 18th cycle of the Council. Consequently, the President informed the Council that, since there was more than one candidate for the position of President, the election should be conducted by secret ballot in January 2024. On 4 January 2024, the Bureau composed of four Vice-Presidents reiterated the relevant UNGA provisions as contained in rules 103, 125 and 132 rules of procedure. Given the possibility for the Council to proceed with the elections in-person, the meeting took place on 10 January 2024 as a result of which the new President for the 18th cycle was elected.[140]

KHAN, Permanent Representative of Fiji; and His Excellency Mr. Ulugbek LAPASOV, Permanent Representative of Uzbekistan.

138 H.E. Nazhat Shameem Khan was elected with 29 ballots while H.E. Mr. Yusuf Abdulkarim BUCHEERI, Permanent Representative of Bahrain obtained 14 ballots and His Excellency Mr. Ulugbek LAPASOV, Permanent Representative of Uzbekistan 4. The required majority according to UN rules was 24 ballots.

139 H.E. Mr. Omar Zniber, Permanent Representative of the Kingdom of Morocco in Geneva; and H.E. Mr. Mxolisi Nkosi, Permanent representative of the Republic of South Africa in Geneva.

140 H.E. Mr. Omar Zniber, Permanent Representative of the Kingdom of Morocco in Geneva obtained 30 ballots and H.E. Mr. Mxolisi

6.5.2 Members of the HRC Advisory Committee

Since its establishment, the Council has created a number of bodies or mechanisms which report regularly to the Council. The only body membership of which has to be the subject of elections by the Council is the Advisory Committee under the provisions of the IBP which provides in its paragraph 70 that 'the Council shall elect the members of the Advisory Committee, in secret ballot, from the list of candidates whose names have been presented in accordance with the agreed requirements'. Paragraph 73 provides for the geographic distribution among the members and paragraph 74 specifies that 'The members of the Advisory Committee shall serve for a period of three years. They shall be eligible for re-election once. In the first term, one third of the experts will serve for one year and another third for two years. The staggering of terms of membership will be defined by the drawing of lots.'

In view of the foregoing, elections to the Advisory Committee take place at every September Session of the Council.

Rule 132 of the UNGA rules of procedure specifies that 'when only one person or member is to be elected and no candidate obtains in the first ballot the majority required, a second ballot shall be taken which shall be restricted to the two candidates obtaining the largest number of votes. If in the second ballot the votes are equally divided and a majority is required, the (President) shall decide between the candidates by drawing lots'.

Annex V to the UNGA rules of procedure[141] specifies in its paragraph 16 that 'the practice of dispensing with the secret ballot for elections to subsidiary organs when the number of candidates corresponds to the number of seats to be filled should become standard'.

Accordingly, when the number of candidates in a given region corresponds to the number of vacant positions, the secret ballot is dispensed with and the list of candidates endorsed by acclamation. However, when

Nkosi, Permanent representative of the Republic of South Africa in Geneva obtained 17 ballots. The required simple majority was 24.

141 Decision 34/401 on the rationalization of the procedures and organization of the General Assembly.

the number of candidates in a given region is higher than the number of vacant seats, a secret ballot is held. The candidate who receives the highest number of votes is elected.[142]

6.5.3 Other Bodies: The Principle of Non-election

HRC Resolution 5/1 provides for the establishment the Working Group on Situations composed of five representatives of Member States to deal with the Complaints Procedure. Similarly, it also provides for the establishment of the Consultative Group of the Council entrusted with responsibilities in regard of the selection of special procedures mandate-holders is composed of five Members. In both cases, the Members are appointed by their respective regional groups.

Difficulties arose in a number of circumstances regarding the appointment of one or more members of these two bodies given difficulties arising within the concerned regional group. At times, it was argued or proposed by concerned regional groups' coordinators or other States that the difficulties were so serious that they should be dealt with at Council level. However, the letter and spirit of the Institution-Building Package being clear and providing the regional groups with the entire responsibility of designating their representatives in both working groups, these difficulties were never dealt with by the Bureau and/or decided by the Council. It is obvious that proceeding otherwise would alter de facto the IBP and would introduce a further element of polarization or politicization in an already complex working environment.

6.6 Selection and appointment of mandate-holders

The process of selection and appointment of mandate-holders is governed by the IBP. In particular, paragraph 52 of Resolution 5/1 states that 'On

---

142 Such elections were held at the Council 7th Session (paras 113–116 and Annex VI of A/HRC/7/78) for the members from the Eastern European Group and the Western European and Other States Group; at the Council 24th Session (paras 22–27 and Annex IV of A/HRC/24/2) for members of the Western and Other States Group; and at the Council 36th (para.18 and Annex IV of A/HRC/36/2) and 42nd (report not yet available) Sessions for members of the Asian Group.

the basis of the recommendations of the consultative group and following broad consultations, in particular through the regional coordinators, the President of the Council will identify an appropriate candidate for each vacancy. The President will present to member States and observers a list of candidates to be proposed at least two weeks prior to the beginning of the session in which the Council will consider the appointments'. More importantly, paragraph 53 indicates that 'if necessary, the President will conduct further consultations to ensure the endorsement of the proposed candidates. The appointment of the special procedures mandate-holders will be completed upon the subsequent approval of the Council. Mandate-holders shall be appointed before the end of the session'. Importantly, Members of commissions of inquiry, fact-finding missions or investigatory mechanisms not being alluded to in the IBP, they are selected by the President without a requirement for a formal approval by the Commission.

The crucial elements in the above-mentioned paragraph 53 is the use of the term 'approval' in connection with the role of the Council. While the outcome of the work of the Consultative Group, the President and the Council is well-known and publicized, this is not the case insofar as the 'consultations' referred to in paragraphs 52 and 53 are concerned. While some of them may be held in a public manner, several discussions held by the President take place behind closed doors, with either a State, a group of States and coordinators of groups of States or representatives of civil society. The viewpoints of some of these stakeholders may be shared by the posting of note verbales or Letters on the Extranet. In practical terms they are often not shared publicly and thus cannot be disclosed in the context of this analysis.

The salient points of this procedure are that, whereas the list of the President is to be considered on a legal standpoint as a 'proposal' submitted to the Council and therefore subjected to relevant provisions of the UNGA rules of procedures, it needs to be endorsed by the Council without a vote. The rationale behind such an imperious requirement is as follows.

The Council's Special Procedures are made up of Special Rapporteurs, independent experts of working groups composed of Members appointed by the Council. They are independent, impartial and serve in their personal capacity. Should their selection be the subject to a vote, they would necessarily lose their ability to operate in a constructive environment and their appointment would be subjected to heavy political considerations. Their views and opinions would be challenged and the outcome of their work perceived and/or presented as the personal opinions of a mandate-holder deprived of the fundamental support of the Council as a whole. The overall system of Special Procedures would be weakened.

Additionally, the list being presented for the approval of the Council is a proposal by the President. Hence, subjecting it to a vote would undermine the status of the President and delegitimize his/her work.

The process of selection and appointment of mandate-holders is governed by law but operates in a very politicized and polarized environment. However, this reality is also a clear testimony to the importance and seriousness of the work of special procedures. Should their work be purely theoretical, deprived of impact on the ground, and with no consequence whatsoever, the process of selection would be ritualized and undertaken in only a few minutes.

In view of the foregoing, the following practice has emerged:

- The list of mandate-holders presented by the President to the Council for adoption is often the result of intense negotiations.
- The list is considered as a package. Should there be insurmountable difficulties concerning one only of the mandate-holders included in the list, the process would nevertheless be considered in its entirety and, if needed, postponed to a later opportunity, normally the next Organizational Meeting, with the proviso that the current mandate-holders are extended on an exceptional basis until the selection of their successors.

- In certain instances, a list may be adopted with one or more countries disassociating themselves from the process (for issues disconnected with the mandate-holder him/herself).[143]
- In practical terms, the selection and appointment process concludes with the approval of the list by consensus.[144]

143 For instance when a country differs from the consultative group and the President on the interpretation of the principle of non-accumulation of mandates.

144 Examples of sensitive and complex processes may be found in documents A/HRC/14/37, paras 37 and 38 (18 June 2010); A/HRC/25/2, paras 28–34 (28 March and 8 May 2014) and minutes of the Bureau of 25 April 2014; A/HRC/27/2, paras 20–22 (26 September and 6 November 2014) and minutes of the Bureau of 24 October 2014; and A/HRC/32/2, paras 28–34 (1 and 8 July 2016). It is of importance to note that the Presidential lists considered at the 25th and 27th Sessions were approved at a subsequent Organizational Meeting. It is also of interest to note the discussion at the 32nd Session when a disagreement occurred after the gavelling by the President. This made it necessary to convene an Organizational Meeting to ponder whether delegations wanted to reconsider the President's proposal under the provisions of Rule 123 of the UNGA rules of procedure. Since this was not the case, the list was deemed approved as such. The relevant webcast archives provide more concrete information on the information alluded to in this section. For a more recent case which unfolded during the summer of 2022, please refer to Chapter 3.2.3.

7 The change management process as it applies to the Council and previously the Commission

The respiratory system brings oxygen from the air to the body and excretes carbon dioxide back into the air. In this chapter an analysis is made of the ways and means by which the Council adjusts to the fluctuating nature of circumstances, getting rid of what has become irrelevant while injecting new working methods and tools into its apparatus.

7.1 The Commission on Human Rights' failed attempts at reforming itself

As has been discussed earlier, one of the reasons the Commission was eventually abolished and replaced by the Council lay in the inherent difficulties it faced in adjusting to the evolving nature of circumstances. A number of documents related to the enhancement of the working methods of the Commission were included in the eponymous Compilation. However, a closer look reveals that the proposed measures were of an extremely low-key nature, went backward, or were not approved by the Commission as a whole.

The most ambitious of these texts was the Annex to Decision 2000/109 of 26 April 2000, which had been subjected to an intense two-year negotiation process. While there is no doubt that the intention of all concerned was genuine, it remains that the Commission failed to adopt broad and concrete measures in relation to the rationalization of existing mandates (with the exception of the merging of two mandates and the termination of another one[1]). Neither did it propose recommendations aimed at instilling flexibility into its programme of work. Its yearly six-week session remained packed with endless and sterile general debates marked by lengthy statements and a large number of agenda items (21). In certain regards, it even went backwards – for instance insofar as the Sub-Commission was concerned – by depriving it of its right to consider country issues not dealt with by the Council.

As far as later documents were concerned, it is sufficient to note that one of the technical documents proposed by the Bureau in 2001 to streamline the Commission's working methods was only partially adopted,[2] while another document, although comprehensive, including a set of recommendations by the 2003 Bureau, could not be formally endorsed by the 2004 Commission.[3]

These facts underscored the inability of the successive Commission Expanded Bureaux[4] to convince the plenary of the appropriateness of the change management measures. Alternatively, possibly the fact that all such documents required the formal approval of *all* members of the Commission provided a de facto veto right to each and every one of them. Attempts by successive Expanded Bureaux failed to crystallize agreements and the status quo remained untouched, leaving limited space for developments in practice.

7.2 The constant efforts of the Human Rights Council to reform itself

7.2.1 The IBP

The change-management process as it applied to the Council in its initial phase (from 2006 to 2011) has to be read against two major factors: first, the above-mentioned extreme rigidity of the Commission in envisioning

1 See paras 14 and 21 of the Annex to Decision 2000/109.
2 See Section F of the compilation, which includes the agreed provisions in document E/CN.4/2002/16.
3 See para 17 of the Commission's report on its 60th session (E/CN.4/2004/127).
4 A fact which appears retrospectively quite awkward since expanded Bureaux included representatives of regional and political groups.

any review or reform with a view to addressing the contemporary world's challenges in a meaningful manner and revisiting its working modalities and functions; and second, the necessity for the Council to implement UNGA Resolution 60/251, which had been subjected to a full year of difficult negotiations and had thus left many blanks in the text.

Immediately after the Council was established, it thus had to find ways and means to translate the UNGA's resolution into deeds. This process took a whole year, during which the Council focused mainly on institutional matters, somewhat to the detriment of substantive human rights matters.

This was particularly the case regarding the UPR set up by operative paragraph 5(e) of the said resolution. However, it extended to the elements alluded to in operative paragraph 6, namely that the Council should 'assume, review and, where necessary, improve and rationalize all mandates, mechanisms, functions and responsibilities of the Commission on Human Rights in order to maintain a system of Special Procedures, expert advice and a Complaint Procedure; the Council shall complete this review within one year after the holding of its first session'. In practical terms, this meant that the Council had to set up its own new sets of procedures and mechanisms while discussing how to assume the Commission's previous responsibilities as well as its working methods – which, it should be recalled, had been sharply criticized and had led to its abolishment. Additionally, this had to be accompanied by a discussion of the Council's agenda and annual programme of work, which had been highly politicized in the past, particularly insofar as the Middle East issues were concerned.

While the main Commission's functions were to be assumed by the Council, nothing in the resolution provided any indications as to what its working methods and arrangements should be. Determining this proved to be a daunting task and the Council spent a whole year discussing these matters to the detriment of substantive matters, which were left aside.

In the first year of its existence, the Council thus engaged in a heavy process of negotiations, which led eventually to the adoption of Resolutions 5/1 and 5/2. Read together with Resolution 16/21 adopted at the end of the 2011 review process, they constitute the IBP.

The modalities resorted to by the Council during this period followed, although in appearance only,[5] the methods usual in the multilateral system, namely the establishment of intergovernmental Working Groups. The first one on the agenda was the annual programme of work, methods of work and rules of procedure. The second was the UPR and the third the issue of reviewing, and when necessary, improving and rationalizing all mandates, mechanisms, functions and responsibilities in order to maintain a system of Special Procedures, expert advice and complaints procedure.

These Working Groups met several times during the year without much success in terms of outcome.[6] Unsurprisingly, the polarization of the Council membership and beyond on issues of significance relating to the role and functions of the Council led to sterile formal discussions where delegations reiterated their positions in a comprehensive and rigid manner.

In order to overcome this situation, a transfer operated between the former modus operandi (Working Groups) and new negotiation strategies – mostly imported from the UN UNGA: the President and his Bureau had no other choice but to adopt a more flexible and informal process by appointing facilitators[7] with a view to collecting ideas, discussing them with all concerned and feeding the above-mentioned Working Groups with the appropriate papers, including recommendations.

This hybrid process enabled the Council to identify conclusions that were refined and eventually consolidated into the IBP. Resolution 5/1 provided quite exhaustive descriptions of the Council mechanisms and bodies, namely the UPR, Special Procedures, the Advisory Committee,

---

5 See Chapter 3.

6 The first session took place from 10 to 13 April, the second from 16 to 20 April, and the third from 23 to 27 April 2007.

7 Working methods and rules of procedures (Permanent Representative of the Philippines); Agenda and Annual Programme of Work (P.R. of Guatemala); UPR (P.R. of Morocco, Vice-President); Special Procedures (P.R. of the Czech Republic, Vice-President); expert advice (P.R. of Jordan, Vice-President); and Complaint Procedure (P.R. of Switzerland, Vice-President).

the Complaints Procedure and the agenda and working methods of the Council – which have been described in previous chapters.

Once the IBP was eventually adopted on 18 June 2007, the Council had to continue devoting time to negotiating various elements which had been introduced into the Council's Resolution 5/1. In particular, the Council had to engage in a time-consuming process of 'reviewing, rationalizing and improving' process whereby all Special Procedures mandates had to be considered against a comprehensive list of criteria referred to in Section II B. The Council also had to work on a number of complex modalities relating to the newly designed UPR, as well as launching the revisited Complaints Procedure and the Human Rights Council Advisory Committee. This was done somewhat at the expense of the substantive Council's work.

7.2.2 The 2011 Review of the Council Work and Functioning (the Geneva Review)

Four years later, the Council engaged in a review process which had been envisioned in paragraphs 1 and 16 of the UNGA Resolution 60/251, which stated respectively that 'the Assembly shall review the status of the Council within five years' and 'the Council shall review its work and functioning five years after its establishment and report to the General Assembly'.

The hybrid nature of the review process, which touched both the status and the modus operandi of the Council but was devolved to two different entities, namely the UNGA, exacerbated difficulties in its own terms.

In particular, it should be borne in mind that discussing the review of the status of the Council (the New York Review) – whether the Council should be upgraded to a principal UN body or remain a subsidiary body of the UNGA – almost automatically leads to the consideration of matters relating to its modus operandi. Indeed, upgrading the Council to a main body of the United Nations on a par with the UNGA, the Security Council and the ECOSOC may only be achieved by way of amending the UN Charter, a process that is both legally and politically difficult. It is self-evident that this is not a plausible course of action. Accordingly, since intergovernmental work, by nature, hates a vacuum, reviewing the status of the Council can only lead to the consideration of other matters of substance relating in particular to the relationship between the Council and New York bodies.

There existed, therefore, a political environment pleading for discussion at the UNGA level of a number of issues that went far beyond the mere status of the Council.

In the non-paper of the UNGA co-facilitators at the start of the process,[8] reference was therefore made to the institutional status of the Council as well as its size, composition and membership, including the practice of pledges and commitments, the relationship between the Council and the Third Committee, the reporting cycle of the Council, the relationship between the Council and the Fifth Committee, and the interplay between the budget of the OHCHR and that of the Council.

From the very start, it became apparent that it was unthinkable to discuss some of these issues without proper input from the Council and a high level of interaction between the New York and Geneva processes. This was made necessary, on the one hand, because the future of the Council was at stake and it was therefore only fair to get its views on the matter, and on the other hand, because discussing the status of the Council invariably led to discussions of the Council's functioning and vice versa.

Accordingly, an agreement between the President of the UNGA and the President of the Council was circulated on the coordination between the two processes according to which it was understood that the 'two processes would be conducted... in a manner that fully reflect(ed) the authority of the two bodies in their respective areas of work. Given the complementarity of these areas of work and the thematic overlap of some of the topics under discussion it (was) of the utmost importance to ensure coordination and coherence between the review processes in Geneva and New York'.[9]

8 See the attachment to the letters of the P.R. of Morocco and the P.R. of Liechtenstein dated 23 November 2010: http://www.un.org/en/ga/president/65/issues/non-paper241110.pdf.

9 The agreement may be found at www.un.org/en/gapresident/65/issues/hrccouncil.shtml.

During the subsequent months, there was ample coordination between the two bodies with exchanges between the President of the UNGA, the President of the Council and the New York and Geneva facilitators. The New York co-facilitators visited Geneva on several occasions and the President of the Council appointed a coordinator to link with the New York review process, whose proposals were included in the Council Working Group report.

In setting up the parameters for the review of the Council's work and function (the Geneva review), use was made of the same methodology as the one that was followed in discussing the IBP, namely setting up an open-ended intergovernmental Working Group and appointing several facilitators. Unsurprisingly, the process was tainted with the same level of politicization and polarization with extremely divergent views between delegations. The Working Group, which was established pursuant to HRC Resolution 12/1, met twice[10] but was unsuccessful in reaching any form of consensus between the Members. The facilitators[11] and the Coordinator[12] appointed by the President of the Council's fifth cycle led the discussion at the Working Group level but conducted many informal consultations and meetings.

From the very beginning, a disagreement emerged over the nature and scope of the review. Some delegations entertained the view that the review should be conceived as a broad exercise to look at how to enhance the effectiveness of the Council in discharging its mandates and consequently that all proposals should be placed on the table as long as they were deemed relevant to the work and functioning of the Council. Others saw the review as a limited fine-tuning exercise to be confined to the parameters of the IBP.

Accordingly, the President took a fine line, which the Council eventually endorsed, that the review would be based on the IBP but in the context of

10 From 25 to 29 October 2010 and on 7, 17/18 and 23/24 February 2011.

11 UPR (P.R. of Morocco, VP); Special Procedures (P.R. of Finland, VP); HRC Advisory Committee (Romania); agenda and framework for a programme of work (P.R. of India, VP); and methods of work and rules of procedure (P.R. of Brazil, VP).

12 Coordination with the Council Review process in New York (P.R. of Algeria).

the mandates that had been given to the Council. Also, it was agreed that all proposals would be open to consideration but that the review would proceed on the basis of consensus and convergence.[13]

Nevertheless, in addition to the agenda of the Council, one specific issue caused a major impasse in the discussion at the initial stage, namely that of Council membership. The question raised was whether the election process should be altered by way of introducing criteria for membership or not. After much discussion, and in view of the entrenched positions of both sides, this issue was set aside on the understanding that it would come under the scope of the review of the status by the UNGA.

Also, the issue of the relationship between the Council and the OHCHR was raised, generating considerable debate. It was resolved by recognizing that this would have to be taken out of the review process in order to be dealt with independently.

Given the extent of the disagreements between the various groups of countries, the President convened a Retreat in Bangkok in December 2010[14] in the hope of overcoming these difficulties. Prior to this retreat, the President convened informal meetings, which he stewarded in order to discuss a possible emerging consensus. However, the Retreat showed that an agreement on most proposals made by delegations would be extremely difficult, if not impossible to reach. Consequently, upon return from Bangkok, the President conducted several informal consultations at the Permanent Mission of Thailand in Geneva. During the last week of these consultations, it became apparent that there was no other choice than to drop most of the innovative features proposed by delegations during the negotiation process. The final agreement contained in Resolution 16/21 was thus lacking the most contentious issues.[15]

Compared with the compilation of contributions by the facilitators circulated at the second session of the Working Group, the following matters were, inter alia left out of the final document:

---

13 Statement by the President of the Council at the informal plenary meeting of the UNGA on the review of the status of the Council on 30 March 2011.

14 See Chapter 2.

15 HRC Resolution 16/21 of 25 March 2011.

- UPR
  - The plenary sessions of the Council for the consideration of the outcome of the UPR review were proposed to be held together with the UPR Working Group sessions or in the context of mini-sessions.[16]
  - There were references to the follow-up to the UPR recommendations and implementation of the UPR outcome.
  - There was also a request for the recommendations contained in the Working Group reports to be clustered.
- Special Procedures
  - An encouragement was included for Special Procedures to draw the Council's attention to situations and issues deserving urgent preventive and proactive action.
  - There were also various references to the need for coordination and cooperation between mandate-holders, including the strengthening of the Coordinating Committee of Special Procedures.
  - The need to accord greater emphasis on the follow-up to recommendations of Special Procedures was highlighted.
  - A whole section was proposed on the importance of cooperation with Special Procedures.
  - The need was also recognized for the enhancement of the accountability of Special Procedures by requesting States to make better use of existing formal and self-regulatory mechanisms and arrangements.
- The Human Rights Council Advisory Committee
  - A proposal was made for completely new modalities for the appointment of Members with an important role to be played by the Consultative Group in this regard.
  - Several suggestions were made to enhance the role of the Committee.
- The Complaints Procedure
  - The facilitator's contribution was not incorporated into the new text. It included elements requesting the Working Group on

16 In his statement to the informal meeting of the UNGA (ibid.), the President explained that this proposal unravelled 'because agreement could not be reached as to whether the mini-plenary sessions to adopt UPR outcome could also be used to take up other issues, such as urgent human rights situations'.

Communications and the Working Group on Situations to meet during the same period of time to facilitate their interaction and inviting the Working Group on Situations to brief the President of the Council after each one of its sessions.

- Agenda and Framework for a Programme of Work
  - There again, the facilitator's contribution was not incorporated into the text. It included a framework of two sessions of four weeks per year, moving the consideration of the UPR outcome out of the plenary sessions, reinstating individual two-hour interactive dialogues with special rapporteurs, and reducing the number of panels per year.[17] Of significant importance, an earlier proposal had been made to merge agenda items 4, 7 and 10 concerning which the President later indicated to the UNGA that 'it failed to gain the needed support for reasons that are obvious to you'.[18]
- Methods of work and rules of procedure
  - There were proposals relating to the special sittings and other work formats and outcomes, as well as avoiding the duplication of initiatives in the Council and the Third Committee.

The few changes that remained in Resolution 16/21 concerned, inter alia, the role of National Human Rights Institutions, the modalities of the second cycle of the UPR Mechanism, including its extension from four to 4.5 years to allow more time for the dialogue with the country under review, the encouragement for countries to provide clear positions on UPR recommendations they can accept or not accept and provide voluntary midterm updates, the strengthening of funding for technical assistance and capacity-building, the improvement of the selection process of mandate-holders, the enhancement of cooperation between States and Special Procedures in parallel with ensuring more equitable and transparent funding for all Special Procedures, and the organization of an annual interagency penal discussion on mainstreaming. Other more technical issues were approved, such as the change of the Council cycle

17 There again, the President explained to the UNGA that a number of countries felt that reducing the number of main sessions from three to two would result 'in reducing the capacity to react to urgent human rights situations'.

18 Ibid.

year, the establishment of an Office of the President, the improvement of the secretarial support and the use of information technology.

In his final words to the UNGA, the Council President stated,

> some may say that this outcome is below their expectations in one way or the other. I agree that it might not be as ambitious that we had thought. But I would beg to differ with those who say that it is a minimalist outcome. All of us know that it reflects the best we could achieve under the present circumstances. More importantly, it reflects the realities of the Council. Nonetheless, I still feel that the review was a worthwhile exercise that allowed us to engage in dialogue on all pertinent issues. I also believe that the outcome will, in many respects, serve to enhance the work and functioning in promotion and protection of human rights.

Such candid remarks shed light on the difficulty of any change management process at the Council level given the complexity of the current arrangements, the unavoidable level of politicization of many, if not all of its components, and the understanding that 'nothing will be deemed adopted until everything is agreed'.

Since there was not much potential for a universal agreement around a comprehensive and formal review of the Council's work and functioning, the many changes that were introduced in subsequent years in the Council's modus operandi were based on pragmatic and pointed negotiations aimed at tackling immediate issues in a flexible and informal manner – usually by way of gavelling a President's proposal negotiated beforehand. There was indeed not much chance for a mid- to long-term apprehension of the Council's work in all of its dimensions. Only short-term but incremental changes could be envisioned at this current stage of the multilateralism system – and this is what is usually referred to as the efficiency and effectiveness process.

7.2.3 The 2011 Review of the Council Status (the New York Review)

Subsequently, the UNGA faced comparable challenges in its review of the Council's status. Mutatis mutandis, this led to the same type of low-key agreement at the end of the New York review.[19]

---

19 See UNGA Resolution 65/281 of 17 June 2011.

An understanding had been reached on 30 September 2010 between the President of the UNGA and the President of the Council, according to which the New York review would consider the issue of the status after the Council had concluded its review of its work and functioning. Close cooperation was established between the two processes, particularly insofar as overlapping issues were concerned. This related prima facie to the relationship between the Council and the UNGA and its Third Committee.

A non-paper of the co-facilitators was attached to the invitation dated 23 November 2010 to the first open-ended informal plenary meeting to discuss the scope of the review of the status of the Council on 1 December 2010. That document anticipated three categories of topics in connection with the status of the Council: (a) institution's standing; (b) the relationship between the Council and the Third Committee; and (c) the relationship between the Council and the Fifth Committee.

Of interest, the first basket included issues relating to 'the status of the Council at the time of its establishment (e.g. size, composition, membership of the Council, including a consideration of the current practice of pledges and commitments)'.

As was mentioned above, the membership issue had reached a stalemate in Geneva and an understanding had been reached that it would come under the New York leg of the review. It crystallized a strong disagreement between the various stakeholders. Among them were matters relating to possible new options for the implementation of paragraphs 8 and 9 of Resolution 60/251, including, for instance possible pledges by candidates to the Council, such as requesting them to declare their intent to fully and effectively cooperate with the Council and its mechanisms during their membership.[20]

Not fewer than nine informal meetings were convened by the co-facilitators. Beyond the membership issue, constructive meetings were held on various other matters relating to the relationship between the Third Committee and the Council, the alignment of the cycle of the Council

[20] Ibid.

with that of the UNGA, consideration of the Council report in New York and financing.[21]

In the zero draft dated 31 May 2011, which was presented for discussion by the co-facilitators, almost all matters relating to the Council membership or composition had disappeared with the exception of a proposed paragraph 11 which, if adopted by the Assembly, would have 'underlined the importance of creating an opportunity for States to present to the membership their voluntary pledges and commitments made in connection with their candidatures to the Human Rights Council'. Even such mild language was eventually taken out of the version circulated on 14 June 2011. This underscored, if needed, the high level of politicization of this matter as well as that of items 4 and 7, both at the Council and UNGA levels.

It may be of interest to refer to the sole oral statement posted on the website of the President of the UNGA, which sheds some light on the matter from the viewpoint of one group of negotiators:

> We are aware that some distinguished colleagues have other preferences to be discussed under this review process. We acknowledge their noble ideas and objectives but the wider membership has expressed its desire to stay within the specific mandate of the Resolution 60/251. We are also aware of the argument that these proposals are for operationalization of specific paragraphs, which does not amount to re-opening the resolution. However, we would respectfully argue that the same logic could be applied to almost all paragraphs of the resolution. Let's not involve in a cherry picking exercise and through you request all distinguished colleagues to concentrate on the mandate i.e. status stricto sensu. Only by following this approach we will be able to finalize the given task within the stipulated time frame of 15th June. We stand ready to help you reach this milestone. (...) Concerning elements for further discussion, we have clearly stated our preference on how to deal with these issues. Discussions on these issues would only involve unnecessary delays and complicate progress on even those issues, which are ripe for consensus. I can assure you distinguished co-facilitators that my delegation could easily comment on the merits of each proposal as well as bring to fore a range of new ones for consideration. However, in our view, the best way

21 See the non-papers circulated by the co-facilitators' letters of 14 February and 11 April 2011.

forward is to park these issues for a future discussion, as and when decided by the GA.[22]

The outcome of the review of the Council's status was Resolution 65/281 adopted on 17 June 2011. It included a number of technical issues aligning the Council cycle with that of the UNGA, clarifying that the Council President would henceforth present the Council Report to the plenary of the UNGA and the Third Committee while holding an interactive dialogue with the latter only, and confirming that the Fifth Committee would consider all financial implications emanating from the Council's resolutions and decisions. Naturally, it did not include any reference to the membership of the Council nor its agenda.

7.2.4 Future Reviews of the Human Rights Council

In considering future formal review processes, it is of importance to note that in the 2011 review, which was prescribed in paragraphs 1 and 16 of the UNGA Resolution 60/251, there is no mention of a Council review of its work and functioning. Whereas in paragraph 3 of Resolution 65/281, the UNGA decided to 'consider again the question of whether to maintain this status at an appropriate moment and at time no sooner than ten years (2021) and no later than fifteen years (2026)', it did not request the Council to proceed in a similar manner. Additionally, the very timid request contained in paragraph 13 of the zero draft prepared by the co-facilitators, which the Council would have been encouraged to continue reviewing its work and functioning, taking into account the provisions of Resolution 60/251, was dropped shortly before the consideration of the final draft.

However, given the interpretation by the UNGA co-facilitators during the 2011 review process, which touched on issues relating inter alia to the coordination of the Council's and the Third Committee's work, as well as the reporting lines and processes, it is fairly clear that some forms of involvement of the Council in the New York review process would be of importance, at least to ensure that the crucial issue relating to the

22 Statement by Pakistan of 15 April 2011 on the second non-paper circulated by the co-facilitators on the Council Review. There is no other written statement posted on the PGA website.

Geneva–New York relationship would not be dealt with solely from a Headquarters viewpoint.[23]

Additionally, the appropriateness of the Council revisiting or assessing its work under Resolutions 5/1 and 16/21, including that of its subsidiary bodies, might be the subject of consideration by the Council at the time of the New York review based on parameters which it would have to decide upon.

It is of importance to note that the formal change of review processes in 2007 and 2011 were very complex, polarized and politicized, and of a hybrid nature, which made it very difficult for the UNGA and the Council to agree on texts introducing significant changes to the existing status and structure as well as working methods, agenda and programme of work. Given the fact that the current underlying political environment combined with a very serious liquidity and budgetary crisis remains quite comparable, if not worse with that prevailing in 2006 and 2011, it may be advanced that the same difficulties will be faced should the work and functioning of the Council ever be reviewed in a formal manner again.

Many of the proposals that individually might have reached a high degree of approval in an informal setting could not be incorporated into the final Council review resolution in 2011. The same rationale will ipso facto apply to future circumstances. This is due to the fact that some of the proposals advanced by delegations relate to extremely controversial matters that could not be agreed upon when the Council was established and do not stand a chance of being agreed upon when multilateralism is in crisis.

Unsurprisingly, a non-comprehensive list of these matters would involve the quality of Council membership and the possible restrictions thereto, the agenda item 4 on human rights situations that require the Council's attention, the agenda item 7 on the human rights situation in Palestine

23 The President of the 13th cycle invited delegations on 28 March 2019 for an exchange of views on the topic of the 2021/26 Review. The discussions emphasized a very moderate appetite for any review of the work and functioning of the Council as well as emerging disagreements on the involvement of the Council in the General Assembly Review of the Council's status.

and other occupied Arab territories, the role and prerogatives of special rapporteurs and investigative bodies, the contribution of non-governmental organizations to the work of the Council and the issue of reprisals against human rights defenders, the inter-sessional activities by the Council, the interaction with the OHCHR and the preventive role of the Council.

This does not mean at all that there will not be calls for profound reviews of the Council's status, particularly insofar as its composition or agenda is concerned. What it does mean is that proposing profound changes in these matters will automatically trigger opposite proposals suggesting significant changes in other areas of the Council's work. For instance, if a delegation were to propose the abolishment of agenda item 7, others would immediately react by proposing the abolishment of item 4. Similarly, any proposal relating to criteria for membership will face insurmountable difficulties as to what these criteria should be all about. Proposing a qualified majority, for instance, a two-thirds majority, for elections to the Council will trigger a counter-proposal to have a similar qualified majority to adopt country resolutions or convene a Special Session.

More broadly, whenever a change-management process is to be envisaged in the Council realm, three factors need to be taken into consideration. First, delegations need to consider the *legal aspects* of any proposal: could the process be envisaged under the existing framework (for instance, UNGA Resolution 65/281 or Resolutions 5/1 and 16/21)? What would be its terms of reference? And what kind of substantive changes may be anticipated that would not run against the Council rules and practices (changes in the UPR modalities, streamlining of the Special Procedures' work and functions, revision of the Advisory Committee's terms of reference or adjustments to the Complaints Procedure's modus operandi)?

Secondly, the *political environment* in which the Council is operating needs to be taken into serious consideration: it bears a considerable impact on the possibility of envisioning a review of the Council's work and functioning. Even if there were no legal obstacle to the discussion of a series of possible changes, it would remain to be seen whether the level of polarization would nullify any such attempt. Given the likelihood that a discussion of substantive issues may automatically raise tensions and trigger entrenched positions, this may be deemed redhibitory by any delegation advocating changes in the Council's modus operandi.

Thirdly, there is a *psychological element* that needs to be borne in mind: given the considerable amount of time and energy spent in previous reviews either at the Commission or at the Council level – at the expanse of substantive human rights work – and taking into account the modest outcome of the 2011 process, the immediate reaction to any delegation urging for a review or reform will be dubious and sceptical.

Additionally, this should also be read in conjunction with the well-known and well-understood Pavlovian reaction prevalent in the human rights intergovernmental machinery: given the unavoidable and unfortunately growing mistrust between delegations, any proposal advanced by one particular group of States will always be considered against the background of the presupposed ultimate goal of the group. Even if there were to be a genuine and common interest in adjusting the working arrangements in relation, for instance, to the contribution of civil society, Special Procedures, or international organizations to the work of the Council or to the organization of general debates or interactive dialogues, the reading of such proposals will always go beyond the mere appearance and focus on what may be (mis)interpreted as lying beneath the appearance.

Accordingly, based on the assumption that perception plays a key role in multilateral negotiations, whenever a delegation advances a recommendation in any of these areas, or even in different areas but which may be conceived as having an indirect and remote link with these matters, it is likely that other delegations will compensate by advancing diverging or opposite recommendations concerning this matter or any other one that may be deemed controversial. In this regard, the inventiveness of delegations knows no boundaries.

In view of these impediments, it is the opinion of the author that the optimum way for the Council's working methods to be adjusted is through a pragmatic and flexible methodology, which is often referred to as the efficiency and effectiveness process.

Enhancing the Efficiency and Effectiveness of the Council Through a Pragmatic Approach

The Bureaux that were established after the 2011 review opted for such a pragmatic approach, focusing on issues of efficiency and targeting several matters requiring urgent action and setting aside any matter that would or could be interpreted as touching on the above-mentioned controversial issues.

The fact that the natural expansion of the Council's work led to a growth in the number of meetings held to more than 150 per year[24] with increasingly heavier and longer sessions and that this number far exceeded the United Nations Office's capacities and played a significant role in narrowing the scope of any revisiting of the Council's work and functioning to issues directly or indirectly linked to related organizational matters. Such change processes thus more often than not led the Presidents', Bureaux's and stakeholders' attention to efficiency measures.

These processes were considered as remaining within the ambit of the IBP and the formal framework and programme of work of the Council and were not tainted with the solemnity, complexity and formalism of a full-fledged Council-driven process. It was often mentioned that they did not constitute any precedent, that they should be deemed as pilot or test exercises, and that they were in line with the IBP.

It is to be understood that they were proposed by the Presidents with the support of their Bureaux and, when no Council member expressed prior disagreement, they were gavelled without further ado. This was particularly the case with successive measures taken regarding time-management,[25] the organization of panels, interactive dialogues and general debates, the bi- or tri-ennialization of resolutions and the improvement of the information technology available to the Council's stakeholders.

---

24 In the Joint Task Force on the Workload of the Human Rights Council, dated 24 August 2017, it is recalled that the Council held 128 meetings over its three regular sessions in 2012 and 2013, 144 in 2015 and 154 in 2016. UNOG serviced 227 Council-related meetings in 2016.

25 At the time of writing this chapter, the speaking time limits were two minutes for participants in panel and interactive dialogues, two minutes 30 seconds for Member States and one minute 30 seconds for Observers during general debates. As far as the UPR discussion in the plenary goes, it is often reduced to one minute 30 seconds for all. During the UPR Working Group discussions, the very high number of speakers often kept the speaking time to around one minute for all participants.

Successive Bureaux thus managed to secure modest but important agreements on matters relating to the enhancement of the effectiveness of the Council. They were often preceded or accompanied by informal retreats organized by the Council's Presidents outside the UN premises to provide a convenient and discrete forum where ideas could be expressed in a Chatham House rules environment.[26]

Among the improvements gained or made possible through such processes, it is of interest to highlight the following:

- The Presidential Statement 29/1 of 3 July 2015 included elements relating to the voluntary yearly calendar for thematic resolutions, the biennialization and tri-ennialization of the initiatives, the duration of the mandates of special rapporteurs, the operation of the Consultative Group, the Council website and the principles of transparency and inclusiveness with regard to the consultative process.
- The Note to the Bureau dated 29 April 2016 included measures that were later implemented to improve the issuance compliance of the Council documentation.
- The Annex to the minutes of the Bureau of 24 August 2016 included a rolling list of 53 proposals on efficiency gains to be implemented if and when circumstances so permit.
- A letter from the President to the President-elect on 7 December 2016 included a consolidated list of proposals for the reduction of meetings of the Council concerning such areas as general debates, panels, UPR, Special Procedures, resolutions and initiatives.
- The annex to the Bureau meeting of 7 September 2017 included the final report of the Joint Task Force on the Workload of the Council to

26 The very first such retreat was organized by the Thai President in December 2010 in Bangkok with the presence of representatives of all Member States as well as regional or political group coordinators. This was considered extremely helpful in assessing the gaps that persisted in the position of many delegations despite two years of formal or informal negotiations. The same format was used by the German President in Berlin in May 2015, the Korean President in Evian in 2016, the Slovenian President in Ljubljana in October 2018, the Senegalese President in Dakar in October 2019, the Czech President in Prague in November 2023 and the Moroccan President in Rabat in November 2024.

be read in conjunction with the letter of the President to the regional coordinators on the Bureau's proposal of 13 September 2017. The proposals endorsed by the Bureau related to the UPR, the general debates and interactive dialogues, and a request for additional fully serviced meetings to be made available to the Council.

- The revised Bureau proposal of 16 February 2018 made proposals relating to the clustering and staggering of general debates in what was criticized as a short-term measure aimed at enhancing the efficiency of the Council.
- The Presidential Statement of 3 December 2018,[27] which referred to the development of a three-year programme of work, strengthened the interaction with the UNOG Director-General, consolidated the practice of limiting the duration of panel discussions to two hours and the number of panellists to four including the moderator, ensured a proper gender and geographic balance among panellists, expanded significantly on the practice of bi- and tri-ennializing initiatives, and encouraged the progressive and full implementation of measures on the use of modern technology to improve efficiency that had been annexed to the Presidential Statement.
- At the start of the 13th Human Rights Council Cycle, the President continued the efforts deployed by his predecessors and appointed facilitators to consider the necessary implementation of the Presidential Statement of 3 December 2018 and make appropriate additional recommendations relating to the Council programme of work and the UPR.[28]
- With the COVID-19 pandemic, efforts aiming at making the Council more efficient and effective continued. Remarkably, the Council managed to adopt a Presidential Statement codifying the methods of work of the Consultative Group.[29] However, the logistical considerations made it difficult for co-facilitators and focal points to embark on more ambitious reforms, which would have required holding numerous bilateral or multilateral informal meetings. Accordingly,

---

27 See Document A/HRC/PRST/OS/12/1.

28 See minutes of the Bureau meetings of 17 June and 23 August 2019, as a result of which the Council approved the introduction of the e-deleGATE system used by delegations to table and co-sponsor resolutions and the 'HRC Clinics' for assistance to small delegations during the Council sessions.

29 See Presidential Statement PRST OS/14/2 of 17 December 2020.

the measures contained in document PRST OS/13/1 were extended at each one of its Organizational Sessions held in December 2020, 2021 and 2022 respectively.[30]

- In recent years, the co-facilitation process strengthened in view of the continuing increase in the Council's work and the ensuing pressures on the programme of work. It was also broadened to encompass new aspects of the Council's work. To the typical areas of work such as efficiency, rationalization of working methods, and improvements of the UPR process, were added new areas such as the use of modern technology, and support to the small missions, particularly the Small Island Developing States (SIDS) and Least Developed Countries (LDCs). In 2024, the President added a more substantive segment on new technologies, artificial intelligence and the digital divide with a view to defining challenges and opportunities from a human rights perspective. This came alongside the milestone work done by the Focal Points on the participation of women in all Council-related activities and the Chairs of the Task Force on Accessibility. Additionally, the Council also requested the secretariat to do a mapping of existing initiatives with a view to assisting delegations in avoiding duplications, overlapping and redundancies. More importantly, it also requested the Office of the High Commissioner to create a knolwedge management tool - named AccessHRC - that would combine digital platforms into one user-friendly tool and develop a live information-sharing tool about the activities of the Council. Whether such requests will be met by an Office facing numerous bureaucratic and budgetary difficulties remains however to be seen.

This working methodology, which departed from the formalism and heavy nature of the past, introduced a high level of pragmatism into the work of the Council. At times, when agreement could not be reached either at the Bureau or Council level, the Presidents had no other recourse than to send letters or Notes Verbales commenting on matters of some importance that had to be tackled but were not ready for consensus.[31]

It should be pointed out in conclusion to this section that quite a number of measures were taken regarding organizational matters by way

30 See PRST/OS/14/1, 15/115/1 and 16/1 of 7 December 2020, 8 December 20212021, and 9 December 2022, respectively.

31 See the above developments on the role of Presidents in this regard.

of mere oral decisions (or gavelling) by the President, thus extricating them from the above-mentioned strenuous negotiations. This is to be considered patchwork diplomacy, highly effective indeed, where matters relating to the Council's modus operandi are not dealt with by keeping in mind a grandiose and future-orientated vision but by implementing a grounded case-by-case approach. This ad hoc policy of one step at a time has proven to be highly successful, particularly in view of the fact that all other options have been exhausted without much success. One of the most negative consequences of such a policy, however, is the difficulty which the analyst, researcher or delegate faces in getting hold of the related rulings or decisions which may be available in remote parts of the Council's extranet or in the files of the Secretariat only.

It should not be assumed that any future formal consideration of the Council's work and functioning should be set aside. No one, including the author, can be led to the conclusion that major Council reviews should not be contemplated in the future simply because previous ones were not entirely successful. There is virtue in repetition and courage in initiating processes of such a Sisyphean nature even in the most dire and hostile set of circumstances. However, realism and a good sense of timing should never be disregarded. Even the highest ambitions should not preclude or disdain the above-mentioned discrete 'patchwork policy'. To eliminate the possibility of the Council doing so, thus enabling it to adjust its working methods slowly but surely to circumstances, would have major consequences. Moving forward is always important, even if the pace is slow and the path arduous, and is always better than remaining at a standstill.

The practice of successive Presidents to appoint facilitators and focal points[32] to cover a broad number of issues linked with the efficiency and effectiveness of the Council is thus of crucial importance. It is quite clear that their efforts will never lead to automatic transcriptions of their consultations into new Presidential Statements or Resolutions of a highly substantive nature. However, it creates a sense of ownership among the Permanent Representatives from various regions selected to play such roles. It also raises the level of trust among delegations since it is well understood that no change will occur if there is no major agreement

32 See minutes of the Bureau meeting of 25 May 2022, 7 February 2023 and 2 February 2024.

from all regions. Transparency and cross-regional cooperation are thus maximized by the efforts initiated even if, at the end of the day, a sense of frustration may be felt among those leading these processes.

As was mentioned in several parts of this anatomy, there are many areas of improvement in the Council work and functioning. The author has not hesitated to propose some medium- to long-term courses of action relating, for instance to: (i) the setting up of five special procedures (special rapporteurs or working groups) dealing with each of the five UN regions in complement to the work of the existing country mandates, (ii) enabling the Council to meet on a continuing basis with a budget that enables it to overcome the heavy nature of the UN bureaucracy, (iii) changing the nature of the complaints procedure by merging the Working Group on Communications and the Working Group on Situations, (iv) adjusting the Advisory Committee's modus operandi, (v) ensuring better coordination between all of the Council's mechanisms and making their work more field-oriented and less headquarters-driven, or (iv) taking steps to reduce the overly important place taken by GONGOs or similar lobbies in the work of the Council.

Others proposals relate to the imperious need of building bridges between delegations, particularly at the Ambassadorial level, strenghtening trust and confidence, and enabling a soft and informal diplomacy to emerge within and around the intergovernmental system, far away from the diktat and misinformation that too often prevails in the social networks. Informal, discrete and frank meetings of Ambassadors on delicate issues outside the United Nations but not far from it represent a concrete way to build bridges and raise up trusts between Ambassadors. This discrete human rights diplomacy needs to be strengthened in this delicate period of time.

These and other proposals deserve to be considered or at least borne in mind, given the importance for the Council to always move ahead in the interest of the best possible protection of human rights worldwide. At a time when multilateralism is considered to be in crisis, it is of crucial importance to suggest ways of improvement and uphold the leading role of the HR Council in the UN architecture.

In guise of an imperfect conclusion

It would be presumptuous and intellectually inadequate to offer any conclusion to a book that aims at proposing an anatomy of one of the most important but challenging UN bodies. Making a fair diagnosis and proposing an adequate therapy may be a reachable goal for a medical doctor. It is not, however, for someone grappling with the Council or any other comparable intergovernmental machinery.

To put it otherwise, assessing a situation and offering recommendations imply that the assessment is a fully objective one and the intention perfectly candid. Although the latter is a prerequisite, no writer can even start to pretend to be able to fulfil the former goal. Any writing is influenced by a multiplicity of factors and variables; neutrality is not a quintessential human quality and humility commands the writer to be cognizant of their own limitations. Any assessment, whatever it is, is thus profoundly marked by subjectivity.

However, what may be done is an ever-deeper dissection until some form of imperfect clarity comes to light. This was the goal that the author set himself when he started writing this book.

The objectives that were set for the Council by the UNGA were rooted in decades of work of the Council's predecessor, the Commission, and more importantly, by international circumstances that dramatically changed the political and legal environment surrounding the international human rights system. Decolonization, the Cold War, the changing and at times shocking shape of our societies, genocides and gross and massive human rights violations, which have marked the past 75 years with dark milestones, have provided a background against which the drafters of Resolution 60/251 worked. In contrast, the significant progress that was made during the same period of time was not, and will probably never will be, taken into full consideration given the quasi-impossibility of computing or factoring in what works well.

Several years later, 19 years at the time of writing the second edition of this book, contemplating what has been achieved and pondering whether and how the system should be shaped in the future is a difficult goal.

What may be one of the least challengeable prisms through which this could be done is surely the lens of the victims or potential victims of human rights violations. Reading what has or has not been done from this perspective offers some pointers in the right direction. Against this background, it is possible to observe subjectively a few elements which the author deems of interest and leave it to the reader to draw his or her own conclusions.

One of the major challenges that have always had to be faced is the identification of actions that worked well in the human rights area. How can it be determined that, in a certain country, a number of individuals or groups were not exposed to a type of human rights violation? And even if it were possible to do this, how would it be possible to link this achievement with specific actors, particularly at the international level?

Another challenge lies in the consequences of flexibility, realism and transparency – in other words the multiplication of mechanisms and tools established by the Council – for the efficiency and effectiveness of the human rights system. It is fair to ponder whether by their mere superposition or juxtaposition, these various layers do not create confusion and lack of visibility, which may ultimately be detrimental to the protection of human rights.

It remains equally challenging to grasp the extent of polarization prevailing within the Council, or to unpack how this has evolved over the past two decades, particularly since the onset of the COVID-19 pandemic.

A deeper, more existential challenge lies in assessing how the Council – as the successor to the Commission on Human Rights – has addressed human rights violations everwhere and anywhere. In this respect it is certainly difficult to avoid the conclusion that double standards and the privileges linked to a country's economic, military or political weight may significantly influence the way in which its human rights violations are addressed by the intergovernmental human rights system.

Ultimately, the main challenge is to what extent the above-mentioned ultimate judge of the human rights system, namely the individuals as subjects of international human rights law and the victims of human rights violations and abuses, trust the human rights system that was developed to promote and protect their rights and prevent any form of human rights violation. Since perfection is sometimes a goal but never a reality, frustrations are met, the nature of which deserves some form of analysis.

A very incomplete list of success stories

There is no doubt that since its establishment, the Council and its work have had a significant impact on the human rights landscape and consequently helped improve the human rights situation of millions of individuals. However, there are no clear criteria as to how to quantify this statement, which in itself may only be considered a subjective one. Any action by or achievement of a national authority is never the result of a single factor. In most cases, it is the result of a combination of factors, from the demands of public opinion, trade unions, NGOs or political parties, deliberations of the legislative power, conclusions of the judicial power, initiatives by the executive power, and pressures or directives from external sources such as other governments, international civil society and regional or international organizations.

It is probably correct to assume that the Council and its mechanisms have had an important impact on the prevention, promotion and protection of human rights at the domestic level. It is, however, far more complex to identify what their exact contribution has been to these changes. Human rights cannot be reduced to equations – and if they were, they would surely be added to the list of unsolved millennial problems.

Accordingly, attempting to draw up a list of significant achievements can only be incomplete and tainted with subjectivity. The following pointers may, nevertheless, be advanced:

- Since its establishment, the Council has tackled numerous issues, including very controversial ones, and has kept them in focus. In many senses, the Council has served as an early warning system by sounding alarm bells ahead of impending or worsening crises. The Council has been effective in responding to crises – both protracted and emerging – in many places. This was particularly evident in the wake of the Arab Spring when the Council held a series of Special Sessions and urgent meetings and thus sharpened its focus on the crises in the region. But, this extended to many other places where gross and massive human rights violations were observed, whether country or thematically based, through the organization of a large number of Special Sessions and urgent debates.

- The Council has given a voice to the voiceless by providing a vital setting where their views can be heard, often views which would otherwise be drowned out or ignored altogether. It has also helped to unlock frustrations largely felt during the days of the Commission on Human Rights, when there were often uncertainties on how to address human rights situations. The UPR Mechanism is considered to be one of its most prominent innovations. This has proven to be a powerful tool to promote change and reflection on sensitive issues for each community, region and country. This has been particularly the case since the reviewed States have supported an average of two-thirds of all recommendations extended by other UN States – much more than what they would have agreed to in other circumstances.[1] This in turn, has provided an extremely helpful entry point for the consideration of delicate human rights issues at the domestic level.
- The UPR mechanism has also triggered countless examples of country successes covering a wide range of themes, from the abolition of the death penalty to laws on combating domestic violence, to strategies to eradicate poverty, to policies on adequate housing, among many others.
- Over half of the 128 States that have extended a standing invitation to all thematic Special Procedures have done so over the course of the Council's existence. The 70 States that have entered into this agreement since 2006 were prompted to take this important step by pointed recommendations at the UPR working group, Special Procedure mandate-holders themselves, and through the High Commissioner,

---

1 Mostly as a matter of face-saving, in order to support at least as many recommendations as neighbouring States or States in comparable situations supported during their own review.

who has strongly advocated at Council meetings for access to countries to allow independent human rights monitoring.

- Special Procedures have played an invaluable role in highlighting crucial thematic or country issues around the globe and have triggered constructive actions at the domestic level, which have impacted positively on the lives of numerous people. These experts have helped shape the Council's agenda and its decisions.
- Since the publication of the first edition of this book, the following examples of breakthroughs were achieved by the action of Special Procedures:[2] Kyrgyzstan withdrew a contentious mass media bill following review by the Special Rapporteur on freedom of opinion and expression; Lebanon adopted a Standard Unified Contract for migrant domestic workers further to action by the Special Rapporteur on Slavery; Argentina passed a bill legalizing abortion thanks partly to the action of the Working Group on Discrimination against Women and Girls; El Salvador provided collective reparations to victims of the El Mozote 1981 massacre after the visit of the Special Rapporteur on the promotion of truth, justice, reparations and guarantees of non-recurrence; and the Advisory Opinion of the International Tribunal for the Law of the Sea reflected the amicus brief submitted jointly by the Special Rapporteurs on Human Rights and Climate Change and Human Rights and the Environment.
- Additionally, the issuing of urgent communications or statements by Special Procedures, as well as their mission reports, had a cumulative effect and often led to significant outcomes such as the release of detained persons, the halting of torture or ill-treatment, the launching of domestic investigations into abuses, the adoption of laws or decrees, and even changes in mindset by initiating discourses on delicate societal issues (for instance, sexual orientation).
- The Council has played an instrumental role in human rights mainstreaming on issues not traditionally seen as human rights issues, per se. By creating mandates and generating discussions in the human rights forum on subjects such as new technologies, climate change, toxic waste and pesticides, the human rights angles to these issues are increasingly evident today compared with a decade ago.

2 See https://www.ohchr.org/en/special-procedures-human-rights-council/making-difference-special-procedures-human-rights-council.

- More generally, the Council has been increasingly active with regard to the realization of sustainable development. These texts covered a variety of topics relating to economic, social, and cultural rights, as well as climate change, administration of justice, corruption, digital technologies, international cooperation, illicit funds, foreign debt, arms transfers, slavery and unilateral coercive measures.
- On the impact of climate change on human rights, discussions were held at the highest levels when the Heads of State of Tuvalu and Kiribati participated in a panel discussion on the issue, drawing particular attention to the plight of people in their small island nations and the vulnerabilities faced by others in similar situations. The consideration of this matter is only growing more important, as was testified by the multiplication of instances when related matters were considered, and a Special Procedure mandate-holder was eventually appointed.
- The Council has played an important role in promoting respect for diversity and for different religions or beliefs, as well as struggling against any form of discrimination. Recommendations from the Special Procedure on freedom of religion or belief have stimulated much-needed discussions at local and national levels to help promote tolerance and combat discrimination. The holding of an urgent debate on the premeditated and public acts of religious hatred provided a forum to exchange on this matter.
- The Council's Special Procedures have also produced ground-breaking reports on emerging issues such as lethal autonomous weapons (aka 'killer robots'), the use of drones in combat, the right to privacy, freedom of expression online, and access to the internet. These reports have in turn generated important debates at local, national and international levels and have helped usher in new policies.
- Since the Council began working, 22 States have abolished the death penalty. This has largely been attributed to the strong focus on the use of the death penalty applied at the Council, vis-à-vis numerous UPR recommendations, sharp recommendations by a host of Special Procedure mandate-holders, and through the regular panel discussions held at the Council where State practices are routinely highlighted, aiming to encourage the abolition of the death penalty.
- States have also taken concerted measures to improve prison conditions and address challenges in their detention policies as a result of the Council's spotlights.
- The Council has devoted more time over the years to addressing the challenges of dealing with non-State actors and violations committed

by them. The Council's Special Session on Boko Haram and numerous reports spotlighting these violations, including the report of the Working Group on mercenaries addressing the recruitment of children by non-State actors, are examples.

- Since its inaugural session in 2006, the Council has adopted the International Convention for the Protection of All Persons from Enforced Disappearance, the Optional Protocol to the International Covenant on Economic, Social and Cultural Rights, the Optional Protocol to the Convention on the Rights of the Child, and the Declaration on the Rights of Indigenous Peoples, thus playing a leading role in normative work on human Rights. In Argentina, the Working Group on Enforced Disappearances has been instrumental to the families of people who disappeared during the military dictatorship and the organizations working on their behalf, ensuring that they are fully supported by the State in their efforts to obtain the truth.
- The Council's vigilant stance on reprisals against those cooperating with the UN and its mechanisms is also noteworthy. Since 2010, the Council has commissioned and heard the presentation of nine Secretary-General reports containing information on alleged acts of intimidation and reprisals broken down by State. Testament to the increased attention to this matter since September 2018, the Council held an interactive discussion on the latest Secretary-General report.

This impressive list may not be considered cast in stone and could probably be expanded quite significantly.

However, the most crucial measure of the Council's impact does not lie with the actions by the governments or other actors at the domestic level but rather in their omissions. If gross and massive human rights violations are prevented, if their scope is narrowed down significantly, if controversial measures are not translated into action, or if steps backward regarding the implementation or interpretation of certain human rights are avoided or halted, how can the Council's contribution to such incredibly important achievements be measured in a tangible manner?

It is clear that in a number of instances, the recommendations of the Council and its mechanisms have led to such achievements, but it is hard to quantify them. For instance, if political prisoners are released, the action by security forces restrained, discrimination against groups or individuals less prevalent, or the number of victims in a conflict reduced, to what extent can it be considered that this is the result of a Council's resolution or of a statement of intervention by the High Commissioner? Of the UPR review? Of Special Procedures mandate-holders' interventions? Of the Complaints Procedure deliberations? Of commissions of inquiry reports? Of treaty bodies' recommendations? Of other international, regional, or national stakeholder action? Of a combination of some of them, of all of them, or even of none of them? In reality, this may well be presented as a spontaneous decision of the national authorities irrespective of the pressure brought to bear by national and international actors.

In certain cases, a government may attribute to the Council and/or its mechanisms the benefit of a certain domestic policy out of convenience or given certain national or international circumstances, whereas in reality, the main contributors were demonstrators and civil society at home. Conversely, in other dramatic cases, the authorities may deny any form of influence by the Council and take entire ownership, where the contrary was absolutely true.

It is often mentioned that whatever the usefulness of these listed achievements, the international human rights system does not impact sufficiently on human reality. It needs, however, to be borne in mind that the contemporary world, being what it is with its numerous cases of human rights infringements and a noticeable deterioration of the human rights situation in various countries or regions, expecting the Council and its mechanisms to redress all such situations would be overly utopian.

Whatever the accomplishments of the Council and its mechanisms – which the author, in his subjectivity believes are numerous – what matters is the importance of it constantly refining its working methods, focusing on the implementation of its work, developing its ability to react to all violations of human rights, whatever they are and wherever they occur, and strengthening its ability to meet at all times to address them.

It is quite clearly inappropriate to consider that all is well in the best of all possible worlds.[3] Given the fact the Council is the only universal intergovernmental human rights body having such an impact on the promotion, prevention and protection of human rights, every possible effort

3 Leibniz, *Theodicy* and Voltaire, *Candide*.

needs to be constantly made with a view to enhancing the efficiency and effectiveness of the Council.

That being the case, the whole universal intergovernmental machinery needs to go one step further and take into account fully the role which the Council and its mechanisms play in the prevention of conflicts. It is quite clear that they are among the first to note a deteriorating domestic situation which, if not addressed, will invariably degenerate into further crisis and possibly conflict. Conflict prevention needs to rely on the signals from the human rights system and act early rather than suffer later. Preventing human rights violations represents an integral component of conflict prevention. After all, none of the conflicts that arose in the past few decades were detached from human rights violations at their very start. This is a reality which is far too often disregarded, making it possibly one of the worst blind spots of the international community.

Flexibility, realism and transparency vs. confusion and lack of visibility

The Council is a body composed of Member States. It is thus no stranger to politicization or polarization, quite the contrary. Whereas human rights and freedoms are often the source of intense speculation, discussion, struggle and conflict in domestic societies, they cannot be expected to meet a general sense of plenitude and consensus at the international level.

The only situation where consensus would be reached on all human rights issues would be if the concerned body were totally anodyne, inconsequential and insignificant. In such a case, it would be plausible to set up a body whose deliberations would be applauded by all – or none. Statements would be pronounced and adhered to by all participants and smiles and plaudits would be a constant feature of its work.

Fortunately, this is not how the Council works. Politicization and polarization will always be well-rooted components of the Council and in turn, it will always have to adjust its course to avoid collision with the coalitions of the many.

Accordingly, it will have to constantly invent new mechanisms, tools, procedures and/or working methods, or develop the existing ones with a view to bypassing and overcoming the numerous problems at hand. New layers will be added to the existing ones and the system will grow in complexity and opacity.

Humility should be our guide: what cannot be described easily in less than 400 pages cannot really be considered clear and coherent. Despite the fact that the Council is assuredly one of the most transparent bodies in the intergovernmental arena, the juxtaposition of so many layers and the inventiveness of all stakeholders in dealing with problems by generating new tools and methods can only lead to confusion. In a bizarre twist of events, the efforts made to strengthen transparency at all levels as well as the ability of the Council to address as many types of human rights violations as possible have undoubtedly generated a high level of opacity – leaving ample room to the GONGOs, illiberal groups and other lobbies to undermine in their social networks the Council's achievements simply due to the sheer complexity of the Council's work.

When dozens of experts, bodies or procedures are dealing with issues which, although they may not be qualified as similar, remain quite comparable in nature, this prevents the end-users, namely the potential victims or the public at large, from grasping the rationale and coherence of the system as a whole. Facing the over-complexity of the Council system, the commentators are almost forced to summarize, paraphrase and, at times, lightly interpret what has actually been done. Since it is quite difficult to explain in a few words what the differences are between the system of Special Rapporteurs, the UPR mechanism, the commissions of inquiry and fact-finding missions, the panels, and numerous experts dealing with human rights matters, there is an unavoidable appetite to cluster and regroup them under the overarching term 'United Nations'.

Accordingly, the richness, inventiveness and complexity of a system that has been developed over decades of tireless activity by many players, lead, in a strange turn of events, to over-simplification, approximation and generalization. In turn, this can only lead to a lack of visibility.

If the Council were a human being, the problems he or she faced would be of an existential nature. Since it is not a human being, this challenge remains of a political or policy nature. This can only be addressed in the context of the above-described change management efforts. Surely, this lofty goal cannot be achieved in a short timespan, but continuing to address it is vital.

The emergence of a complex and multilayered polarization

As has been repeatedly underlined in the previous pages, particularly in Section 2.2.11, the Council is dealing with complex issues that touch upon the very core of human societies. Hence, it is not and will never be averse to political controversies since they are mere reflections or mirrors of the state of the world at the present juncture.

More problematic is the phenomenon of deep polarization which has remained a constant feature of the Council since its inception. In the early years of the Council, this polarization was extremely severe and opposed regional and political groups as solid blocs of power. Groups' coordinators led strong attacks against one another to the detriment of human rights and not much was left to the initiatives by individual actors.

The groups' logic and the resulting deep polarization were severely affected by the Arab Spring in the early 2010s. From that moment onwards, the cohesion within some of the regional and political groups started to crumble. Added to the renewed interest in the Council by the United States following the election of President Obama, this provided a springboard upon which the Council could revisit its modus operandi. A calmer and more constructive working atmosphere started to emerge. Given the years of groups' confrontation and logic, a new practice started to develop wherein draft resolutions were no longer supported by individual States affiliated with or close to a regional or political group. For almost every resolution, a cross-regional group of sponsors was henceforth established, thus reducing the risk of groups re-instating themselves as the leading drivers within the Council. Certainly, individual States and political or regional groups continued to steward a number of initiatives, but this is now a minority of them. Such a policy move created the conditions for a new solidarity to appear, crossing the regional or political boundaries and based on the perception by all that the Council had to overcome extreme polarization.

In the wake of the COVID-19 pandemic and the wars in Ukraine and Gaza, many expressed their surprise that the Council managed to retain its capacity to act forcefully in the field of human rights. Some might have expected the Council to sink into irrelevance. Others sceptically considered that being part of a complex UN bureaucracy, there was simply no other outcome than a reduction of the Council's ability to operate in a complex and increasingly fragmented environment. On the contrary, for the reasons explained in the previous pages, while many – if not most – other UN bodies started to crumble and became for a while inconsequential, the Council blossomed and gained a high level of visibility and recognition for its role and functions. The main reason why it maintained its ability to operate in such a delicate and tense multilateral environment was precisely the understanding by all delegations of a common goal, thanks to its culture of dialogue and de-polarization which had been enshrined in its work for more than a decade.

The by-now well-established practice of cross-regional groups of sponsors behind almost every single Council resolution might have saved the Council in this regard. Indeed, given the high number of resolutions adopted every year, this practice implied that many States became parts of a complex web of groups of sponsors for several resolutions each.

In practice, each delegation part of a core group of sponsors works closely with the other members to get 'their' common resolution adopted. Obviously, this does not prevent them from being on the opposite side of the political, legal or societal spectrum when it comes to other resolutions. It is therefore very common for a delegation, whichever it is, to work with other delegations towards a common goal in the morning on one specific country or thematic topic while opposing them in the afternoon on a different topic. This provided the breeding ground for a new culture of cooperation and constructive dialogue to emerge. Hence, the prevalence of courtesy and respect between delegations and the practice of avoiding embarrassing each other by triggering endless procedural motions. Indeed, how would it be possible for a given delegation to stubbornly and viciously attack one or several delegations on one topic during one meeting and few hours later work hand in hand with the same delegations but on a different topic?

Thus, this multilayered and complex polarization which by now is almost impossible to decrypt, led in the past few years to a much more efficient and balanced Council, a conclusion which is certainly not self-explanatory.

This should also be considered against the background of a constant increase in the number of new initiatives resulting from the higher standing and status of the Council. Given the paralysis of the Security Council and the difficulties faced by many other bodies of the UN system during and following the COVID-19 pandemic, many have come to realize that the Council is the 'place to be' in raising initiatives or topics.

Although this may not necessarily be the body best placed to deal with the various matters at stake, it is at least a mechanism that works reasonably well and has a satisfactory level of visibility, at least much higher than most other UN bodies. Hence, there is a tendency to bring an increasingly high number of issues to the Council. The increase in the number of new initiatives requires more cross-regional groups of sponsors to be established, and consequently it further increases the number of States involved in working constructively with other delegations – and further complexifies the polarization of the Council.

The Council may thus be qualified as a place where polarization is unavoidable and omnipresent. But, at the same time, it is also a place where this very polarization has been somewhat contained and its consequences limited. What was a vicious circle at the start of the Council's history has by now become a virtuous one.

For this to continue working, it requires that as many States as possible join core groups of sponsors, thus diversifying and broadening their composition and contributing to diluting the impact of polarization.

It may even be suggested in the context of this Anatomy that core group of sponsors be opened to States that bear a strong interest in the initiative but do not necessarily share the same views on all of its aspects. This may lead to simplifying and shortening the negotiations' process and targeting more precisely and openly the issues of disagreements.

From a simple type of polarization in its infancy, the Council has grown into a very complex body with extraordinarily sophisticated and nuanced polarization. This is by no means a minor affair.

The arduous task of tackling human rights violations everywhere and anytime

The world events that unfolded since the end of the COVID-19 pandemic clearly showed that the international community, as it is reflected in the work of the Human Rights Council despite its 18 years of activities, has not yet overcome the difficulties faced in dealing with multiple forms of gross and massive human rights violations in various regions and multiple countries around the world.

There is a general sense of double standards which are largely prevalent in civil society and often referred to by States and non-governmental societies alike. How can it be the case, it is often asked, that a situation is dealt with differently or not dealt with at all depending on where and when it occurs?

One need only reflect on the qualifications attributed by various parties to the massive violations of human rights that have occurred in Ukraine and in the occupied Palestinian territories, as well as in Sudan, or the Democratic Republic of Congo, to name just a few of the current conflicts. An outside observer would find it quite difficult to understand the differences in terminology used by different but important parties regarding often very comparable situations, whether concerning the nature of the gross and massive violations committed or the suffering endured by the concerned populations. Is there not an equality in death and pain? And should not the perpetrators and accomplices of such tragedies face the full force of the law, regardless of their position on the global political chessboard?

It is painfully true for the lay person to note that many of the numerous human rights crises denounced by the High Commissioner, the Council's mechanisms, the treaty bodies and the Council itself in its multiple resolutions are considered unevenly, if at all.

Several centuries ago, the famous French writer La Fontaine wrote that as power or misery defines your state, the courts will judge you harshly or absolve you. He also stated that the reasoning of the strongest is always the most convincing. This probably sums it up in a broad and non-academic manner.

It is, for instance obviously clear that focusing attention on the human rights situation in a Permanent Member of the Security Council or a member of the Group of Twenty[4] (G20) is extremely difficult, to put

4 Argentina, Australia, Brazil, Canada, China, France, Germany, India, Indonesia, Italy, Japan, Republic of Korea, Mexico, the

it mildly. Until 2022, none of these countries or political groups had ever been the focus of attention via a specific Human Rights Council resolution.

In an ideal world, this would be considered an oddity since, with special power, should come special responsibilities. Obviously, being a country of importance in the geopolitical world does not mean that there should be a presumption that there are violations of human rights of importance which should be considered automatically by this body. But, in such an ideal world, being among the leaders of the world should imply that human rights are better promoted and protected and violations prevented in a much more efficient manner than in other countries and those concerned might even request the Council or any comparable body to scrutinize the effectiveness of their human rights policies. However, the world we are living in is far from being ideal. It is clear that if and when gross and massive human rights violations occur as a result of the actions – or lack of – of one or more of these countries, dealing with them at the Council level is extremely hard, thus creating a feeling that some may be immune from scrutiny while others are not.

It is topical in this respect that the conflicts or human rights situations which arose since the start of the twenty-first century in which one or several powerful countries were involved in whichever capacity, were never dealt with evenly, broadly and convincingly by the Human Rights Council despite their impacts on human rights. It is enough, I presume, to take a moment to think about the situation of migrants desperately seeking to reach a supposedly safer host country and/or one more conducive to finding a means of subsistence, or that of oppressed minorities, Indigenous populations, victims of violent forms of racism by law enforcement officials, and, of course, all those who have so tremendously suffered due to the occupation or aggression by foreign troops or various coalitions. Is it not deeply regrettable that when such actions are carried out by influential countries, they largely go unnoticed or are dismissed as gross and massive human rights situations – a euphemism for saying that there is generally no reaction from the international community and, consequently, from the Human Rights Council?

Russian Federation, Saudi Arabia, South Africa, Türkiye, the United Kingdom of Great Britain and Northern Ireland, the United States of America and the European Union.

It is sufficient to note in this regard that during the years 2023 and 2024, only one Special Session – on the situation of human rights in Sudan – and one urgent debate – on the alarming rise in premeditated and public acts of religious hatred – were organized. What about all the numerous other situations the account of which is repeatedly mentioned in UN press communiques and tormenting our sleepless nights? What about the sum of all tragedies faced by millions of victims of human rights violations and their families and loved ones? In certain cases, silence becomes a evocative roar which may haunt us for decades.

Still on the issue of double standards, but in a different understanding, it is also obvious that those situations that do not make the headlines in the international media are less likely to be flagged at the Council, whatever the level or intensity of the violations – thus transforming worldwide media into de facto drivers of what may or may not be raised at the Council. It is topical to note in this regard the oral update of the High Commissioner for Human Rights at the 55th session in March 2024, when he referred to 55 conflicts in the world and their unbearable consequences on the state of human rights worldwide. Among them, many unfortunately only receive token attention during general debates or interactive dialogues.

Even worse, when such situations are the subject of specific consideration by the Council, the arguments advanced by some stakeholders against these mandates about double standards might lead to ending the concerned mandate. It is sufficient in this respect to note by way of example that a draft resolution aiming at renewing the mandate of a commission of inquiry on Yemen was defeated in October 2021. Similarly, calls to abolish agenda item 7 on the human rights situation in Palestine and other occupied Arab territories – based on claims by a few that it reflects a bias within the Council – seem incongruous in light of the gross, massive and systematic human rights violations affecting Palestinians in the occupied territories, particularly Gaza.

Another ominous weakness of the international human rights system is the unfortunately common uneven qualifications of comparable violations depending on where they are registered, and more importantly, which government is allegedly responsible. Depending on such geopolitical circumstances, certain violations may be depicted, or not, as war crimes, crimes against humanity, and gross and massive violations of human rights and international humanitarian law, and even as acts constituting apartheid or genocide.

In trying to address the double-standards problem, the international community established the Universal Periodic Review Mechanism, which was considered one of the most realistic ways to deal with all human rights violations wherever they occur when UNGA Resolution 60/251 was adopted.

However, it is fair to state that this did not solve the matter once and for all. Unless one becomes a utopian and considers that one day all human rights violations will be considered equally and immediately by the international community whenever and wherever they occur, there are not that many options available to deal with the discrepancy between the world reality and the way it is analysed and dealt with by the Council.

This is naturally due to the fact that in order for a situation to be dealt with by the Council, it requires a draft resolution to be tabled. For a draft resolution to be tabled, it requires a country – and not a non-governmental organization or another Council stakeholder – to initiate it and take full responsibility for it. For a country to take such a responsibility, it requires a solid and principled approach towards human rights and immunity towars any possible economic, trade or financial retaliation.

This sole observation explains why a body composed of States within an Organization established by the UN Charter cannot easily deal with human rights violations everywhere. The consequences of tabling of a draft resolution on a country situation cannot be neglected or undermined. They are multifaceted, diverse, and heavy and do not need to be presented here.

However, as is usually the case with the Human Rights Council, even those situations that appear the most intangible or immutable may suddenly change depending on circumstances. Hence, despite decades of non-condemnation of G20 members or Permanent Members of the Security Council by the Human Rights Council or its predecessor, one of its members, the Russian Federation, was subjected to very close scrutiny by the Council following its aggression against Ukraine. This led to the convening of an urgent debate, a Special Session, the establishment of an Independent International Commission on Ukraine and the creation of a mandate for a Special Rapporteur on the situation of human rights in the

Russian Federation. It also lost its membership rights following action by the General Assembly.

It may, however, appear far-fetched to consider that this may serve as a precedent concerning the actions of other powerful countries in future circumstances. The above action clearly broke a very important glass ceiling, but it may not be replicated elsewhere easily.

To ease the burden on States that remain the sole initiators of resolutions at the Council, the author proposed in Section 2.2.2 on procedures for dealing with violations of human rights the establishment of five Working Groups or Special Rapporteurs with the role of reporting on the human rights situations in each one of the five UN regions. This would be a complement and not a substitute for the existing network of special procedures. It would be flawed to consider that this objective may be easily achievable, but it remains a possibility that might deserve serious consideration. Another complementaty option, but outside the remit of this anatomy, would be to consider the possibility for the OHCHR to be invited to establish field presences in each Permanent Member of the Security Council.

As mentioned in the preface of this second edition, there is no alternative to multilateralism in the field of human rights. Nothing can replace the painstaking yet essential and beneficial effort of so many States to agree on norms and apply them universally. Transactional diplomacy, or the law of the strongest, is a relic of the past that should be viewed only as a temporary discomfort. This must prompt the Council to move forward with even greater strength and urgency, leaving behind the remnants of past decades. Humanity and universality must be at the centre of its actions, with a methodology focused on peer negotiations, the pursuit of the common good, the difficult struggle for accountability of all responsible for gross and massive human rights violations, and the practical realization of human rights for everyone and for the benefit of everyone. The specific responsibilities of the most powerful countries in the world regarding the consideration of their human rights situation is an essential precondition for the betterment of human rights protection worldwide. It does not mean at all that until such time this goal is achieved other situations should not be considered, but on the contrary, that all human rights situations, whichever their location and those responsible for them, should be dealt with at the Council level.

The fluctuating nature of frustrations

Never before have human beings been so well versed in the rights and freedoms from which they benefit, either directly or as a component of society. Almost nothing can evade the scrutiny of individuals via traditional or social media. In parallel, fake news has become a reality and its proliferation may unfortunately not be easily halted.

Information is thus everywhere. Yet it may as well be said that information is nowhere.

Facing a plethora and variety of news, or so-called news, on so many distinct issues, many of them abounding with human rights connotations, it is unrealistic to anticipate that no expectation is expressed, hasty judgement passed and final conclusion drawn. Frustration is the norm, and indulgence the exception. The human rights world is not excluded from this phenomenon which affects many human activities – in fact, it is right at the core of it.

Against this background, it is of crucial importance to analyse the nature of the frustrations developed by the public at large against the ways and means that human rights are being promoted and protected and violations and abuses prevented. There can be no full satisfaction with any human rights system, whatever it has been, is, or may develop in the future; it is indeed humanly impossible to reach the ultimate goal of zero violations or zero abuse. Such is the nature of human societies. The accumulation of conflicts, the proliferation of gross and massive human rights violations, the deep economic and social crises and the resulting injustice and inequality, the impact of technology on human lives and the environment, to quote just a few instances, can only provoke resentment.

Despite the Council's achievements, it is therefore very hard not to perceive a general sense of frustration insofar as the outcome of its activities and those of its mechanisms are concerned.

While it is very easy to take note of this overwhelming sense of frustration, it is much more difficult to describe objectively the whys and wherefores. In this regard, one area deserves to be pointed out, an area that has always elicited passionate interest, namely that of the prevention of human rights violations.

If indeed a system were to be established that would be sophisticated enough to detect almost immediately any potential defect in the situation of human rights in a given country or territory, thoroughly analyse it, develop a set of recommendations and have them implemented at once, this would change forever the face of our international society and the international human rights system.

What may be advanced is that, despite flaws, omissions and inappropriate actions, the Council and its mechanisms have enabled significant and positive changes to occur. This is largely due to the fact that the toolbox of Council mechanisms has grown to encompass a multiplicity of steps which may be taken in isolation or together to prevent the occurrence of human rights violations or limit their nature, impact and possible growth.

It may very well be argued that there is not a single human rights situation which has not been brought to the attention of the Council. The High Commissioner, in her various statements or reports, complemented by the documents produced by her Office, spotlights numerous human rights situations, thematic or country-wise, and calls upon the Council for action whenever deemed necessary.

Special Procedures are reporting on hundreds of situations, from the very general to the extremely specific, and with no shyness or reluctance to engage the Council on such matters. They also send a large number of urgent appeals, communications, and press releases.

The UPR mechanism allows for the consideration of 193 States over a period of four and a half years and in turn provides ample information prior to, during, and after the reviews. This probably represents the most accurate and objective mapping of human rights situations in the world. The Complaints Procedure enables the Working Group on Situations to brief the Council on specific situations.

Panels shed light on country or thematic situations. Dignitaries address the Council with the necessary level of solemnity and draw attention to what they consider to be the issues of primary importance in terms of the prevention, promotion and protection of human rights. Hundreds of joint or individual statements by States, international organizations and civil society are delivered with a specific focus on issues at the national level. The numerous side events organized on the margins of the Council sessions alert Council participants to numerous issues of concern. The media, new or traditional, follow the debates and are extremely forthcoming in relaying information to the public at large.

In brief, the alarm bells are ringing during any given session. In response to these various calls for action, the Council has set up an intermingled network of procedures, mechanisms and tools designed to analyse this information, dissect it closely and assess the matters brought directly or indirectly to its attention.

Since the establishment of the Council, a large number of Special Sessions have been convened; urgent debates organized; informal conversations and formal dialogues and debates held with the High Commissioner underlining a multitude of country or thematic situations; sessional or intersessional panels on specific countries organized; stand-alone or enhanced interactive dialogues with Special Rapporteurs or the High Commissioner convened on a multiplicity of subjects; and an average of 250 recommendations formulated during each one of the UPR reviews.

The Council has adopted hundreds of resolutions, decisions and Presidential Statements, including a large number of comments, observations, conclusions and recommendations. Commissions of inquiry, fact-finding missions and an accountability mechanism have been established. The High Commissioner has been requested to investigate matters directly or indirectly through the appointment of experts. Special Procedures mandates have been established. Investigation missions have been sent to many countries. The UNGA, the Council's parent body, has been briefed by the Council with numerous calls for action, as well as the entire UN system.

It is therefore fair to state that in many cases the Council and its mechanisms rang, rang, rang and rang the alarm bell in a forceful and extremely precise manner. It studied the matters in depth, formulated recommendations, and alerted all concerned with the dire situations prevailing in certain countries or regarding certain themes.

This is exactly the opposite of the situation that prevailed in the Commission in the second part of the twentieth century when genocides, atrocities and mass murder of the population in countries such as Rwanda and Cambodia occurred.

The Council's modus operandi has indeed enabled it to adjust its response to each and every situation with a variety of responses, and there is probably no human rights crisis which evades the Council's scrutiny.

However, and this is a big however, many human rights crises have not been overcome despite the Council's action, and many gross and massive human rights violations are still being registered throughout the world, in both hemispheres and in many different forms. All human rights and fundamental freedoms are far from being implemented.

There is a palpable feeling of despair regarding the apparent inability of the international community to resolve large-scale – not to mention the numerous small-scale – human rights crises.

The author will comment no further and leave the following to the consideration of the readers:

- To what extent can it be contended that all human rights situations have been treated equally and fairly by the Council with similar responses to comparable situations?
- Has the universality of human rights been translated into deeds with equal attention paid to all human rights violations, whether civil, cultural, economic, political and social or other rights and freedoms, including the right to development?
- Have the responses proposed by the Council been effective and to what extent has it been in a position to efficiently and swiftly address them? In particular, has it been possible for the Council to set up an adequate timeline to consider matters which, by definition require urgent attention and action?
- Should the Council not have established further tools between the mere consideration of reports and the action by Commissions of inquiry or Special Rapporteurs? In particular, have the roles and responsibilities of successive Presidents and their Bureaux been fully recognized?
- There is virtue in repetition since it often leads to changes at the domestic level, but when repetition does not lead to any meaningful change, does it not become a sin?
- Have all of the Council's partners, within the UN system and beyond, who were briefed with urgent requests for action in devastating cases, responded with the full force of their respective mandates to the matters at stake?

Besides the responses which may be reached, it may be observed that attempting to look beyond the near horizon is, by definition increasingly difficult in an international society and culture marked by a strong appetite for short-sightedness.

The nature of frustration has indeed changed during recent decades. In the past, frustration emanated from the inability of the human rights system to shed light on many crises. Issues were not brought to the fora before it was too late. Many devastating situations were not brought to the attention of anyone, and in the rarest cases when they were, this was mostly too little and too late.

Currently, even though it may be acknowledged that human rights situations are rightly highlighted and analysed, and that forceful recommendations are often pronounced by the Council, a new form of frustration is developing, a deep and powerful sense of frustration that the international community's responses to such crises have been and remain largely ineffective.

Undeniably, the alarm bells rang forcefully; the public at large has been made aware of what is being done and considered by the Council and its mechanisms,[5] the issues are debated, considered, and analysed deeply and publicly, recommendations are made, and urgent calls extended to various contenders. However, a brief overview of the current situation of human rights in the world, particularly the multiple crises which have been alluded to or referred to in the present text, shows that the outcome of such action in the field has been somewhat limited.

When the alarm bells ring, and ring, and ring, when the reports accumulate, when the Council's recommendations multiply, when the calls for precise and strong action remain unanswered, and when the situation of victims of human rights violations and abuses does not change concretely, the frustration on the part of the public, the world conscience, grows exponentially.

5 Although in far too many instances this is reported as an action by the United Nations in general terms, the matter is too complex to allow for an appropriate dose of adequacy in the terminology used.

Lack of information is no longer regretted, but lack of prompt and efficient action by the United Nations is. In this regard, far too often, the Human Rights Council is unfortunately deemed responsible for an inadequate translation of its findings or deliberations into deeds. However, what is almost systematically missed is that the Human Rights Council is not, and never will be, the principal body in charge of peace and security or of development. These are the two other pillars of the Organization. Human rights represent the remaining one, strong in its principles but deprived of implementation tools adequate to its roles and functions – and incidentally lacking an appropriate budget to deal with.

The fluctuating nature of frustration is thus an issue that will need to be tackled soon enough by the international community to avoid the emergence of a passive and silent rejection of an absolutely essential international and multilateral human rights system, the first cornerstone of which was laid in a famous Universal Declaration adopted in Paris on 10 December 1948.

It may be topical to conclude this anatomy written in dire international circumstances by reminding ourselves of the first paragraphs of the Preamble of the Universal Declaration, which recognized that the inherent dignity and the equal and inalienable rights of all members of the human family are the foundation of freedom, justice and peace in the world; that disregard and contempt for human rights have resulted in barbarous acts which have outraged the conscience of mankind, and the advent of a world in which human beings shall enjoy freedom of speech and belief and freedom from fear and want has been proclaimed as the highest aspiration of the common people; and that it is essential, if humans are not to be compelled to have recourse, as a last resort, to rebellion against tyranny and oppression, that human rights should be protected by the rule of law.

May we never forget these powerful words and strive to implement them into deeds at last.

Index